DOMINANCE, AGGRESSION AND WAR

DOMINANCE, AGGRESSION AND WAR

Edited by Diane McGuinness

An ICUS Book

Paragon House Publishers

New York

Published in the United States by

PARAGON HOUSE PUBLISHERS
2 Hammarskjold Plaza
New York, New York 10017

An International Conference on
the Unity of the Sciences Book.

Library of Congress Cataloging-in-Publication Data

Dominance, Aggression, and War.

  "An ICUS book."
  Bibliography:
  Includes index.
  1. Inter-male aggression. 2. Dominance (Psychology)
3. Power (Social sciences) I. McGuinness, Diane.
BF575.A3D66 1986   302.5'4   86-8191
ISBN 0-89226-035-1

Contents

Introduction

The Function of Status and Rank in Inter-Male Aggression and War

The Project

The history of this volume began in 1982 at a meeting in Palo Alto of myself, Karl Pribram, Keck Moyer and Peter Reynolds. We had convened to discuss the research from a variety of disciplines on the nature of aggression. Could these findings shed some light on the origin and expression of human warfare? The puzzle of human warfare is that, in contrast to rage, war is premeditated and prolonged. Most human aggression is produced by proximal causes, such as frustration, jealousy and threat. Such "reactive" aggression is typically immediate and short-lived. But soldiers are not in a rage when they face the enemy. It is not anger that propels them into battle, but a conscious decision. What force or forces can embolden the resolve to commit one's life to a purpose or cause? Who decides these causes and convinces others that they are worthy?

Research on non-human species had indicated that there were several types of aggression. Each form had the same outcome, but this outcome was produced by different kinds of triggers. Some of these are obvious, such as an immediate threat to life or severe frustration. Others are more specific, like the fury of a female towards anyone who attacks her infant, or one form peculiar to males termed "Inter-male Aggression" by Moyer (1976) because it does not fit any of the types of aggression that have obvious triggers. In general, types of aggression can be placed into three major categories: 1) Reactive aggression, a response to any threat or frustration from any source; 2) Inter-species aggression, of which predatory aggression is the major form; and 3) Intra-species aggression which includes sexual aggression and inter-male aggression.

The major characteristic of inter-male aggression is that it is directed solely to members of one's own species. Furthermore, inter-male aggression is not haphazard. It is triggered by highly specific events in the environment, such as the sudden appearance of a strange male of the same species, inadequate proximal spacing of troupe members, or distal spacing *between* the various troupes (sometimes called "territoriality"), the shortage of food and the presence of a female in estrus. These factors could be considered as constituting a threat to survival or to reproductive success, but if these triggers were really life threatening, then the obvious result would be a violent combat to the death. This would immediately remove the problem of access to space, food and females, leaving one male triumphant and at peace with his harem. This, however, is not what occurs, because this solution would destroy genetic variation, without which a population or species would become extinct.

The mechanism by which inter-male aggression is controlled is through the formation of dominance (or status) hierarchies. These are achieved and maintained largely through threat and bluff, and only occasionally through physical combat. Inter-male aggression in non-human species rarely results in death. This is because it is held in check by a panoply of rituals and gestures of appeasement. For example, male chimpanzees acknowledge defeat in status by permitting the dominant animal to perform a "bluff-over," in which the submissive animal crouches to allow the dominant animal to step over him (deWaal, 1982). The ultimate result of these interactions, is that males come to form a linear "dominance" hierarchy, often bolstered by coalitions. One male achieves top status (the "alpha male"), while others, due to lesser strength, guile, or cunning, rank below, and still others, for reasons not understood, seem perfectly content to remain near the bottom of the heap. Dominance ranks function to prevent and contain aggression that could run out of control and decimate the male population. It is only when the threat is really severe, such as during a drought, that the dominance order begins to crumble, and it is "every man for himself" (Southwick, 1969).

The outcome of this initial meeting was to take seriously the information that was available from non-human primate studies, and compare the mechanisms and the behavior to various human groups. This raised the fundamental question: Is it a struggle for dominance and the management of coalitions that leads ultimately to the outbreak of human war, rather than, as has been suggested, "the aggressive nature of man?" This latter view leaves us with no hope, and with feelings of inevitability regarding the ultimate destruction of the planet. On the other hand, if we had a better understanding of human behavior, especially with respect to primate behavior as a whole, we might have some clues concerning the genesis of warfare, and the germ of a solution.

As we searched for a method to begin to unravel this mystery it was suggested that not only did we need to involve the primatologists in our quest, but that representatives from every discipline that studied human aggression should be involved. As a first step, we set up another meeting to study film material from primate research, anthropology, sociology and psychology. These disciplines rarely come together to discuss problems of common interest, and to our knowledge had never convened to view film material. What would a primatologist make of films of the Yanomamo or New Guinea tribal wars? How would anthropologists react to films of chimpanzees, gorillas, or macaques? And for those of us who studied human behavior in our own "civilizations," could we discern any common elements in this material that could be applied to our own societies?

In April of 1983, we convened a small group of primatologists, anthropologists, psychologists, and an expert in International Relations, to watch films on aggressive encounters in primates and humans. The discussions were often heated. Was "dominance" even a viable concept? Could one begin to compare non-human primate behavior with human behavior that is so much more complex? Were the reasons for inter-male conflict in the chimpanzee or macaque remotely similar to those for aggressivity in the Yanomamo, or in the Dani, who's "warfare," as illustrated in the amazing film "Dead Birds," looked more like a jousting tournament or a football match than "real" war?

In November of the same year we expanded our membership, presented selected examples of the film material and invited formal presentations. The papers that are included in this volume are the outcome of the participants' reaction to these meetings. We are not entirely in agreement, as is to be expected. But what has been exciting throughout this process, is the gradual understanding that it is not possible to understand the problem of aggression in its entirety from only one perspective.

Terminology

Terms from one discipline are not readily transportable to another. But it is vitally important, that we can all agree on what we mean when we use the words "aggression," "dominance" or "status." The group reached a consensus in accepting Moyer's (1976) definition of aggression. This is: "an action with the intention to harm another." The critical aspects of this definition are that aggressive behavior is intentional and not accidental. Furthermore, this intention is a deliberate attempt to harm someone or some*thing*, as in the case of displaced aggression. Agreement was also reached with respect to my contention that aggression should be considered to be more like an *instinct* than a *drive* (McGuinness, 1981.) Whereas a "drive" is triggered by internal stimulation, such as lowering glucose level inducing hunger, or rising levels of saline inducing thirst, an "instinct" is induced by an external stimulus. An example would be "any moving object," in the case of Konrad Lorenz's geese. A drive state is most characterized by random behavior, whereas an instinct is characterized by precise and stereotypic behavior.

The purpose of making this distinction is that it has not been fruitful to view aggression as a product of an internal state. The "hydraulic" model of aggression, in which aggression builds up over time, has not been borne out in research. People are not aggressive without cause, unless they are suffering from brain damage or a biochemical disorder. This is not to say that everyone has the same threshold for aggressivity. Human males are considerably more aggressive than females. This means that their tolerance for events that trigger aggression is much less, that there are *more* triggers, and that they are more likely to become aggressive when they are provoked.

Drives and instincts are not mutually exclusive. They often interact. Hunger, combined with competition for the last piece of fruit on a tree, will inevitably result in a fight. Sexual feelings are triggered from within by the action of hormones, inducing bodily reactions. But sexual *behavior* is triggered by a stimulus: an attractive and eligible mate. However, we know of no condition, at least in the normal brain, where aggression wells up for no reason. This means that if we want to understand how to control and contain aggression, we must be aware of it's triggers in the environment. We have already mentioned the triggers that have been observed in non-human primate colonies, such as a strange male of the same species. These same triggers seem to be operating similarly in humans, as any school boy who has had to change schools will attest. One trigger omitted by Moyer, because it is not observed in animals who are solitary feeders, is hoarding of surplus. Jane Goodall's research showed that when chimpanzees are provisioned by a large cache of bananas, with abundance for all, fighting will frequently break out. Similarly, humans are envious of others who have excess wealth and possessions. Many ancient wars (e.g., Sumer) were fought as often over gold and gems as over boundary disputes for irrigated land.

The concept of "dominance" proved to be much more problematic. For most psychologists and primatologists "dominance" refers to an intent to gain and maintain control over others. It is expressed in behaviors in which the dominant animal, or human, has greater access to desirable commodities and locations, such as food, a special resting place, females, and in our society, wealth and material goods. For others, "dominance" has overtones of aggessivity. It implies force or coercion and for this reason they prefer the term: "status." (For a fuller argument on this issue, see Angst and Reynolds in this volume.) Despite this, the dictionary definition of the two terms is nearly identical and the *result* of high status or dominance is essentially the same. Nevertheless, status does have the further connotation that it can be conferred by additional factors, such as birth into a specific kinship group. In the non-human primate this often occurs by virtue of being born to a "dominant" or high-ranking female. Here, status is given automatically and does not have to be won. In humans, the line of succession of royal families is a familiar example of obtaining automatic status.

Where status cannot be guaranteed, dominance may be, perhaps, the better term. Most interactions in our complex modern societies are carried out between individuals who are not related by birth or position. In interactions between strangers of equal status, all males of all ages (see Savin-Williams this volume) will form dominance hierarchies. This fact has been established by scientists from observations of reactions to any win-lose encounter. Dominance can be won by coercion, by guile, or by receiving some gesture of submission on the part of a less dominant individual. In addition, some humans actively seek subordinant status by a number of, seemingly unnecessary, acts of submission such as seeking approval, help, or advice, and by offering service.

Linear dominance or status ranks do not imply that individuals act in isolation. When the group is considered as a whole, the frequent observation has been in both non-human and human primates, that the common group pattern involves one or more coalitions. These coalitions are almost inevitably built by members close in dominance ranks. For example, "best friends" in Savin-Williams studies on human adolescents, tended to be adjacent in rank. Linear ranks within coalitions is a feature of male dominance patterns in distinction to females. In the non-human primate, female dominance is based largely upon kinship, whereas human female strangers tend to form "cliques." These cliques may be arranged in some sort of dominance order, but within each clique is no predictable ranking within the group (see Savin-Williams, this volume; Knudsen, unpublished data).

The Biology Versus Psychology Versus Sociology Trap

Most anthropologists (and the anthropologists in this volume are no exception) are uncomfortable with attempts to search for global explanations. What they observe in their field work is often so idiosyncratic that is almost defies explanation. They especially object to biological theories that universalize patterns of human behavior, attribute them to an animal origin and hence backward in time to some evolutionary design. In our debates we tried hard to avoid what could be called the "evolutionary trap." Instead we attempted to focus on a comparative analysis without resorting to teleological futility. Inter-male aggression and warfare is a fact. One need not consider *why* it originated, or even what purpose it serves. What is important is to understand the situational factors common to triggering hostilities, the patterns of behavior, the structure and formation of coalitions, the function of the alpha male, and so forth. The major question is: Can we derive any basis for making species and cultural comparisons that will help us understand our own behavior?

When cultures elaborate a biologically based activity, the results can be quite extraordinary. Nevertheless, it is still possible to determine which elements of the behavior are biologically based and which are ramifications of cultural elaboration. As an example, I asked the group to consider a universal behavior with less negative connotations: eating. Eating is the outcome of a biological drive state that induces organisms to seek food and consume it. In psychology we use the terms "stimulus" and "response," to represent the inducement to action and the behavior which follows. In animal research the relationship of stimulus to response is easily observed in the laboratory because the behavior studied is simple and the stimulus and response are contiguous, that is, they are obviously temporally related. We say an animal is hungry if we put down some food and the animal eats it. We say it is not, if the food is refused. But the moment that stimulus and response become separated in time, the exact biological state is less obvious. For example, some animals store food. Here the stimulus (the sight of a nut) and the response (eating the nut) do not co-occur. We assume that a squirrel is not hungry when the nut is collected, but is hungry when it is eaten.

For humans, eating is influenced by the strong propensity to share food. The food is collected, prepared and cooked, shared out among family members, and then eaten. Here we have the biological fact of hunger, the social fact of sharing, and the additional cultural fact of preferences in what is eaten and how the food is cooked. In modern societies, we go to the supermarket to buy food that is grown, packaged, and marketed by a host of different people. Are we hungry when we buy it? Are farmers hungry when they harvest it? Not necessarily. But the complexity does not disguise the biological fact that hunger is involved. Humans have an amazing capacity to delay gratification. In addition they have an equally amazing capacity to elaborate simple biological states into rituals.

We not only sit down to dinner, but we enjoy feasts on special days, which are only marginally related to how hungry we are. We enjoy social interactions at cook-outs, cocktail parties, and restaurants which have the dual purpose of assuaging our hunger and promoting friendship. There are even more elaborate gestures of good will, which have less to do with food than with the politics of dominance, such as state banquets where the major function is to impress visiting dignitaries. State banquets are more benign forms of tribal dances (see Meltzoff this volume).

In every case, for both animals and humans, all of these actions include needs, desires, preferences, and intentions. Only humans add beliefs (some foods are taboo, and some are "healthy"), traditions (sit at tables not on the floor), rules (no boarding house reach permitted), values (feed the sick and needy), and symbols (the President sits at the head of the table). None of this, however, is to deny that the biological basis of all of this elaborate behavior is the hunger drive. This basic behavior is amplified by the human capacity for sharing, which involves the appreciation that eating is as necessary and as pleasurable to others as to oneself. Sharing stems from the capacity for self-reflective consciousness (a property of human brains) which gives rise to empathy. But the gift of food can be used in the service of other motives such as to seek or seal accord for a political action.

When we encounter other behaviors that are ubiquitous across species, such as inter-male aggression and dominance, then there is reason to suspect that these have a biological basis. How this biology is expressed and elaborated is still at issue (see Moyer and Delgado this volume). Nevertheless, the goal of this volume is to begin to discover the principles underlying the mechanism and expression of dominance and its function in the control and prevention of aggressive encounters. Each of the contributors addresses these issues in his or her own way, from their experience with animals or through their studies of peoples around the world. It is our hope that this endeavor will lead towards a more coherent science of conflict and conflict resolution.

Diane McGuinness
Stanford University

Bibliography

DeWaal, F., *Chimpanzee Politics*. London: Unwin, 1983.

Douglas, M., *Natural Symbols*. New York: Penguin Books, 1978.

McGuinness, D., The nature of aggression and dominance systems. From: The Proceedings of the IXth conference of the International Congress of the Unity of the Sciences, New York: ICUS Press, 1981.

Moyer, K. E., *The Psychobiology of Aggression*. New York: Harper and Row, 1976.

Southwick, C. H., Aggressive behavior of Rhesus monkeys in natural and captive groups, in, S. Garattini and E. G. Sigg (eds.), *Aggressive Behavior*. New York: Wiley, 1969.

1.
The Biological Basis of Dominance and Aggression

K.E. Moyer

Introduction

Studies on dominance abound and cover a range of species from the Stellar Jay to the White rhinoceros, though, there is relatively little research on humans. Because of the plethora of studies, it is clearly not possible to cover all of them. Thus, one must be highly selective. The emphasis in this paper will be on human and non-human primates. Because of a variety of problems encountered in experimental design and because of financial considerations, the amount of research in the higher mammals, particularly in the physiological manipulations, is limited. It is therefore necessary, in some cases, to turn to the work on other mammals. Rats and mice, of course, are not people and the results obtained through the study of those subjects may not have any relationship to similar phenomena in humans. Certainly one cannot transfer findings on animals, and particularly lower animals, to humans. However, these studies can provide us with hypotheses that can be tested on humans.

There are situations in which females form dominance hierarchies and engage in threat and fighting behavior if their status is threatened. However, the dominance hierarchy is primarily the province of the male in most species. The antagonists are other males of the same species. Contests between males reflect a dominance interaction whether it involves a fight associated with a particular position in a hierarchy or simply a fight that involves the dominance of one animal over another. The latter type of fighting is frequently called intermale aggression.

There are many different forms of social organization in the various animal species. Professor Itani has provided us with an excellent introduction to the many social organizations in primates. It will therefore not be necessary to include that material in this report.

Definitions:

An individual may be said to be dominant if it has a high probability of winning hostile encounters. A win occurs when one subject leaves the field of altercation, or makes "submissive gestures". Submissive gestures are species-specific responses that operationally decrease the probability of attack by a dominant foe. In the case of humans, the range of submissive responses is very broad and are frequently verbal, such as "I am sorry."

Characteristics of Fighting in Dominance Determining Situations

From mouse to man, with few exceptions, the male of the species is more aggressive than the female[1] and the most frequent target of that hostility is a male conspecific. Intermale aggression is unique and can be differentiated from other types of hostile behavior on the basis of the kinds of stimuli that elicit it, the stimuli that inhibit it, the species-specific topography, and its particular physiological basis.

Although there are particular situations in which the female can display intense and effective aggression (in the defense of the young, for example), in most day-to-day encounters among animals it is the male that shows the highest and most consistent level of spontaneous aggression.

Among non-human primates, most of the aggressive behavior that does occur is manifest by males. For example, Thompson (1967), who studied *fascicularis macaques* and observed dyadic encounters within and between sexes in a laboratory situation, reports that the principal interactions between pairs of males consisted of biting or rough handling of one male by the other.

Pairs of females manifested almost no aggressive behavior, but spent their time in grooming and inspecting one another. In male-female pairs the males initiated most of the social interactions, which involved mounting, grooming, and anogenital inspection with relatively little hostile behavior.

Although there are some species differences, the naturalistic observations of a variety of non-human primates tends to support the laboratory findings that indicate that intraspecific aggression is displayed more by the males than by the females (Kummer, 1968; Chance & Jolly, 1970; Carpenter, 1964). A number of additional studies are cited in Gray (1971).

Humans are no exception to this general zoological principle. Although hostile behavior is by no means an exclusive male province, males are the primary perpetrators of violent crimes. One of the major findings of the National Commission on the Causes and Prevention of Violence (1969) is stated in unequivocal terms, "Violent crime in the city is overwhelmingly committed by males." In 1968, for example, the homicide rate in the United States was five times higher for males than it was for females and the rate for robbery was 20 times higher.

It has been suggested that the trait that has the greatest statistical significance in differentiating criminals from noncriminals is that of sex, (Cressey, 1961). Broom and Selznick (1957, p. 639) summarize the particular propensity of the male for all types of criminal behavior as follows: "Compared with females, males have a great excess of crimes in all nations, all communities within nations, all age groups, all periods of history for which we have statistics and all types of crime except those related to the female sex, such as abortion."[2]

Although actual fighting does not generally occur until endocrine maturation takes place, the males in some species seem to have an early predisposition to rough-and-tumble play that simulates adult aggressive behavior. Among chimpanzees and baboons, males spend considerably more time engaging in aggressive play than do females (Hamburg, 1971a). Infant male rhesus monkeys wrestle and roll and engage in sham biting significantly more than do females, and from 2½ months of age, males show more threat responses than do females. These results were obtained during the study of infant monkeys raised with inanimate surrogate mothers who could hardly transmit cultural differences to the young (Harlow, 1965). Sexual dimorphism in regard to frequency of threat, rough-and-tumble play, and chasing play in the infant rhesus has also been confirmed by Goy (1968); it seems unlikely that this difference between the sexes is due to blood levels of testosterone since that hormone is undetectable in the blood at that age (Resko, 1967). Furthermore, these sex differences are maintained even though the males are castrated at 3 to 4 months of age (Goy, 1966). Field studies have also confirmed the tendency for the young male monkey (old world) to engage in the rough-and-tumble play (DeVore, 1965).

Human children also show sex differences in aggressive tendencies at a very early age. Large amounts of data have been collected in various parts of the United States on the amount and kinds of aggression displayed in relatively standardized doll play situations and there is a clear distinction between the sexes on these variables as early as the age of 3. Boys spend more time in aggressive play than do girls and the type of aggression shown by boys tends to be more vigorous, destructive, and hurtful than that shown by the girls (Sears, 1965). Careful observation of nursery school children reveals that boys more frequently engage in mock hostile play than do girls. This activity involves rough contact with considerable running, chasing, jumping up and down, and laughing (Blurton, 1969). Preschool boys manifest more physical aggression than do girls (McIntyre, 1972). It has also been reported that boys up to the age of 6 or 7 in a Melanesian society show much more rough-and-tumble play than do girls (Davenport, 1965).

Response Topography in Intermale Aggression

A number of authors have emphasized the stereotyped ritualized nature of fights between male conspecifics (Lorenz, 1964; Eibl-Eibesfeldt, 1967, 1970; Fox, 1969b; Ardrey, 1966). The behaviors displayed by fighting males are characteristic of the species and differ considerably from aggressive behavior involved in the capture of prey or defense against predators.

The response sequences characteristic of intermale aggression have been referred to as fixed action patterns, and although there is some increase in the precision of the movements and an increase in coordination with practice, there is little evidence that these response sequences are learned.

The ritualistic aspect of intermale aggression can also be

readily seen in higher animals. An excellent description of the fighting topography in the baboon is given by Kummer (1968):

> Fighting technique consists of each opponent aiming bites at the shoulder or neck of the other. Among hundreds of such scenes we have only seen a male actually take hold of another's coat on two occasions. The analysis of films shows that the animals fence rapidly with open jaws without really touching each other and that the heads are often held back. During a fight each opponent also hits out at the face of the other with his hand, usually missing here as well. The biting and hitting ritual goes on with tremendous speed for a few seconds, silently, the opponents facing each other. Then, one of them turns to flee. At this moment the other often snaps out at him, producing an occasional scratch on the anal region. The vigorous chasing, interrupted by some more fencing, usually lasts no longer than 10 seconds. Most fights come to an end when one opponent flees.

The threat response is also a portion of the topography of intermale aggression. Unless an opponent responds to threat with a submissive posture, a fight is likely to ensue. The threat of the squirrel monkey is particularly easy to observe and consists of a genital display in which one monkey approaches another and bends over it, making penile thrusts toward the second animal (Candland et al., 1970; Ploog, 1967).

Threat Responses in the Chimpanzee.

Once a dominance hierarchy is established, the amount of actual fighting is reduced and the submissive animals respond with the responses of submission. The threat responses in the lower mammals may be relatively simple. In the chimpanzee, the threat responses are quite complex and may be considered ritualistic. This does not mean that they are rigid. In fact, they are remarkably flexible and a full-blown threat response may combine any of the following:

1. Staring directly at another animal and making eye contact.

2. The subject may raise one arm above the head, and/or hunch the shoulders.

3. The dominant animal may show foot stamping.

5

4. It may show hooting, hair erection, and head tipping or jerking.

5. More directly hostile, the dominant member may throw rocks at the animal that is lower in the hierarchy.

6. Finally, it may grab a bush or small tree, shake it vigorously, and even uproot it.

If the opponent does not flee, a full-scale fight may occur (Van Lawick-Goodall, 1968).

The Submissive Response

Fighting for dominance among males is unique in that it can be blocked or inhibited by specific, generally species-specific stimulus input.

The defeated animal successfully avoids serious injury by engaging in particular ritualized behaviors that function to prevent further attack by the superior contestant. These behaviors have been referred to as submissive (Matthews, 1964) or appeasement (Lorenz, 1966) responses. Schenkel (1967) has characterized "active submission" in the wolf and dog as "impulses and effort of the inferior toward the friendly harmonic social integration," or as a request for "love" from the superior animal. It is important to recognize that one need not project such complex cognitive-affective mental states onto animals in order to recognize that a particular behavior in one animal has a high probability of eliciting a particular behavior on the part of a responding animal. The terms *submission, appeasement, love,* and so on, are descriptive of mental states recognizable by humans. They may, of course, have nothing at all to do with the mental states (if any) that occur in animals behaving in the manner described as submissive, appeasing, and so on.

Although the intent and the derivation of these ritualized aggression-inhibiting responses have been variously interpreted, there can be little doubt that active, ongoing intermale aggression can be immediately blocked by the assumption of a particular stance or posture by the defeated animal. The ethological literature is replete with examples (Darwin, 1896; Eibl-Eibesfeldt, 1961, 1970; Cloudsley-Thompson, 1965; Lorenz, 1966). Lorenz (1966) devotes an entire chapter in his *On Aggression* ("Behavioral Analogies to Morality") to descriptions of various aggression-inhibiting signals. The wolf, it is said, turns its head away from its opponent and offers the jugular vein, which immediately inhibits further aggression from its rival. Or when the fight is clearly lost, the weaker wolf throws itself on its back, exposing all the vulnerable parts of the body to the victor, who "cannot" then follow up his advantage (Matthews, 1964).

Such rituals of appeasement exist in most species ranging from the rodent to the great apes. Detailed observations on the mouse indicate that the defeated animal "sits on its rump and rears without displaying the aggressive face." The posture is accompanied by vocalization. The submissive animal does not attempt to bite the attacker, but may push it away with the front feet. This posture reduces the aggressiveness of the attacker. If the defeated mouse attempts to flee, the victor follows for some distance in hot pursuit, with the result that the fleeing mouse is frequently bitten on the rump (Brain & Nowell, 1970). Brain and Nowell also indicate that the inhibition of aggression by posturing is found only in intermale aggression. The submissive posture in several laboratory animals is described by Grant and Mackintosh (1963). Grant (1963) constructed ethograms of the social behavior of the rat and showed that the submissive posture occurs as a response much more frequently than it is responded to. The opposing animal most frequently reacts to submission by refraining from further social behavior and by moving away from the social interaction. Aggression-inhibiting postures have also been described in detail by Barnett (1963) and Seward (1945).

As one might expect, the submissive behaviors in the chimpanzee are more complex. The defeated animal may raise its rump toward the opponent in a sexual presentation or it may reach out to be touched. The submissive chimp may bow or crouch or bob. Another common gesture is to retract the lips, exposing the teeth and gums (Van Lawick-Goodall, 1968).

The submissive postures, in general, tend to be quite different from those displayed during threat or actual fighting, and it may be that there are few components in the submissive posture that elicit aggression. Darwin (1896), in developing his principle of antithesis in emotional expression, emphasized that gestures of greeting and gestures of affection present a stimulus pattern that is quite the opposite of the pattern presented during threat. In the anecdotal methods of the times he presents some rather convincing examples. "When a dog approaches a strange dog or man in a savage or hostile frame of mind, he walks upright and very stiffly; his head is slightly raised, or not much lowered; the tail is held erect and quite rigid; the hairs bristle, especially along the neck and back; the pricked ears are directed forward and the eyes have a fixed stare."

Darwin suggests that the demeanor of the friendly greeting dog is just the reverse of threat. Instead of walking upright, the body sinks downward or even crouches, and is thrown into flexous movements; his tail, instead of being held stiff and upright, is lowered and wagged from side to side; his hair instantly becomes smooth; his ears are depressed and drawn backwards, but not closely to the head; and his lips hang loosely. From the drawing back of the ears, the eyelids become elongated, and the eyes no longer appear round and staring.

An analysis of many of the submissive postures manifest by mammals seems to indicate that, at least in a general way, Darwin's principle of antithesis appears to hold (Eisenberg, 1963). The animal that appears large in threat appears small in submission. The erect stance of threat is replaced by the supine posture of submission. The canines, which in many species are prominently displayed during threat, are hidden, covered, or turned away during gestures of appeasement.

Submissive Behavior as a Remotivating Display

However, it seems likely that more is involved in the act of submission than merely the absence of aggression-eliciting stimuli. Lorenz (1966) makes the salient point that in the aroused and "angry" animal there is considerable emotional momentum, and that the shift from one motivational state to another tends to be gradual rather than abrupt. Thus it seems that the appeasement postures provoke direct response inhibition on the part of the attacking animal.

Nothing is known as yet about the neurological mechanisms underlying the aggression-inhibiting capacity of submissive postures. However, the descriptive literature available suggests the possibility that elements of the submissive pose function to activate neural systems that are incompatible with the neural system for intermale aggression. Morris (1964) has referred to the submissive gestures as "remotivating displays"; that is, the submissive posture elicits from the attacking animal a response that is incompatible with further attack behavior. He suggests that an important component in the display in many species is pseudoinfantile and pseudosexual behavior. The behavior of the submissive wolf is frequently identical to the food begging of a puppy. Or, as indicated previously, the wolf may roll on its back and remain still. Such behavior does expose the vulnerable belly, but perhaps more important, it constitutes a "ritualized presentation for cleaning of the anal region," as is common in puppies (Fox, 1969). The submissive wolf may urinate, which elicits an actual cleaning response on the part of the dominating victorious animal (Eibl-Eibesfeldt, 1970).

A frequent component of submissive behavior in a number of subhuman primates involves sexual presentation. That is, the submissive animal turns and presents the hindquarters to the dominant animal (Kreveld, 1970; Chance & Jolly, 1970; Altman, 1962; Hall & DeVore, 1965). The presentation posture results in the elicitation of a perfunctory mounting response, which is incompatible with continued attack.

Aggression-inhibiting postures have not evolved in all species of animals. Neither the cotton rat (Bunnell & Smith, 1966) nor the dove (Lorenz, 1966), for example, seem to have developed such mechanisms; consequently, when escape is not possible, aggression may lead to the death of one of the animals. In general, however, in those species in which efficient weapons of defense or of predation have evolved, there has been a parallel development of aggression-inhibiting mechanisms. The resultant value to the species is obvious in that intraspecific confrontations do not generally have serious or lethal consequences.

Limited Wounding from Intermale Encounters.

One of the most remarkable characteristics of intermale aggression is the relatively small amount of injury that occurs during fighting. In other kinds of aggression, the animal uses its available weapons as effectively as possible to dispatch the antagonist. The terminal behavior in the predatory aggression sequence is the killing of the prey. Most typically, there is a bite directed at the cervical spine, which is both efficient and lethal. In contests between males, however, the fighting behaviors have evolved in such a way that the encounters result in a demonstrable superiority of one animal over the other with little physical damage. At a given stage in the conflict, one of the animals may flee and his opponent is unlikely to pursue for any distance, or the defeated animal may assume a posture that results in the inhibition of aggression on the part of the victor. In other instances the attack is aimed at portions of the opponent's anatomy that have evolved in such a way as to minimize injury.

Fighting among male elephant seals, for example, is vigorous and intense. It is conducted with the large upper canine teeth, which have considerable potential for damage. The bulls are frequently wounded and the older, more dominant veterans of many encounters display a large number of wrinkled scars in the neck region, where the attacks are directed. However, the elephant seal is well equipped by tough skin and fat pads to take a great deal of punishment in that part of the body (Matthews, 1964).

The agonistic behavior between males of the same species is highly ritualized and stereotyped. Again, the nature of the response is such that the possibility of serious wounding is minimized. Among fallow deer (*Dama dama*), rival stags engage in vigorous fighting. Their encounters consist of headlong charges against one another. However, they charge only when facing, with the result that the contact is antler to antler. An attack is never directed against the more vulnerable parts of the body. Fighting among male giraffes is common. They engage in neck-to-neck pushing matches or they swing their heads against the opponent's body or legs. They do not, however, attack with their sharp and dangerous hooves, which are reserved for defense against predators. The oryx and other antelopes may have extremely sharp horns for use in interspecific defense. In intraspecific interactions they are used only to lock the heads of the animals together during intermale pushing contests (Cloudsley-Thompson, 1965).

Another aspect of the hostile interactions among male conspecifics that tends to minimize serious injury is the role of learning. As indicated above, after a limited number of agonistic contacts between a given pair of animals, a dominance-submission relationship is set up between them. When this is accomplished, the probability of actual fighting is diminished because the more submissive animal has learned to respond to anticipatory aggressive responses (threat behavior) with submission or escape, which terminates the encounter. Thus the threat gestures functionally replace actual fighting.

In spite of several safeguards that have evolved to minimize serious consequences from intraspecific conflict, "fractricidal accidents" do occasionally occur and some animals are badly wounded. Pedersen (1962, quoted in Matthews, 1964) reports that a bull musk-ox is sometimes killed as a result of fractures in the frontal part of the skull received during an intermale head-butting match. Bull elephants have been killed as a result of tusk stab by a rival. Defeated hippos have died from heart penetration by the tooth of another male (Cloudsley-Thompson, 1965). In the fights between seals an eye may be burst or knocked out, and rarely an animal is killed (Bartholomew, 1967). Fights between male gibbons sometimes result in serious wounds, including broken bones (Carpenter, 1940). All these examples, however, are the exception rather than the rule.

As with most behaviors, the two major factors influencing dominance include environmental inputs and physiological processes. Other things being equal, any factor that increases the probability of other types of aggression occurring will also have a probability of increasing a given subject's rank in a dominance hierarchy, or of increasing the likelihood that it will defeat any given individual.

Environmental Variables:

There are a multitude of environmental inputs, from a drunken father to the observation of the "A TEAM" on television that may have an influence on dominance. Learning, in the broadest sense, is important. The functions of reward and punishment are obvious, as are the influences of various types of modeling. Conditioning in some circumstances may also influence the status of a given individual in a dominance submission relationship. Miller et al. (1955) have clearly shown that it is possible to manipulate social hierarchies in monkeys by punishing a dominant animal in the presence of a subordinate.

There are a variety of environmental inputs consisting of sign stimuli that may alter dominance relationships. Humans, of course, use many signs. Some are verbal and quite straight forward, such as "Now I shall have to kill you." Meltzoff (see pg.

201), in the paper *Lethal Dance,* describes a variety of signs used by New Guinea tribesmen to express dominance and designed to intimidate others.

Southwick (1969) has shown that the physical and the social environments are of the utmost importance in the aggressive behavior of the Rhesus monkey. Animals in forest habitats are less aggressive than are those living in rural villages and temple areas. A captive group showed the greatest number of aggressive interactions. The social climate had a more profound effect on aggression than did the physical environment. When strangers were introduced to the group, agonistic behaviors increased as much as tenfold, presumably in an attempt to reorganize the social order. Also see Teas et al. (1982) in this regard.

An important environmental variable that has an influence on dominance relationships is territoriality. It is generally agreed that aggressive encounters that occur within the territory (or central home range) of an animal will usually be won by the resident. The win occurs even though the resident, in other situations, may be subordinate. Although the relationship between dominance and territoriality is an interesting one, there are a number of problems with the concept of territoriality. One of the earliest definitions suggested that "territory is any defended area" (Noble, 1939). Many authors have adopted this definition (Ruffer, 1968; Jewell, 1966; Brown, 1966; and many others). For an historical account of this concept, see Carpenter's excellent review (Carpenter, 1958).

It has been repeatedly pointed out that home ranges may overlap, but territories generally do not because the various animals under study "defend" their territories and "protect" them from encroachment by conspecifics, or by male conspecifics, or by any intruder. How intensive a "defense" the animal puts up depends on the species under consideration and on how broad the experimenter wishes to make the definition.

Motivational states are not only attributed to the territory holder but are also not uncommonly attributed to the intruder. For example, Hamilton (1947, quoted in Wynne-Edwards, 1962, p. 187) suggests that the blue wildebeest (*Gorgon taurinus*) "strongly resents" encroachment on its grazing land. He also describes an instance in which intruders are chased by a territory-holding bull and then says, "Not the least remarkable phase of the incident was the *sense of wrong-doing* exhibited by the trespassers, which displayed not the smallest tendency to offer any resistance." (Emphasis added.)

Defend, protect, and *resent* are all terms that are descriptive of human motivational states. When these terms are applied to animals they are inferred from the behavior, and there can be no assurance that the animal has any mental process even remotely similar to those implied by such words. Observation indicates only that many kinds of animals live within certain restricted areas and that some of them engage in fighting behavior. It can also be said that, in general, the closer they are to the center of their territory, the more intense will be threatening gestures and fighting responses to an interloper. It is really no more reasonable to suggest that the animal is "defending" his territory than it is to believe that the intruder is defending his God-given right to territorial expansion. Crook (1968) makes the important point that, "In animal societies, individuals do not fight because they have territories; they have territories because, among other things, they fight."

It contributes very little to our understanding of the phenomenon to suggest that certain animals have an innate tendency for territorial defense. Understanding comes only when we can specify the variables of which this behavior is a function. We need to spell out specifically the stimulus characteristics that elicit this kind of behavior in a given animal. Further, since many animals engage in aggression within the home range only at particular times in the seasonal or life cycle, it is necessary to specify the physiological state of the animal during that aggressive period.

One need not impute unobservable need states, or motivations in order to understand the phenomenon of territoriality. There are alternative explanations.

There is evidence, of course, that animals do confine their activities to particular geographical locations and within a given location many animals spend a greater amount of time in so-called core areas. There is also abundant evidence that many animals engage in intraspecific fighting within home ranges and that many species tend to win encounters that are fought close to their core areas; that is, the animals on unfamiliar ground are chased away, infrequently injured, and on very rare occasions killed.

It is of little explanatory value to suggest that the large variety of factors contributing to fighting within an animal's home range are related to an innate tendency or need to defend a territory. The fact that the animal closest to the center of its home range is more likely to be successful in an encounter with an intruder is certainly not evidence that territorial defense is involved. Barnett (1969), for example, has suggested that aggressive behavior in the rat is territorial because the animal must be on familiar ground before it will attack a conspecific. By the same reasoning, one should refer to territorial sexual behavior and territorial eating behavior.

Animals are more "successful" in all their behaviors when they are on familiar ground. If one wishes to study sexual behavior, predation, or simply eating and drinking, it is essential that the animal be adapted to the environment. In a strange area the predominant behavior of most animals is cautious investigation, which is incompatible with aggressive, sexual, or consummatory behavior. Exploratory behavior overrides eating or drinking even under conditions of extreme deprivation. It has been repeatedly reported that a mouse in its home cage is more likely to initiate and to win a fight against an introduced intruder. However, Urich observed in 1938 that the stranger spends most of its time investigating the unfamiliar cage whereas the home cage mouse concentrates on fighting.

There are a variety of stimulus conditions that facilitate the tendency for one male to attack another. There is also a tendency on the part of most animals to investigate and/or escape from unfamiliar situations. There are a variety of ways in which motivational states can be mutually inhibitory. Thus if an animal is on unfamiliar ground, it has investigatory and escape tendencies that are incompatible with a full-blown aggressive response of whatever kind. If, under the pressure of attack, the animal flees to the familiar stimuli of its own core area, the factors producing escape and investigation tendencies are eliminated and the stimulus of its attacker elicits full and uninhibited aggressive proclivities. It is now likely to win an encounter with the aggressor, who is now itself on unfamiliar ground and has escape and investigation tendencies to compete with its hostile behaviors. In a series of chases and counterchases it would be expected that the animals might end up at the borders of their home ranges manifesting a combination of escape and aggressive behaviors that are frequently components of the threat response.

Since, as Carpenter (1958) suggests, the so-called territorial behavior is a higher-order construct that results from the action of a variety of sub-systems, it is not possible to attribute this behavior to particular physiological mechanisms. In different seasons and in different species, fighting in relation to a geographical location may be primarily between males, as in the Uganda kob (intermale aggression); restricted to a nest area and confined to lactating females, as in certain female mice (maternal aggression); or related to the herding of a harem, as in the Pinnipedia (sex-related aggression). The amount and intensity of fighting must also undoubtedly be a function of the success or failure of these various aggressive interactions and is therefore partly instrumental aggression.

Physiological Factors Include Neural and Hormonal Mechanisms.

The two basic physiological methods used for the neurological study of dominance and related problems have been brain stimulation and brain lesions. It has been shown repeatedly that brain lesions may reduce a subject's status in the hierarchy. The areas lesioned have included the amygdala, the orbital frontal area, as well as the prefrontal and temporal lobe. It is important to note that the situation in which the animals are tested is critical to the outcome. Amygdalectomized animals tested in the laboratory manifest no aggressive tendencies toward humans. However, if the amygdalectomized animals are released among normal animals in a natural setting, or in a natural group in a large cage, the subjects generally show a lack of fear or escape responses in relation to humans. At the same time, they tend to avoid social interactions with other animals and become social isolates. The dominance rank of the operated animals is reduced and they manifest inappropriate social behaviors which elicit aggression from the normal animals (Kling & Cornell, 1971; Kling et al., 1968). In a completely natural setting, operated animals released into their own group withdrew from all attempts by their peers to interact with them. The operates appeared fearful and eventually left the group (Kling et al., 1970). Briefly, the amygdalectomized animals in a fairly normal social setting appear to show an increase in fear in all social interactions.

In an attempt to resolve the discrepancy between the apparent loss of fear of man and the increase in fear of normal social interactions with other monkeys, Kling (1972) offers the hypothesis that the removal of the amygdala results in an inability to modulate an emotional response on the basis of context-specific information. This inability may result in a state of "depersonalization" such as has been reported in some human patients after amygdalectomy.

The studies on the orbital frontal area (Snyder, 1946), the prefrontal area (Brody & Rosvold, 1952), and portions of the temporal lobe (Plotnik et al., 1968), carried out on non-human primates, show that the lesions interfere with social adjustment and cause the social status of the individual to drop.

One cannot assume, however, that because dominance is affected by a given brain lesion, that the damaged area is responsible for dominance behavior. The relationship may be a circuitous one indeed. In addition to the suggestions of Kling, the actual effect may be due to neurological systems removed from the lesion. Some other deficiency, partial facial paralysis for example, may prevent the monkey from giving adequate social signals. Or, some other unmeasured variable may be critical to the finding, such as a reduction of spontaneous activity. The effect may also be due to the dependent variable used. Dominance relationships may very well lack stability if a single measure is used to represent the complex interactions between two or more animals. One can only begin to understand the subtle relationships if the details of the behavioral mechanisms are observed. Benton (1982) puts it well when he says,

The problem remains that those who have used competitive measures of dominance often did so because they were unable to observe overt fighting. One answer may be to take more detailed ethological descriptions of social interactions.

Benton (1981) noted that too frequently, the complex dynamic interaction between animals is reported as one measure. An additional benefit from a more ethological analysis of behavior is that drugs and hormones do not influence all behavioral postures usually described as characteristically dominant or subordinate in the same way. It seems likely that the ethological approach will demonstrate that subcategories of dominant behavior have different biological bases. Alternatively, if subcategories of behaviour are influenced in a similar way by particular drugs or hormones, then we may feel safer in using a range of behavior in composite scores.

Stimulation Studies:

Stimulation studies are equally problematic and can be difficult to interpret. Frank Ervin (Ervin et al., 1969, pp. 54–55) has indicated many of these interpretation problems:

1. A synchronous electrical discharge is quite different from the exquisitely patterned afferent volley of physiologic signals.

2. In a complex neural aggregate the electrical input may activate excitatory and inhibitory, afferent, efferent, and integrative, or cholinergic and adrenergic systems indiscriminately.

3. The instantaneous state of cerebral organization—i.e., all the other influences acting on the object structure at the time of stimulation—is unknown.

4. At best, the site stimulated is part of an integrated system, so that the stimulus is like a rock thrown in a pond —perhaps influencing by waves a distant lily pad. The stimulation of a structure says what it can do under certain circumstances, not what it does do normally.

5. It should be further emphasized that ablation is not the reciprocal of stimulation in other than very simple input and output systems.

   It might best be said that both stimulation and ablation experiments should be described with the emphasis on how the organism functions in the new state of cerebral organization necessitated by the experimental intervention.

In spite of the above cautions, stimulation studies do provide us with some insights into the neurological mechanisms involved.

Robinson, et al., (1969) have produced what clearly seems to be an example of intermale aggression in the primate *M. mulatta*. An electrode was implanted in the anterior area of the hypothalamus. It was bolted to the animal's skull and connected to a radio receiver that the subject wore on its head. When the stimulated animal was confined to a primate chair it made no attempt to attack the experimenter, nor did it manifest a random type of aggression against inanimate objects. When in a colony situation, however, the brain stimulation resulted in an attack on another male that was dominant to the experimental monkey. Other investigators have found that it is difficult to change a dominance hierarchy by brain stimulation (Delgado, 1965). In this case, however, the attacks by the experimental animal were so intense that the formerly dominant subject became submissive.

This appears to be a rather clear cut case of an intermale activity that resulted in dominance change. The experimental animal showed no tendency to attack. Although it is complex and, without doubt interacts with other neurological mechanisms, there appears to be an identifiable neurological system associated with intermale aggression, and thus with the systems relating to dominance. It is characteristic of the nervous system that active neural systems have associated with them inhibitors which tend to block the active system when the inhibitors are active. A series of studies by Delgado (1963, 1965) indicate that inhibitory systems also exist for the intermale aggression mechanisms. Delgado also used a telestimulation device so that the animal could be stimulated by remote control.

In a classic experiment, it was shown that remote stimulation of the caudate nucleus of the boss monkey in a colony blocked his spontaneous aggressive tendencies. His territoriality diminished and the other monkeys in the colony reacted to him differently. They made fewer submissive gestures and showed less fear. When the caudate was being stimulated it was possible for the experimenter to enter the cage and catch the monkey with bare hands. During one phase of the experiment, the button for the transmitter was placed inside the cage near the feeding tray and thus made available to all the monkeys in the colony. One of the submissive animals learned to press the button during periods when the boss monkey showed aggressive tendencies. When the boss made threatening gestures, the smaller monkey would frequently look him straight in the eye and press the button, thus directly calming him down and reducing his hostile tendencies (Delgado, 1963, 1965).

Winning an encounter may be its own reward regardless of other rewards, such as availability of sex or food. That is to say, the win may produce positive affect in and of itself. Since animals do not respond well to questioning, it is difficult to get good data; however, at least one study has shown that monkeys will press a bar in order to receive stimulation that produced intermale aggression (Robinson et al., 1969). One might infer from this that the activation of the intermale system produced positive affect because the animal would work to turn it on. However, there are other possible interpretations. The current may activate more than one neural system at the same time. These systems may be functionally discrete even though they are anatomically proximal. Thus the affective state generated by the stimulation may be irrelevant to the manifest behavior. More definitive information on this problem must come from work with humans who can provide verbal reports on the affective states that accompany dominance oriented responses. There are other animal experiments, however, that do give some insight into the problem of the reward value of intermale aggression.

There are several lines of evidence to indicate that the opportunity to engage in intermale aggression may be positively reinforcing to the participants. The opportunity for one male to attack another will suffice to support the learning of new response patterns. Male mice trained as fighters using the "dangling" procedure of Scott (1958) learned a positive response in a T-maze when the only reinforcer used was the opportunity to attack a "victim" mouse. When the reinforcer was withdrawn, the response extinguished and the position response was reversed when the victim mouse was moved to the opposite side of the T (Tellegren et al., 1969).

It has also been shown that trained fighters run faster in a runway if the running behavior results in a 5-second opportunity to attack a victim mouse. The starting latency for these animals is shorter than that of controls; they acquire the running response in fewer days and take longer to extinguish than do control subjects (Legrand, 1970). Further, Fredericson (1949, 1951) showed many years ago that the latency for "spontaneous" fighting between male mice decreased over days when they were permitted to fight once a day. If a fight between mice is interrupted, the victorious mouse will push open a door and run from one compartment to another to get at its opponent, as will one of a pair of evenly matched mice. The only reward for this behavior is an opportunity to continue the fight. The latency of this response is significantly shorter than that of either defeated mice or mice not involved in an aggressive incident (Lagerspetz, 1964). If a fight immediately precedes a trial, aggressive mice will also cross an electrified grid to get at a defeated opponent. Again there is no reward available except the opportunity to fight (Lagerspetz, 1964).

Endocrine Mechanisms

Only recently have adequate measures of androgens and other hormones in the blood stream become available. The behavioral effects of hormones must operate through their effects on the brain and these interactions are, of course, incredibly complex. Additionally, experiments and clinical observations on humans frequently present problems in interpretation. Because experiments frequently lack some desirable controls, it is difficult to determine the role of variables not specifically considered in a particular study. Manipulations of blood chemistry, either experimental or natural, do not occur in a vacuum; a large number of factors are constantly interacting to affect the changes in aggression potential that result from blood changes. Additionally, there are wide individual differences in susceptibility to various hormones.

Changes in hormone levels cause changes in subjective experience that may be interpreted differently by different individuals because of their prior learning. The individual's expectations may strongly influence his behavior, and the experience he has after a given manipulation will be influenced by his interpretations of the expectations of others about how he should be affected.

For these reasons one must be cautious in the interpretation of the many studies which demonstrate that social hierarchies are influenced by various endocrine mechanisms. A given preparation may serve as a precurser to the actual active hormone, and it may influence more than one endocrine system. For example, one of the corticosteroids (hormones from the adrenal cortex) may reduce the amount of ACTH put out by the pituitary.

In spite of all the difficulties, however, it is possible to draw some tentative conclusions about the role of blood chemistry changes and aggressive behavior in humans. Much of the evidence in this section is clinical and some of the studies have a small number of subjects and fewer controls than one would find with comparable animal experiments. Although one must be cautious about the meaning of these findings, the results are frequently suggestive of hypotheses that should be followed up and tested more carefully in the future.

While endocrine studies are relatively easy to do, interpretation is always problematic. Whereas it is generally the case that changes in hormonal balance which increase intermale aggression also show a measurable increase in social dominance, it is not necessarily so. The treated subject may be a violent isolate that will win a one to one encounter but removes itself from social interactions, thus having no position on the dominance scale.

Androgen Levels and Dominance

Indirect evidence of the relationship between levels of androgens and aggressive behavior can be derived from studies of the seasonal fluctuations of this type of behavior in primates. Wilson and Boelkins (1970), in a study of the colony of rhesus monkeys on Cayo Santiago Island, have shown that high levels of aggression (as measured by amount of wounding and deaths) occur most frequently in males during the mating season and in females during the birth season. These authors cite evidence to show that the testes are larger during the breeding season (Sade, 1964) and that the relative spermatogenesis occurs during the spring birth season and maximum spermatogenesis during the mating season (Conaway & Sade, 1965). They conclude from these data that the most plausible interpretation of the elevated frequencies of aggression during the mating season is indirectly due to the hormonal changes at that time in the mature males. Alexander (1970) also reports seasonal changes in the behavior of adult male Japanese monkeys, indicating that increases in affiliative behavior result from the seasonal withdrawal of androgens.

The plasma testosterone levels of male rhesus monkeys have been shown to correlate with a number of agonistic behaviors. Threatening and chasing behavior and being submitted to by another member of the colony all correlate significantly with testosterone plasma levels. Submissive behavior is negatively correlated with testosterone level, but not significantly so. This is interpreted as indicating that an animal with a high frequency of aggressive contacts with its subordinates will generally show a higher testosterone level, regardless of how frequently he responds submissively to those above him in the dominance hierarchy. (See Table 1). Dominance rank within the colony is also correlated with plasma testosterone concentration. The animals in the highest quartile had significantly higher testosterone levels than those animals lower in the hierarchy (Rose et al., 1971).

Table 1

Testosterone and Behavior

A. Testosterone and behavioral correlations

Total aggression	0.469
Non contact aggression	0.515
Receives submission	0.516
Tension	0.534
Dominance rank	0.350 (rho)
Submission	−0.320 NS

B. Behavioral intercorrelations

Aggression and receives submission	0.543
Aggression and dominance rank	0.710 (rho)
Submission and dominance rank	−0.650 (rho)
Aggression and tension	0.334 NS
Tension and dominance rank	0.490 (rho)

All correlations listed are Pearson's r except those shown as p, which are Spearman's rank-order correlations. All are significant to at least $p < 0.05$, except those followed by NS. For all correlations, n = 34.

From R. M. Rose et al., "Plasma testosterone, dominance rank and aggressive behavior in male rhesus monkeys," *Nature* (1971), *231*, 367.

There are numerous studies that show an increase in intermale aggression scores when the subject is treated with one of the androgens, while, conversely, gonadectomy results in a reduction of such scores. Much of this information has been collected on rodents and it must be recognized that the same findings do not necessarily apply to primates (See Dixson, 1980) for an excellent and detailed review). Recent evidence also indicates that endogenous levels of androgens are influenced by the subject's fighting behavior. In general, winning an aggressive encounter results in an increase of the circulating levels of testosterone and other steroids. This has been shown in mice (McKinney & Dejardins, 1973). Animals defeated in a fight have lower levels of circulating plasma testosterone (Bronson & Dejardins, 1971). This general finding has been substantiated in the male rhesus monkey. Defeat in dominance encounters causes a significant decrease in testosterone levels. Rose et al. (1971, 1972) indicate that dominant males show relatively high circulating levels of testosterone. Although there are wide individual differences, there appear to be dramatic increases in testosterone and androstenedione (a biologically active form of testosterone) levels in adolescent human males. There are differences between the sexes prior to puberty, but after the age of 9, boys show a gradual increase in testosterone levels. At ages 10 to 15 the increase is on the order of tenfold. Adolescent boys do, of course, show an increase in aggressive behavior, but the increases in testosterone levels have not yet been related to any measures of aggression in adolescents (Hamburg, 1971b).

Until recently, essentially no information had been available relating the endocrine function and affective response tendencies in man. However, with improvement in assay techniques (see Hamburg & Lunde, 1966), such studies are beginning to appear. A suggestive relationship was found between the activity of the pituitary (luteinizing hormone) testicular axis and feelings of hostility, anger, and aggression (Persky et al., 1968). A further study was undertaken on the basis of those findings, using more refined techniques involving the measurement of plasma testosterone level and testosterone production rate (Persky et al., 1971). Two groups of men were studied. The 18 individuals in the younger group ranged from 17 to 28 years of age, and the 15 older men were between the ages of 30 and 66 years. The average testosterone production rate of the older men was about half that of the younger men and when all the subjects were considered as a group, a significant negative correlation ($r = -.062$) was shown between age and testosterone production rate. This is an interesting finding in itself, inasmuch as it has been shown that violent crime in the United States is most prevalent among males between the ages of 15 and 24.

This study also showed that in the younger men the production rate of testosterone was highly correlated with a measure of aggression derived from the Buss-Durkee Hostility Inventory,[3] and a multivariate regression equation was obtained between the testosterone production rate and four different measures of aggression and hostility. This equation accounted for 82 percent of the variance in the production rate of testosterone for the younger men. In the older age group the only variable that correlated highly with testosterone production was age, and the regression equation that was highly predictive for the young men was not valid for the older age group.

In another study aggressive behavior and plasma testosterone were assessed in a young criminal population (Kreuz & Rose, 1972). The subjects were selected to provide a high-aggression and a low-aggression group using the number of times that an individual had been placed in solitary confinement as the index for assignment to the two groups. That index was associated with fighting behavior and resulted in highly differentiated groups. Fighters were defined as those individuals who had been in more than one fight during their imprisonment. Plasma testosterone was measured in six plasma samples taken within one hour of awakening. Although there was a significant difference between the two groups in terms of actual fighting behavior and verbal aggression, the differences on plasma testosterone were not significant. Paper and pencil tests were also given to the subjects. Hostility was measured by the Buss-Durkee Hostility Inventory but no significant correlation was found between the hostility test scores and fighting in prison, and the hostility scores did not correlate with plasma testosterone. However, an investigation of the type of crime for which the subjects were incarcerated revealed that those individuals who had committed violent and aggressive offenses during adolescence had a significantly higher testosterone level than men who had not committed that type of offense. There was also a significant correlation between the age of the first conviction for a violent crime and the plasma testosterone level. However, the past history of assaultive behavior was not correlated with either fighting in prison or hostility as measured by the paper and pencil test.

The results of the Kreuz and Rose (1972) study are somewhat surprising in light of the Persky et al. (1971) study, which used the same hostility inventory. It may well be that a variety of potent pressures in the prison setting influence the instrumental aggression of the subjects. Reinforcement in the prison tends to be swift and severe and may be a more important determinant of actual behavior than whatever internal tendencies to hostility are set up by the testosterone level. The behavior that did correlate with plasma testosterone took place outside the prison. The reasons for the lack of relationship between the scores on the Buss-Durkee inventory and testosterone level are not clear at the moment.

The preceding studies on blood levels of testosterone and aggressive tendencies use males as subjects, but it is not possible from the data to determine whether the hostility measured is a form of *intermale or irritable aggression*, or some combination of both.

Although uncontrolled clinical studies must be interpreted with caution, several reports on humans offer support for the idea that exogenous androgens enhance aggressive tendencies. One series of schizophrenic patients showed a decrease in fearfulness and apprehension and increased self-confidence when treated with Diandrone (dehydroisoandosterone) (Strauss et al., 1952). A decrease in feelings of inferiority, timidity, and apathy with an increase in self-confidence occurred in young males with "inadequate personality" after four days to four weeks of therapy with the same preparation (Sands & Chamberlain, 1952). Diandrone is also reported to exert an androgenic effect in the social and psychological rather than in the physical or sexual field. Masculine activity, aggression, and self-confidence are enhanced. The timid "shrinking violet" becomes more adequate, and aggressive tendencies in individuals with manifest hostility are made flagrantly worse (Sands, 1954).

Although the evidence is far from conclusive, it certainly suggests a relationship between testosterone level in the male and some indications of aggressive behavior. This is what one might expect from the numerous studies on animals. One could also expect the relationship to be less powerful because learning is such a potent factor in aggressive behavior in humans. Learned inhibitions can, of course, prevent an individual from acting on relatively strong aggressive feelings that might occur because of the sensitivity produced in the neural systems for aggression by a relatively high androgen level.

A more recent study (Elias, 1981) investigated the levels of testosterone and cortisol (a steroid from the adrenal cortex) in male wrestlers after either a win or a loss. Winners of competitive matches showed greater increases in both cortisol and testosterone than losers. The author concludes, "These findings indicate that humans, like other social mammals may undergo specific endocrine changes in response to victory or defeat."

Can Aggression be Inherited?

The answer to that specific question must be "no." However, the concept must not be discarded too easily. One cannot inherit behaviors or behavioral tendencies. One inherits only structures. However, if, as clearly indicated above, there are a variety of physiological mechanisms, both neural and endocronological, on which aggression is based, it can be seen that the inheritance of particular structures or patterns of structures will, of course, predispose the individual to the expression of aggression. If that is true, it should be possible to breed aggressive types of subjects and non-aggressive subjects.

There can be no doubt that animals can be bred specifically for particular kinds of aggression; for example, fighting cocks, fighting bulls, and pit dogs have been selectively bred for fighting behavior. There are clear-cut strain differences in the probability of predatory attack. Seventy percent of Norway rats kill mice, whereas only 12 percent of the domesticated Norways do (Karli, 1956). A significantly higher percentage of Long-Evans hooded rats kill chickens than do Sprague-Dawley albinos (Bandler & Moyer, 1970).

There are also strain differences in intermale fighting (Scott, 1942; Southwick & Clark, 1968). A number of experimenters have shown that it is possible, through selective breeding, to develop aggressive and non-aggressive strains of animals. In these cases the behavior studied was also intermale aggression (Hall & Klein, 1942; Lagerspetz, 1964; Stone, 1932; Yerkes, 1913). The most extensive study of the genetics of aggression has been done on mice selectively bred for high and low aggressiveness according to a seven-point scale of behavior during a period in which formerly isolated mice were paired. It is interesting to note that the selection process was carried out only on males, since the females did not show enough aggression to score. Table 2 shows the mean aggression score for each successive generation. As McLearn (1969) points out, "In combination with the differences among inbred strains in aggressiveness, this success in selective breeding for aggressive behavior constitutes unassailable evidence of the importance of hereditary factors in determining individual differences in mouse aggressiveness."

There are, of course, no comparable data on humans. However, there must be hereditary factors contributing to the determination of individual differences of some kinds of aggression in

Table 2

The Selective Breeding Experiments

Genera-tion	Number of selected males		Age at selec-tion (Months)	Range of test scores of selected animals		Number of successful matings		Number of offspring			
	A	N		A	N	A	N		A		N
P	3	3	3–6	5.3–7.0	1.8–2.1	4	3	10	8	12	8
S₁	4	4	4½	4.1–5.9	1.5–1.9	5	4	25	8	7	10
S₂	6	4	4½	4.1–6.6	1.3–2.4	7	7	29	22	22	19
S₃	6	6	4½	5.0–6.2	1.1–1.9	7	7	20	15	22	14
S₄	7	7	4½	6.1–7.0	1.0–1.7	6	6	30	24	27	23
S₅	7	8	4½	5.9–6.9	1.4–1.7	9	9	31	37	26	31
S₆	9	9	4½	6.4–6.9	1.0–1.6	10	13	34	30	28	34

humans. Certainly there are vast inherited differences in the human nervous and endocrine systems. If, in fact, there are specific neural systems which are responsible for particular types of aggression, one would expect genetic variability in the sensitivity of those structures. If, as appears to be the case, the sensitivity of these systems varies as a function of the level of certain circulating hormones, one would also expect genetic variability in the factors that contribute to the determination of the hormone levels in the blood stream.

A consideration of the concept that there is the possibility of innate mechanism that may increase the probability that aggressiveness in humans frequently leads to conclusions about the inevitability of war. And, the concept that the mafia and the beast of Buchenwald must, then, forever be with us is concluded. Philosophical questions are raised: Are humans innately evil, and are the discussants at scientific meetings born with the hostility they so frequently display?

Human aggression of any kind is not inevitable. There are no behaviors based on physiological mechanisms (as all behaviors must be) that cannot be modified through a multiplicity of environmental inputs. These include all kinds of learning. It can be convincingly shown that aggressive responses can be learned. The inhibition of aggression can also be learned, as it has been by hundreds of millions of people around the world. The probability of innate mechanisms for aggression is food for thought, but not despair.

References

Alexander, B.K., "Parental behavior of adult male Japanese monkeys," *Behaviour.* 1970, *38*, 543–547.

Altman, M., "Naturalistic studies of maternal care in the moose and elk," in H.L. Rheingold (ed.), *Maternal behavior in mammals.* New York: Wiley, 1963, pp. 233–253.

Ardrey, R., *The territorial imperative.* New York: Atheneum, 1966.

Bandler, R.J., & Moyer, K.E., "Animals spontaneously attacked by rats," *Communications in Behavioral Biology.* 1970, *5*, 177–182.

Barnett, S.A., *A study in behavior.* London: Methuem, 1963.

Barnett, S.A., "Grouping and dispersive behavior among wild rats," in S. Garattini & E.B. Sigg (eds.), *Aggressive behavior.* New York: Wiley, 1969, pp. 3–14.

Bartholomew, G.A., Jr., Discussion of paper by K.S. Norris, "Aggressive behavior in Cetacea," in C.D. Clemente & D.B. Lindsley (eds.), *Aggres-*

sion and defense: Neural mechanisms and social patterns, Vol. V, Brain function. Los Angeles: University of California Press, 1967, pp. 232–241.

Benton, D., "Is the concept of dominance useful in understanding rodent behavior?" Aggressive Behavior. 1982, 8, 104–107.

Benton, D., "The measurement of aggression," in P.F. Brain & D. Benton (eds.), The Biology of Aggression. Alphen aan den Rijn, The Netherlands: Sijthoff/Noordhoff, pp. 487–502.

Blurton Jones, N.G., "An ethological study of some aspects of social behaviour of children in nursery school," in D. Morris (ed.), Primate Ethology. London: Doubleday, 1969, pp. 437–463.

Brain, P.F., & Nowell, N.W., "Some observations on intermale aggression testing in albino mice," Communications in Behavioral Biology. 1970, 5, 7–17.

Brody, E.B., & Rosvold, H.E., "Influence of prefrontal lobotomy on social interaction in a monkey group," Psychosomatic Medicine. 1952, 14, 406–415.

Bronson, F.H., & Dejardins, C., "Steroid hormones and aggressive behavior in mammals," in B. Eleftheriou & J. Scott (eds.), The Physiology of Aggression and Defeat. London: Plenum Press, 1971, pp. 43–64.

Broom, L., & Selznick, P., Sociology: A text with adapted readings. New York: Harper & Row, 1957.

Brown, L.E., "Home range and movement of small mammals," in P.A. Jewell & C. Loizos (eds.), Play, exploration and territory in mammals. London: Academic Press, 1966, pp. 85–107.

Bunnell, B.N., & Smith, M.H., "Septal lesions and aggressiveness in the cotton rat" Sigmodon hispidus, Psychonomic Science. 1966, 6, 443–444.

Buss, A., The psychology of aggression. New York: Wiley, 1961.

Candland, D.K., Bryan, D.C., Nazar, B.L., Kopf, K.J., & Sendor, M., "Squirrel monkey heart rate during formation of status orders," Journal of Comparative and Physiological Psychology. 1970, 70, 417–423.

Carpenter, C.R., "A field study in some of the behavior and social relations of howling monkeys," Comparative Psychology Monographs. 1940, 10, 1–168.

Carpenter, C.R., "Territoriality: A review of concepts and problems," in A. Roe & G.G. Simpson (eds.), Behavior and evolution. New Haven: Yale University Press, 1958, pp. 224–250.

Carpenter, C.R., Naturalistic behavior of non-human primates. University Park, PA: Pennsylvania State University Press, 1964.

Chance, M., & Jolly, C., Social groups of monkeys, apes, and men. New York: Dutton, 1970.

Cloudsley-Thompson, J.L., Animal conflict and adaptation. Chester-Springs, PA: Dufour, 1965.

Conaway, C.H., & Sade, D.S., "The seasonal spermatogenic cycle in free ranging Rhesus monkeys," Folia Primatologica. 1965, 3, 1–12.

Cressey, D.R., "Crime," in R.K. Merton & R.A. Nisbet (eds.), Contemporary Social Problems. New York: Harcourt Brace Jovanovich, 1961, pp. 21–76.

Crook, J.H., "The nature and function of territorial aggression," in M.F.A. Montague (ed.), *Man and aggression*. London: Oxford University Press, 1968, pp. 141–178.

Darwin, C., *The expression of emotions in man and animals*. New York: D. Appleton, 1896 (authorized edition).

Davenport, W., "Sexual patterns and their regulation in a society of the southwest Pacific," in F.A. Beach (ed.), *Sex and behavior*. New York: Wiley, 1965, pp. 164–207.

Delgado, J.M.R., "Cerebral heterostimulation in a monkey colony," *Science*. 1963, *141*, 161–163.

Delgado, J.M.R., *Evolution of physical control of the brain*. New York: The American Museum of Natural History, 1965.

DeVore, I. (ed.), *Primate behavior: Field studies of monkeys and apes*. New York: Holt, Rinehart & Winston, 1965.

Dixson, A.F., "Androgens and aggressive behavior in primates: A review," *Aggressive Behavior*. 1980, *6*, 37–67.

Eibl-Eibesfeldt, I., "The fighting behavior of animals," *Scientific American*. 1961, *205*, 112–122.

Eibl-Eibesfeldt, I., "Ontogenetic and maturational studies of aggressive behavior," in C.D. Clemente & D.B. Lindsley (eds.), *Aggression and defense: Neural mechanisms and social patterns*, Vol. V, *Brain function*. Los Angeles: University of California Press, 1967, pp. 57–94.

Eibl-Eibesfeldt, I., *Ethology: The biology of behavior*. New York: Holt, Rinehart & Winston, 1970.

Eisenberg, J.F., "The behavior of heteromyid rodents," *University of California Publication in Zoology*. 1963, *69*, 1–114.

Elias, M., "Serum cortisol, testosterone, and testosterone-binding globulin responses to competitive fighting in human males," *Aggressive Behavior*. 1981, *7*, 215–224.

Ervin, F.R., Mark, V.H., & Stevens, J., "Behavioral and effective responses to brain stimulation in man," in J. Zubin & C. Shagass (eds.), *Neurobiological Aspects of Psychopathology*. New York: Grune & Stratton, 1969, pp. 54–55.

Fox, M.W., "The anatomy of aggression and its ritualization in Canidae: A developmental and comparative study," *Behaviour*. 1969, *35*, 242–258.

Fredericson, E., "Response latency and habit strength in relationship to spontaneous combat in C57 black mice," *Journal of Psychology*. 1950, *29*, 89–100.

Fredericson, E., "Time and aggression," *Psychological Review*. 1951, *58*, 41–51.

Goy, R.W., "Role of androgens in the establishment and regulation of behavioral sex differences in mammals," *Journal of Animal Science*. 1966, *25*, Supplement, 21–35.

Goy, R.W., "Organizing effects of androgen on the behaviour of Rhesus monkeys," in R.P. Michael (ed.), *Endocrinology and human behavior*. London: Oxford University Press, 1968, pp. 12–31.

Grant, E.C., "An analysis of the social behaviour of the male laboratory rat," *Behaviour*. 1963, *21*, 260–281.

Grant, E.C., & Mackintosh, J.H., "A comparison of the social postures of some common laboratory rodents," *Behaviour*. 1963, *21*, 246–259.

Gray, J.A., "Sex differences in emotional behaviour in mammals including man: Endocrine bases," *Acta Psychologica.* 1971, *35,* 29–46.

Hall, C.S., & Klein, S.J., "Individual differences in aggressiveness in rats," *Journal of Comparative and Physiological Psychology.* 1942, *33,* 371–383.

Hall, K.R.L., & DeVore, I., "Baboon social behavior," in I. DeVore (ed.), *Primate behavior.* New York: Holt, Rinehart & Winston, 1965, pp. 53–110.

Hamburg, D.A., "Psychobiological studies of aggressive behavior," *Nature.* 1971a, *230,* 19–23.

Hamburg, D.A., "Recent research on hormonal factors relevant to human aggressiveness," *International Social Science Journal.* 1971b, *23,* 36–47.

Hamburg, D.A., & Lunde, D.T., "Sex hormones in the development in sex differences in human behavior," in E. Maccoby (ed.), *The development of sex differences in human behavior.* Palo Alto, CA: Stanford University Press, 1966, pp. 1–24.

Hamilton, J.S., *Wildlife in South Africa.* London: Cassell, 1947.

Harlow, H.F., "Sexual behavior in the Rhesus monkey," in F.A. Beach (eds.), *Sex and behavior.* New York: Wiley, 1965, pp. 234–266.

Jewell, P.A., & Loizos, C. (eds.), *Play, exploration and territory in mammals.* London: Academic Press, 1966.

Karli, P., "The Norway rat's killing response to the white mouse," *Behaviour.* 1956, *10,* 81–103.

Kling, A., "Effects of amygdalectomy on social-affective behavior in nonhuman primates," in B.E. Eleftheriou (ed.), *The neurobiology of amygdala.* New York: Plenum, 1972, pp. 511–536.

Kling, A., & Cornell, R., "Amygdalectomy and social behavior in the caged stump-tailed macaque (*M. speciosa*)," *Folia Primatologica.* 1971, *14,* 190–208.

Kling, A., Dicks, D., & Gurowitz, E.M., "Amygdalectomy and social behavior in a caged-group of vervets (*C. aethiops*)," *Proceedings of the 2nd International Congress of Primateology.* Atlanta, GA., 1968, *1,* 232–241.

Kling, A., Lancaster, J., & Benitone, J., "Amygdalectomy in the free-ranging vervet," *Journal of Psychiatric Research.* 1970, *7,* 191–199.

Kreveld, D.A., "A selective review of dominance-subordination relations in animals," *Genetic Psychology Monographs.* 1970, *81,* 143–173.

Kummer, H., *Social organization of Hamadryas baboons: A field study.* Chicago: University of Chicago Press, 1968.

Lagerspetz, K., "Studies on the aggressive behavior of mice," *Annales Academiae Scientiarum Fennicae.* 1964, Series B, *131,* 1–131.

Legrand, R., "Successful aggression as the reinforcer for runway behavior of mice," *Psychonomic Science.* 1970, *20,* 303–305.

Lorenz, K., "Ritualized fighting," in J.D. Carthy & F.J. Eibling (eds.), *The natural history of aggression.* New York: Academic Press, 1964.

Lorenz, K., *On aggression.* New York: Harcourt, Brace, Jovanovich, 1966.

Matthews, L.H., "Overt fighting in mammals," in J.D. Carthy & F.J. Ebling (eds.), *The natural history of aggression.* London: Academic Press, 1964, pp. 23–32.

McIntyre, A., "Sex differences in children's aggression," *Proceedings of the Annual Convention of the American Psychological Association.* 1972, 7, 93–94.

McKinney, T.D., & Dejardins, C., "Androgens, fighting and mating during postnatal maturation in male house mice," *Biology of Reproduction.* 1972, 7, 112.

Meltzoff, S.K., "Lethal dance." Paper presented at the 12th International Conference on the Unity of the Sciences. Chicago, Ill., November, 1983.

Miller, R.E., Murphy, J.V., & Mirsky, I.A., "The modification of social dominance in a group of monkeys by interanimal conditioning," *Journal of Comparative and Physiological Psychology.* 1955, 48, 392–396.

Morris, D., "In discussion of L.H. Matthews—overt fighting in mammals," in J.D. Carthy & F.J. Ebling (eds.), *The natural history of aggression.* London: Academic Press, 1964, pp. 33–38.

National Commission on the Causes and Prevention of Violence, "To establish justice, to insure domestic tranquility" (Final Report). Washington, DC: U.S. Government Printing Office, 1969.

Noble, G.K., "The role of dominance in the social life of birds," *Auk.* 1939, 56, 263–273.

Payne, A.P., & Swanson, H.H., "Agonistic behaviour between pairs of hamsters of the same and opposite sex in a neutral observation area," *Behaviour.* 1970, 36, 259–269.

Pedersen, A., *Polar animals* (translated from the French by Gwynne Vevers). London: Alwin, 1962.

Persky, H., Smith, K.D., & Basu, G.K., "Relation of psychologic measures of aggression and hostility to testosterone production in man," *Psychosomatic Medicine.* 1971, 33, 265–277.

Persky, H., Zuckerman, H., & Curtis, G.C., "Endocrine function in emotionally disturbed and normal men," *Journal of Nervous and Mental Disease.* 1968, 146, 488–497.

Ploog, D.W., "The behavior of squirrel monkeys (*Saimiri sciureus*) as revealed by sociometry, bioacoustics, and brain stimulation," in S.A. Altman (ed.), *Social communication among primates.* Chicago: University of Chicago Press, 1967.

Plotnik, R., King, F.A., & Roberts, L., "Effects of competition on aggressive behavior of Squirrel and Cebus monkeys," *Behaviour.* 1968, 32, 315–332.

Resko, J.A., "Plasma androgen levels of the Rhesus monkey: The effects of age and season." *Endocrinology,* 1967, 81, 1203–1212.

Robinson, B.W., Alexander, M., & Bowne, G., "Dominance reversal resulting from aggressive responses evoked by brain telestimulation," *Physiology and Behavior.* 1969, 4, 749–752.

Rose, R.M., Gordon, T.P., & Bernstein, I.S., "Plasma testosterone levels in the male rhesus: Influences of sexual and social stimuli,"*Science.* 1972, 178, 643–654.

Rose, R.M., Holaday, J.W., & Bernstein, I.S., "Plasma testosterone, dominance rank and aggressive behavior in male rhesus monkeys," *Nature.* 1971, 231, 367.

Ruffer, D.G., "Agonistic behavior of the northern grasshopper mouse

(*Onychonys leucogaster breviauritus*)," *Journal of Mammalogy*. 1968, *49*, 481–487.

Sade, D.S., "Seasonal cycle in size of testes of free ranging *Macaca mulatta*," *Folia Primatologica*. 1964, *2*, 171–180.

Sands, D.E., "Further studies on endocrine treatment in adolescence and early adult life," *Journal of Mental Science*. 1954, *100*, 211–219.

Sands, D.E., & Chamberlain, G.H.A., "Treatment of inadequate personality in juveniles by dehydroisoandrosterone," *British Medical Journal*. 1952, *5*, 66–68.

Schenkel, R., "Submission: Its features and functions in the wolf and dog," *American Zoologist*. 1967, *7*, 319–329.

Scott, J.P., "Genetic differences in the social behavior of inbred strains of mice," *Journal of Heredity*. 1942, *33*, 11–15.

Scott, J.P., *Aggression*. Chicago: University of Chicago Press, 1958.

Sears, R.R., "Development of gender role," in F.A. Beach (ed.), *Sex and behavior*. New York: Wiley, 1965, pp. 133–163.

Seward, J.P., "Aggressive behavior in the rat: I. General characteristics; age and sex differences," *Journal of Comparative Psychology*. 1945, *38*, 175–197.

Snyder, D.R., "Fall from social dominance following orbital frontal ablation in monkeys," *Proceedings of the 78th Annual Convention of the American Psychological Association*. Washington, DC: American Psychological Association, 1970.

Southwick, C.H., "Aggressive behaviour of Rhesus monkeys in natural and captive groups," in S. Garattini & E.G. Sigg (eds.), *Aggressive Behaviour*. New York: Wiley, 1969, pp. 32–43.

Southwick, C.H., & Clark, L.H., "Interstrain differences in aggressive behavior and exploratory activity of inbred mice," *Communications in Behavioral Biology*. 1968, *1*, 49–59.

Stone, C.P., "Wildness and savageness in rats of different strains," in K.S. Lashley (ed.), *Studies in dynamics of behavior*. Chicago: University of Chicago Press, 1932, pp. 3–55.

Strauss, E.B., Sands, D.E., Robinson, A.M., Tindall, W.J., & Stevenson, W.A., "Use of dehydroisoandrosterone in psychiatric treatment," *British Medical Journal*. 1952, *2*, 64–66.

Teas, J. Feldman, H.A., Richie, T.L., Taylor, H.G., & Southwick, C.H., "Aggressive behavior in the free-ranging rhesus monkeys of Kathmandu, Nepal," *Aggressive Behavior*. 1982, *8*, 63–77.

Tellegren, A., Horn, J.M., & Legrand, R.G., "Opportunity for aggression as a reinforcer in mice," *Psychonomic Science*. 1969, *14*, 104–105.

Thompson, N.S., "Some variables affecting the behavior of irus macaques in dyadic encounters," *Animal Behaviour*. 1967, *15*, 307–311.

Wilson, A.P., & Boelkins, R.C., "Evidence for seasonal variation in aggressive behaviour by *Macca mulatta*," *Animal Behaviour*. 1970, *18*, 719–724.

Wynne-Edwards, V.C., *Animal Dispersion in Relation to Social Behavior*. New York: Harper, 1962.

Yerkes, R.M., "The heredity of savageness and wildness in rats," *Journal of Animal Behavior*. 1913, *3*, 286–296.

Notes

1. Exceptions to this general rule include hamsters and gibbons. When hamsters are tested in pairs in a neutral area, considerable agonistic behavior occurs with overt fighting in about half the cases. However, no sex differences are discernible (Payne & Swanson, 1970). After extensive field observations, Carpenter (1940) has concluded that male and female gibbons are generally equally dominant and aggressive.

2. In humans, of course, there are potent social and environmental influences on the aggressive behavior displayed by the males, but the sex differences are clear.

3. The Buss-Durkee inventory provides a measure of aggression and hostility. It was developed through the use of standard test construction techniques. It was subjected to an item analysis and factor analysis and a collection of norms are available. Responses to the items on the inventory seem to be relatively free from the influence of the social desirability variable. (See Buss, 1961.)

Commentary: Aggressiveness and Hierarchy in Monkeys

Jose M.R. Delgado

Aggressive behavior is heterogeneous in its causality, neurological mechanisms, and observed manifestations, but some elements are shared by all forms of aggression, including the need for sensory inputs, neuronal activation, and release of preestablished patterns of emotional and motor responses. Understanding and prevention of aggression require the simultaneous study of its genetic, social, cultural, and economic aspects at parity with an investigation of its neurological bases. Codes of information, frames of reference for sensory perception and for evaluation of threats, and formulas for aggressive performance in general are not established genetically but must be learned individually. Human beings are born with the capacity to learn aggressive behavior but not with established patterns of violence. Mechanisms for fighting, which are acquired by individual experience, may be triggered in a similar way by sensory cues, volition, and by electrical stimulation of specific areas of the brain.

To investigate the neurological mechanisms of aggressive behavior, the phenomenon may be considered a sequence of interrelated events requiring (a) reception of sensory inputs; (b) processing of the received information by means of cerebral throughputs; (c) triggering of emotional reactivity; and (d) expression of motor outputs resulting in social conflict.

In a monkey colony, peaceful relations may last until the occurrence of such aggression-triggering events as the delivery of food. It should be remembered that the chemical mechanisms of muscle contraction are not specialized for aggression: the same movements may be used in different activities such as grooming, walking, or attacking. We may ask whether the neurological mechanisms involved in hostile acts are specific or are shared with other types of behavior. In the working hypothesis of "fragmental behavior" (Delgado, 1964,1967,1969) we postulated that each behavioral category is formed by a series of motor fragments which have anatomical and functional representation within the brain. In food intake, the successive acts cannot be considered specific of alimentary behavior because the animal may orient itself toward different stimuli, may use its limbs for many purposes, may swallow water or simply salivate if it is anxious, and may bite during playing or fighting. The combination of successive acts and their aim together constitute the specific category of alimentation.

Aggression can be analyzed in a similar manner. Single behavioral fragments may form part of many categories and therefore they have a different significance in each context. Fragments of behavior may have a functional affinity, forming a sequence like the notes of a melody. This linkage is reinforced by use and weakened by disuse. Emotional behavior, including rage, is expressed by a variety of autonomic, somatic, and behavioral phenomena which may be shared by non-emotional manifestations. Fear, for example, produces increased heart rate comparable to the tachycardia induced by other emotions or by non-emotional exercise. Motor performance is related to kinetic formulas learned through past experience and modified by individual skills. An enraged person may display aggressive behavior but performance and efficiency will be very different if he is a sedentary professor or a jujitsu champion. It is highly improbable that motor activities have multiple cerebral representation only because they may be used for many purposes. It is more likely that the same cerebral mechanism is activated for the performance of similar motor acts which form part of different behavioral sets.

The theory of fragmental representation postulates that motor performance of behavioral fragments depends on a set of cerebral structures which is different from the set responsible for coordination of these fragments. The elements forming each behavior category should be studied separately to determine the cerebral representation of each fragment and to identify the brain areas which coordinate and integrate these elements. Depending on the site of cerebral stimulation, it should be possible to elicit isolated fragments of responses without purpose or context; or, alternatively, to elicit well organized, purposeful behavioral sequences. It should also be possible to modify hostility in a selective way without changing other aspects of individual reactivity.

Extensive studies in monkeys support the above mentioned theory. As described in detail elsewhere (Delgado, 1967), different facial expressions and vocalizations, which appeared as isolated fragments of aggression, have been evoked in the same animal by electrical stimulation of points 5 mm. apart in the nucleus olivaris superior, lateral lemniscus, nucleus reticularis, superior part of the nucleus reticularis, and superior colliculus. Facial expression of aggression has been induced by stimulation of the brain stem without offensive or defensive behavior. This response could not be conditioned, had no positive or negative reinforcing properties, and did not modify social behavior in the monkey colony.

In another series of experiments (Delgado and Mir, 1969), fragmental responses ranging from closing the ipsilateral eye (amygdala stimulation) to vocalization (fimbria stimulation) were characterized by their lack of purpose and adaptation, being generally stereotyped in contrast with other responses evoked by pedunculus cerebellaris medius excitation, which evoked complex, well organized aggression requiring skillful performance and adaptation to the location and reactions of the target animal.

Activation of the cerebral areas involved in the onset and organization of aggression may be *secondary* to the reception of nociceptive stimuli, or may be related more directly to the activation of *primary* cerebral representation of aggressive behavior. One location of these primary structures could be the hypothalamus. Most brain stimulation has produced only *secondary* aggressive responses.

One characteristic of electrically evoked aggression is the normality in processing of sensory information and the perfect adaptation to changes in the environment during performance of induced behavior. As previously suggested (Delgado, 1975), brain stimulation probably activates an "aggressive *drive*" in these cases because the offensive intent is constant, whereas strategies and motor activities vary. This aggressive drive may depend on a set of cerebral structures that are activated directly in "primary" aggression or "secondarily" when nociceptive perceptions evoke an alarm, inducing escape from a potentially harmful stimulus or attack to remove the danger.

Most reported experimental results do not support the idea of one "aggressive center" in the brain and it is more logical to hypothesize the existence of a "constellation" of neuronal structures with close functional interactions, resulting in a dynamic equilibrium of activating and inhibitory influences. The hypothalamus, amygdala, tectal area, caudate nucleus, posteroventral thalamus, cerebellum, and other cerebral areas probably interact in the motivation and performance of aggression, and hostility can be induced by electrical—or sensory—stimulation of different elements of interlacing neuronal circuits.

Aggression evoked by brain stimulation is indistinguishable from spontaneous hostilities, indicating that electricity triggers preexisting physiological mechanisms that interact with information from the environment. This hypothesis is supported by results of experiments in a monkey colony in which social hierarchy was manipulated (Delgado and Mir, 1969). Female monkey Lina was tested in three colonies where she ranked lowest, next to lowest, and finally was #2 below the boss. Ranking was evaluated by priority in food getting, territoriality, and the number and direction of threats and aggressive acts. In each colony, Lina was radio stimulated in the nucleus posterolateralis of the thalamus with the same parameters (100 Hz, 0.5 msec, 0.3 mA). In Colony I where Lina ranked lowest, these stimulations induced considerable increase in attacks against her, whereas in Colony III when Lina ranked #2, the same stimulations resulted in a marked increase in her attacks against other monkeys. This experiment demonstrated the essential role of social rank in the expression of aggression evoked by brain stimulation, since excitation of the same cerebral point produced different effects, even with opposite social consequences, depending on the hierarchical position of the test animal.

Similar results were produced in pairs of monkeys (Plotnik et al., 1971), stimulating monkey "A6" in a nociceptive region (nucleus corporis geniculate medialis) when in the company of a dominant or submissive animal. When "A6" was dominant, it attacked the submissive partner following stimulation, whereas in the company of a dominant monkey, the same cerebral excitations induced grimacing and submissive gestures in "A6" and this reaction often caused it to be attacked by the dominant animal.

In these studies, brain stimulation induced effects depending on the social structure of the group. Responses were not blind or stereotyped but were well integrated with other behavioral determinants. The performance of secondary aggression should have longer latency and more flexibility than primary aggression, in which triggering of hostility can be evoked out of context, inducing animals to appear hostile to a dominant partner regardless of its previous experience and personal risk. Responses of primary aggression have been evoked by stimulation of the hypothalamus: for example, false rage in cats (Delgado, 1964), and attacking by submissive monkeys (Alexander and Perachio, 1973), which disrupted and even reversed group ranking. Permanent reversal of dominance was also reported by Robinson et al. (1969) following aggressive behavior induced by stimulation of the lateral and anterior hypothalamus in monkeys. In experiments with cats attacking anesthetized rats (Flynn, 1974), stimulation of the lateral hypothalamus elicited affective attack resembling behavior induced by tail shock which was evaluated as being related to nociception, whereas medial hypothalamic stimulation evoked quiet biting without emotional or hunger components which resembled predatory behavior.

Pharmacological studies in monkeys have also demonstrated the importance of individual and social variability in the evaluation of psychoactive drugs (Delgado et al., 1976). As a model, the effects of oral administration of Diazepam were tested in Rhesus monkeys in three situations: (1) alone, (2) paired with a dominant partner, and (3) paired with a submissive animal. Spontaneous mobility of the test animal was similar in all three situations, demonstrating its independence of social conditions. Diazepam reduced mobility markedly when the animal was submissive. Food intake of automatically delivered pellets decreased significantly from situations (1) to (3). Some other behavioral categories were also closely related to social rank. Small oral doses (0.1—0.3 mg./kg.) of Diazepam had significant effects on the behavioral profile only when the animal was submissive. When dominant, 0.1 mg./kg. of Diazepam decreased the monkey's aggressive acts by 50% but doses as high as 10 mg./kg. did not cause a reversal of dominance. These studies indicate that social status is of great importance in the behavioral effects of psychoactive drugs.

Hierarchy also plays an important role in the rhythmicity of spontaneous behavior, as shown in monkey colonies where animals were instrumented for continuous telemetric recordings up to 48 hours of EEG, EOG, EMG, mobility, and behavior. Each test animal was placed in different colonies where its social status was high, medium, or low. Results showed that in the low agonistic situation, Stage 1 sleep was displaced to midday, while in the medium and high agonistic situation, it was displaced to night time. REM appeared to have some correlation with subsequent aggressive manifestations. Rank was more important during the day than during the night as a factor influencing characteristics of wakefulness and sleep stages (Fernández-Gonzalez and Delgado, in preparation).

The hope is often expressed that research on animal aggression may provide clues for the understanding and prevention of human hostilities. It is true that many basic motor and emotional mechanisms are shared by animals and man.

For example, results about neuronal depolarization investigated in frogs are directly applicable to humans. The physiology of muscle contraction, neuronal timing in the motor cortex, ideo-kinetic formulas, cerebellar coordination of movements, and many other functions have been investigated in mammals and applied to the explanation of human behavior. There are, however, essential differences in the organization of behavior and in the supporting neuronal mechanisms which must be emphasized: animals do not have ideological conflicts, do not write books, and do not invent atomic weapons. One essential difference is that human beings are born with very immature brains and that sensory inputs are totally necessary for their neuronal development. Frames of reference for evaluation of environmental information are provided by culture and must be learned by individual experience.

For the understanding of human aggressive behavior we must differentiate activities which require personal contact, including verbal and physical threatening and fighting which may resemble agonistic behavior in animals, from the most dangerous kinds of human aggression which are related to the use of intellectual power, indeological domination, industrial development, economic subjugation, and military confrontation. Animal experimentation is most useful, but it should not be unduly generalized to aspects of behavior with exclusive human qualities. At the same time the intellectual aspects of aggression require working neurons and cerebral mechanisms which can and should be investigated.

Research on the neurological bases of aggression should be closely related with the analysis of its genetic, social, cultural, and economic aspects. The prevention of human hostilities is not dependent on the organization of motor performance, but on the neurological traces of hates and ideological conflicts which trigger the destructive application of learned behavior.

References

Alexander, M. and A.A. Perachio, "The influence of target sex and dominance on evoked attack in rhesus monkey." *Amer. J. Phys. Anthrop.*, 38:543–548, 1973.

Delgado, J.M.R., "Free behavior and brain stimulation." Pp. 349–449 in: *International Review of Neurobiology*, Vol. VI, C.C. Pfeiffer and J.R. Smythies (Eds.), New York: Academic Press, 1964.

Delgado, J.M.R., "Social rank and radiostimulated aggressiveness in monkeys." J. nerv. ment. Dis., 144:383–390, 1967.

Delgado, J.M.R., "Physical Control of the Mind: Toward a Psychocivilized Society," Vol. XLI, World Perspectives Series, New York: Harper & Row, 280 pp., 1969.

Delgado, J.M.R., "Inhibitory systems and emotions." Pp. 183–204 in: *Emotions—Their Parameters and Measurement*, L. Levi (Ed.), New York: Raven Press, 1975.

Delgado, J.M.R., C. Grau, J.M. Delgado–García, and J.M. Rodero, "Effects of Diazepam related to social hierarchy in rhesus monkeys." *Neuropharmacol.*, 15:409–414, 1976.

Delgado, J.M.R. and D. Mir, "Fragmental organization of emotional behavior in the monkey." Ann. N.Y. Acad. Sci., 159:731–751, 1969.

Flynn, J.P., "Experimental analysis of aggression and its neural basis". Pp. 53–61 in: *The Neuropsychology of Aggression*, R.E. Whalen (Ed.), Vol. 12 in *Advances in Behavioral Biology*, New York: Plenum Press, 1974.

Plotnik, R., D. Mir, and J.M.R. Delgado, "Aggression, noxiousness and brain stimulation in unrestrained rhesus monkeys." Pp. 143–221 in: *Physiology of Aggression and Defeat*, B.E. Eleftheriou and J.P. Scott (Eds.), New York: Plenum Press, 1971.

Robinson, B.W., M. Alexander, and G. Bowne, "Dominance reversal resulting from aggressive responses evoked by brain telestimulation". *Physiol. Behav.*, 4:749–752, 1969.

2.

Some Basic Biological Terms and Concepts of Primate Aggression, With a Focus on Aggressive Alliances

Walter Angst

Introduction

In discussing inter-male aggression and dominance systems in primates there is a need for a definition of terms and their underlying concepts. Though the focus of this paper is on macaques, the definitions and most of the concepts are meant to be applicable to all primates, including man.

Many topics central to aggression and dominance are treated only briefly or not at all because they have been dealt with in other papers in this volume. (For a more systematic, detailed and comprehensive analysis, see Angst, 1980.) However, the important and generally neglected issue of aggressive alliances is dealt with in some depth and special consideration is also given to behaviors of appeasement and reassurance.

On the Term 'Aggression'

A real definition of the term 'aggression' seems rather impossible. However, there are consistencies across disciplines in descriptions of what is commonly called aggression. These make it possible to provide a basis for arriving at a determination which comes close to a definition of the term 'aggression.' Such a determination would be as follows:

'Aggression' is a behavior which is directed towards inducing a detrimental effect on the integrity of a partner or oneself.

Following the framework of ethology, aggression is always considered to be a *behavior*. Unobservable dreams and fantasies are therefore excluded, whereas speaking is clearly included. *Directiveness* in animal behavior can either be observed or inferred. By the use of 'cluster analysis' (see Wiepkema 1961; Van Hooff, 1973) one can determine the motivation of different behavior patterns and on that basis arrive at a descriptive definition of aggressive behaviors of a species. In humans, the relation between motivation and behavior is less clear cut. But in man, directiveness has the ingredient of a conscious intention and thus the observer has, as an additional source of evidence, asking the subject.

If we used the effect of an action rather than directiveness as a criterion, we would run into difficulties. For example, we would have to include accidental harm such as may occur in a car crash. In addition we would miss an act such as a purposeful bombing if the bomb, due to a technical fault, does not explode. By '*inducing a detrimental effect on the integrity,*' we mean effects that range from the reduction of biological fitness (reproductive success) to minor psychological inconveniences. Again in accord with ethology, predation is not included in aggression. Therefore the determination concludes: '. . . *of a partner or oneself.*' However, the possibility is not excluded that the partner is a social companion of a different species to the aggressor. Clearly distinct from 'aggression' is the word 'aggressivity,' meaning a readiness for aggressive behavior, i.e. internal variables leading to aggression, as opposed to external variables.

The word '*fight*' is limited to interactions in which both partners engage in physical aggression against each other. For any kind of disruptive interactions, including flight, submission and their combinations, the common term is: '*agonistic behavior*' (Scott, 1972).

Dominance and Inferiority as Components of Personal Relationships

Observations of any established primate group show that the

types of interaction, their duration, frequency and interrelation differ between various dyads of individuals. This leads to the conclusion, that primates maintain *personal relationships*, which are based on mutual recognition and experience. Hinde (1975) and Hinde and Stevenson (1976) have thus defined social relationships as the *content, quality* and *patterning* of interactions.

A component of such a relationship is the patterning of agonistic interactions. Agonistic interactions are patterned in a comparable way to affiliative and sexual interactions. In a dyadic relationship we call the one who regularly wins in a conflict the '*dominant*' individual, and the one who regularly loses the '*subordinate*' individual. This component of the relationship is the '*dominance relationship*' (Angst, 1975). The term 'dominance' therefore should be reserved for established relationships; correspondingly 'dominant' should not be substituted for 'stronger,' 'more aggressive' and the like, to describe individuals which have not yet established a relationship.

The system of dyadic dominance relationships in a given group results in the social *hierarchy*, which in turn is a component of the group's social structure.

In small, well established groups of macaques, the dominance hierarchy is primarily linear. But even here we may find inversions, such as: monkey A dominates monkey B, and monkey B dominates C, but C dominates A.

In macaques not living under extremely artificial conditions, all adult males are higher in rank than the rest of the group. Just below are the subadult males. Further down, the age-sex classes are interwoven, and we find adult females, subadult females, juvenile males and juvenile females intermingled. Infants are usually at the bottom of the hierarchy, but are well protected.

These relationships can be clarified by looking at the ontogeny of dominance. The baby is efficiently protected, and socially nurtured by its mother. However, when the infant moves independently and engages in agonistic interactions, its mother can only support her offspring successfully against subordinates. So, by enlisting help from its mother, the young macaque can at least chase away all partners which are dominated by its mother. In females, this support, if consistently performed, leads to a mother-independent dominance of the young macaque over all partners inferior to its mother. But this transfer of dominance from mother to daughter is a process, which requires varying lengths of time to develop in different partners. In close associates of the mother and very low ranking females, the dominance of the daughter is more readily accepted than among less familiar and high-ranking females (personal observation, primarily in M. fascicularis). In several macaques, e.g. the Japanese macaque, the support by the mother of her youngest can even lead to the inversion of the hierarchy among the daughters: dominance rank then is negatively correlated to age.

Of course, in many primate species we find dominance relationships on an inter-group level as well. Important variables in determining group dominance are the number of adult males in the group and, less frequently, intergroup dominance-relationships of specific males (personal observation in M. fascicularis and M. sylvanus).

The maintenance of dominance relationships as a result of earlier experience, helps all individuals involved to avoid the risk of being wounded, as well as spending time and energy unnecessarily. So it is not aggression, which, as often stated, represents an organizing force or advantageous aspect of a group, but instead, the establishment and maintenance of personal relationships, including dominance relationships.

Reassurance and Appeasement

Most primates have signals which enhance friendly contact. Some of these signals, like grooming and lip-smacking in many macaques, are used by any individual toward any other, irrespective of dominance relationships. Other signals are correlated with the dominance relationship: in the Macaca fascicularis only inferior individuals perform the grimace and the teeth-chattering face.

The friendly (affiliative)—and often also fearful—behavior of an inferior individual toward a dominant one, by which the dominant's aggression is reduced and/or his friendliness enhanced, is called *submissive* or *appeasing*. The friendly behavior of a dominant individual towards an inferior one, by which the inferior's flight (fear) is reduced and/or his friendliness enhanced, is called *reassuring*.

Appeasement and reassurance both constitute a friendly component in motivation, and create a reduction of tension as well as an enhancement of friendly contact.

The effectiveness of submissiveness and reassurance depends

extensively on the relationship existing between the partners involved. For example, submissiveness may not be effective at all among strangers.

Instead of describing the totality of these behaviors, it may be more useful to look at one specific behavior pattern in detail. A monkey 'presents,' then it stands or crouches in front of a partner with its hindparts directed to the partner. Presenting can occur within six different contexts, and accordingly, serves six different functions. Again, the focus in the following listing will be on macaques.

1. Sexual Presenting: Females may, by presenting, invite a male to approach, to inspect its genital area and finally to copulate. The sexual context can be identified by the reaction of the male, but even better by other signs, such as sexual swelling, indicating the estrus of the female.

2. Presenting for Grooming: A would-be groomee of either sex may present in front of a partner with the effect of triggering grooming to the exposed hindquarters. Contrary to all other forms of presenting, the presenter in the grooming context does not look at his partner and stands or crouches very rigidly.

3. Presenting for Riding: In a number of species, such as the Barbary macaques (Macaca sylvanus), mothers, and other infant carriers as well, may invite infants to take a ride on their back by presenting to them. In this context the hindquarters are typically lowered and the presenter shows intensive friendly facial expressions. The presenter may even reach back and help the infant climb onto its back.

4. Submissive Presenting: Within the context of submissive presenting it is useful to distinguish two versions:

a. Reactive Submissive Presenting: A dominant individual threatens or mildly attacks a subordinate one. The aggressed monkey flees a bit and then stops and presents. The aggressor is thus more likely to end his aggression and even to address friendly signals to the aggressed partner than if the aggressee just flees or turns round and screams. The aggressor may even mount the presenter and/or invite him for grooming. Reactive submissive presenting, used by both sexes and all ages, reduces aggression and enhances friendly behaviour.

b. Initiative Submissive Presenting: A subordinate monkey approaches a dominant one without receiving any aggression. Nevertheless, at a short distance, he turns round and presents, or he may even continue his approach by walking backwards. It is highly probable, though not yet proven, that performing initiative submissive presenting increases the individual's probability of being accepted by the dominant partner. This second type of submissive presenting is much rarer than the first one, but often reactive phases are interwoven with more initiative ones, which makes it hard to draw a clear line between them. Both types are usually accompanied by friendly facial signals.

5. Reassuring Presenting: In tenseful encounters or after an aggressive episode in some species, and during friendly and relaxed interactions in other species, the dominant of two males may present to the other one and consequently may be mounted. This can be interpreted as the dominant individual reducing the tendency to flee in his partner, and, furthermore, increase the probability of a friendly approach, eventually leading to mounting.

6. Playful Presenting: In the context of play, presenting can trigger a playful performance of all reactions mentioned above. But, in addition, it can lead to playful chasing. Contrary to all other contexts, in play, the presenter often runs away as soon as the partner approaches and thereby starts a "cat-and-mouse" chase.

In all contexts, presenting enhances non-aggressive approach, and it is a much used antagonist to aggression.

Contexts of Aggression

Nearly twenty years ago, Moyer (1968) made a pioneering effort to categorize the contexts enhancing aggression. Because this list was based mainly on rodents in a laboratory situation and also included predation, it cannot be transferred to primates. However, using Moyer's list as point of departure, I developed a preliminary list of aggression provoking contexts for non-human primates: (Angst, 1980)

1. Competition for food.

2. Sexual competition.

3. Territoriality (competition for living space).

4. Competition for a place (to rest or pass through).

5. Competition for dominance.

6. Encounters with outgroup individuals (including intergroup competition).

7. Take-over of alpha-male position (leading to infanticide in several species).

8. Receiving aggression (leading to retaliation or redirected aggression).

9. Preferred partner being aggressive (leading to joining in, equals 'social facilitation').

10. Preferred partner receiving aggression (leading to protective aggression).

11. Unaccepted proximity of a partner.

12. Non-sexual competition for proximity with a partner.

Besides these twelve widespread and common contexts, there are a number of rarer ones, most of which are confined to a few species. Here are six examples:

13. Sexual frustration.

14. Female of harem is too far away (male triggers its return by threatening it).

15. Rape (Orang-Utan).

16. Unattentiveness of subordinate partner.

17. Passing by in flight.

18. Bizarre behavior without locomotion (e.g. being trapped, having seizures).

Numbers 16–18 have been added in this paper. It is important to note that "Crowding" is not listed because crowding does not consist of a unique context, but is a condition that increases the frequency and intensity of aggression in several contexts (Angst, 1980). If an attacked individual cannot flee out of sight, and if proximity of others is such that they easily can join in the attack, then long lasting and damaging aggression is almost inevitable.

Proximate Causes of Aggression, Focus: Secondary Aggression.

Proximate causes of aggression on the physiological level are dealt with by Delgado (. . . this volume) and therefore need not to be discussed here.)

On the behavioral level we can distinguish external from internal variables that cause aggression. Since internal causes can not be observed, external stimuli are more valid for categorizing behavioral causes of aggression. Thus the above given list of contexts at the same time provides the categories of aggressive behavior.

Rather than attempt to cover all categories, I will focus on numbers 8 to 10, which can be summarized as 'secondary aggression'. Due to problems in observation, secondary aggression has been too often neglected. Nevertheless, it is extremely common in most primate species and has great social impact.

1. Retaliation: In a monkey group the aggressor normally is dominant, the aggressee subordinate. Unidirectionality of threat is part of most dyadic relationships in macaques. However, the subordinate aggressee can adopt various means of retaliation. The most common one is loud screaming, which is likely to enlist the support of others against the dominant aggressor. If supporters are near or are actually supporting, the screamer may counterattack the dominant aggressor. On rare occasions, I have seen females ganging up against a dominant male and, in captivity, even overwhelming him. In the wild, however, I have never seen a dominant macaque or baboon being brought down by a gang of subordinates. But I did observe several cases in which a subordinate individual pursuing a fleeing dominant one, was able to bite him from behind.

In less established relationships, a subordinate individual may fight back at the moment, when serious injury is imminent. Bernstein and Gordon (1974) have reported the following observations: Newly introduced male Rhesus monkeys were aggressively subdued by the resident males. They remained submissive, as long as they were bitten only with the incisors. But as soon as canines were used, which can inflict mortal wounds, the bullied males resumed fighting.

If a dominant individual is attacked by a subordinate, this generally takes the form of a supported counterattack as described above. The dominant monkey will always threaten the inferior attacker, but will intermittently retreat or flee to the extent necessitated by the supporting individuals. If one or several supporters are even higher ranking than the 'dominant' monkey, then, as is common in Macaca sylvanus, he will start to scream at his subordinate opponent. In M. sylvanus, this even applies to the highest ranking male. The appeal for support prevails over the manifestation of dominance. This will be dealt with later in the chapter.

Finally, there are the relativly rare, but important and systematically occurring situations, in which a subordinate individual challenges the dominance of his partner by either attacking him or by resisting his aggression without resuming screaming. Especially if the two opponents are of the same age-sex class, a severe fight may ensue. But more often such a challenge is found between a growing hitherto subordinate male and a dominant female that he is attempting to subdue. In these cases, females do not generally engage in a fight. Instead they scream and may counterattack with support of others. These behaviors indicate the female's loss of dyadic dominance.

2. Aggressive support: As stated above, screaming can trigger support, but this is only one stimulus that induces support. There are a number of different contexts inducing support, and these will be treated separately (see Fig. 1).

The first context comprises all the cases in which a subordinate monkey is helped by others through directing threats or attacks to that monkey's aggressor. This kind of support can be labelled as 'protective aggression'. A well-known example of this type of protection is that of an infant by its mother. In macaques, at least, infants generally receive protection from adults against other adults, subadults or juveniles. But as De Waal (1977) first demonstrated in the captive Macaca fascicularis, there are more than just random frequencies of protective aggression in many triadic relationships which do not include infants. These will be discussed towards the end of this chapter.

To be aggressively protective usually presupposes dominance over the opponent, but 'ganging up' by two or more subordinate individuals against a dominant animal is included in the category of protective aggression, as long as the primary aggressor is higher ranking than the supported individual.

At this point it becomes evident that there is no clearcut boundary between protective aggression, which is defined as reactive, and an aggressive coalition of subordinates, which is meant to be more initiative (Fig. 1). All of these variations have in common a support of the subordinate against the dominant animal. The remaining types of support relate to support of the dominant animal against the subordinate. Here, the most frequent case is a monkey joining another in threatening and chasing a subordinate. This I call an aggressive coalition of dominants. If a subordinate attacks a dominant animal who is under pressure by another dominant animal, one can speak of 'opportunistic support' (Fig. 1). However, this term does not imply any other criteria than the descriptive ones mentioned above.

A rare case, known as 'support of the dominant,' is one in which a subordinate is the initial aggressor against a dominant animal. The dominant animal will always retaliate or defend himself, and another dominant individual may join him in doing so (Type B.a) in Fig. 1.) In all primate groups consisting of more than a pair of individuals, the question of 'who *supports* whom against whom' is at least as important in understanding intragroup aggression as the question of 'who behaves aggressively against whom.'

There are several reasons why this is the case. First, intensive aggressive interactions in a primate group more often involve three or more animals rather than only two. In other words, aggressive episodes are more often polyadic than dyadic.

Second, most species have elaborate means to enlist support by others. High pitched vocalizations and positioning one's body between the opponent and the potential supporter are the most common. Besides the 'open-mouth threat,' in crab-eating macaques (M. fascicularis) there is a specific threat pattern, called the 'white-pout threat' (Shirek-Ellefson, 1967), 'Hetzen' (Angst, 1974), or 'pointing' (De Waal, Van Hoof and Netto, 1976) which is highly effective in enlisting support. In Barbary macaques, which lack 'pointing,' adult males engage in 'scream battles,' where any expression of dominance is suppressed in favor of an appeal for support. Typically this behavior is restricted to established males with several potential supporters (personal observation).

Third, long-term observations of primate groups reveal the importance of coalitions in establishing and maintaining a dominance hierarchy. In macaques, young females generally attain a rank in the dominance hierarchy just below their mother (e.g., Kawamura, 1965; Sade, 1967; Angst, 1975). This is the result of continuous protective aggression and aggressive coalition within the matriline. In some species, e.g., the Japanese macaque, preferential protection of the youngest by the mother generally makes the younger daughters rise in the hierarchy above their older sisters (Kawamura, 1965; Koyama, 1967).

At least in some species, e.g., the Rhesus monkey, the protection by the mother is not limited to direct intervention, but is also indirect. Close female relatives, especially sisters, are as effective as the mother. (Berman, 1980; Datta, 1983). Females in high ranking lineages may enjoy the special advantage of having more close kin protectors because they have better reproductive success than lower ranking lineages and therefore tend to be more numerous. Furthermore, it is interesting to note that a feature of high ranking individuals, at least in Rhesus monkeys, is that they are more likely to provide protective support to kin than low ranking individuals (Datta, 1983). This appears to be a strategy related to the risk of the supporter's being attacked himself. The higher a female's rank, then the less there are dominant potential interferers and the less the risk for the female to be attacked herself as a consequence of her aggressive support. In males the effect of protection is less pronounced. However, coalitions are exceedingly important for the establishment of the adult male hierarchy.

From the evidence on longitudinal observations of Macaca fascicularis, I have proposed (Angst, 1975, 1980) the following hypothesis: The aggressiveness towards a partner of the same sex and age category is negatively correlated with the degree of familiarity between the two. Familiarity means the result of acquaintance and the reinforcement of attraction. In other words, the more familiar two monkeys are, the less likely they are to engage in aggression against each other. This only holds true for individuals of the same sex and similar age, where infant-attraction and sexual attraction are not a factor. Kin of the same matriline are most familiar with each other because, as a consequence of the mother-infant relationship, they cluster and groom each other frequently, and in some cases, even exclusively. Due to the high amount of proximity, they appear to have a high frequency of aggressive interactions (Kurland, 1977). But if one corrects this frequency by the factors of proximity and weaning, the resulting relative frequency is low, and furthermore, there is hardly ever intensive aggression within the matriline.

Another source of long-lasting familiarity, beside kinship, is the playmate effect, especially in young males. Since young monkeys prefer individuals of equal sex and age as playmates, one can expect a relatively high familiarity at least among some males of the same age. My own observations support this view, but these are still unsystematic and cannot support a hypothesis.

A further step in the analysis of the relationship between familiarity and aggressiveness is to re-examine aggressive alliances. There are innumerable observations, especially in captivity, that members of a group form aggressive coalitions against strangers and newcomers. Some authors therefore have postulated that primates are 'xenophobic' (Southwick, et. al., 1974). But within groups, aggressive support is also patterned. A monkey is more likely to support a specific partner against a particular animal than vice versa. Each agonistic interaction is a type of double-choice situation for the third party: In any encounter, each animal will chose whom they prefer.

We still lack analyses of support relationships which also consider the context in sufficient detail. However, the following rules may be anticipated from published studies and from my own personal observations:

a. Quite irrespective of context, high familiarity, primarily meaning close matrilineal kinship, is the dominant decisive factor determining who supports whom against whom.

b. With higher consideration of the risks involved, sex partners may be supported.

c. Opportunistic alliances result largely from a strategy to reinforce or even increase one's rank with minimal risks. I remember a juvenile male crab-eating macaque who consistently joined in attacks against a rival just one position higher in the hierarchy. However, when he had finally risen above him, he ceased doing so. A fascinating, very complex example of opportunistic alliances can be seen in the agonistic behavior of the chimpanzee 'Yeroen,' as described in De Waal's book, *Chimpanzee Politics* (1982).

d. Infants enjoy a high probability of being supported against older opponents by nonrelatives, in addition.

e. If a macaque interferes in an agonistic interaction of less familiar individuals, it will still support the more familiar one against the less familiar one. This becomes most evident in inter-group aggression.

f. 'Policing,' i.e., breaking up agonistic episodes by the intervention of a very dominant male, does not work well in small cages. But in large enclosures and in the wild, where a party is able to flee out of sight of its opponents or at least move to a remote place, policing is more effective. The policing male does not support any animal specifically but rushes to the middle of the scene with the effect of driving away all other animals. 'Policing' corresponds in part to the 'control role' as described by Bernstein (1964, 1966).

g. If a chased macaque flees through the group, many onlookers threaten it or even participate in the chase for a moment. Here, just the flight of a less familiar individual, rather than the action of a more familiar pursuer, appears to elicit aggression. This is further evidenced by the fact that these onlookers often start to threaten the escaping individual before they can see or hear any pursuer.

This discussion of aggressive support has demonstrated that the term 'social facilitation' is of little value. However, it is a well established term and I have included it in my list of contexts above. 'Social facilitation' was coined to describe behaviors which involve joining an activity of social partners, and which lead to a synchronization of behavior within the group. While not fulfilling the second criterion, the term can be used descriptively for agonistic behavior in all cases in which an individual is joining an attack on another. But the term explains little because it has become clear that the underlying strategy of joining an aggressive encounter is a goal-directed behavior in support of a specific partner, rather than merely joining a fracas due to a kind of 'behavioral infection'. Even the effect of aggressive appeals works in a very differentiated manner, depending on the existance of personal relationships between the individuals involved.

3. Redirected Aggression: In most species of monkeys and apes, one can frequently observe interactions typified by this example: An individual is threatened or attacked by a dominant partner. It flees and does not retaliate, but goes on to attack and chase a third individual, which had nothing to do with the previous interaction. This type of secondary aggression is labelled 'redirected aggression' (Bastock, Morris and Moynihan, 1954). This term derives from a common interpretation that the individual which is attacked develops a tendency to retaliate, but because of fear of the aggressor, redirects his aggressiveness towards another more suitable partner. Indeed, this substitute is almost always a subordinate individual who just happens to be nearby.

Under captive conditions, but not in the wild, chains of redirected aggression may develop, which commonly end up with an attack on one of the lowest ranking individuals. This effect has been compared to human interactions where such behavior results in finding a scapegoat. However, 'scapegoating' in humans requires considerable cognitive elaboration, and is not simply the result of passing on aggression down the social hierarchy. Therefore, and because it is not typical of wild groups of monkeys, it should not be considered a basic aspect of primate social organization. In the non-human primate 'scapegoating' is the outcome of specific unnatural conditions, especially an inability to reach and maintain the necessary inter-individual distances.

Redirecting aggression serves a beneficial function in that it diverts the attention to another individual. In some cases the main protagonist even joins in and turns his attack on the secondary target.

Related cases exist where no primary aggression is actually observed: Typically, in macaques and baboons, two or more males may show increasing tension by approaching and monitoring each other (though carefully avoiding eye contact) and yawning. Suddenly, one of the males may very noisily attack and chase a nearby female or juvenile and then return to its former position. This behavior may be repeated, with the opponent following suit. While this kind of redirected aggression may indirectly intimidate the opponent, it certainly is not a display like branch-shaking, or 'herding,' as has also been suggested. This final type of redirected aggression is typically observed in one of two contexts: a. Competition of males for females in estrus, and b. meeting of two groups (personal observations).

Ultimate Causes of Aggression

1. Aggression and The Concept of Evolutionarily Stable Strategy: Aggression serves as a means of attaining an advantage at the cost of another. This happens in a wide range of contexts, but all are in the framework of interindividual competition within the species. Natural selection can function via interindividual competition on the basis of differential reproductive success. According to the modern sociobiological theories, competing alleles, (the different versions of a given gene) are selected and thus differentially propagated. It seems obvious that in primates, alleles which

55

permit an efficient and variable use of aggression are selected positively, as against alleles which lead to a weak or rigid strategy of aggression. However, it is less obvious, in considering this explanation, why unlimited, lethal aggression strategies do not regularly evolve.

Under the models developed by game theory and population genetics (Parker, 1974; Maynard-Smith, 1976; and Maynard-Smith and Parker, 1976), extreme strategies of aggression cannot evolve because they would not be evolutionarily stable. In other words, if by mutation a lethal aggression strategy appeared in a population, this strategy would not be able to compete successfully with non-lethal aggression strategies. Also, as single aggression strategy, it could not be maintained in a population. The models even show that single aggression strategies generally cannot become evolutionarily stable; only mixed strategies can achieve that. A mixed strategy consists of either one individual employing more than one strategy, or different individuals using different strategies. Thus, a macaque male in its prime may rely on actual fighting because its chance to win is relatively high, while a weaker (younger or older) animal may specialize in bluff, display, and enlisting support in order to avoid actual fighting. These conclusions only relate to reciprocal aggression systems, such as inter-male aggression, but not unilateral aggression systems, as in infanticide. However, despite the elegance of these models it must be borne in mind, that there is still a huge gap between their simplicity and the complexity of the observed behavior.

2. Inclusive Fitness and Coalitions: It was Hamilton (1964, 1971) who first developed a theory explaining the ultimate causes of what he termed 'altruistic behavior.' Altruistic behavior is any behavior which benefits the fitness of a partner at costs to the fitness of the actor. Biological fitness always means reproductive success.

Hamilton suggested, for example, that if a mother takes risks for the benefit of her offspring, this may well be an evolutionarily stable strategy, under the condition that her loss in fitness is statistically not greater than the benefits of her offsprings' fitnesses. Hamilton's theory is quite precise. For the positive selection of an allele causing altruistic behavior. Hamilton put forward the following formula: $k > \frac{1}{r}$, where k stands for the ratio of gains in fitness versus loss of fitness, and r for the degree of relatedness.

In other words, the loss of fitness in the actor must be smaller than the benefit in the partner, multiplied by the degree of relatedness. The resulting total 'fitness,' that is, the fitness of the actor plus the combined fitnesses of his kin, multiplied by their various degrees of relatedness, Hamilton termed 'inclusive fitness' (Hamilton, 1964). Thus, the evolutionary success of an allele underlying altruistic behavior depends upon its effects on inclusive fitness and not only upon the immediate effect on an individual.

The model of inclusive fitness provides us with the best existing explanation of all types of aggressive support in which monkeys take risks to protect kin, especially against dominant opponents. Opportunistic support can, in some cases, be explained by the model of 'reciprocal altruism' (Packer, 1977).

However, it may not be necessary to incur a specific model for explaining mutual and opportunistic alliances. The 'selfish' aggression-strategy, plus its modifications through learning, have sufficient explanatory power. In many cases, the model of 'reciprocal altruism' can only be inferred because the kinship structure is not known.

The mechanism which ensures the support of kin is based on familiarity (see Chapter 5). This extends to adopted infants who are treated the same as offspring (personal observations). It has been found that more familiar partners of lower relatedness were preferred to less familiar partners of higher relatedness (Fredrickson and Sackett, 1984). This all supports the conclusion that familiarity is the critical intervening variable leading to kin-related behavior. It is familiarity that guarantees the recognition of relatedness beyond the mother-offspring relation. Even within the mother-offspring relation, the fundamental infant-mother attraction is probably evidenced solely between the mother and her youngest offspring. The persistence of the bond may also rely on familiarity.

Summary

1. The term 'aggression' was determined to be: a behavior which is directed at inducing a detrimental effect on the integrity of a partner or oneself.' For any kind of disruptive behavior, the term 'agonistic behavior' is employed.

2. The dominance relationship is the component of the personal relationship, which consists of the patterning of agonistic interactions.

3. An antagonist of aggression is affiliative behavior. Some affiliative behavior patterns are independent of rank, others are rank-dependent. Dominance-dependent affiliative behavior is called reassuring; inferiority-dependent, submissive or appeasing. The pattern of 'presenting' is discussed as an example of multifunctional behavior pattern which also has affiliative functions.

4. A preliminary list of aggression-contexts in nonhuman primates consists of 18 categories.

5. Aggressive coalitions are an element of polyadic relationships and therefore, an extremely important issue of primate group organization. The principles and variations of aggressive support were outlined, together with two other forms of secondary aggression: retaliation and redirected aggression.

6. Except for infant-bonding and sexual attraction, familiarity is the key factor determining who aggresses against or supports whom. Familiarity acts as an intervening variable between matrilineal kinship and kin-dependent behavior. The more closely related two monkeys are, the more familiar they are, the less they are aggressive against each other, and the more they support each other in agonistic episodes.

7. The models of 'evolutionarily stable strategy' and 'inclusive fitness' provide the best current explanations for the ultimate causes of the observed consistencies in primate aggression.

References

Angst, W., "Basic data and concepts on the social organization of Macaca fascicularis," in: *Primate behavior IV* (L.A. Rosenblum ed.). Academic Press, 1975, p. 325–388.

Angst, W., *Aggression bei Affen und Menschen.* Springer-Verlag, 1980 190 pages.

Bastock, M.; Morris, D. and Moynihan, M., "Some comments on conflict and thwarting in animals", *Behavior.* 1954 6, p. 66–89.

Berman, C.M., Early agonistic experience and rank acquisition among free-ranging infant Rhesus monkeys," *Tntl. J. Primatol.* 1980, 1, p. 153–170.

Bernstein, I.S., "The role of dominant male Rhesus in response to external challenges to the group," *J. Comp. Physiol. Psychol.* 1964; 57, p. 404–406.

Some Basic Biological Terms and Concepts of Primate Aggression

Fig. 1 Elementary types of aggressive support

A. Support of the subordinate

    a) Protective aggression

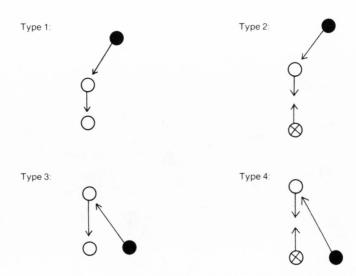

Type 1:   Type 2:

Type 3:   Type 4:

    b) Aggressive coalition of subordinates

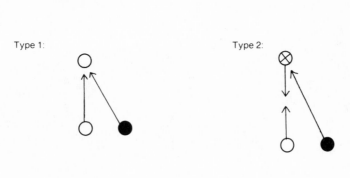

Type 1:   Type 2:

59

B. Support of the dominant

a) Joining retaliation

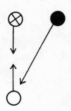

b) Aggressive coalition of dominants

Type 1:

Type 2:

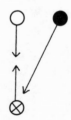

c) Opportunistic support

Type 1:

Type 2:

Symbols:

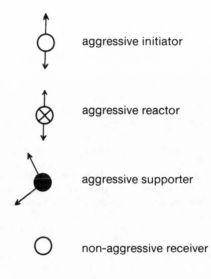

    aggressive initiator

    aggressive reactor

    aggressive supporter

    non-aggressive receiver

level of symbols:

    higher = dominant

    lower = subordinate

    even = dominance rank not relevant

Bernstein, I.S., "Analysis of a key role in a capuchin (Cebus albifrons) group," *Tulane Stud. Zool.* 1966; 13, p. 49–54.

Bernstein, I.S. and T.P. Gordon, "The function of aggression in primate societies," *Amer. Scientist, 62.* 1974; p. 304–311.

Datta, S.B., "Relative power and the maintenance of dominance," in 'Primate social relationships', 1983. R.A. Hinde, ed., Blackwell Scientific Publications, p. 103–112.

Fredrickson, W.T. and Sackett, G.P., "Kin preferences in primates (Macaca nemestrina): Relatedness or familiarity?" *J. Comp. Psychol.* 1984; 98, p. 29–34.

Hamilton, W.D., "The genetical theory of social behavior," (I and II), *J. theor. Biol.* 1964; 7, p. 1–52.

Hamilton, W.D., "The genetical theory of social behavior (I and II), extreme models," in: *Man and Beast: Comparative social behavior* (J.F. Eisenberg and W.S. Dillon, eds.). Smithsonian Institution Press, 1971; p. 57–92.

Hinde, R.A., "Interactions, relationships and social structure in non-human primates," in: *Symp. 5th Cong. IPS* (S. Kondo, M. Kawai, A. Ehara and S. Kawamura, eds.). Japan Science Press, 1975; p. 13–24.

Hinde, R.A. and J. Stevenson-Hinde, "Towards understanding relationships: dynamic stability," in: *Growing Points in Ethology* (P.P.G. Bateson and R.A. Hinde, eds.). Cambridge University Press, 1976; p. 451–479.

Hooff, J.A.R.A.M. Van, "A structural analysis of the social behavior of a semi-captive group of chimpanzees," in: *Social Communication and Movement* (M.V. Cranach and I. Vine, eds.). Academic Press, New York and London, 1973; p. 75–162.

Kawamura, 5., "Matriarchal social ranks in the Minoo-B troop: A study of the rank system of Japanese monkeys," in *Japanese Monkeys*, S.A. Altmann, ed. 1965; p. 105–112. Published by S.A. Altmann.

Koyama, N., "On dominance rank and kinship of a wild Japanese monkey troop in Arashiyama," *Primates.* 1967; 8, p. 189–216.

Kurland, J.A., "Kin selection in the Japanese monkey, *Contributions to Primatology* 12, S. Karger. 1977; 145 pages.

Moyer, K.E., "Kinds of aggression and their physiological bases," *Behav. Biol.* 1968; 2, p. 65–87.

Packer, C., "Reciprocal altruism in Olive baboons," *Nature.* 1977; 265, p. 441–443.

Parker, G.A., "Assessment strategy and the evolution of fighting behavior." *J. theor. Biol.* 1974; 47, p. 223–243.

Sade, D.S., "Determinants of dominance in a group of free-ranging rhesus monkeys," in *Social communication among Primates*, S.A. Altmann, ed. 1967; p. 99–114 Univ. of Chicago Press.

Scott, J.P., "Animal behavior." University of Chicago Press, Chicago, London, 2nd revised edition 1972.

Maynard-Smith, J., "Evolution and the theory of games," *Amer. Sci.* 1976; 64, p. 41–45.

Maynard-Smith, J. and Parker, G.A., "The logic of asymmetric contests," *Anim. Behav.* 1976; 24, p. 159–175.

Shirek-Ellefson, J., "Visual communication in Macaca irus." Unpublished Ph.D. thesis. 1967.

Southwick, C.H.; Siddiqui, M.F.; Farooqui, M.Y. and Pal, B.C., "Xenophobia among free-ranging rhesus groups in India," in: *Primate Aggression, Territoriality and Xenophobia*, R.L. Holloway, ed. Academic Press, 1974; p. 185–209.

Waal, F. De., "The organization of agonistic relations within two captive groups of Java-monkeys (Macaca fascicularis)," *Z. Tierpsychol.* 1977; 44, p. 225–282.

Waal, F. De., *Chimpanzee Politics*. Jonathan Cape, 1982.

Waal, F.; De, Van Hooff, J.A.R.A.M. and Netto, W.J., "An ethological analysis of types of agonistic interaction in a captive group of Java-monkeys (Macaca fascicularis)," *Primates*. 1976; 17, p. 257–290.

Wiepkema, P.R., "An ethological analysis of the reproductive behavior of the Bitterling (Rhodeus amarus Bloch)," *Arch. nedrl. Zool.* 1961; 14, 103–199.

Commentary: Aggressive Interactions in Non-Human Primates: Some Genetic and Environmental Factors

Diana L. Mendoza and J. Martin Ramirez

During the 1980 biannual meeting of the International Society for Research on Aggression, which took place at Groningen, we watched the Dutch film, "Bij de beesten af," made by Bert Haastra, one of the foremost documentary film makers in the world. This film, nominated for an Oscar, used shots taken in the wild and in the laboratory to show how important ethological studies in animals are for the understanding of the mechanisms underlying human behavior. Ethology, rather than using inadequate standardized tools for the evaluation of aggressiveness (tools which provide information on only a few measures or behavioral categories), provides a comprehensive picture of complex behaviors, such as aggressive interactions in primates. As Benton (1981) pointed out, ethology has the advantage of describing the variety of behavioral elements shown simultaneously in any complex social interaction and their variable sequence, timing and orientation. This is why our own psychobiological research on human and animal aggressiveness has taken a bioethological approach, involving construction of ethograms of agonistic patterns and submissive postures shown by pigeons, rats, squirrels and monkeys (Ramirez, Delius, 1979; Ramirez, 1980; Mendoza, submitted).

Here we wish to share our insights on aggressive interactions, with special emphasis on non-human primates.

Although biased, like every behavior, by genetic determinants, aggressive behavior is developed and modified through interactions with other life forms and with physical environment, i.e., though a variety of sociological and ecological inputs. (On the importance of genetics and learning to behavior, see Ramirez, 1978.)

Before we discuss the variety of potential influences involved in aggressive interactions, let us make one point of a general introductory nature on the concept of aggression.

Nature of Aggression

Although people generally seem to be in agreement about what the word "aggression" stands for, research workers are in considerable disagreement about its meaning. Aggression has been defined many ways, ranging from "an overt response that delivers noxious stimuli to another organism," to an internal state, such as a personality trait (Hinde, 1974). With a term so broadly used, it becomes virtually impossible to formulate a single and comprehensive definition (Ramirez, 1981).

In order to better understand this complex phenomenon, it would be more convenient to consider each dimension or strategy and its conceptualization in terms of its functional value (see, for instance, Bandura, 1974; Nagel, Kummer, 1974), or in terms of how it is expressed; Stokes and Cox (1970) consider it as a group of behaviors that lead to attack, more than to retreat. Others have defined aggression in terms of the performers' intention: "an action carried out with the intent to harm another individual or object," (Moyer, 1976).

In the real world, aggressivity is articulated by a number of different types of behavior, subsumed under the general rubric of "aggression". Among the several tentative classifications are those that have focused on dichotomies (for instance, Valzelli, 1981, distinguished spontaneous from induced aggression), or those that consider the situations which trigger an aggressive response (Moyer's eight classifications, 1968). We propose, following McGuinness's (1981) suggestion, three types: interspecific, intraspecific and reactive aggression, the latter representing an indiscriminate response to frustration or threats from any source. Details have been presented elsewhere (Ramirez, 1981).

The major emphasis here shall be on intraspecific aggression, especially in primate males.

Genetic Factors of Aggression

Aggressive interactions are affected by genetic factors. Since one of us has recently written on the physiological factors (Ramirez, Nakaya, Habu, 1980), we wish to focus here on species-specified differences and differences related to sex in the expression of aggression.

1. Species-Specific Differences: Moyer (this volume) has reviewed the more characteristic agonistic patterns of several primate species: baboons, squirrel monkeys, chimpanzees . . . , showing how fighting topography, threat patterns and dominance systems are species-specific. Itani (this volume) has shown how sociability and aggression vary among species and provides us with a very interesting taxonomy of the many forms of social organization in primates: a) "elemental" or "asocial" societies, consisting only of solitaries with few social interactions (ex., nocturnal prosimians and orangutan), and b) "stable family groups", with a basic social unit, a bisexual unit which allows inflow and outflow of certain individuals. Itani distinguishes two kinds of primate societies as well: one based on the inequality principle, having a very clear linear dominance system (ex., Japanese monkeys), and the other based on the equality principle, sharing a sense of social identity. The prevalence of either principle would depend on situational structure and phylogeny. If we accept this point of view, and it is very attractive indeed, it would be more valid than the old dominance concept, initially defined as a social behavior, according to which all groups were thought to be organized in a linear hierarchy. (For a more detailed comment on dominance see the recent review by Snowdon, 1983).

Although differences in aggression among different species are obvious, there are few studies where aggression has been compared for several species sharing the same habitat. Hakk, 1965, and Jolly, 1972 observed that in free living conditions macaques and baboons were in general more aggressive than other Old World monkeys such as Patas monkeys or guenons. However, baboons seem to adjust better to captivity: killings are less frequent in them than in guenons (Rowell, 1971); probably this is related to the frequent appeasement and conciliation behaviors (lip smacking and presenting) shown by baboons, but not by guenons (Nagel, Kummer, 1974). The cercopithecoids are probably the most aggressive among the primates.

There are also conspicuous differences in regard to aggression and sociality among closely related species, as Bertrand (1969) found comparing stumptails and liontails living with equal group composition in the same captive conditions, and Sorensen (1974) studying several tree shrew species living in semi-captive conditions.

2. Sex Differences: Naturalistic observations support laboratory findings that in most primate species, including humans, males are generally far more aggressive and the more frequent target of hostility than females. There are, however, exceptions, such as gibbons, where males and females are equally dominant and aggressive (Carpenter, 1940).

This prominency of male aggressiveness has been documented at very early ages. Two month old male Rhesus displayed more threat responses than females of the same age (Harlow, 1965; Goy, 1966). Field studies (Devore, 1965) have also confirmed the tendency for the young male monkeys to engage in rough-and-tumble play. Infant male chimpanzees and baboons spend considerably more time than females engaging in aggressive play (Hamburg, 1967). In humans, boys also spend more time in aggressive play and have a more physical, vigorous, destructive and hurting type of aggression, as Sears (1965) observed in 3 year-old children and we confirmed in 7 year-olds (Mendoza and Ramirez, in press).

The quality of aggression also shows sexual dimorphism in primates. In tree shrews, males chase and bite more often than females do and, in turn, the latter display more lunges, slaps, threat calls and postures (Sorenson, 1974). In Rhesus monkeys, females show milder forms of agonistic behavior, such as threatening gestures (Mallow, 1981) and more instigation than males (Teas, Feldman, Richie, Taylor, Southwick, 1982). In general, then, males seem to compensate for their strength and danger by giving ample warning before they attack (Nagel, Kummer, 1974), and their confrontations are quick, clean and directed to one individual at a time. (Erwin, personal communication, August, 1982), whereas female aggressiveness is sometimes less predictable and, in this sense, more dangerous. Someone once said, speaking about another primate species (the human one): "A woman does not fight fairly because she does not know how to be a gentleman."

Finally, there is evidence that males may inhibit aggression among females; in the direct presence of males, there is seldom any reciprocal fighting by females, and their eventual aggressive encounters usually consist of a single act such as a grab or bite (Erwin, 1979).

Environmental Factors

A number of potential social and ecological variables of utmost importance on the aggressive behavior of primates have been suggested (see Southwick, 1969; Nagel, Kummer, 1974; Erwin, 1979). Let us comment on a few of them.

1. Social Factors

a. Social Bonds: Although there are so-called asocial species, such as the already mentioned prosimians, whose level of social interaction is very low, one of the general characteristics of most monkeys is their social nature, which allows a relatively stable social organization that varies little from one group to another. For many primate species, the maintenance of group integrity and cohesion appear to be based in part on specific long-term emotional bonds between individuals within groups (Erwin, 1979). These social bonds may develop at any age or sex: the earliest bond is established between the infant and its mother, and later by increasing the interaction with peers. These peer relationships are typically closest among individuals of the same gender.

Studies in captive macaques have found that the familiarity —unfamiliarity dimension influences aggressiveness: animals who know each other form coalitions against unfamiliar intruders, who are attacked and repelled, with the exception of infants, who are accepted and even adopted (Bernstein, 1964; Southwick, 1967; Erwin, Flett, 1974; Erwin, Mitchell, 1975). Familiarity, therefore, endures as a deterrent to violence and unfamiliarity contributes to the risk of violence.

Fieldwork (Bernstein, 1967; Richard, 1970) has shown that in free ranging primates, overt interactions between different species are minimal and physical contact is particularly rare. There is a social organization only within groups of conspecifics. William's studies (1983) have shown that wild hybrid macaques were socially integrated in their respective groups. They formed an integrated social unit similar to that of a non-hybrid macaque group although with less proximity and contact and without the female social nucleus.

In sum, familiarity between animals creates social bonds which in turn permit a stable organization of social relationship between individuals of the same species.

b. Social Deprivation: Rearing conditions have a large influence on the socialization of primates. These early influences are not only maternal, but also paternal: males play an important role in socialization. Parental behavior may be described as varying along two scales: one from overprotective and possessive mothering, to brutal responses to the infant's demands (see details in Arling, Harlow, 1966; Mitchell, 1968). An incompetent parental behavior would result in neglect and abuse of offspring (Suomi, 1978), aggression to the offspring to promote their independence (Negayama, 1981) and even infanticide (Hrdy, 1979).

A well known study of maternal deprivation comes from the classical research done by Harlow and Harlow (1969) on the behavioral effects of social isolation of the infant Rhesus monkeys from their mothers in the early stages of development. Animals deprived of social experience (especially tactile) at an early stage of life become fearful and disturbed and less socially active, partake in less social exploration and play, and display increased intensity of aggressiveness. On the contrary, an assessment of the effects of short-term maternal deprivation (12 weeks) in Papio monkeys followed by peer group rearing showed that the nursery-reared infants were less aggressive and dominant than those reared by the mother and in contact with other infants (Coelho, Bramblett, 1981).

One of us has had the occasion to observe the case of an orphaned infant squirrel monkey, which we will consider in some detail. This monkey lost his mother when he was two weeks old and was hand-reared up to the age of two months, and then reintroduced into his former colony. At the beginning of this stage, he was extremely fearful and threated any individual who walked near him. Later, at the age of three months, he seemed to readjust and threatened less than before. After being back in the colony, his social interaction was almost nil, except when any other monkey approached him. In these instances he threated and screamed. At this stage, abnormal behaviors were also observed such as thumb (or any other digit) sucking as well as penis sucking. After a month of reincorporation into the colony, most of these behaviors ceased and he seemed to behave almost like any other of his peers. The data obtained up to the age of six months indicates that he remained more likely to threaten other animals than any other member of the colony. He was characterized by a low rate of activity, while the normal reared infants of the group were the most active of the colony. The point of this illustration is that there is a very low level of social interaction in the orphan monkey. This is consistent with the results obtained by Fairbanks (1974), who indicated that the normal-reared juvenile and infant males in her study were involved in 83% of the 401 recorded behavioral interactions.

Most infanticide cases (Hrdy, 1979) reported for many primate species (Sugiyama, 1965, in langurs; Fossey, 1979, in gorillas; and Sing Pirta, Sing, 1981, in Rhesus monkeys) occurred during inter-groups episodes. In these situations, more male infants were killed by conspecifics than females, especially when the captors of the infants were males (Kawanaka, 1981). According to Sackett (1981), fetal gender appears to influence the aggression received by pregnant pigtail monkeys. Female-pregnant mothers receive more bites than male-pregnant mothers. The explanation given is that something in their appearance or physiology is linked to the sex of the fetus and is in some way detectable by other monkeys.

2. Environmental Factors

Although social factors usually outweigh environmental ones, some ecological variables have been reported to have had profound effects on aggressive behavior in primates. Let us comment on how aggressiveness varies according to season and space.

a. Space: Although the supposition that crowding produces an increase in aggressiveness in many species is well accepted (summarized by Archer, 1970), results are ambiguous at the present time; for instance, experimental studies on crowding effects on non-human primate aggression (Bernstein, Gordon, 1974) have failed to produce more than temporary increases in intragroup aggression. This may be partly due to an unclear formulation of problems related to crowding. There should be differentiations between spatial density (by changing the available space while the number of individuals is not changed) and social density (by changing the group size while the available space remains unchanged).

In macaques: 1) a higher spatial density resulted in an increase of dyadic male aggressive interactions and in a decrease of the female ones. Alexander and Roth (1971) suggest that the more crowded conditions lowered the risk of trauma due to contact aggression, and 2) the social density has not yet been experimentally investigated, but field observations on growing populations suggested that the tension resulted from its increase was normally resolved by group fusion (Furuya, 1969; Nagel, Kummer, 1974). In humans, McGrew (1971) has compared both kinds of density changes in preschool children, finding that: 1) at higher spatial density, proximity and peer contacts increased proportionally, whereas 2) at higher social density, the children tended to avoid each other. For a more detailed summary of non-human studies on density effects on stress, see Elton (1979).

b. Captivity: Although fighting is a fairly common occurrence even in a natural wild setting, captivity intensifies the destructive violence of primates. For instance, Hamadryas baboons in the Zurich Zoo and Savanna baboons in the Vincennes Zoo were nine to fifteen times and three to ten times, respectively, more aggressive than the wild population of the same species (Kummer, Kurt, 1965; Masure, Bourliere, 1971). The greatest aggressive interaction in captive groups may be caused, among other possible factors, by: 1) spatial limitations and excessive social density (it is very important to keep this in mind for adequate maintainance of captive primates), with their subsequent restriction of movements; and 2) "artificial" composition of groups, forcing a familiarity between individuals previously alien or even incompatible, which is uncommon to feral populations that solve such incompatibilities in the wild by emigration. The distortions of social rules, imposed by captivity, may result in probably the most devastating problem encountered in captive primates: their social disruption.

Final Remarks

We are conscious of the high risk of a premature assessment

before doing careful research based both on biological findings and on social and physical environments operating within the still poorly understood agonistic interactions and other social processes. Let us conclude, however, saying that aggressiveness cannot be assessed as a merely negative drive to be avoided. On the contrary, it seems to be an essential element in the organization of a social group. Interacting with other forces, such as social attraction, escape, submission, rearing conditions, space availability, and familiarity to a place, aggressive behavior plays an important role as an organizing factor, which serves to establish and maintain the social structure (Nagel, Kummer, 1974; Erwin, 1979). The cercopithecoids are a good example for this assertion: as already mentioned, they are probably the most aggressive, and they have the most clearly organized societies among non-human primates.

The biological aim of aggressiveness is to provide a means of competition for vital resources (food, territory, partners . . .). The aggressive intraspecific episodes in non-human primates tend to result in the submission of the loser and rarely cause severe damage or death. However, this strategy is effective only at distances short enough to perceive appeasing signals and submissive gestures. That is why in fighting at too long distances, as in human wars, where weapons are used (lances, arrows, bombs, rockets . . .), aggression becomes impersonal. A distortion of the positive function of aggression produces those terrible massacres that destroy mankind.

Bibliography

Alexander, B. K., and Roth, E. M., "The effects of acute crowding on aggressive behavior of Japanese monkeys," *Behaviour* 39: (1971) 73–90.

Arling, G. L., and Harlow, H. R., "Effects of social deprivation on maternal behavior of rhesus monkeys," *J. Comp. Physiol. Psychol.* 64: (1967) 371–377.

Bandura, A., *Aggression: a social learning analysis*. Englewood Cliffs: Prentice Hall, (1973).

Benton, D., "The measurement of aggression," in P.F. Brain & D. Benton (eds.), *The Biology of Aggression*. Alphen aan den Rijn, The Netherlands: Sijthoff/Noordhoff, (1981) pp. 487–502.

Bernstein, I., "The integration of Rhesus monkeys introduced to a group," *Folia Primatol* 2: (1964) 50–63.

Bernstein, I. S., "Intertaxa interactions in a Malayan primate community," *Folia primat.*, 7: (1967) 198–207.

Bernstein, I. and Gordon, T., "The Function of aggression in primate societies," *Am. Sci* 62: (1974) 304–311.

Bertrand, M., "The behavioral repertoire of the stumptail macaque," *Bibl. Primat.* No. 11. (1969).

Carpenter, C. R., "A field study in Siam of the behavior and social relations of howling monkeys," *Comparative Psychology Monographs*, 10. (1940) 1–168.

Coelho Jr. A. M., and Bramblett C. A., "Effects of rearing on Aggression and Subordination in *Papio* Monkeys," *Am. J. Primat.* vol 1, Nº 4, (1981) pp 401–412.

Devore, I. (ed.) *Primate behavior: Field studies of monkeys and apes.* New York: Holt, Rinehart & Winston, (1965).

Eaton, G.G.; Modahl, K.B.; Johnson D.F., "Aggressive Behavior in a Confines Troop of Japanese Macaques: Effects of Density, Seasun a Gender," *Aggressive Behaviors.*, vol 7, Nº 2: (1981) pp 145–164.

Itani, J., "Inequality versus equality for coexistence in primate societies," 12th I.C.U.S. (in press).

Jolly, A., *The Evolution of Primate Behavior.* MacMillan, New York, 1972.

Kawamaka, K., "Infanticide and cannibalism in chimpanzees, with special reference to the newly observed case in the Mahale Mountains," "*Afr. Stud. Monogr.*" 1: (1981) 69–99.

Kummer, H. and Kurt, F., "A comparison of social behavior in captive and wild Hamadryas baboons," in H. Vagtborg (ed.) *The Baboon in Medical Research*, vol. 2, Univ. Texas Press, Austin, 1965, 65–80.

Masure, A.M., and Bourlière, F., "Surpeuplement, fécondité, mortalité et aggressivité dans une population captive de *Papio papio*," "*Terre et Vie*" 25: (1971) 491–505.

McGrew, W.C., *An Ethological Study of Children's Behavior*, Academic Press. New York, 1972.

McGuinness, D., "The nature of aggression and dominance systems", in *Absolute Values and Search for the Peace of Mankind*, ICF, New York, 1981.

Mendoza, D.L., "El modelo animal en las depresiones infantiles," *Revista de Neuropsiquiatría Infantil* (in press).

Mendoza, D.L., "A new interpretation of the communicative meaning of *Saimiri sciureus*' Genital display (submitted).

Mendoza, D.L.; Martín Ramírez, J.; "Ethological observations of hostility in children," *Aggressive Behavior* (in press).

Mallow, G.K., "The relationship between aggressive behavior and menstrual cycle stage in female Rhesus monkeys (*Macaca mulatta*)," *Horm. Behav.*, 15: (1981) 259–269.

Moyer, K.E., "Kinds of aggression and their physiological basis," *Commun. Behav. Biology*, 2: (1968) 65–87.

Moyer, K.E., *The Psychobiology of Aggression.* Harper & Row, New York, 1976.

Moyer, K.E., "The biological basis of dominance and aggression," 12th I.C.U.S. (in press).

Morris, D., *The Naked Ape* (1967).

Nagel U., and Kummer, H., "Variation in cercopithecoid aggressive behavior," in R.L. Holloway (ed.), *Primate Aggression Territoriality and Xenophobia. A comparative Perspective.* Academic Press, New York 159–184 (1974).

Negayama, K., "Maternal aggression to its Offspring in Japanese Monkeys," *J. Human Evolution,* 10: (1981) 523–527.

Richard, A., "A comparative study of the activity patterns and behavior of *Alouatta villosa* and *Ateles geoffrovi,*" *Folia primato.* 12: (1970) 241–263.

Rowell, T.E., "Organization of caged groups of *Cercopithecus* monkeys," Ramirez, Martin J., *Einführung in die Anthropobiologic,* Peter Lang Verlag, Frankfurt, Bern, Las Vegas, 1978. *Animal Behav.* 19: (1971) 625–645.

Ramirez, Martin J., "Towards a conceptualization and classification of animal aggression," *"Hiroshima Forum for Psychology"* 8: (1981) 11–21.

Ramirez, Martin J., and Delius, J.D., "Aggressive behavior of pigeons: suppressions by archistriatal lesions," *"Aggressive Behavior"* 5: (1979) 3–17.

Ramirez, Martin J.; Nakaya, T.; Habu, Y., "Physiological models for several types of aggression," *"Japanese J. Psychology"* 18: (1980) 183–207.

Sackett, G.P., Receiving severe aggression correlates with fetal gender in pregnant pigtail monkeys, Psychobiol., 14: (1981) 267–272.

Sears, R.R., "Development of gender role", in F. A. Beach (ed.), *Sex and Behavior.* Wiley, New York, 1965, 133–163.

Singh Pirla, R.; Singh, M., "Forcible swatching and probable killing of infants by a Rhesus (*Macaca mulatta*) alpha male in wild habitat," *Behav. Anals. Lott.,* 1: (1981) 339–344.

Sorenson, M.W., "A review of aggressive behavior in the tree shrews," in R.L. Holloway (ed.) *Primate Aggression Territoriality and Xenophobia. A comparative Perspective.* Academic Press, New York (1974) 13–30.

Southwick, C., "An experimental study of intragroup agonistic behavior in Rhesus monkeys (*Macaca mulatta*)," *Behaviour.* 28: (1967) 182–209.

Southwick, C., "Aggressive behaviour of Rhesus monkeys in natural and captive groups," in S. Garattini & E.G. Sigg (ed.) *Aggressive Behaviour.* Wiley, New York (1969) 32–43.

Sugiyama, Y., "On the social change of hanuman langurs (*Presbytis entellus*) in their natural condition," *Primates.* 6: (1965) 381–418.

Teas, J.; Feldman, H.A.; Richie, T.L.; Taylor, H.G. & Southwick, C.H., "Aggressive behavior in free-range Rhesus monkeys of Kathmandu," *Aggr. Behav.* 8: (1982) 63–77.

Valzelli, L., "Psychobiology of Aggression and Violence, Raven Press, New York, 1981.

Williams, L.E., "Sociality among captive hybrid macaques, *Behavioural Processes,* 8: (1983) 177–187.

3.
Inequality versus Equality for Coexistence in Primate Societies

Junichiro Itani

Introduction

In an analysis of vocal sounds of Japanese monkeys, I pointed out that there are social interactions based on an *inequality* principle and those based on an *equality* principle (Itani, 1963). They can be recognized in two types of face-to-face vocal sounds in the category of "sounds generally emitted in peaceful states of emotion." One of them is emitted when a subordinate individual attempts to "win a superior's favor, to please him, or to beg his pardon." The other vocalization resembles it in the sound itself, but is emitted in a totally different situation. This vocalization is mutually exchanged, in which no inequality appears between the two individuals (Itani, 1963). What is important here is that both vocal sounds are emitted in non-aggressive interactions, al-though one is based on the inequality principle, the other on the equality principle, and that in either case a peaceful coexistence of the two individuals is assured.

Besides sexual interactions and mother-offspring interactions, the social coexistence of individuals is based on either of the two principles. The inequality principle urges an individual to behave in accordance with its dominant/subordinate relationships with others, while the equality principle works as if there were no dominant/subordinate inequality between individuals. Prevalence of either principle not only depends on the situational structure of the given event, but also on the phylogeny of the given species.

The inequality principle and the equality principle can be metaphorically compared to a pair of Japanese words, "honne" (personal learning) and "tatemae" (norm expected by convention). The latter, which is a social norm, is expected to be performed for some reason or purpose. Here, I would like to ascribe the peaceful coexistence of individuals to the reason or purpose for the equality principle. By reviewing the dominance systems based on the inequality principle among cercopithecids, I will probe into possible bases of social interactions based on the equality principle, and then trace the breakdown of the inequality principle and rise of the equality principle in the societies of the genus *Pan*, i.e., chimpanzees and pygmy chimpanzees.

Thus, this paper focuses on behaviors, whether active or passive, in which individuals are affirmative and tolerant to others and in which some social organization is assumed. Cases of negative interactions typically represented by aggression are taken for exposures of breakdowns of the assumed social organization. Since there are many societies of primates with structures in which individuals do not coexist, I will first briefly review the variations of social structures in primates.

Social Structures of Primates

Primate societies include those consisting of only solitaries and those comprising stable groups. I called the former "elemental societies" (Itani, 1972, 1977a). This type of society has few social interactions; solitary males and females come together only during the short mating season, and the following breeding period is also short. Therefore, the present article does not deal with this type of society, found only among nocturnal prosimians. Note, however, that all other higher primate societies also originate in this type of elemental society. The orangutan, as the sole exception among the simians, has a society without stable groups. Although this cannot be considered the same as the prosimian elemental society, it is not within the scope of the present paper.

In considering the societies made of stable groups, I would like to propose the concept of "basic social unit (BSU)" (Itani, 1972, 1977a). Although the group size, composition, and their maintenance mechanism vary from species to species, the basic social unit has the following common features: It is a bisexual unit with a half-closed structure which allows inflow and outflow of certain individuals. It has a mechanism of maintaining a stable structure, and is antagonistic to other conspecific units (Itani, 1981). A *specia* (species society, Imanishi, 1950) can be schematized as consisting of BSUs which exist by keeping some social distance from one another, and of solitaries which do not belong to any BSU (Itani, 1977a).

Table 1 (page 97) summarizes the types of primate social structures. Although this table is not complete, it summarizes fairly well the results of field studies made to date. There are three types of BSU compositions: one-male/one-female, one-male/multi-female, and multi-male/multi-female. The type of BSU composition is generally species-specific. The mechanism of maintaining the group structure further divides the latter two types into two each to give a total of five types. This is determined by the elements (male and/or female) which transfer between BSUs, and is closely related to the mechanism of incest avoidance.

1. $\overline{MP}_1$ (nonmatrilineal-nonpatrilineal-1): This type of society has only one-male/one-female pair type groups. The young of both sexes mate out; thus incest is avoided and the pair type group structure is maintained. All nocturnal prosimians which have stable groups belong to this category. Also indris, callithricids, approximately one half of cebids, and gibbons have this type of society. Both sexes are tolerant of the presence of the same sex in the BSU, which is succeeded through neither the maternal line nor the paternal line.

2. M_1 (matrilineal-1): This is a one-male/multi-female type, and incest is avoided by the males' desertion of groups. Male offspring leave their natal groups before they become sexually mature, and the only male in the BSU is replaced by another within five years (Sugiyama, 1965; Hrdy, 1974). This structure is found only among cercopithecids.

3. M_2 (matrilineal-2): This is the same as M_1 in that the group matrilineally perpetuates, but differs in that this has a multi-male/multi-female structure. Males leave before they sexually mature. Adult males usually stay in a group for less than five years

and then transfer to another. Males which stay in their natal groups even after sexual maturity notably avoid incest with their mothers or sisters (Takahata, 1982a, b). This structure is found in *Lemur* and about one half of cebids and cercopithecids. *Presbytes entellus* has both M_1 and M_2 types (Yoshiba, 1968), indicating their continuity; however, it is unknown what determines whether the dominant male tolerates another males' presence in the BSU.

4. $\overline{MP}_2$ (nonmatrilineal-nonpatrilineal-2): This resembles M_1 in composition, which is one-male/multi-female, but differs in that females move between groups while males do not. The gorilla is the only primate species which has this type of structure (Harcourt et al., 1976). However, the gorilla's society also includes one-male/one-female and multi-male/multi-female groups (Schaller, 1963). These three types of groups represent different stages of the gorilla's BSU; the one-male/one-female structure is the early stage, which becomes one-male/multi-female by immigration of additional females. It is said that there is only one patriarchal male in a multi-male/multi-female group and the other males are his sons (Harcourt et al., 1976; Fossey, 1979; Veit, 1982). Since most males leave their natal groups, here I classified the gorilla's BSU as a nonmatrilineal-nonpatrilineal type. However, it is still possible for a gorilla BSU to be succeeded patrilineally; this issue awaits future studies (Harcourt et al., 1976; Veit, 1982; Yamagiwa, 1983).

5. P (patrilineal): This is the second kind of multi-male/multi-female structure, which is found in the common chimpanzee and the pygmy chimpanzee (Itani, 1980). In this type of BSU, in contrast to M_2, incest is avoided by the young females' mating out (Nishida & Kawanaka, 1972).[1] Although father-daughter incest remains possible before the daughter leaves her natal BSU because of the multi-male/multi-female structure, adolescent sterility (Tutin, 1980; Goodall, 1983) seems to prevent births resulting from such mating. Also, observations to date seem to indicate that mother-son sexual interactions are psychologically inhibited (Goodall, 1968, 1983; Pusey, 1980).

The five types listed above can be grouped into two: M_1 and M_2 which are matrilineal and $\overline{MP}_1$, $\overline{MP}_2$ and P which are nonmatrilineal. The latter group is probably of the same structure originating from $\overline{MP}_1$ (Itani, 1972, 1977a). However, clarification of the phylogeny between the five types of structures requires further studies. For example, as to M_1 and M_2, one may conclude that M_1 is more complex than M_2 while another may evaluate the coexistence of several males in the M_2 type of BSU. It is also possible to conclude that M_2 is the more general structure because M_1 cannot be found among prosimians and ceboids.

Among the cercopithecids, which were believed to have only matrilineal types of structures, two exceptions have been reported. They are *Presbytes potenziani* (Colobinae) and *Cercopithecus neglectus* (Cercopithecinae) both of which have $\overline{MP}_1$ type of BSUs (Watanabe, 1981; Gautier-Hion & Gautier, 1978). This may be related to the fact that in the genus *Lemur*, only *L. variegatus* has the $\overline{MP}_1$ type of BSU. Furthermore, this is probably related to the fact that all prosimians which have groups are of the $\overline{MP}_1$ type; this is inferred to be the oldest type of primate BSU. This is probably related to the fact that primitive taxa in cebids generally have $\overline{MP}_1$ type of BSUs, while presumably more advanced taxa have M_2 type of BSUs. These must be studied with reference to the origin of matrilineal structure in primate societies.[2]

The present paper deals with the societies which have one-male/multi-female or multi-male/multi-female compositions, especially those with M_2 and P types of BSUs.

Coexistence Based on the Inequality Principle

One of the most important findings in the early studies of wild Japanese monkeys was confirmation of the presence of a definite mating season (Itani & Tokuda, 1958). Since the group structure comprising both sexes persists during the long asexual period of the year, the formation of a group cannot be explained by sex as Zuckerman (1932) did. In short, the BSU of Japanese monkeys consists of the matrilineally related females tied to a particular home range and the immigrant males which live in the BSU for a while. Therefore, the males and females, which have different life cycles, share the home range and membership of the same troop. The recognition of the troop members can be seen clearly in the reactions to solitary males by the troop (Itani, 1954), behaviors of emigrant males entering another troop and attitudes of the troop members to them (Nishida, 1966), different attitudes shown to individuals of the same or different troop in intertroop encounters (Kano, 1964; Kawanaka, 1973), etc.

The mutual recognition of members of the same troop is based on both the recognition of the dominance system, which is basic to the inequality principle, and the recognition of kinship, which can be regarded as basic to the equality principle. In this section, I will discuss the former.

In many primate species the existence of dominant/subordinate relationships between individuals is known; in particular, there are many reports on the dominance system seen among the cercopithecids with M_2 type of BSUs (DeVore & Hall, 1965; Kaufmann, 1967; Kawai, 1958a, b, 1965a; Southwick et al., 1965). This section will present primarily the important findings from the studies of Japanese monkeys.

When we succeeded in provisioning the Koshima troop and began the identification of individuals, we found a linear rank order among the five males in accordance with their ages. There was another male aged between the third and fourth; being semi-solitary, he was outside the dominance system of the troop (Itani & Tokuda, 1958). In the next year I began observing the Takasakiyama troop which consisted of about 200 monkeys. They also had a linear rank order (Itani, 1954). The dominance relationship can easily be recognized by the facial expressions and attitudes when two individuals meet. However, I judged the dominance by a simple test of throwing some food between the subject individuals. The dominant always took the food, no matter how many times the test was repeated. When the food was thrown closer to the subordinate, the uneasiness of the subordinate increased, but the dominant took it. The non-aggressive relationship between the two is maintained by the inhibition of the subordinate (Kummer, 1971). Table 2, pages 98–99, shows the linear rank order among 44 males of this troop in 1955, as well as that seven years later in 1962. In the meantime, although several individuals left the troop and two died and the troop divided into two troops A and B (Sugiyama, 1960), the order changed little among the high-ranking individuals who remained in the A troop except for a few cases of reversals. The rank order among males is very stable.

Following these findings, the studies of the Minoo B troop consisting of about 30 monkeys (Kawamura, 1958) and the Arashiyama troop, of 125 monkeys (Koyama, 1967, 1977), revealed that the rank order among females is also stable. Adult females are subordinate to mature males (Kawai, 1969; Furuichi,

1983a, b). Although little study has been done on the qualitative difference between male and female rank, the rank gap between adjacent ranking individuals seems smaller among females (Itani, 1954). Dependence on a third individual (Kawai, 1958a, b, 1965a) which affects the social interactions between the subject individuals is far more prominent among females than among males.

The assumption of such a male-female difference in dominant/ subordinate relationships leads naturally to the conclusion that there are two dominance systems according to sex in a troop. In 1973, the Takasakiyama A troop consisted of about 1000 monkeys and the B troop consisted of about 300. Mori (1977) compared the female ranks of the two troops and concluded as follows: In the B troop, dominance between individuals adjacent in rank was unclear, while in the A troop dominance was unclear between individuals quite far apart in rank. This indicates that unstable interindividual relationships increase as the troop size becomes large; especially when the troop size exceeds 100, in which unstable relationships drastically increase. This is an interesting result showing the limit of mutual recognition of dominant/subordinate relationships among females.

In addition to the dominance systems among males and females, Kawamura (1958) showed the correlation between rank and lineage in a study of the Minoo B troop. He proposed the rule of "youngest ascendancy" which schematized the rank order within a lineage, and illustrated the mechanism of rank formation between kin-related groups (Kawamura, 1958). This predicts that if A is dominant over C and A has an offspring B, the rank order among them will be $A > B > C$. Youngest ascendancy means that this relationship holds even if B and C are sisters, i.e., both are offspring of A, but B is younger than C.

Koyama (1970, 1977) reported that Kawamura's rule holds also for the Arashiyama troop where the mother was dominant over the daughter in 60 mother-daughter pairs, and the younger was dominant over the older in 28 pairs of sisters. In addition, he showed a linear rank order among 16 lineages, within which 50 females formed a linear rank order generally in accordance with Kawamura's rule. Kawamura's hypothesis does not apply to the males, which separate from their mothers and sisters as they grow and finally leave their natal troop. Even while they are still in their natal troop, it is rare that a male is dominant over his older brother (Norikoshi & Koyama, 1975). In this way, the formation of rank order among females is based on recognition by C that B is an offspring to A and that B can depend on A, who tolerates this dependence. In a study of the nonprovisioned Yakushima M troop, however, Furuichi (1983a, b) found that in all four pairs of sisters, the older sister was dominant over the younger, and proposed that such a rank order exists because the monkeys do not need to depend on their mothers in a natural feeding situation. Nevertheless, he confirmed the existence of dominant/subordinate relationships between lineages.

Among infants born in the same year, a rank order parallel to that of their mothers is formed, irrespective of sex, by the time they reach one year of age (Koyama, 1977). In other words, until two years of age, males also follow the rank order formation process within the matrilineal dominance system, and they generally maintain this rank order, although they gradually separate from this dominance system at the age of three years.

Between troops, too, there are dominant/subordinate relationships. At Takasakiyama, three troops, which formed after fissions, shared the same provisioning site by feeding at different times according to the troop's dominance (Itani et al., 1963; Itani, 1975). The home ranges of the three troops overlapped with one another to include the provisioning site, and the most dominant A troop used the provisioning site until noon. The second dominant C troop used it in the afternoon, and the lowest B troop used it in the evening and early in the morning.

Kawanaka (1973) analyzed the intertroop dominant/subordinate gap between the three troops. The fourth and fifth-ranking males of the A troop were even with the first and second-ranking males of the C troop, and the first and second males of the B troop were even respectively with the 20th male of the A troop and the 10th male of the C troop. Differing from intra-troop social interactions between individuals, intertroop encounters often involve antagonistic interactions, in which dominant/subordinate relationships are difficult to discern between individuals of different troops. Nevertheless, he showed that the even-ranked males who were dominant over most males of other troops maintained their overwhelming dominance and seldom had encounters with subordinate males of different troops (Kawanaka, 1973).

Such extratroop even interindividual relationships are also

observed between troop males and solitary males (Itani, 1954). Until approximately 1955, many solitary males approached the Takasakiyama troop. Among them, *Miminashi* and *Ushi*, respectively, were even with the first and second-ranking troop males, *Taku* and *Kuma* were even with around the 10th-ranking male, and *Mimikire* was even with around the 20th-ranking male. In 1962, a solitary male named *Yama* approached the A troop and repeatedly fought with its peripheral males. Some of them later came to follow *Yama*, and they formed a new troop, C, with lower ranking females of the A troop (Kano, 1964).

In the society of Japanese monkeys, the inter-BSU, inter-lineage, and inter-individual dominance systems are based on the inequality principle with which coexistence of individuals within the neighboring BSUs, lineages, and a BSU is maintained through the individuals' mutual recognition of the membership and identity of each. Although there may be some variation from species to species, these may be regarded as the main features of the M_2 type of society.

Limit of Coexistence Based on the Inequality Principle

Kin relationships within the P type of BSU of chimpanzees differ greatly from those of the M_2 type BSU, e.g., of Japanese monkeys. From the observations so far at the Mahale Mountains, it is known that since young females leave their natal troop, the mother-daughter bond lasts only 9–10 years (Nishida & Kawanaka, 1972; Kawanaka & Nishida, 1974; Nishida, 1979, 1983). Therefore, there is no kin-related group consisting of mothers and daughters[3]. About mother-daughter relationships, Nishida (1979:105) stated: "If we show the degree of association of a daughter with her mother by a familiarity index so as to categorize developmental stages of female chimpanzees, we can roughly define individuals between 0 to 4 years of age as in the stage of 100% dependence (infant), from 4 to 8 years of age as 85% dependent (juvenile), from 8 to 10 years of age as 50% dependent (adolescent) and from 10 to 12 years of age as 20% dependent (subadult)." Although Nishida (1983) pointed out that females which immigrated from the same BSU often associate within their new BSU, he stated that there is little possibility of kin selection even if sisters immigrated to the same BSU because their age differences are too great to have significant familiar relationships owing to the long birth interval. Thus, female-female relationships are rather "cool." This is well reflected in their grooming relationships. In the K group at Mahale, while there were recorded 218 sessions of male-male grooming and 180 sessions of male-female grooming, there were only 49 sessions of female-female grooming (Nishida, 1979). Similar figures were also reported from Gombe (Goodall, 1965). In the chimpanzee society, the matrilineal lineage does not work as the frame for the dominance system.

Although Goodall (1965) and Reynolds & Reynolds (1965) wrote that males are dominant over females without exception, Nishida (1970, 1979) stated that some old females are dominant over low-ranking males owing to their personalities, individual histories, and kin relationships. The rank of a female fluctuates. The female's rank goes up by her becoming estrous and mating with high-ranking males. When a dominant female babysits an infant of a subordinate female, their dominant/subordinate relationship is reversed. A mother with a newborn becomes timid and lower-ranking. Nishida (1979) reported, however, an example of a past-prime female who was dominant over any other female for seven years, and stated that old females are generally dominant over young females and there is a linear rank order among the adult females within a BSU.

Among males, the rank order is easier to recognize than among females. Since it is not so rigid as that found in an M_2 type of BSU, judgement of dominance by means of throwing food is impossible. Although the one expressing submissive behavior in an antagonistic interaction is judged to be the subordinate, the grimaces of the dominant caused by the explosive display of the subordinate often leads to misjudgement. The example of a male who acquired a higher rank by throwing and hitting a kerosene can (Goodall, 1971) represents one aspect of the chimpanzee male's rank. Nevertheless, there can be assumed a stable linear rank order among them. In the K group at Mahale, the rank order among four males was stable from 1966 to 1969, and after the alpha male disappeared in 1969,[4] the order among the remaining three males was stable until 1975. However, the young adult male who was the fifth-ranking in 1966 often reversed its rank with the higher-ranking males. At Gombe, Bygott (1979) grouped the males into the alpha male, three high-ranking males, six middle-ranking males, and five low-ranking males, and he stated that as they develop from youth to prime age, they become more dominant, and then become lower-ranking as they grow older. Many researchers admit that their fierce displays are related to the rise of their ranks. Nishida (1979) said that this display behavior is prominent among high-ranking males and young adult males.

Although there is no report on the dominance rank in the pygmy chimpanzee, Kuroda (1980) inferred from the high tension among males that there is a definite rank order among them. By confirming the rank order of the first 8 males of the 15 males in the E group, composed of 59 pygmy chimpanzees at Wamba, he also pointed out that the rank gap between pygmy chimpanzees is far less than that found in Japanese monkeys (Kuroda, 1982). Among females, it was possible to distinguish between high, middle, and low-ranking individuals; but further individual rank could not be determined because of their peculiar social interactions which are described later. Nevertheless, as in common chimpanzees, old females are dominant over young ones and males seem to be dominant over females (Kuroda, 1980).

The pygmy chimpanzee society is the same as that of the common chimpanzee in that young females move from one BSU to another (Kano, 1982; Kuroda, 1982; Kitamura, 1983), but it differs in the intra-BSU structure. Kuroda (1982) stated that the mother-son bond persists until the son reaches the age of 11–16 years. There is no sexual interaction between mothers and sons.[5] The mother-son bond within a BSU is so stable that the son is often observed to depend on her on occasions of inter-male interactions. In this society, the rank of the mother could greatly influence that of her son; this seems to be the crux of the subgroup formation mentioned by Kuroda (1982). Another difference between the two species of *Pan* is seen in the interindividual relationships in the BSU. The relative affinity index based on grooming data is highest between males and females in pygmy chimpanzees, and setting this to be 100, the index is 81 between females and 42 between males (Kuroda, 1980). On the other hand, in common chimpanzees, the index is highest between males, and setting this to be 100, the index is 17 between males and females and only 5 between females (Nishida, 1977). This contrasting difference corresponds to the strong male bond in the common chimpanzee society and the "routinely daily frequent sexual interactions" (Kuroda, 1982) in the pygmy chimpanzee society. At any rate both societies have features which cannot be understood simply by the interindividual dominant/subordinate relationships based on the inequality principle.

Between neighboring chimpanzee BSUs, there are clear dominant/subordinate relationships (Nishida & Kawanaka, 1972; Kawanaka & Nishida, 1974). The K and M groups at Mahale overlap their home ranges, and M is dominant over K, which avoids being close to M. On occasions, there have been observed antagonistic intergroup encounters, which I will discuss later. The case reported from Gombe that males of the Kasakela community attacked and killed males of the Kahama community (Goodall et al., 1979) could be an example in which the intergroup balance was lost. Kano (1982) reported that neighboring pygmy chimpanzee groups greatly overlap their home ranges up to 40–64%. The overlapping area often abounds in food sources, and each group use this area by temporarily segregating from the others. Although groups encounter only infrequently as expected, there appears to be intergroup dominance (Kano, 1982).

It is evident from the foregoing that coexistence based on the inequality principle in the genus *Pan* differs greatly from that seen of the M_2 type of society. The very rigid structure as in the Japanese monkey society is not found. They cannot rely on the structure for group integration. Rather it may be better described by saying that they need a multiplex social organization for coexistence.

Budding Coexistence Based on the Equality Principle

I have stated that the equality principle originates in kinship. It originates in that animals recognize their kin among those they live with, and that they exchange interactions different from those with non-kin. While the relationships between non-kin are ruled by dominance, the relationships between kin are biased to fill up or obscure interindividual dominance gaps through sharing the same identity of kinship. The relationships between kin of being depended on and dependent, such as seen between the mother and offspring, are thought to be the original forms of the bonds based on the equality principle. They are relationships in which the two individuals are ideally identical rather than equal. Even after becoming two individuals by parturition, the mother and offspring are psychologically and socially unseparated for a certain period of time. The importance of this period for the offspring's development is evident from the cases of orphaned chimpanzees under the age of 4.5 years, who are for the most part reported to become inactive, playless, and eventually die (Goodall, 1983), and the cases of orphaned Japanese monkeys (Hasegawa & Hiraiwa, 1980).

These relationships are extended to between non-kin. They are seen in all nonaggressive interactions not based on the dominant/ subordinate relationships. While the dominance/subordinate relationships realize the coexistence through inhibition of the subordinate, these relationships assure the coexistence by facilitating the interactions of both individuals concerned. While the former are primarily asymmetrical relationships, the latter are symmetrical. The vocal greeting sounds referred to in the Introduction are symmetrical since both individuals exchange greetings face to face. Most social play is performed as if the playmates were equal. Except for one-directional grooming based on dominant/subordinate relationships, the grooming is mutually exchanged while not exposing the dominant/subordinate inequality. In some monkeys, such as *Macaca fuscata* and *M. sylvana,* relationships similar to those between mothers and offspring are found between some adult males and particular juveniles (Itani, 1959; Deag & Crook, 1971). These are outside the social relationships governed by the dominance system, and are based on the equality principle or indicating the trends toward egalitarianism.

I took more than 10 pages to discuss play behavior in *The Monkeys of Takasakiyama* (Itani, 1954), in which I described play as separated from the world of usual social interactions. This could be rephrased as a world in which unusual rank distinctions do not apply. This separation from the world ruled by dominance means interactions based on the equality principle. It is unknown why social development requires a period which seems contrary to the behavioral development in accordance with the dominance system and why this period is limited to the early stage of the growth from one to three years of age. In species that have prolonged duration for development of young, such as apes, the period spent in play is longer and the social interactions are more complex.

Play is impossible without the participants behaving as if they were equal. Social play requires not only this but also some kind of mood. Even if one solicits another to play, play does not occur if the latter does not share the mood to play. Hayaki (1983), in a discussion of play, pointed out that some self-inhibition works not to force the partner to play, that the dominant restrains its dominance toward the subordinate, and that when one stops moving, the other also stops its move and the play enters a pause. In rough and tumble play (Mori, 1974), which appears an aggressive interaction at first sight, a fictitious world unfolds in which the subordinate chases and holds down the dominant.

Formerly, I thought that play interactions eventually formed the rank order among juveniles (Itani, 1954). Mori (1974: 316) criticized my interpretation and stated, "The most important relationship seen in play is that which provides the equal ground for the participants," which seems correct. After my early studies at Takasakiyama, it was shown that the rank order among infants is formed within 12 weeks after births as if their mothers' rank order were copied (Norikoshi, 1974). In other words, when play becomes most prominent in the developmental stage, the rank order is already firmly established, and play occurs as if such a rank order were nonexistent.

However, play partners are more easily formed if the rank gap is less, so as to put them on equal terms. The infants less than one year of age choose their play partners from the cohort group or those one year older. Juveniles of 1.5–2 years also choose their partners from among their cohorts; those three or more years different in age are seldom chosen as play partners (Mori, 1974). Koyama (1977) reported that 45% of play occurred between the same-aged and 38% between those with one year of age difference, and that 42% occured between males, 35% between females, and 23% between males and females. Between kin-related individuals, the incidence of play was 31.5%—much greater than expected—within the fourth degree of consanguinity (Koyama, 1977). These results suggest that smaller rank gap and closer kin relationship are more suited for the realization of interindividual equality, which is prerequisite for play. However, it should be noted that play sometimes occurs between an adult male and an infant (Itani, 1954). This kind of interaction is more frequent among chimpanzees (Nishida, 1981), although this may be better labelled as "babysitting."

Social grooming is also one of the social interactions based on the equality principle. The one-directional grooming by a mother of her infant is like an extension of self-grooming. Koyama (1977) showed that 50% of grooming occurs between individuals of first degree consanguinity and 15% between those of second degree consanguinity while only 32% occurs between non-kin, which indicates that grooming originates from maternal behavior. However, 27% of grooming between mothers and infants is directed from infants to their mothers, which indicates that grooming gradually becomes mutual as infants grow up. Eventually, this "service behavior" to clean the body surface of another is extended to facilitate non-kin relationships and becomes an important medium of social interactions based on the equality principle. Japanese monkeys cannot give others something valuable to them, but they can treat others with grooming.

Finally I would like to mention peculiar interactions exchanged between non-kin. In the Takasakiyama troop I noticed the peculiar behavior of some high-ranking males taking care of particular 1-year-old juveniles during the birth season, and I called this behavior "paternal care" (Itani, 1959). These peculiar relationships are established between high-ranking males and some 1-year-old juveniles whom their mothers have to leave for parturition. Of the juveniles so cared for, 28 were males and 34 were females; there was little difference by sex. The caretaker's positive attitudes are prominent. The guardian becomes mild and shows high tolerance to his particular juvenile with maternal-behavior-like grooming, caring, cofeeding, etc. Some males attempt to enter the central part of the troop by holding a juvenile in its arms. Similar behavior was observed for the Barbary ape and called "agonistic buffering" (Deag & Crook, 1971).

Later, Kitamura (1977) noticed at Takasakiyama that particular females stay close to some high-ranking males, and that there are some "effects of proximity" between the individuals which have such relationships. Takahata (1982a, b) called this a "peculiar proximate relationship (PPR)," and studied this in detail in the troop at Arashiyama. According to him, more than half the females were in PPR with at least one adult male. High-ranking males are in PPR with females of several lineages. The first-ranking male was in PPR with 18 females of six different lineages, and the second-ranking male with 14 females of five lineages. Between individuals in PPR, intimate interactions as if between kin were observed; they mutually approach and groom each other. He showed that some male-female pairs that developed during the mating season became PPRs in the following non-mating season, and thereafter they seldom interacted sexually with each other (Takahata, 1982a, b).

PPR is notable as a relationship which assures the equality-principle-oriented interactions between non-kin in the society ruled by the dominance system. However, as with the other equality-oriented behaviors, this is far from the ideal social order which can be shared equally by all members of the society. The equality principle in the society of Japanese monkeys does not apply to the whole of their group.

Toward an Egalitarian Society

I have already pointed out that the dominance system is not almighty in the societies of the genus *Pan*. Its breakdown can be seen in every aspect of their social interactions. However, where the P type of society differs most from the M_2 type of society is the sharing of food in response to begging. Although Japanese monkeys also beg for food by stretching their hands with palms up toward humans (Kawai, 1965b, 1969), this behavior is never directed to other monkeys, probably because they know well that they never do nor can share food, or because their dominance system prohibits begging and sharing. By contrast, in the societies of the genus *Pan*, i.e., common and pygmy chimpanzees, valued things are transferred by begging and sharing. This also may be regarded as originating in mother-offspring interactions, although it also occurs between non-kin and adults.

Kortlandt (1962) first reported food sharing among wild chimpanzees. Since then, many cases have been reported from the habituated common chimpanzees at Gombe and Mahale (Goodall, 1968; Nishida, 1970; McGrew, 1975; Silk, 1978). Among pygmy chimpanzees, even more frequent food sharing is reported (Kano, 1980; Kuroda, 1980). Here I will review the outline of this interaction. Kano (1980: 250) stated: "Food sharing was considered to have occurred when one individual obviously possessing a food item, by holding it in his hand, foot or mouth, transferred a part or whole to another individual without any overt antagonism. . . . Food was distributed over all age-sex classes, except from infants." The donor-recipient relationships are summarized by Kano (1980), who analyzed 261 cases of food sharing. Recipients are often subordinate. Although the gestures of begging and mostly expressions of submissiveness, such as grinning and grimacing, food possessors may, though rarely, even show positive food sharing by breaking off a portion of the food and letting the recipients take it. Nevertheless, Kano (1980: 250) noted, "Food was usually shared with reluctance to a craving recipient, although the donor exhibited no hostile rejection in most cases."

Kuroda (1980: 189) summarized the responses of donors as: "1. letting the food fall from the mouth, 2. letting the beggar take as much as it wants, or 3. handing some portion to the beggar." However, possessors do not always share the food. They may ignore begging, turn away from the beggars, firmly rehold the food, slap the beggars' outstretched hands, or run away from the spot; they express their refusal. Note, though, that these are neither hostile rejections nor aggressive interactions. Even dominant possessors sometimes express submissive grinning to subordinate beggars' persistent request (Kuroda, in press). Food items that can be the objects of begging are favorite foods of pygmy chimpanzees, and possessors would certainly hesitate to give them away; psychological ambivalence would cause the dominant possessors to show a submissive expression. The subordinate recipients move away from others and eat the distributed food. By contrast, dominant males seem to hesitate to do so, and remain there, allowing females and immatures to continue to beg (Kuroda, in press).

Food sharing poses some important problems. First, their favorite food items move between individuals. This never occurs in Japanese monkeys. Direct consumption of food from hand to mouth is delayed through transfers between individuals, and the food is consumed also by some individuals who have not originally obtained it. Although it is an exaggeration to say that this is the origin of economic flow of goods, it is true that without this, economic system in the human society would not work. Moreover, the objects flow from those who have to those who do not have; this flow is opposite to that of exploitation found in an inegalitarian society. The objects which move become the media to assure the budding equality in their society. In an egalitarian society of hunter-gatherers, they seem to visualize their principle of egalitarianism in the distribution of objects (Woodburn, 1981; Ichikawa, 1981). Similarly, the pygmy chimpanzee society seems to have stepped toward this egalitarian society and away from one based on the inequality principle.

Second, begging individuals are psychologically free from the inhibitions that maintain the coexistence of subordinate and dominant individuals in the Japanese monkey society. Therefore, begging is a social interaction irrelevant to the inequality principle. Furthermore, food sharing indicates their recognition that one's favorite food is another's favorite food too, which is a mentality related to sympathy and objectification. Only on the basis of sympathy, food sharing becomes possible. As opposed to the inequality principle, this bud of mentality is oriented toward some social system based on the equality principle.

One of the features which facilitate such social interactions in the societies of *Pan* is their wide repertory of food. The food repertory of pygmy chimpanzees includes fruit, such as *Annonidium mannii* and *Treculia africana*, which are especially favored and large enough to be shared by several individuals (Kano, 1980), and that of common chimpanzees include meat of various mammals (Goodall, 1963; Teleki, 1973; Nishida et al., 1979; Nishida, 1981; Kawanaka, 1982). I agree with Nishida's (1981) proposition that large fruit for pygmy chimpanzees and meat for common chimpanzees facilitate food sharing among them.

Besides food sharing, there are many social interactions based on the equality principle in the societies of *Pan*. Employing varieties of facial expressions, vocal sounds, gestures, they have greeting, appeasement, and assurance behaviors, which not only make up for the breakdown of social interactions due to the non-rigid support of their dominance system but also make their societies multiplex. While asymmetrical interactions are prominent in Japanese monkeys, mutual and symmetrical interactions are prominent in the societies of *Pan*. Of these symmetrical interactions, I would especially like to mention the unique "genito-genital contacts" of pygmy chimpanzees.

Kano (1980) and Kuroda (1980) first described this behavior, and Kitamura (in press) attempted an analysis of this. Kano (1980: 253) explained this behavior as follows: "Female *A* approaches female *B*, stands or sits nearby, and stares into *B*'s face. If *B* shows no response, *A* may demand attention by touching *B*'s knee or foot with her foot. *B* may then respond by a slight gesture, such as turning to meet *A*'s gaze. Then either of them may invite the other, by falling on her back, or hanging from a branch. They embrace face to face, and begin to rub each other's genitals together (probably clitoris) rhythmically and rapidly. Genital rubbing lasts for just a few seconds to 20 seconds. On rare occasions, it may last over a minute. . . . Estrous females with genital swellings were the majority of those involved, but anestrous females were not excluded. . . . This suggests that this behavior does not occur exclusively in a sexual context, but has some other social significance."

This behavior usually occurs in a tense situation such as within five minutes of meeting each other in the provisioning site. Both Kano (1980) and Kuroda (1980) concluded that this behavior is related to relieving tension or anxiety and that this is appeasing or friendly behavior rather than homosexual behavior. The difference between common chimpanzees and pygmy chimpanzees in the female familiarity index (Nishida, 1977; Kuroda, 1980), mentioned earlier, is probably due to the absence in the former of this peculiar behavior.

Genito-genital contacts also occur between male pygmy chimpanzees. Male-male mounting, which is well known in Japanese monkeys, is also present in pygmy chimpanzees. In addition, pygmy chimpanzees have a more symmetrical contact called "rump-rump contact" in which two males touch their anal regions while standing on all fours (Kuroda, 1980). Kitamura (in press) classified various genito-genital contacts into four categories: 1. male-mature female, 2. mature male-infant, 3. female-female, and 4. mature male-mature male," and concluded that the latter two categories, being "interactions occuring within a set," are not sexual interactions.

Pygmy chimpanzees have more frequent true copulations than common chimpanzees, and the sexual skin swelling of cycling pygmy chimpanzee lasts 14-20 days (Kano, in press), more than twice as long as the common chimpanzee's 6.5 days of swelling period (Goodall, 1968). Since the birth interval of pygmy chimpanzees is 5–6 years (Kuroda, 1982; Kano, in press), most of the frequent copulations do not result in conception. Kuroda's (1982) description that "pygmy chimpanzees routinely daily have sexual behavior" may be better rephrased by "they perform even sexual behavior in the context of interactions based on the equality principle."

Few agonistic interactions resulting in injuries, which are frequent in common chimpanzees, have been observed in pygmy chimpanzees. With the exception of young females who emigrated, there has been only one missing individual from the BSU studied over 6 years (Kuroda, personal communication). The socionomic sex ratio is close to one (Kuroda, 1979, 1982; Kano, 1982) and there seems to be little sexual difference in the death rate. These factors seem to be related with their overdeveloped varieties of appeasement behaviors, and probably with the rise of the equality principle to rule social interactions.

Thus far I have reviewed the systems supporting the coexistence of individuals within a BSU and traced the transition from the system based on the inequality principle to the system based on the equality principle by comparing M_2 and P types of primate societies. If we assume the hunter-gatherers' egalitarian society (Lee, 1979; Tanaka, 1980; Woodburn, 1981; Ichikawa, 1982) as an ideal model based on the equality principle, we see that the P type of primate societies already have some of its important features. This trend probably cannot be reversed unless the multi-male/multi-female group composition is resolved. In the hominid evolution, this orientation toward equality between BSU members for coexistence probably permeated into every aspect of daily life, and various sharings have been intensified. The solution to the old anthropological problem of the origin of human family could be sought along these lines.

Negated Coexistence

The topic of this symposium session is male aggression, which I have hardly discussed so far. Most aggressive interactions can be understood in the context of failure to conform to the social systems for coexistence of individuals—whether inequality-based or equality-based. However, interactions between groups which do not come under the rules of such systems cannot be understood in the same context. Aggressive interactions within a group are mainly trifles due to social mismanagement. On the other hand, intergroup interactions may result in serious episodes even involving some individuals' deaths (Itani, 1982). Since there are many varieties, it is not easy to draw out general characteristics of these intergroup interactions. Nevertheless, they indicate that the social mechanism for maintaining intergroup relationships is far less developed than that for intragroup relationships. Since I have summarized the types of intergroup aggressive interactions elsewhere (Itani, 1982), here I will only briefly point out the main features.

Many students have recognized the presence of firm, coherent ties between male chimpanzees within a BSU (Itani & Suzuki, 1967; Nishida, 1979). Many episodes recorded from Gombe and Mahale seem to indicate that this is related to the fierce inter-group relationships (Goodall et al., 1979; Nishida, 1979; Itani, 1977b; Itani et al., 1983). Such a male bond has not been noticed in pygmy chimpanzees. The male bond of chimpanzees even has characteristics of those of a combat troop; this strongly suggests fierce antagonism between males of different BSUs. Males born in a BSU become involved in the male bond as they grow up. Goodall (1973) ascribed sibling relationships as an important factor in the formation of male coalition. Nishida (1979: 93) emphasized the ambivalent psychology between subordinate and dominant individuals and discussed the mechanism of maintaining and reinforcing the male bond: "complex sequences of threat-submission-reassurance interaction may strengthen the male bond."

At Gombe, the Kasakela community exterminated the Kahama community. At Mahale there had been a dominant/subordinate relationship between the M and K groups, and they seem to have been in balance; however, now the M group appears to have almost exterminated the K group. How can we interpret these two cases in which the neighboring BSUs could not coexist? Each BSU exists provided that females immigrate from neighboring BSUs; then, what does the extermination of the females' natal BSUs imply? If there is no psychological or social constraint on extermination of other BSUs, the only way left for each BSU to survive is to have a strong male bond within it. The systems maintaining coexistence of individuals within a BSU are not supported by aggressiveness; but it is the male bond that coun-terpoises the aggression directed to the males of enemy BSUs. This means that inter-BSU balancing by means of uncompromis-ing antagonism is the only way of assuring that neighboring BSUs coexist. Therefore, those which cease to resist will be eventually wiped out.

At Gombe, since the Kahama community was exterminated, the Kalande community further south had begun to interact with the Kasakela community (Itani et al., 1983). At Mahale, the M group had begun to intrude into the former core area of the K group, and there the M group once happened to encounter the B group of about 100 chimpanzees in the north (Nishida, 1981; Itani et al., 1983). We have to wait for further studies to see what now happens between these strong BSUs. One of the most important and not yet solved problems in the evolutionary pathway of primate societies is how the antagonism and conflict between males of different BSUs could have been resolved.

Most cases of infanticide, which have been recently reported from many primate species, are inter-BSU episodes. The infanticide seen in Hanuman langurs (Sugiyama, 1965) is performed by the new male after the male replacement; this also should be distinguished from ordinary intra-BSU interactions. Although there has been much individual-centered selectionist argument on this phenomenon, I will not join in that argument here. Most cases of infanticide have occurred in societies with BSUs of one-male/multi-female compositions. It cannot be denied that the infanticide can be possibly interpreted, in the context of elimination of offspring resulting from father-daughter incest, inevitable due to the one-male/multi-female structure by a non-father male. Another notable feature is that the infanticide occurs as a symbolic event characterizing the birth of a new BSU (Fossey, 1979) or rejuvenation of a BSU (Sugiyama, 1965) in the initial phase or final phase of the aging cycle of the BSU. These features are shared by the two types of societies with the same one-male/multi-female BSU composition, M_1 and $\overline{MP}_2$, although the two types of societies have different diachronic structures.

On the other hand, the infanticide in common chimpanzees which have BSUs of multi-male/multi-female composition does not seem to have these features. Chimpanzees differ from langurs or gorillas in that the killing sometimes results in cannibalism and that their infanticide is not exclusively an inter-BSU episode (Goodall, 1977; Kawanaka, 1981). Kawanaka (1981: 83) attempted to analyze infanticide in detail with 12 cases including his own observations, and stated: "It seems that more male infants were killed by conspecifics than females, and this trend was more apparent in the cases where the captors were males." Two of the 12 victims could not be sexed, seven of the other ten were males and three were females. Four of the six victims reported from Gombe were killed by a particular female named *Passion* (Goodall, 1977). Another victim was not consumed, which differed from the other cases. Excluding these five cases, the remaining five sexed victims were males. Of course we have to wait for future studies. Nevertheless, at present it is undeniable that male infants may be selectively killed. Although implications of this are not clear, its effect on the BSU composition is not negligible.

I have briefly reviewed the three types of intraspecific killings in primate societies especially from a sociological viewpoint. All of these indicate negation of coexistence. It also should be noted that in effect, primates themselves modify their own societies, and that this is more prominent in higher primate taxa and more highly developed *specia* (Itani, 1982). In continuing sociological studies of wild primates, we have been observing societies which they themselves have "artificially modified". Implications of the negated coexistence and its seemingly paradoxical links with humanistic characteristics are important topics in future studies of human evolution.

Table 1

Social structure of non-human primates.

Group composition	Incest avoidance mechanism		Social structure	
	Mother-son	Father-daughter		
One-male/one-female	Mate out (m)	Mate out (f)	Nonmatrilineal-Nonpatrilineal	$(\overline{MP_1})$
One-male/multi-female	Mate out (m)	Mate out (m)	Matrilineal	(M_1)
	Mate out (m)	Mate out (f)	Nonmatrilineal-Nonpatrilineal	$(\overline{MP_2})$
Multi-male/multi-female	Mate out (m) and PA	Mate out (m)	Matrilineal	(M_2)
	PA	Mate out (f)	Patrilineal	(P)

(m): By male   (f): By female   PA: Psychological avoidance

Table 2

Rank order of 44 males of the Takasakiyama troop in 1955, and changes up until January 1972.

Individual	Rank in 1955	Leave or death up to Dec. 1962	Rank* in Dec. 1962	Leave or still in troop, Jan. 1972
Jupiter	1	D-1961, 1		
Tatan	2		A-1	L-1964, 5
Pan	3	L-1956, 4		
Monk	4	L-1956, 7		
Bacchus	5		A-2	L-1967, 5
Boor	6		A-3	L-1967, 8
Achilles	7		A-5	L-1964, 11
Dandy	8		A-6	L-1969, 12
Yubi	9		A-7	L-1964, 8
Uzen	10	L-1960, 9		
Kuro	11		A-4	L-1963, 2
Sharaku	12	D-1959, 4		
Utamaro	13	L-1960, 3		
Aome	14		A-10	L-1970, 12
Saruta	15		A-8	L-1970, 11
Cyrano	16		A-9	L-1967, 6
Soba	17	L-1956		
Gon	18	L-1962		
Gen	19	L-1955		
Sibu	20	L-1962		
Pac	21	L-1955		
Don	22	L-1956		
Shiro	23	L-1959	B-2	L-1969, 9
Hoshi	24	L-1959	B-1	L-1965, 8
Curi	25	L-1959	B-3	L-1966, 7
Akutare	26	L-1958, 7		
Tamo	27		A-22	L ?
Zin	28	L-1959	B	L ?
Pong	29	L-?1961		
Nula	30		A-31	A-7
Tion	31	L-1955		
Kin	32	L-1955		
Oro	33		A-11	L-1963, 2
Goemon	34		A-23	L-1963, 1
Ali	35	L-1956		
Gata	36		A-12	L-1963, 1
Jose	37		A	L-1968, 2

Table 2 (Continued)

Rank order of 44 males of the Takasakiyama troop in 1955, and changes up until January 1972.

Individual	Rank in 1955	Leave or death up to Dec. 1962	Rank* in Dec. 1962	Leave or still in troop, Jan 1972
Los	38	L ?		
Peke	39		A-29	L-1970, 12
Toku	40		A-13	A-1
Ika	41		A-26	L-1968, 2
Tanc	42		A-34	L-1971
Idi	43	L ?		
Bob	44	L-1955		

*Main group split to A and B troops in 1959. The alphabet indicates the troop and the number indicates the rank in each troop.

Notes

1. Sugiyama & Koman (1979) and Sugiyama (1981) reported cases in which male chimpanzees might have migrated between groups in the Budongo Forest of Uganda and Bossou of Guinea; these could be the sole exceptional reports if any.

2. Starin (1981) reported that females are dominant over males in multi-male/multi-female groups of *Colobus badius* and that all females and most males migrate between groups. Also for *Papio hamadryas*, which has a multi-layered social structure, complex moves of individuals have been reported (Sigg et al., 1982). However, the process and meaning of their deviation from the M_2 type of structure have not been clarified.

3. In contrast with this, at Gombe three generations of a maternal lineage comprising *Flo* and her daughter are known to live in the same community (=BSU). Recently from Mahale also, J. Hasegawa and M. Hasegawa reported two lineages consisting of three generations from the grandmother to the grandchild within the large M group containing 106 chimpanzees. Thus, large BSUs could contain such lineages. This issue needs further research (Itani et al., 1983).

4. Nishida (1979) ascribed the disappearance to his death by old age.

5. Out of about 2,000 observed cases of copulation, there were only a few cases of mother-son copulation (Kano, personal communication).

Acknowledgements.

I would like to thank: Dr. Diane McGuinness, who gave me the opportunity to participate in this symposium; Dr. Toshisada Nishida, Dr. Takayoshi

Kano, and other colleagues, who have been studying primates, especially the African great apes, together with me; Mr. P. Scarabaeus, who drafted the English translation of my manuscript for this article; and Dr. Pamela J. Asquith, who corrected the English.

References (Titles in Japanese are indicated by J in parentheses.)

Bygott, J. D., "Agonistic behavior, dominance, and social structure in wild chimpanzees of the Gombe National Park," in: *The Great Apes* (Hamburg, D. A., & McCown, E. R., eds.). Benjamin/Cummings, Menlo Park, California, (1979) pp. 405–427.

Deag, J. M. & Crook, J. H., "Social behavior and agonistic buffering in the wild Barbary macaque (*Macaca sylvana* L.), *Folia Primat.*, 15: (1971) 183–200.

DeVore, I. & Hall, K. R. L. "Baboon ecology," in: *Primate Behavior* (DeVore, I., ed.). Holt, Rinehart and Winston, New York (1965).

Fossey, D., "Development of the mountain gorilla (*Gorilla gorilla beringei*): The first thirty-six months," in: *The Great Apes* (Hamburg, D. A., & McCown, E. R., eds.). Benjamin/Cummings, Menlo Park, California, (1979) pp. 139–185.

Fossey, D., "A grim struggle for survival: The imperiled mountain gorilla," *National Geographic.* April, 1981: 501–523.

Furuichi, T., "Dominant-subordinate relationships in the social life of Japanese macaques," *Iden.* (1983a) 37(4): 3–9. (J)

Furuichi, T., "Interindividual distance and influence of dominance on feeding in a natural Japanese Macaque troop," *Primates.* (1983b) 24(4) in press.

Gautier-Hion, A. & Gautier, J. P., "Le singe de Brazza: Une stratégie originale," *Z. Tierpsychol.*, (1978) 46: 84–104.

Goodall, J. "Feeding behaviour of wild chimpanzees: A preliminary report," *Symp. Zool. Soc. Lond.*, (1963) 10: 39–47.

Goodall, J. van Lawick-, "Chimpanzees of the Gombe Stream Reserve," in: *Primate Behavior* (DeVore, I., ed.). Holt, Rinehart and Winston, New York, (1965) pp. 425–473.

Goodall, J. van Lawick-, "The behaviour of free-living chimpanzees in the Gombe Stream Reserve," *Anim. Behav. Monogr.*, (1968), 1: 161–311.

Goodall, J. van Lawick-, *In the Shadow of Man.* Collins, London (1971).

Goodall, J., "Infant killing and cannibalism in free-living chimpanzees," *Folia Primat,* (1977) 28: 259–282.

Goodall, J. "Population dynamics during a 15 year period in one community of free-living chimpanzees in the Gombe National Park, Tanzania," *Z. Tierpsychol.*, (1983) 61: 1–60.

Goodall, J.; Bandora, A.; Bergmann, E.; Busse, C.; Matama, H.; Mpongo, E.; Pierce, A.; & Riss, D., "Intercommunity interactions in the chimpanzee population of the Gombe National Park," in: *The Great Apes* (Hamburg, D. A., & McCown, E. R., eds.). Benjamin/Cummings, Menlo Park, California, (1979) pp. 13–53.

Harcourt, A. H.; Stewart, K. J.; & Fossey, D., "Male emigration and female transfer in wild mountain gorilla," *Nature, Lond. (a(1976) 263:* 226–227.

Hasegawa, T. & Hiraiwa, M., "Social interactions of orphans observed in a free-ranging troop of Japanese monkeys," *Folia Primat.* (1980) 33: 129–158.

Hayaki, H., "Social play of infant Japanese monkeys," *Iden*, (1983) 37(4): 44–50. (J)

Hrdy, S., "Male-male competition and infanticide among the langurs (*Presbytis entellus*) of Abu, Rajasthan," *Folia Primat.*, (1974) 22: 19–58.

Ichikawa, M., "Ecological and sociological importance of honey to the Mbuti net hunters, Eastern Zaïre," *Afr. Stud. Monogr.*, (1981) 1: 55–68.

Ichikawa, M., *Forest Hunters: The Life of the Mbuti Pygmies*. Jinbun-shoin, Kyoto. (1982) (J)

Imanishi, K., "A survey of the society of semi-wild horses." In: *The Group and Environment of Organisms* (Minka Biological Research Group, ed.) Iwanami, Tokyo, (1950) pp. 1–9. (J)

Itani, J., "Japanese Monkeys in Takasakiyama." In: *Social Life of Animals in Japan* (Imanishi, K., ed.) vol. 2, Kobun-sha, Tokyo. (1954) (J)

Itani, J., "Paternal care in the wild Japanese monkey," *Macaca fuscata fuscata. Primates*, (1959) 2(1): 61–93. Also in: *Primate Social Behavior* (Southwick, C. H., ed.) Van Nostrand, Princeton, (1959) pp. 91–97.

Itani, J., "Vocal communication of the wild Japanese monkey," *Primates* (1963) 4(2): 11–66.

Itani, J., *Social Structure of Primates*. Kyoritsu-shuppan, Tokyo. (1972). (J)

Itani, J., "Twenty years with Mount Takasaki monkeys." In: *Primate: Utilization and Conservation* (Bermant, G. & Lindburg, D. G., eds.) John Wiley and Sons, New York, (1975) pp. 101–125.

Itani, J., "Evolution of primate social structure," *J. Human Evol.*, (1977a) 6: 235–243.

Itani, J., *The Chimpanzee Savannah*. Heibonsha, Tokyo. (1977b) (J)

Itani, J., "Social structures of African great apes." *J. Reprod. Fert., Suppl.*, (1980) 28: 33–41.

Itani, J., "Development of the mind—Society and behavior," in: *Modern Psychology* (Fujinaga, T., ed.) (1981) vol. 1: 91–155, Shogaku-kan, Tokyo. (J)

Itani, J., "Intraspecific killing among non-human primates," *J. Social Biol. Struct.*, (1982) 5: 361–368.

Itani, J. & Suzuki, A., "The social unit of chimpanzees." *Primates*, 8: 355–381.

Itani, J & Tokuda, K., *Japanese monkeys on Koshima Island*. in: *Nihon Dobutsuki III* (Social Life of Animals in Japan, Vol. 3) (Imanishi, K., ed.) Kobun-sha, Tokyo, (1958) 242pp. (J)

Itani, J.; Tokuda, K.; Furuya, Y.; Kano, K., & Shin, Y., "The social construction of natural troops of Japanese monkeys in Takasakiyama," *Primates*, (1963) 4(3): 1–42.

Itani, J.; Goodall, J.; & Nishida, T. "Twenty years of chimpanzee studies in Africa," *Anima*, (1983) 121: 48–54. (J)

Kano, T., "Social behavior of wild pygmy chimpanzees *(Pan paniscus)* of Wamba: A preliminary report," *J. Human Evol.*, (1980) 9: 243–260.

Kano, K., "The second division of the natural troop of Japanese monkeys in Takasakiyama," in: *Wild Japanese Monkeys in Takasakiyama* (Itani, J., Ikeda, J., & Tanaka, T., eds.) (1964) Keiso-shobo, Tokyo, pp. 42–73. (J)

Kano, T., "The social group of pygmy chimpanzees *(Pan paniscus)* of Wamba," *Primates*, (1982) 23: 171–188.

Kano, T. (in press) "Reproductive behavior of the pygmy chimpanzees *(Pan paniscus)* of Wamba, République du Zaïre," in: *The Primate Sexuality* (Maple, T. & Nadler, R. D., eds.) Van Nostrand, Princeton.

Kaufmann, J. H., "Social relations of adult males in a free-ranging band of rhesus monkeys." in: *Social Communication among Primates* (Altmann, S. A., ed.) Univ. of Chicago Press, Chicago, (1967) pp. 73–98.

Kawai, M., "On the rank system in a natural group of Japanese monkeys: I. The basic rank and dependent rank," *Primates*, (1958a) 1: 111–130. (J)

Kawai, M., "On the rank system in a natural group of Japanese monkeys: II. In what pattern does the rank order appear on and near the test box?" *Primates*, (1958b) 1: 131–148. (J)

Kawai, M., "On the system of social ranks in a natural group of Japanese monkeys: (1) Basic rank and dependent rank," in: *Japanese Monkeys: A Collection of Translations* (Imanishi, K. & Altmann, S. A., eds.) S. A. Altmann, (1965a) Chicago, pp. 66–86.

Kawai, M., "Newly acquired precultural behavior of the natural troop of Japanese monkeys on Koshima Island." *Primates*, (1965b) 6: 1–30.

Kawai, M. *Ecology of Japanese Monkeys*. Revised Ed. (1969) Kawade-shobo-shinsha, Tokyo. (J)

Kawamura, S., "Matriarchal social ranks in the Minoo-B troup: A study of the rank system of Japanese monkeys," *Primates*, (1958) 1: 149–156. (J) Also in: *Japanese Monkeys* (Imanishi, K. & Altmann, A., ed.) S. A. Altmann, Chicago, (1958) pp. 105–112.

Kawanaka, K., "Intertroop relationships among Japanese monkeys," *Primates*, (1973) 14: 113–159.

Kawanaka, K., "Infanticide and cannibalism in chimpanzees, with special reference to the newly observed case in the Mahale Mountains," *Afr. Stud. Monogr.*, (1981) 1: 69–99.

Kawanaka, K., "Further studies on predation by chimpanzees of the Mahale Mountains," *Primates*, (1982) 23: 364–384.

Kawanaka, K., & Nishida, T., "Recent advances in the study of inter-unit-group relationships and social structure among chimpanzees of the Mahali Mountains," in: *Proc. Symp. 5th Congr. Int. Primat. Soc.* (Kondo, S., Kawai. M., Ehara, A., & Kawamura, S., eds.) Japan Science Press, Tokyo, (1975) pp. 173–189.

Kitamura, K., "Persistent spatial proximity among individual Japanese monkeys," *Kikan Jinruigaku*, (1977) 8(3): 3–39. (J)

Kitamura, K. "Pygmy chimpanzee association patterns in ranging," *Primates*, (1983) 24: 1–12.

Kitamura, K. (in press), "Genito-genital contacts in the pygmy chimpanzee *(Pan paniscus),*" in: *The Primate Sexuality* (Maple, T. & Nadler, R. D., eds.) Van Nostrand, Princeton.

Kortlandt, A., "Chimpanzees in the wild." *Sci. Am.*, (1962) 206: 128–138.

Koyama, N., "On dominance rank and kinship of a wild Japanese monkey troop in Arashiyama," *Primates*, (1967) 8: 189–216.

Koyama, N., "Social structure of Japanese monkeys," in: *Primates* (Itani, J., ed.), *Jinruigakukoza* vol. 2, Yuzankaku, Tokyo (1977) pp. 225–276. (J)

Kummer, H., *Primate Societies*. Aldine and Atherton, Chicago. (1971)

Kuroda, S., "Grouping of the pygmy chimpanzees." *Primates*, (1979) 20: 161–183.

Kuroda, S., "Social behavior of the pygmy chimpanzees," *Primates*, (1980) 21: 181–197.

Kuroda, S., *The Pygmy Chimpanzee: Its Secret Life*. Chikuma-shobo, Tokyo, (1982) 234pp. (J)

Kuroda, S. (in press), "Interaction over food among pygmy chimpanzees," in: *The Pygmy Chimpanzee: Evolutionary Morphology and Behavior* (Susman, R. L., ed.) Plenum, New York.

Lee, R. B., *The !Kung San: Men, Women, and Work in a Foraging Society*. Cambridge Univ. Press, Cambridge. (1979)

McGrew, W. C., "Patterns of plant food sharing by wild chimpanzees," in: *Proc. Vth Int. Congr. Primatol. Soc*, Karger & Kodansha, Basel & Tokyo, (1975) pp. 304–309.

Mori, A., "The social organization of the provisioned Japanese monkey troops which have extraordinary large population sizes," *J. Anthrop. Soc. Nippon*, (1977) 85: 325–345.

Mori, U., "The inter-individual relationships observed in social play of the young Japanese monkeys of the natural troop in Koshima Islet," *J. Anthrop. Soc. Nippon*, (1974) 82: 303–318.

Nishida, T., "A sociological study of solitary male monkeys," *Primates*, (1966) 7: 141–204.

Nishida, T., "Social behavior and relationship among wild chimpanzees in the Mahali Mountains," *Primates*, (1970) 11: 47–87.

Nishida, T., "Chimpanzees of the Mahale Mountains. I. Ecology and social structure of unit-group," in: *The Chimpanzee* (Itani, J., ed.) Kodansha, Tokyo, (1977) pp. 543–638. (J)

Nishida, T., "The social structure of chimpanzees of the Mahale Mountains," in: *The Great Apes* (Hamburg, D. A. & McCown, E. R., eds.) Benjamin/Cummings, Menlo Park, California, (1979) pp. 73–121.

Nishida, T., *The World of Wild Chimpanzees*. Chuokoron-sha, Tokyo. (1981) (J)

Nishida, T., "Social relationships of immigrant females in the chimpanzee society," *Anima*, (1983) 121: 45–47.

Nishida, T. & Kawanaka, K., "Inter-unit-group relationships among wild chimpanzees of the Mahali Mountains," *Kyoto Univ. Afr. Stud.*, (1972) 7: 131–169.

Nishida, T.; Uehara, S.; & Nyundo, R., "Predatory behavior among wild chimpanzees of the Mahale Mountains," *Primates*, (1979) 20: 1–20.

Norikoshi, K., "The development of peer-mate relationships of free-ranging Japanese monkeys in food-getting situations," *Primates*, (1974) 12: 113–124.

Norikoshi, K. & Koyama, N., "Group shifting and social organization among

Japanese monkeys," in: *Proc. Symp. 5th Congr. Int. Primat. Soc.* (Kondo, S, Kawai, M., Ehara, A., & Kawamura, S., eds.) Japan Science Press, Tokyo, (1975) pp. 43–61.

Pusey, A. E., "Inbreeding avoidance in chimpanzees," *Anim. Behav.*, (1980) 28: 543–552.

Reynolds, V. & Reynolds, F., "Chimpanzees of the Budongo Forest," in: *Primates* (DeVore, I., ed.) Holt, Rinehart and Winston, New York, (1965) pp. 368–424.

Schaller, G. B., *The Mountain Gorilla.* Univ. of Chicago Press, Chicago (1963).

Sigg, H.; Stolba, A.; Abegglen, J. J.; & Dasser, V., "Life history of hamadryas baboons: Physical development, infant mortality, reproductive parameters and family relationships," *Primates*, (1982) 23: 473–487.

Silk, J. B., "Patterns of food sharing among mother and infant chimpanzees at Gombe National Park, Tanzania," *Folia primat.*, (1978) 29: 192–141.

Southwick, C. H.; Beg, M. A.; & Siddiqi, M. R., "Rhesus monkeys in North India," in: *Primate Behavior* (DeVore, I., ed.) Holt, Rinehart and Winston, New York, (1965) pp. 111–159.

Starin, E. D., "Monkey moves." *Natural History*, (1981) 90(9): 37–42.

Sugiyama, Y., "On the division of a natural troop of Japanese monkeys at Takasakiyama," *Primates*, (1960) 2(2): 109–148.

Sugiyama, Y., "On the social change of hanuman langurs *(Presbytis entellus)* in their natural condition," *Primates*, (1965) 6: 381–418.

Sugiyama, Y., *The Society of Wild Chimpanzees.* Kodansha, Tokyo, (1981) 222pp. (J)

Sugiyama, Y. & Koman, J., "Social structure and dynamics of wild chimpanzees at Bossou, Guinea," *Primates*, (1979) 20: 323–339.

Takahata, Y., "Social relations between adult males and females of Japanese monkeys in the Arashiyama B troop," *Primates*, (1982a) 23: 1–23.

Takahata, Y., "The socio-sexual behavior of Japanese monkeys," *Z. Tierpsychol.*, (1982b) 59: 89–108.

Tanaka, J., *The San, Hunter-Gatherers of the Kalahari: A Study in Ecological Anthropology.* Univ. of Tokyo Press, Tokyo. (1980)

Teleki, G., *The Predatory Behavior of Wild Chimpanzees.* Bucknell Univ. Press, Lewisburg (1973).

Veit, P. G., "Gorilla society," *Natural History*, (1982) 91(3): 48–58.

Watanabe, K., "Variations in group composition and population density of the two sympatric Mentawaian leaf-monkeys," *Primates*, (1981) 22: 145–161.

Woodburn, J., "Egalitarian societies," *Man* (n.s.), (1981) 17: 431–451.

Yamagiwa, J., "Diachronic changes in two eastern lowland gorilla groups *(Gorilla gorilla graueri)* in the Mt. Kahuzi region, Zaïre," *Primates*, (1983) 24: 174–183.

Yoshiba, K., "Local and intertroop variability in ecology and social behavior of common Indian langurs," in: *Primates—Studies in Adaptation and Variability* (Jay, P. C., ed.) Holt, Rinehart and Winston, New York, (1968) pp. 217–242.

Zuckerman, S., *The Social Life of Monkeys and Apes.* Routledge and Kegan Paul, London (1932).

Commentary: Social Regulation for Individual Coexistence in Pygmy Chimpanzees (Pan Paniscus)

Takayoshi Kano

Ⅰn the outline of the paper to this meeting submitted by Dr. J. Itani, it was said that the coexistence of groups in non-human primate societies was established on the two principles of equality and inequality. He said, further, that the dominance of either one or the other was generally determined by the primate's phyletic status. He went on to illustrate that among Cercopithecids, inequality is dominant, while in the genus *Pan*, for the first time, we can see the establishment of equality. He confirmed a difference, too, between the two species *Pan troglodytes* (common chimpanzee) and *Pan paniscus* (bonobo or pygmy chimpanzee). He hypothesized that in the latter, especially, one can discern the first steps towards an egalitarian society of hunting and gathering people.

P. paniscus and *P. troglodytes* have the same "basic social unit" (BSU), a fact reflecting their phylogenetical closeness. First, in both species the basal social unit is a unit group (or community) comprised of a plural number of males and females. Second, there is social fluidity; the members of the unit group undergo fission and fusion in response to social and ecological demands, forming diverse sizes of temporary associations (parties). Third, the rule is that as the female matures, she emigrates to another group while the male does not.

The first characteristic is not unusual in non-human primate societies. But the second and third points are special characteristics seen only in the genus *Pan*. However, in their sub-basic social organization, these two species evidence a number of important differences. The members of the basic unit among *P. troglodytes* have a strong tendency to fission off into many small size parties. The temporary lone individual is common.

For example, in the Kasakela group in Gombe National Park, parties of six or less comprised 82%; those of ten or more members, only 9% (Goodall, 1968). In particular, many females with dependent offspring separated into their own ranges where they foraged independently. Males and estrus females overlapped these mother-offspring ranges and foraged more widely. Accordingly, the opinion has even been advanced that the unit group and its range must apply only to the males (Wrangham, 1979). In contrast, there is the tendency among *P. paniscus* for larger-sized parties. For example, in the Wamba E group, which is comprised of approximately 70 members, the size of which corresponds to that of the Kasakela group, parties with five or fewer animals were seen in only three instances among a total of 172 (Kano, 1982). The distinguishing characteristic of the *P. paniscus* party—with rare exceptions—is that, regardless of the party's size, they include all kinds of age and sex classes (adults of both sexes, adolescents, juveniles and infants). Further, the relative ratio of males to females is about 1:1 (Kano, 1982). The equalization of the sex ratio can be applied not only to the party but to the unit group (Kano, 1982). From 1979 to 1982, in two censuses conducted of adults and juveniles in E group, there was a sex ratio of 1:1, but among the adolescents the number of females greatly exceeded that of males (Table 1, page 117). However, that could be attributed to the fact that the adolescent females wandered between unit groups.

Among nonhuman primates, the large incidence of an equal sex ratio in the BSU is found only in *P. paniscus* (Itani, in a paper submitted to this meeting). In *P. paniscus*, too, there is evidence that more environmental pressure is working against the males than the females. In a 1982 census of E group, the proportion of individuals with permanent physical impairment (partial or total lack, dislocation, etc. of digits, hands or feet) among the adult females was 56% (n=25) and among adult males 86% (n=28). The sexual difference was significant (p=0.0146, also see Kano, in press). But this environmental pressure does not seem to result in effective selection pressure because since 1977, of the identified males, no member has been recorded as having disappeared or died.

The above differences between *P. paniscus* and *P. troglodytes* show that, as regards the former, there is more development of social regulations for member coexistence.

The purpose of this paper is to consider the differences in inter-group and inter-individual interactions in these two species and to discuss how these are reflected in the species-specific characteristics of social organization. Such a discussion, however, is somewhat hypothetical and preliminary, the reason being that much of the recorded data have not been analyzed yet and, concerning several important points, a longer, more detailed study is considered necessary.

Individual Coexistence

Coexistence of Kin

Regarding the coexistence of offspring and mother in *P. paniscus*, a clear sex difference can be seen. In both sexes, from infancy (0–2 years) through juvenility (3–6 years), dependence on the mother slowly decreases, but late juveniles still move completely with the mother. Upon the advent of adolescence with the first signs of genital swelling, however, the female offspring abruptly sever their connection with the mother and leave the natal group.

All the male offspring, on the other hand, pass through adolescence, and even after entering young adulthood, continue to travel with the mother. (Some small parties comprise only a young adult male and an aged female. They are the mother and her oldest male offspring.) Between them there is frequent co-feeding and mutual grooming; it is also not unusual for the mother to exhibit protective and food-sharing behavior. It is conjectured that their close affiliation probably lasts until one dies.

The writer has never observed any dominant behavior on the part of the offspring towards the mother, or fear or deference on the part of the mother towards her male offspring. Among *P. troglodytes* there are not a few instances of a female remaining in or returning to her natal group once she had separated from her mother (Goodall, 1977). In *P. troglodytes* a male having entered

107

the adult period is incorporated into the male bond and its connection with its mother becomes weak. Sometimes, the mother comes to fear such a male offspring (Goodall, 1971). Sexual difference in affiliation between an offspring and mother is not as great in *P. troglodytes* as in *P. paniscus.*

Immature males, from their infancy on, frequently copulate with adult females. However, in *P. paniscus*, sexual inhibition between male offspring and its mother seems established in early infancy. Apart from some exceptional examples of two pairs, there is no recorded instance of copulation between a mother and her offspring. In contrast, it is not unusual to find copulation occurring between mother and immature male offspring among *P. troglodytes* (Nishida, pers. comm.). The occurrence of sexual interaction between mother and male offspring may have some connection with the term of male offspring dependence on the mother and the dominance relationship between them.

By emigration of the female, coexistence of siblings of different sexes comes to an end at a time when either is of an immature age. In contrast to *P. troglodytes*, there had been no clear observation of alliance between male siblings in *P. paniscus* (without exception, the older brother is dominant). One pair of male siblings, however, during the same period fell in rank within a group. Male siblings frequently engage in mutual grooming and never show severe aggression to each other. However, as concerns agonistic interaction with non-kin males, there has been no definite observation of mutual support among male siblings. It seems that they are bound together only through the mother. As for their ties after the death of the mother, we must wait for further research or clarify that problem.

Coexistence within the Group of Non-Kin

As for the relation between mature, non-kin members within the unit group, excepting male and estrus females, competition has been thought to be the dominant state of affairs. The expression of competition and its regulation, that is, social interaction, is different from class to class.

Coexistence between Males

Compared to that between males and females, or between

females only, there is an overwhelmingly high frequency of agonistic episodes between males (Kano, 1980). Aggressive behavior towards the target often takes the form of threat, pseudo-charge, charge, and chase. Instances of attack (including such forms of physical contact as kicking, slapping, grappling, and so on) are far fewer. Even if attack should occur, when the victim responds, not by running away but by crouching, the attacker immediately moves to the substitute activity of mounting or of rump contact (two animals joined firmly together at their rumps; Kano, 1980), or alternatively, the attacker leaps over the victim while avoiding direct physical contact. The attacker does not usually attack violently (such as by biting).

While feeding, agonistic interactions take place much more frequently between males than between females, or between females and males. Compared to feeding, there seems to be far less sexual competition though the highest ranking males engage in sexual interaction with females regardless of place, while lower ranking males lure females away from the others for copulation (Kano, in press c).

Submissive behavior also occurred with the highest frequency among males. The ranking was not necessarily in linear order. In the E group males, at least two alliances were noted. One was when five members formed a high ranking group; however, when the fourth and fifth ranked males were separated from their comrades, they sometimes showed submissive behavior (expression of grimace, screeching, avoidance, etc.) to the males whom they usually threatened. One other alliance consisted of three low-ranking males who always traveled together and showed no agonistic behavior to one another. Among the males in these two alliances none was suspected of still having a mother.

There were 12 adult males not in the alliance. Of these, 8 young males often traveled together with a female thought to be the mother. Two males were aged; the other two were physically handicapped and socially inactive. Among the young males, three, plus one late adolescent male, were for a time extremely assertive among the other males. They were similar in having an aged mother who received respect from the other members. For a while, one of them was even alpha-male (Kitamura, pers. comm.), but when the mother became timid after giving birth, he dropped in rank, returning to the group of males of the lowest rank. A late adolescent male, whose mother rose to the rank occupied by the previous female, became dominant to all the other males which associated frequently with him. Also, in the case of another young male, he received the actual support of his mother. One day he suddenly began direct and persistent charging displays towards the second ranking male. At first the latter ignored him, but then began to punish the attacker by slapping or chasing him. At this time, the attacker's mother restrained the second ranked male by barking at or attacking him, sometimes receiving help from other females until she repelled him. A few days later, the second ranked male, when faced by a charge from the same young male, instantly ran away. This episode shows that the young male's sudden rise in rank was a sham, depending as it did on the mother's assistance.

This kind of sudden assertiveness is thought to be prompted by a young male's need to enter the ranks of adults, stemming from his physical and social development. But the mother's presence and intervention delays his settling into his proper rank.

Among *P. troglodytes*, within the unit group, males form a firm bond and among them their ranks are strictly linear. Through frequent social grooming etc., they strengthen their "we-feeling" and cooperate in confronting males of other groups (Nishida, 1979). Among *P. paniscus*, however, the rank order is not as strict nor is the grooming between males nearly as common as that between males and females and between only females (Kano, 1980; Kuroda, 1980). From this we can deduce that the male's "we-feeling" is correspondingly weaker in *P. paniscus*.

Coexistence between Adult Males and Adult Females

P. paniscus and *P. troglodytes* are similar in that the external genital organs of the females have a swelling cycle. But there are two points of difference between them.

1. The maximum swelling phase of *P. troglodytes* averages 7–10 days (Goodall, 1969; Nishida, 1977; Tutin, 1979) whereas it is not unusual for that of *P. paniscus* to continue more than 20 days (Kano, in press b). One past-prime female even maintained maximum tumescence for about ninety consecutive days.

2. *P. troglodytes* females neither resume their sexual cycle nor engage in copulation for an average of three years following parturition. *P. paniscus* females, by contrast, recommence the swelling cycle anywhere from two to three months to a year after

110

parturition and then engage actively in sexual interaction (Kano, in press b).

Females of both species copulate during the period of maximum tumescence. The *paniscus* female, as noted above, is sexually receptive more continually and involved in sexual intercourse with males far more frequently than her *troglodytes* counterpart (Kano, in press b).

P. troglodytes become pregnant within two or three cycles after resuming sexual swelling and almost their entire lives are spent either in a nursing or gravid state (Goodall, 1968; Coe et al., 1979). By contrast, *P. paniscus* females, can be said to spend most of their reproductive life in nursing and copulation. The birth interval of both species, however, is similar (4–5 years). That is, the greater part of copulations of *P. paniscus* does not lead to pregnancy. It would seem then that the fact that the *paniscus* female has prolonged sexual receptivity is more for making coexistence possible with the male than it is for reproduction. Several young females frequently solicited high ranking males in order to get food (Kano, in press b). This is one proof of the socialization of sexual behavior.

Social grooming was most frequent between males and females (Kano, 1980; Kuroda, 1980), yet grooming with the mating partner was rare. Mounting or rump contact between male and female was often seen, although its frequency was less than copulation. It took place more often between males and females who were not yet fully in estrus. It may be that such behavior serves as a form of appeasement between males and females who cannot engage in sexual interaction.

Among *P. troglodytes* the male generally dominates the female (Reynolds and Reynolds, 1965; Riss and Goodall, 1977). In *P. paniscus*, however, no clearly dominant/subordinate relationship could be found between an adult female and male. Generally, the *paniscus* adult female does not hesitate in approaching a male in order to obtain food. Even the highest ranking male is disconcerted at such an approach and often leaves, taking some food with him. As a result, the female supplants that male and has free use of the food left behind. Sometimes a high ranking male, occasionally even an alpha-male, is threatened or chased by a female or group of females. Almost all males of middle lower rank are patently more subordinate than the full adult female in all kinds of social situations.

The male *paniscus* even seems to be somewhat psychologically inhibited from demonstrating aggressive or dominant behavior toward an old female. That may very well have some connection to the male's prolonged dependence on its mother.

Coexistence among Females

The adult female *troglodytes* is characterized by unsociability. During the non-estrus period she lives alone with her offspring; only during estrus does she go with the male. *Troglodytes* females seldom associate. There is a minimum of social grooming between females (Nishida, 1970; Sugiyama, 1969).

In contrast, *P. paniscus* females often engage in a variety of social interactions. At times of group excitement, for example when arriving at a feeding site, or when the parties come together, "genital rubbing" (ventro-ventral embracing and rubbing of their sexual organs together) frequently occurs among females (Kuroda, 1980; Kano, 1980). This activity appears to reduce tension among the females and is an activity that permits mutual proximity. This genito-genital contact takes place during the non-swelling phase, too, but is most frequent at the time of maximum swelling. Therefore, the prolongation of the female's maximum tumescence is useful for peaceful coexistence among the females themselves.

Social grooming is more frequent among females than males. Also, there are special females who often associate together. On many occasions females will band together to counter attack when they are confronted with threats from males. There is obviously some kind of "we-feeling" among these females.

It appears that younger females show respect towards older ones but there is no evident dominant/subordinate relationship among females. Aggression between females is at a minimum. When it does occur, they grapple with one another and roll on the ground. Such fights often bring in many other females and cause a general uproar. Whereas aggression among males is unidirected, that is, one always shows aggressive behavior to the other who always shows submission, that between females is more diffuse, a fact which seems to reflect the lack of a clear rank order among females. The bonds among females may be thus formed on something other than dominant/subordinate relationships.

Immigration of Adolescent Females and Its Process

Among both *P. troglodytes* (Goodall, 1968) and *P. paniscus* (Kano, in press b), the genital swelling of adolescent females is smaller than that of adults; adolescent females have no regular cycle and are sterile for 4–5 years. The greatest difference is that among *P. troglodytes*, in which the adolescent swelling is not attractive to the adult male, mating between an adolescent female and an adult male is very infrequent (Goodall, 1968). Among *P. paniscus*, however, the mature males are attracted to the adolescent swelling which exhibits maximum tumescence almost continuously.

In short, it is always possible for the adolescent female to mate with the males and to engage in genital rubbing with other females. This is quite effective in getting them admitted into other unfamiliar groups. The adolescent female is the class that is most active in copulation and genital rubbing. They not only always respond to solicitation for copulation or genital rubbing by presenting or mounting but actively initiate it. They wander to groups other than their natal one and, upon entering late adolescence, become especially close to a certain group. At the time of first parturition (that is, on entry into adulthood) they become a stable member of that group.

It has been the writer's observation that females with offspring have a solid sense of being in the in-group. Only once was a female with young observed associating with an outside group (a P group primiparous female entered the E group for only one day).

Group Coexistence

Among *P. troglodytes*, interaction is represented by antagonism between males. Fights between males of different groups sometimes results in the death of some of the combatants (Goodall et al., 1979).

In *P. paniscus* the group range largely overlaps (between 40% and 66%, Kano, 1982; in press c) and the important food resource is included in that overlapping portion. Through avoidance, however, group encounters are minimized. Between groups of *P. troglodytes*, dominant/subordinate relationships do exist, but, in the case of *P. paniscus*, which group is dominant or subordinate depends on the circumstances of the moment. The size of the party is especially an important factor. When there is an actual encounter between groups, a variety of behavior ensues, from fighting (Kitamura, pers. comm.) to peaceful mixing in the bordering area. Until now, no observation has been made of participants killed during severe intergroup fights.

Discussion

P. paniscus is more gregarious than *P. troglodytes*. For inter-group competition it is an advantage to form a large party, but that may also escalate intra-group competition. Many kinds of primates, through strengthening the dominance hierarchy, lower the outbreak of aggression that may arise from intra-group competition. Dominance hierarchy itself does not promote peaceful coexistence between group members. It only acts to suppress excessive outbursts of aggression. Thus, generally, a species which has a more rigid hierarchy, shows aggressive and/or dominant/subordinate behavior more frequently.

Dominance hierarchy establishes an order of priority in competition. Accordingly, those lower ranking members have fewer opportunities to get food or approach mating partners than higher ranking ones. Within the same species, the male usually makes a stronger dominance hierarchy than the female. This has the effect of making the number of males fewer than females. In the unit group of *P. paniscus*, however, the number of males and females is about equal. This means there is no powerful dominance hierarchy within and between all age-sex classes. To put it another way, this suggests that intra-group competition is neatly avoided.

Let us look first at the mechanism for avoidance of competition from the social and then from the ecological side. In the social group of *P. paniscus*, the dependence of the male on its mother and the long duration of that closeness, the equality of the female vis-á-vis the male, and the coalitions among females, all seem to depress the formation among males of a powerful dominance hierarchy. Among many other primates, grooming is the single important friendly behavior among group members. But with *P. paniscus*, in addition to grooming, a variety of other kinds of behavior have developed to deepen affiliative relations and to dissolve tensions among them. All of those forms include genital contact. That is to say, all originate in copulatory behavior (Kano, in press c). Copulatory behavior itself exceeds the original purpose of reproduction and is employed to develop affiliation between the male and female. Through the socialization of sexual activity in *P. paniscus*, peaceful coexistence of the group members of all age-sex class is made possible. In order to reduce sexual competition between males, to strengthen the bond between male and female, and further to facilitate affiliative relations among the females, it is important that the female has attained a condition of semi-continual estrus.

Much of the major food of *P. paniscus* is produced in giant trees or huge vines covering the tops of those trees in the rain forest. Those foods change seasonally and are not evenly distributed in the forests. Because their food grows in abundance in one place and changes with the season, *P. paniscus*, by organizing themselves into large parties, can maximize their feeding efficiency.

In physical ability, the male is superior to the female, and thus has greater access to food. Further, males have almost no direct role in raising offspring. By foraging independently, *P. troglodytes* females, with their dependent offspring, avoid direct competition with males and effectively utilize the more widely dispersed food. The disadvantage of *P. paniscus* females with young is alleviated by other social means. On reaching a food tree, the low-medium ranking males (which are in most cases in front of the others) first help themselves, but as higher ranking males arrive, they take what food they can carry from the tree and retreat. Females, however, who arrive late, assure themselves of co-feeding through genital rubbing. Some time later, the tree is occupied by two or three high-ranking males and many more females. The result is that these females and their young can enjoy relaxed feeding over a longer time. Thus the higher antagonism between males in a group than between females has a very important bearing on the survival of the females and their young. Because of that, this has a selective advantage.

The fact that the unit group has a large overlapping range in which major food sources are included, increases the efficiency of gathering food occurring in large quantities at one spot.

That males are not lost in *P. paniscus* society suggests in part that inter-group antagonism is not as strong as in *P. troglodytes*. The large degree of overlapping area blurs the value of territorial defense. By enlarging their territory, *P. troglodytes* make available to themselves a larger number of females (Goodall, 1983). But among *P. paniscus*, the "in-group feeling" among females is strong and expansion of territory is not connected with an increase in available females.

With regard to exploitation of food resources, it appears that *P. troglodytes* are better at it than *P. paniscus*. The former has a greater diversity of food and makes use of a larger variety of daily-monthly food (Kano, in press c). They are less conservative in trying new kinds of food (such as crops) and have succeeded in developing a greater variety of animal foods than *P. paniscus*. For hunting and acquiring food, as well as for processing it, reports have come in from many localities of *P. troglodytes'* use of tools (e.g., Goodall, 1965, 1968; Nishida, 1973; Nishida and Uehara, 1980; Nishida and Hiraiwa, 1982; McGrew, 1974, 1979; Sugiyama and Koman, 1979; Boesch and Boesch, 1981). As for *P. paniscus*, no such behavior has been reported except a single instance based on indirect evidence from Lomako (Badrian et al., 1981).

Because of their great ability to exploit food resources, *P. troglodytes* have come to occupy a geographical range (including a diversity and a greater severity of food environments) far wider than that of *P. paniscus* (Kano, in prep.). By contrast, it appears that *P. paniscus* live in a more stable food environment (Kano, in prep.). They spend less time on subsistence activities (Kano, in press c). The remaining time they turn to the development of social behavior for coexistence of members, and have succeeded in raising the survival rate of males to be nearly equal to that of females. Perhaps it has retarded the selection rate against some genes in the male. More than *P. troglodytes* females, *P. paniscus* females completely break their relation with the natal group. This suggests that the inbreeding coefficient in a *P. paniscus* unit group may be lower than that of *P. troglodytes*. This means that the selection rate against certain recessive genes in *P. paniscus* is slower. This, and the fact that genetically the selection rate is slower, suggests that *P. paniscus* may preserve a greater primitivity than *P. troglodytes*.

Table 1

Composition of the E group in 1979 and 1982

	1979	1982
Adult Males	15	21
Adult Females	16	18
Adolescent Males	5	5
Adolescent Females	8	14
Juvenile & Infant Males	10	9
Juvenile & Infant Females	9	9
Total	63	76

References

Badrian, N., Badrian, A., and Susman, R. L., "Preliminary observations on the feeding behavior of *Pan paniscus* in the Lomako forest of central Zaire." *Primates*, 1981, 22(2): 173–181.

Boesch, C., and Boesch, H., "Sex differences in the use of natural hammers by wild chimpanzees: a preliminary report." *J. Human. Evol.*, 1981, 10: 585–593.

Coe, C. L., Connolly, A. C., Kraemer, H. C., and Levine, S., "Reproductive development and behavior of captive female chimpanzees." *Primates*, 1979, 20(4): 571–582.

Goodall, J., "The behaviour of free-living chimpanzees in the Gombe Stream Reserve." *Anim. Behav. Monog.*, 1968, 1: 161–311.

Goodall, J., van Lawick-, "Some aspects of reproductive behaviour in a group of wild chimpanzees, *Pan troglodytes schweinfurthii*, at the Gombe Stream Chimpanzee Reserve, Tanzania, East Africa." *J. Reprod. Fert., Suppl.*, 1969, 6: 353–355.

Goodall, J., van Lawick-, *In the Shadow of Man*. Collins. London 1971.

Goodall, J., "Infant killing and cannibalism in free-living chimpanzees." *Folia Primat.*, 1977, 28: 259–282.

Goodall, J., "Population dynamics during a 15 year period in one community of free-living chimpanzees in the Gombe National Park, Tanzania." *Z. Tierpsychol.*, 1983, 61: 1–60.

Goodall, J., Bandora, A., Bergman, E., Busse, C., Matama, H., Mpongo, E., Pierce, A., & Riss, D., "Intercommunity interactions in the chimpanzee population of the Gombe National Park." In: *The Great Apes*. (Hamburg, D. A., & McCown, E.R., eds.) Benjamin/Cummings, Menlo Park, California, 1979, pp. 13–53.

Kano, T., "Social behavior of wild pygmy chimpanzees *(Pan paniscus)* of Wamba: A preliminary report." *J. Human Evol.*, 1980, 9: 243–260.

Kano, T., "The social group of pygmy chimpanzees *(Pan paniscus)* of Wamba." *Primates*, 1982, 23(2): 171–188.

Kano, T., in press a, "Observations of physical abnormalities among the wild bonobos *(Pan paniscus)* of Wamba, Zaire." *Amer. J. Phys. Anthropol.*

Kano, T., in press b, "Reproductive behavior of the free-ranging pygmy chimpanzees *(Pan paniscus)* of Wamba, on the right bank of the upper Luo River in the Zaire Basin." In: *Sexuality of the Primates*, (Maple, T. L., and Nadler, R. D., eds.) Van Nostrand Reinhold Co., New York.

Kano, T., in press c, "Feeding Ecology of the bonobos *(Pan paniscus)* of Wamba, In: *The Pygmy Chimpanzee: Evolutionary Morphology and Behavior.* (Susman, R. L., ed.) Plenum, N.Y.

Kano, T., in prep., "Geographical distribution and adaptation of the pygmy chimpanzees *(Pan paniscus)* in the central Zaire Basin."

Kuroda, S., "Social behavior of the pygmy chimpanzees." *Primates*, 1980, 21: 181–197.

McGrew, W. C., "Tool-use by wild chimpanzees in feeding upon driver ants." *J. Human. Evol.*, 1974, 3: 501–508.

McGrew, W. C., "Evolutionary implication of sex differences in chimpanzee predation and tool use." In: *The Great Apes.* (Hamburg, D. A., & McCown, E. R., eds.), Benjamin/Cummings, Menlo Park, California, 1979, pp. 440–463.

Nishida, T., "Social behavior and relationship among wild chimpanzees in the Mahali Mountains." *Primates*, 1970, 11: 47–87.

Nishida, T., "The ant-gathering behavior by the use of tools among wild chimpanzees of the Mahali Mountains." *J. Human. Evol., 1973, 2: 357–370.*

Nishida, T., "Chimpanzees of the Mahale Mountains (in Japanese)." In: *The Notes on Chimpanzees. (Itani, J., ed.), Kodansha, Tokyo 1977.*

Nishida, T., "The social structure of chimpanzees of the Mahale Mountains." In: *The Great Apes.* (Hamburg, D.A., & McCown, E. R., eds.), Benjamin/Cummings, Menlo Park, California, 1979, pp. 73–121.

Nishida, T. & Uehara, S., "Chimpanzees, tools, and termites: Another example from Tanzania." *Curr. Anthrop.* 1980, 21: 671–672.

Nishida, T., and Hiraiwa, M., "Natural history of a tool-using behavior by wild chimpanzees in feeding upon wood-boring ants." *J. Human. Evol.*, 1982, 11: 73–99.

Reynolds, V. & Reynolds, F., "Chimpanzees of the Budongo Forest." In: *Primate Behavior* (Devore, I., ed.), Holf, Rinehart and Winston, N.Y., 1965, pp. 368–424.

Riss, D., and Goodall, J., "The recent rise to the alpha-rank in a population of free-living chimpanzees." *Folia Primat.*, 1977, 27: 134–151.

Sugiyama, T., "Social behavior of chimpanzees in the Budongo Forest, Uganda." *Primates*, 1969, 9: 225–258.

Sugiyama, Y., and Koman, J., "Tool-using and -mating behavior in wild chimpanzees at Bosou, Guinea." *Primates*, 1979, 20(4): 513–524.

Tutin, C. E. G., "Mating patterns and reproductive strategies in a community of wild chimpanzees *(Pan troglodytes schweinfurthii)."* *Beh. Evol. Sociobiol.*, 1979, 6: 29–38.

Wrangham, R. W., "Sex differences in chimpanzee dispersion." In: *The Great Apes* (Hamburg, D. A., & McCown, E. R., eds.), Benjamin/Cummings, Menlo Park California, 1979, pp. 481–489.

4.

Animal Intelligence and Human Instinct: Reflections on Psychobiology of Rank

Peter C. Reynolds

T wenty years ago, when I first began the study of monkeys and apes, the nature of behavior was so well understood that it needed no discussion. Higher animals were characterized by learning, lower animals by instinct, and "physical anthropology" was the dissection of primate cadavers by former medical students. In all fields of social science, human nature, while not actually denied, was regarded as a residual category, far off the main line of significant variables. Even Bronislaw Malinowski, the founder of modern anthropology, whose Continental eccentricities included what he called a "biological theory of culture," is most revealing in what he thought a human behavioral biology ought to include: "impulses for oxygen, hunger, sexual coupling, fatigue, restlessness, sleep, urination, elimination, fright, and pain." Not even aggression is on this list, much less anything as abstract as dominance or hierarchy.

Biology itself was not much of a corrective to this point of view. Biology had only two theories of human nature, genetic determination of behavior and neurohumoral control of behavior, and neither theory gave much room to social science. Neurobiology, in fact, had come of age in the same intellectual context as the modern branches of social science, and they both shared the same nineteenth century assumptions about the relationship between nature and nurture. As I have pointed out at length in my book, *On The Evolution Of Human Behavior* (University of California Press, 1981), for almost two hundred years the social and biological sciences have shared a progressive and dualistic concept of human nature that is not only contradicted by the facts but makes impossible any theoretical reconciliation among these different fields.

Take, for example, the illustrations from textbooks in physical anthropology and neurobiology from the 1940's to 1960's. The cerebral cortex, the organ of enlightenment, is either superimposed on the more instinctual side of nature, or, as in Watson's *Behaviorism*, there is an explicit rendering of a two-tack theory of behavior, in which innate behavior appears as unconditioned responses at birth and becomes subordinated to learned behaviors during development. Finally, the culmination of this tradition is in Paul McLean's 1949 paper on the concept of the visceral brain. Here, the instinctual functions are shown as the lowest stratum of a three-story model of the mammalian brain, in which the phylogenetically older "reptilian" parts of the brain are on the bottom while learning and intelligence are on the top, equated with the newer "mammalian" structures that develop later in evolution.

When I first became interested in the biological basis of primate behavior, I confess that I fell in love with McLean's diagram of the neural hierarchy. What a thrill to discover that everything I had been taught in graduate school about the relationship between nature and nurture had been scientifically validated by the exact sciences, neuroanatomy and neurophysiology! In McLean's theory of the nervous system, the concept of human instinct is a residual category, subordinated to phylogenetically advanced mechanisms of learning and culture. Shortly thereafter, I was invited by Dr. Karl Pribram, the Honorary Chairman of this committee, to do my dissertation research in his laboratory at Stanford University, and it was there that I came to see these issues in a very different light. Now I use McLean's theory of the brain as a litmus paper test of a person's neurological sophistication. It fits so neatly into our cultural preconceptions about the nature of human nature that people who know nothing about the brain are immediately attracted to it. Even recently, one can see McLean's illustration reproduced in all seriousness in Carl Sagan's book, *The Dragons of Eden*.

What is wrong with this picture? First of all, it assumes that advanced behaviors can be localized in anatomically advanced brain structures, while primitive behaviors can be localized in anatomically primitive brain structures. Second, it assumes that the relationship between primitive and advanced is one of subordination, with the latter dominating the former. Third, it assumes that anatomy is the best guide to functionally distinct systems in the brain. Virtually all of these assumptions, however, have been negated by the findings of the neurosciences over the past three decades.

- The anatomically primitive parts of the mammalian brain, such as the hippocampus, septum, and amygdala, are critically involved in such advanced behavioral functions as learning and memory.

- The advanced and primitive parts of the brain are not related by subordination but by differentiation of function.

- The physiological properties of the cerebral cortex are determined to a large extent by the activity in lower brain centers.

- The function of anatomical structures is determined in part by the chemical composition of the fluids that bathe them.

- The brain and body are reciprocally related: the brain controls the production of hormones that affect the body, while the brain is itself a target organ for hormones produced by the body.

- Many anatomical structures in the brain, such as sensory cortex, are dependent upon certain kinds of environmental information for normal growth and development.

- Many functional systems, such as visual processing or aggression, involve anatomical structures developed at different evolutionary periods.

- Specifically, human behavioral systems, such as language, tool use, or intellectual processes, may involve subcortical parts of the brain as well as the neocortex.

Biology's own understanding of the nervous system has

changed dramatically in the span of a generation, and any appeals to human nature must refer to this richer concept of the brain. Among the general public, the older neurology of animal instinct and human intellect continues to hold sway, but behavioral science cannot afford to shy away from issues because the conclusions may be misinterpreted by the misinformed or twisted by the malicious. The duty of behavioral science is to present the causation of behavior in all of its empirical complexity. By attempting to assess the role of biological variables in social phenomena, we are expanding the intellectual range of the inquiry, not narrowing it down to preconceived assumptions. The nature of human nature is the last thing that behavioral science will discover, not its point of departure; and our research programs should be designed to discover it, not to assume it.

In primatology, my own field of expertise, the inquiry into the biological determinants of behavior has been a humbling experience, conducive to intellectual growth. Modern primatology began around 1960 as a joint venture among psychologists, zoologists, and anthropologists. At that time, each science was confident that it already knew the significant causal factors that determined why animals behaved as they did.

The zoologists began with a concept of innate behavior patterns derived from the European ethologists, Niko Tinbergen and Konrad Lorenz, and they categorized primate species in terms of the species-specific behaviors they exhibited. Psychologists began with the assumption that a monkey's behavior was determined by its relationship to its mother, and they set about varying childhood experience in a systematic way. Anthropologists were convinced that membership in the social group explained the form and frequency of behavior. They made careful records of social grooming and mapped the statistics against kinship charts of who was related to whom.

After only a few years of this enthusiasm, the research paradigms of all three sciences were demonstrated to be insufficient. The same species with the same species-specific behavior patterns were found to live in different types of social groups in different places and to have localized behavioral variants not easily explained by the innate fixed-action pattern. Primate zoology suddenly shifted from Hobbes to Montesquieu, downplaying ethological models in favor of ecological studies on such environmental issues as predation rates, resource availability, and the effects of climate on behavior. Primate psychology suffered a reversal in the opposite direction. Experimental learning theorists, who had written tomes proving that behavior could be shaped more easily than putty, suddenly found themselves with infant monkeys whose developmental history could be predicted better by biological species than by rearing experience. Even closely related species of macaque monkey differed in their response to maternal deprivation, and these differences continued in the face of cross-fostering experiments in which infants of one species were raised by mothers of another. And the anthropologists? Their studies did indeed demonstrate the pervasive effects of kinship on the social organization of monkeys and apes, but they also underscored the significance of another organizing principle which they were far less happy to validate—the concept of social rank as an independent variable.

At this point, it is necessary to touch on a territory so hedged about with caveats that I have postponed approaching it at all: the characterization of social rank itself. In many respects, it is easier to characterize in a negative way by giving instances of what it is not. It is not, for example, the same as "dominance" in a brute-force sense of the term. In the early days of primatology, when Robert M. Yerkes was the science's nearly sole practitioner, monkeys and apes were believed to have a social organization based on dominance, the monopolization of resources by more aggressive individuals. Abraham Maslow, the humanist psychologist, carried this idea a step further by devising a "pair test" to measure it. He would put two monkeys together in the same cage and toss a peanut between them. The monkey who grabbed the peanut was judged the dominant individual, and if the subordinate objected to the situation, the dominant animal would threaten him. The problem with this method is that it creates the phenomenon one is trying to measure—although it creates it reliably. If one puts monkeys in a winner-take-all situation, a winner will almost always emerge to take it all. However, situations like this are an artifact of concentrated feeding, and the social organization of primates in the wild has scarcely anything that corresponds to the monopolization of resources.

Human beings are the only species of primate that have cooperative economic production, although there are adumbrations of it in chimpanzees, and monkeys and apes forage for themselves on plant food that is scattered about, not concentrated. Even primate children fend for themselves once they are off their mother's breast. In some species, in fact, like hamadryas baboons, where the males are almost twice the size of the females, the sexes occupy different economic niches, with the lighter animals feeding on the tops of bushes, while the heavy adult males are restricted to more accessible food sources. Thus, the direct competition for resources that the dominance theory addresses in fact hardly ever arises in a primate's natural habitat.

Another shortcoming of the classical model of dominance was observed by Japanese primatologists. They found that an animal's dominance status when measured by the peanut tossed between two individuals was not necessarily the same as the dominance rank that could be inferred by watching the animal in its natural social group. The pair-test was not as predictive as it should have been, and additional problems of the dominance concept soon came to light in the first field studies of primate groups in their natural habitats: in most species of primates, dominance is strictly marginal to the social organization. If one measures dominance by one individual giving way or acquiescing to the will of another, then in most species of primates such behavior is rare, and in many species almost nonexistent. In gibbons, siamangs, and many kinds of South American monkeys, for example, where the basic social unit consists of a father, mother, and their dependent offspring, territoriality, not dominance, is the way in which aggression manifests itself. These species give intense displays on the borders of their territories, like male song birds in mating season, but social relations within the group are harmonious and peaceful. Dominance, as defined for laboratory monkeys and chimpanzees, does not apply at all.

After hundreds of field studies on a wide variety of species, a more realistic picture of primate social organization began to emerge. It became clear that "dominance hierarchies" are preferentially associated with a single type of primate society, the multimale troop. The multimale troop is a social group that contains *multiple, unrelated, breeding* adult males. Such a social organization is very rare in mammals, but relatively common in primates. Even so, most species of primates live either in mated-pair societies, where the nuclear family is the largest social unit, or in harem societies, where a single male lives and breeds with a group of females.

In multimale troops, by definition, there are two or more adult males, and these males are unrelated in the sense of not having grown up together as children of the same mother. (Whether they have the same father is usually impossible to say.) Furthermore, these unrelated males have sexual access to females in the troop. In these social situations, it is usually easy to discern a male hierarchy, in which male alpha outranks male beta . . . down to male omega. These hierarchical relationships, once called "dominance hierarchies," are now called "ranking systems" or "status hierarchies" by primatologists, and this alteration of terminology signals an important change in our understanding of how they work.

The classical theory of dominance predicts that rank is primarily motivated by the desire for scarce resources and that it is implemented by aggressive means primarily, but observations on free-ranging animals do not bear out these presuppositions. High-ranking animals are typically not the most aggressive as measured by the frequency of fights and threat behavior, and rank does not usually function in the allocation of resources unless these are artificially concentrated. This fact will prove extremely important in intellectual history because it undercuts conventional sociological theories on the origins of social rank. All the major sociological theories derive rank from the system of resource allocation—the monopolization of the means of production—but systems of social rank are widespread in species of nonhuman primates that have no cooperative economic production and no concentrated resources. If sociology were right, the ranking systems of monkeys would be expected to wither away.

The primatological answer is that social rank is not primarily a system for the allocation of scarce resources—even though it might subserve that function in special circumstances—but a way of integrating unrelated adults into a single social group. This explanation runs as counter to the premises of sociobiology as it does to sociology. Sociobiologists think that the highest ranking individuals should be the most successful at reproduction, but the allocation of sex in primate multimale troops is as refractory to simplistic explanations as is the allocation of material resources. If examined objectively, the primatological evidence is exactly the opposite of what a reproductive fitness model would predict. The species where reproductive success correlates with the boundaries of aggression are the species that have lived in territorial mated-pair societies or in harems with a single breeding adult male. Ranking systems, in contrast, are correlated with sexual democracy. The species that have the most elaborated status hierarchies—macaques, baboons, and chimpanzees—are also the species with the least exclusive system of mating. In none of these species can reproductive success be predicted from the ranking position alone. In primates with elaborate ranking systems, the lower ranks reproduce themselves; what an amazing sociological revelation!

Social rank does not determine reproductive success; it creates a two-tier system of sexuality with a matrimonial component and an adultery component. This can be seen quite clearly in Frans de Waal's monograph, *Chimpanzee Politics*, about sex and power among apes in Aarnhem Zoo. In this case, the high-ranking males attempted to monopolize the females, denying other males access to them, but the females and the lower-ranking males nonetheless indulged in sexual hanky-panky outside the bounds of the ranking system. Similar behaviors have been observed in hamadryas and gelada baboons, where the males have harems, and it suggests that rank is no more involved in the regular allocation of sex than it is in the allocation of resources. Experiments with captive monkeys that purport to show a relationship between male rank and reproductive success cannot be taken at face value until the life cycle is corrected for. Since male rank is correlated with age, up to a point, are they demonstrating the effect of rank or just measuring an age window? Do they represent the situation in nature where low-ranking individuals may move to other troops?

Social rank is not primarily a system of resource allocation, sexual or otherwise, but an adaptation for large-scale social aggregations containing unrelated adults of the same sex. "Unrelated," in this context, means animals who have not grown up together as members of the same family, rather than unrelated in a genetic or genealogical sense. As numerous ethological experiments show, raising animals together as siblings inhibits the expression of aggression, enforcing cooperative relationships, even among predators and their natural prey. In troops of wild primates, all of a female's children tend to form a distinct social group, the "matriline," whose members support one another. These matriline subgroups can become fault lines along which larger groups fracture; but in multimale troop species, the kinship organization is integrated into a larger social framework, the ranking system.

Not all primates have the biological dispositions to form ranking systems. Ranking systems are made possible by the transformation of aggression into display, and fear into submission. In primates without the hierarchical propensity, aggression leads to defeat, and defeat to flight from the scene of battle; but in rank-oriented species, defeat leads to gestures of subordination by the defeated party. Instead of fleeing, as in territorial species, the defeated animal continues to live in the social group as a subordinate member, giving gestures of dominance to those below him and gestures of submission to those above. Ranking systems, in other words, make possible social aggregations of adults by both sexes without any diminution of aggressive motivation on one hand or any reduction in the importance of kin-based subgroups on the other.

Consider the ranking system of Rhesus monkeys, which is composed of at least four subsystems that interact:

- A central hierarchy composed of adult males ranked in linear order.

- A peripheral hierarchy composed of young or old subordinate males who are no longer active.

- A serially ranked system of matrilines composed of adult females and their daughters and granddaughters.

- A linear intertroop hierarchy composed of entire troops that defer to each other when sharing resources and habitat.

Ranking systems, therefore, are not the outcome of unsocialized animal instincts, but a phylogenetically advanced form of social organization that presupposes kin-based social units and the evolution of signals for dominance and submission that are over and above the normal vertebrate repertory of ritualized aggression and fear. Moreover, the manipulation of rank, as careful studies of ape behavior are beginning to demonstrate, is an intentional process in higher primates, based on awareness of the consequences of the behavior and the intelligent assessment of political support. Although dominance and subordination are transacted in the coinage of fear and aggression, they nonetheless are implemented through political alliances that draw on the positive feelings that sustain families and friendships.

Ranking systems are not a recent development, contingent on concentrated resources—although concentration can reinforce existing inequalities as ethological experiments show—but a universal attribute of primate species that have cooperative groups of unrelated adults with high levels of aggressiveness. Human ranking systems, far from being a radical departure from our simian forebears, are in fact one area of continuity. There are clear differences between humans and other primates in language, technology, and art, and these differences are incorporated into human political behavior; but no one reading De Waal's *Chimpanzee Politics* with an open mind can come away convinced of major discontinuity in the underlying motivations.

As a scientific hypothesis, it is far more parsimonious to accept these close behavioral correspondences as evidence of similarity in the underlying brain mechanisms. Far from being a reductionist fallacy, this assumption makes possible a new model of behavior that is far richer than either the cultural or biological perspectives because it can incorporate findings from both traditions into a single intellectual framework. As is now well known, brain mechanisms for the processing of information about the social environment are affected by social input during development (step 1). This is generally consistent with the maternal deprivation experiments in monkeys and cross-fostering experiments in mammals. These same mechanisms are also affected by changes in the hormonal environment (step 2), which are in turn triggered by age, sex, physical stress, and the social context, as indicated by a host of endocrinological experiments (step 3). The brain mechanisms for processing social information, more commonly known as emotions, do not work in a vacuum but interact with the mechanisms for skill acquisition associated with the special senses and the skeletal musculature (step 4). Although there are some innate expressive behaviors specifically associated with the emotions (step 5), as revealed by cinematic and video studies of facial expression, as well as some innate instrumental actions such as biting and hitting (step 6), these behaviors are always combined with nonemotional motor skills that track the target in space and time, and monitor the effect of the behavior (step 7). As a result, the observed behavior is always a composite of learned and innate elements, as the detailed studies of emotional expression indicate. Finally, the brain mechanisms for acquiring learned behaviors are also affected by the social context in higher primates (step 8), leading to the social transmission of skills through observational learning, a phenomenon that is well-documented in home-reared apes.

Can a theory of this type, which takes seriously the interactive model of the brain with which we began this presentation, come to terms with some of the peculiar features of human aggression and rank discussed by anthropologists? It illuminates human behavior as well as that of nonhuman primates. In an intelligent species, selected for an increased ability to perceive the consequences of action, perception of the effects of innate behavior transforms these actions into learned skills. The innate connections between emotional perception and emotional response do not disappear, nor even attenuate, but they come to be represented in the nervous system as both innate programs and as intentional skills. Once a swaggering posture or broad shoulders are perceived as instrumental in the negotiation of rank, they will be simulated by intentional action and culturally elaborated, as with any other efficacious technique, into a body of traditionally transmitted skills.

The Samurai warrior or the nuclear bomb are cultural phenomena by anyone's definition, but their efficacy nonetheless depends upon the underlying mechanisms of social perception that humans share with apes. The unique capacities for language and technology confer to humans a far higher level of consciousness and creativity in the implementation of social behavior than is possible in an ape, but the inherent parsimony of science forbids us from postulating two distinct principles of behavior when one will do. There are not two kinds of social ranking systems, the human and the simian, mediated by two different levels of neural control—the instinctive and the symbolic—but a single functional system that merges affect and instrumentality into composite behavioral strategies. This is not a pessimistic conclusion about the inevitability of war and the inequalities of rank. Primatology, by looking squarely at human nature, gives us the enhanced capacity for action implicit in all good science. If the ranking systems of apes presuppose, as primatology has shown, the intentional control of emotionally salient behaviors and the perception of the consequences of action, do not human beings have at least an equal ability to alter their behavior through a rational assessment of behavioral effects and the communication of their implications to others?

Bibliography

The facts upon which this essay is based are extensively documented in my book on primatological theory:

Peter C. Reynolds, *On The Evolution of Human Behavior: The Argument from Animals to Man.* Berkeley and Los Angeles: University of California Press (1981).

5.
Dominance Systems Among Primate Adolescents

Ritch Savin-Williams

Τhere is probably no fact more antagonistic to developmental psychologists than the realization that humans are animals. It seems to be an embarrassment or, if realized, ignored. Certainly it is underplayed. The "animal nature" of young children not yet properly socialized, or of adolescents still enthralled with the trauma of puberty, is discussed in developmental psychology textbooks, but with humor or with the sense that with proper nurturing "it" will go away.

Others are not so quick to dismiss the interplay of biology with human features. For example, Bouchard's "Minnesota Twins" research project has brought together psychologists, psychiatrists, pediatricians, and physiologists to study identical twins reared apart to explore the interdependencies of medical, psychophysiological, psychomotor, emotional, cognitive, personality, and attitudinal aspects of development (Holden, 1980). Kreuz, Rose, and Jennings (1972) demonstrated how a psychological factor (stress) can affect one's (officer trainee) biology (circulating plasma testosterone).

Although genetists, physiologists, neuroendocrinologists, and others have made inroads in influencing the way developmental psychologists think about human nature on a molecular level, disciplines such as ethology, that emphasize a biological perspective on a molar level, have had little impact. Although ethology has a long history (Eibl-Eibesfeldt, 1975), only recently has the field come of age in terms of textbooks (e.g., Boice, 1983), books of readings (e.g., Omark, Strayer, & Freedman, 1980), and organization (what was to become the International Society of Human Ethology first met in 1974). Much of this ethological research has focused on infants and young children. There have been, however, several recent attempts to develop an ethological theory of adolescent development (Montemayor & Savin-Williams, in preparation; Savin-Williams & Montemayor, in preparation; Weisfeld, 1979; Weisfeld & Berger, 1983).

The first section of this chapter details the basic assumptions of ethology, highlighting its contribution to the "unity of the sciences". The second is a review of what is currently known about male and female dominance-antagonism-aggression among nonhuman primate adolescents. This literature forms the basis for a review of the theoretical assumptions and the empirical research that I have conducted during the last 10 years on dominance behaviors and hierarchies in groups of human adolescents in naturalistic settings. In the final, and fourth section, I draw from the preceding conclusions concerning the nature and study of dominance systems among primate adolescents.

Interactions Among Nonhuman Primate Adolescents

Overview

In 1932, the primatologist Zuckerman asserted that for an adequate primate, whether human or nonhuman, sociology is not possible without reference to the principle of dominance. During a lecture at the University of Chicago 45 years later, ornithologist, Marler, made the same point: "It would be disastrous to discard the concept of dominance to explain group interactions."

Can one conclude the same when describing the internal structure and interactions of adolescent groups? This issue is explored through a descriptive study of dominance and submission behaviors and hierarchies in groups of male and female adolescents. Four major questions are addressed:

1. Can a social system be described in terms of dyadic dominance and submission behaviors?

2. If so, how stable is this group structure over time and across behavior settings?

3. What are the physical, psychological, and social characteristics of those who occupy the various status positions?

4. Are the answers to the above three questions different for adolescent groups of various ages and for girls as opposed to boys? In addition, it is of interest to speculate as to the function(s) such a group structure has for individuals (individual selection) and for the group (group selection). In this quest both objective and impressionistic sources of data will be used.

Definitions

In this paper we use the following terms to mean:

1. Pubescence—the time when the biological processes of sexual and physical growth occur.

2. Adolescence—from the onset of the first external signs of pubescence to the termination of sexual development (procreation may or may not be possible, depending on sterility), but not before physical growth is completed.

3. Subadulthood and youth—from the end of sexual growth to the end of physical growth and the attainment of adult status.

It is difficult, given the impreciseness of most primatological studies, to infer that the same definitions are applied to nonhuman primates. It is nearly impossible to determine the exact beginning of pubescence from field studies of free-ranging primates because the initial external physical changes that signify the onset of pubescence are not easily observable from a distance. For example, the timing of pubertal events in both male and female prosimians is difficult to delineate, due to the scarcity of prosimian studies, as well as to practical difficulties of assessing pubertal status, e.g., fur around the anogenital region hinders viewing (Chandler, 1975). As a result, most field reports define the pubertal period in terms of 1. relative size or age, which are unreliable indicators of pubescence, or 2. gross species-specific pubertal features that occur late in pubertal development, e.g., the hair color of the gorilla, the fatted torso of the squirrel monkey, and the baboon mantle and snout.

Subadulthood begins after full sexual maturity, but not before mature physical growth is achieved, and without the corresponding adult responsibilities in procreation and dominance status. It appears that in most primate species, sexual and antagonistic behaviors are essential components and markers of adulthood. Subadulthood ends when a place is achieved, however lowly, in the adult dominance hierarchy and when heterosexual sexual activity is a possibility, although perhaps prevented by others in

133

the group. Few of the studies cited in this paper distinguish between adolescence and subadulthood; frequently subadulthood is used to cover both periods.

In the nonhuman primate literature, subadulthood is almost exclusively a male phenomenon unless one discusses the higher primates. In most primate species, it is assumed that the female passes immediately from pubescent onset to full adulthood, often attaining social maturity (motherhood) before physical growth maturity. This is not to deny that in most primate species, females experience an adolescence. An earlier recognition of the onset of puberty (pre-menarche) and a more accurate assessment of reproductive sterility during the first swelling periods might in fact demonstrate a chronological time period that should be classified as adolescence.

In female Rhesus monkeys, baboons, and chimpanzees there is a prolonged period of cyclic irregularity and sterility, allowing for a time lag between first swellings and conception (Graham, 1970). This development signifies an evolutionary change, perhaps indicative of the important adaptive function of learning. Such species can afford delaying female entry into reproduction, thereby gaining females who have learned complex skills and cultural traditions.

Finally, it should be emphasized that the behavioral information cited in this paper is derived only from studies of primates in *naturalistic settings*. This "limitation" was, I felt, a necessary one because of our concern with ecological validity: "The extent to which the environment experienced by the subjects in a scientific investigation has the properties it is supposed or assumed to have by the investigator" (Bronfenbrenner, 1979, p. 29). In non-natural situations, such as zoos or laboratories, a subject may react to the strangeness of the setting, thus resulting in atypical behavior. It is also difficult for researchers to create the diversity and uniqueness of an individual's natural environment, introducing extraneous situational factors that might not ordinarily affect behavior (Benson et al., 1980).

Nonhuman Primate Studies

Primatological research reveals to human ethologists the most potentially productive areas and methods for human research. The "message for ethologists," according to Tinbergen (1968), is that the methods, rather than the results, of primate and animal research should be applied to the study of human behavior. Yet, results from nonhuman primate research can generate new hypotheses at a fast rate, hypotheses that are probably nearer the mark in explaining real life occurrences than armchair theory (Blurton Jones, 1972).

Although ethologists recognize that behavior is, in many respects, species-specific, they also recognize that commonalities exist; these should be studied comparatively so as to elucidate the evolutionary process (Tinbergen, 1963). Due to the prevalence of dominance hierarchical structures in mammalian groups, especially in nonhuman primates, Scott (1953, 1969) sees little reason to doubt that human groups are also characterized by dominance hierarchies.

Here, I examine the pubescent years among nonhuman primates in order to identify those characteristics that are typical of most primate genera. This is not to contend that there is *one* primate pattern, but a common thread that runs throughout the primates. It is difficult to define with precision what it means to behave as a primate because behavior is dependent on environmental factors, such as ecological niche, population composition and density, and recent group experiences and history, as well as on taxonomic position (Dolhinow, 1972). Thus, in the following review of the dominance behavior of primates ranging from lemur (*Lemur*) to chimpanzee (*Pan*), the search is not so much for *the* pattern, as for a common theme from which variations are derived.

The value of examining developmental issues in species other than our own has been demonstrated through recent review of nonhuman primate research on the mother-infant relationship (Swartz & Rosenblum, 1981), paternal behavior (Mitchell & Brandt, 1972; Redican & Taub, 1981), peer interaction (Rosenblum, Coe, & Bromley, 1975; Savin-Williams, 1980b), and relations with parents and peers during adolescence (Montemayor & Savin-Williams, in preparation). In these reviews, the adaptive value of various types of associations for children has been identified, along with environmental pressures that might account for the diversity of these relations. Similarly, by examining the pubescent years in nonhuman primates, we gain an understanding of its evolutionary significance and thereby approach the study of human adolescence with a deepened appreciation of its importance for human growth and development. Although this is not the first attempt to present an ethological perspective

135

of adolescence (Weisfeld, 1979; Weisfeld & Berger, 1983), it is the first to systematically review the behavior of pubescent, preadult nonhuman primates as the basis for an ethological perspective of adolescence.

I was assisted in the present review of the literature by R. Montemayer. Although there are many ways in which to organize the evidence—for example, by ecological niche or mating system —we chose the taxonomic method. It reflects our view that dominance interactions become more complex as one moves forward in evolutionary species complexity. Thus, we expect human dominance behaviors to be more similar to chimpanzee than to prosimian interactions.

Prosimians

Prosimian pubescent males may or may not be involved in group dominance interactions. In one group, lemur adolescent males were involved in considerably fewer agonistic interactions (spats, chases, and jump-fights) than one might expect statistically (5 observed vs. 51 expected) (Jolly, 1966). In another troop, they were actively engaged in dominance interactions, especially in lengthy stink fights with subordinate adult males (Budnitz & Dainis, 1975). Of the five group males, the adolescent male ranked fourth and was occasionally involved in dominance interactions. Lemur pubescent males may be prevented from anogenitally marking females by adult males; whenever they approached an estrous female in one group they were chased and cuffed by adult males (Chandler, 1975).

Richard and Heimbuch (1975) found in three groups of *Propithecus* that pubescent males were frequently the recipients of aggression, considerably more often than they aggressed against other group members. For example, in one group the adolescent male aggressed 6 times but was aggressed against 83 times. For the three groups, for every aggressive act initiated, an adolescent received 5.5 aggressive acts (71% of which were from adult females). Only agonistic encounters with juveniles were mutually reciprocated by the adolescent male.

New World Monkeys

New World adolescent male monkeys frequently establish a dominance hierarchy within the adolescent group; when they enter the adult hierarchy they rank low. With increasing physical development they receive increased adult antagonism. While still in the natal group, young squirrel pubescent males are rowdy, but

> . . . when males reach a given age (probably around five years old) they begin to become physiologically and behaviorally adult; but if the maturing males are not able to successfully establish themselves in the troup's adult hierarchy because they are too frequently or seriously chased and fought, they will be forced to avoid the fully adult males and to assume some peripheral or totally separated positions in the troup (Baldwin, 1968; p. 307).

Among themselves, adolescent males establish an internal, ingroup dominance hierarchy based on relative strength, but it is barely detectable and is insignificant when compared to the adult male hierarchy. Adult males generally pay little attention to pubescent males in the troop, at least until pubescent status; then, the number of interactions, primarily antagonistic, increases dramatically (Baldwin, 1968 & 1969).

The same pattern has been detected in a group of golden-lion marmosets (Snyder, 1974). Adults tolerate same-sex juveniles until they become pubescent, then the adults drive the young out of the group. As the young female matures she becomes subordinate to all; she is seldom seen eating with the group and food may be stolen from her.

Jones (1980) reported that among howler monkeys, high-ranking individuals are young adults (perhaps late adolescents); intermediate-ranking individuals, middle-aged adults; and low-ranking individuals, older adults. This exceptional hierarchy is apparently the result of the ecological niche in which these animals live, one that favors individuals with high energy over those with physical growth.

Old World Monkeys

More is known about antagonism among Old World monkeys than in any other group. Shortly after pubertal onset, macaque males assert themselves, first over infants, juveniles, and adult females, and then among themselves (Simonds, 1965). The peer group hierarchy that emerges among adolescents is influentially inferior to the adult male dominance structure, but it is indicative of future relative ranking in the adult male hierarchy (Southwick, Beg, & Siddiqui, 1965). In the group hierarchy adult males dominate all other animals while pubescent males and adult females dominate juveniles, who in turn dominate infants (Dittus, 1979). Further, adult males frequently displace adolescent males to the troop's periphery, away from favored feeding areas.

In most cases, pubescent males rank low in the adult male dominance hierarchy (Yamada, 1971). Based on giving way, fights, and various physical gestures and threats, four adolescent males in a South Indian macaque group were ranked in the four lowest places in the adult hierarchy (Simonds, 1965). In the Cayo Santiago population, Loy (1971) found that the bottom six places in the group hierarchy were occupied by three- or four-year olds, while the top six monkeys were 5 years or older. Thus, in most groups the leaders and sub-leaders are adult males, while the peripheral or follower members are young adult or adolescent males.

During the juvenile and early adolescent periods, a male's status is largely determined by the rank of his mother (Drickamer & Vessey, 1973; Koyama, 1967; Sade, 1967). But after puberty, physical strength and abilities, physique, and assertiveness become more influential. In one group, a male, ranked eleventh at the onset of the study, underwent a dramatic musculature and size growth spurt; 9 months later he was displacing the beta individual (Simonds, 1965).

For the macaca pubescent female, dominance interactions are not crucial for later status or breeding efficiency. As a juvenile, she ranks immediately below her mother; as an adolescent and as an adult, she also ranks immediately below her mother (Koyama, 1967; Sade, 1967).

Among baboons, with the onset of sexual maturation, males become the recipients of increased hostility from adult males. They frequently turn on juveniles and defeat them in aggressive encounters. As a juvenile, age is the prime determinant for winning aggressive encounters, but after the age of 5 years there is little correlation between age and aggressive interactions. Pubescence thus appears to be a time to reassess peers in terms of strength and fighting ability (Owens, 1975). By the fifth year, large adolescents dominate some adult females, and by the seventh or eighth year they begin the climb in the adult male hierarchy. During this period, pubescent males become increasing pugnacious and daring (Hall & DeVore, 1965).

In hamadryas and gelada baboons, an aggressive relationship

develops between the leader male and his male offspring as the latter sexually matures (Dunbar & Dunbar, 1975). Avoidance of the harem leader is the adolescent's usual defense. Toward the end of this period he may become a "young adult leader," working and associating closely with the harem leader to coordinate travel and herd stray females. If the harem leader is exceptionally old, he may then assume leadership and sexual privileges over the harem.

Adolescent vervet (McGuire, 1974; Strusaker, 1967b) and guenon (Bourliere, Hunkeler, & Bertrand, 1970) males rank lowest on the adult male hierarchy. More than 50% of all group agonistic and supplantation encounters involve early adolescent males, usually directed at younger juveniles or adolescent females. They may displace an adult female, something never observed prior to this age. The more sexually advanced the guenon male, the more likely he is to receive adult male aggression, especially during the breeding season. During the nonsexual season, however, both juvenile and adolescent males approach, groom, and mount females without fear of adult male intervention (Bourliere et al., 1970). Many early pubescent talapoin males have minor wounds, missing tufts of hair, and other signs of being aggressed against during the breeding season (Rowell, 1973). Pubescent females, by contrast, are quite passive and nonagonistic (McGuire, 1974).

Toward adult males, mangabey adolescent males more often interact agonistically (attacks, chases, threats) than peacefully. Exactly the reverse pattern is the case for their associations with other group members. In one study they were submissive to adult males (69 of 78 encounters), and dominant over adult females (33 of 50 encounters) and juveniles (29 of 29 encounters) (Chalmers, 1968).

Pubescent male langurs are involved in a considerable number of dominance interactions with adult males and females, but they only dominate other adolescents or those younger (Jay, 1965; Poirier, 1970). During puberty, as a male matures in size and strength, he asserts himself, first over low-ranking females and then, as a young adult, over low-ranking males. These situations, plus the fact that they are also competing through physical contact, aggressive threats, and chases among themselves for food, right of way along paths, tree positions, and estrous females, produce tension among adolescent male langurs. Some, however, avoid these antagonisms by maintaining close proximity to the dominant male, living peacefully in that position. Yoshiba (1968) claims that these males are being groomed for the top leadership positions by the adult male.

Aggression between adult and pubescent male langurs is affected by the relations that adult males have with each other. In troops with one clearly dominant male and few aggressive interactions among adult males, social relations between adults and adolescents are relaxed. In troops with no dominate male and many agonistic interactions among the adult males, relations with adolescents are tense and aggressive (Boggess, 1982). Adolescent langur females are subordinate to all adult females, but they seldom engage in dominance interactions except when in estrus (Jay, 1965; McGuire, 1974).

Old World adolescent male monkeys are rarely observed to directly challenge an adult male, especially a high status one. The attacks, when they occur, tend to be "hit and run" harassments. For example, adolescent male patas monkeys have been observed taunting and harassing adult males during copulations (Loy & Loy, 1977) and feeding (Zucker & Kaplan, 1981). Such behavior indicates a growing boldness coupled with some caution.

Apes

Dominance interactions among gibbons, orangutans, gorillas, and chimpanzees follow many of the same patterns described above. Carpenter (1964) observed that as young gibbons mature, a special and poignant antagonism develops between them and their same-sex parent—in a spirit of intense competition for status and sexual access. Tenaza (1975) substantiated this relationship between males, but not between mothers and daughters.

Similarly, Aldrich-Blake and Chivers (1973) have observed increased hostility among Siamang group males as the offspring reach puberty. Most of the 213 scraps that Chivers (1972) recorded involved adolescent and adult males, usually when the former intruded within the personal space of the latter. Siamang adolescent males, however, are more tolerated by their fathers than are gibbon adolescents.

Little information is available concerning antagonistic behavior in orangutans, perhaps because of their asocial nature. Rodman (1973) observed that as the male orangutan matures, the increased competition between he and adult male visitors effectively forces him away from the mother-centered family group. Galdikas-Brindamour (1975) reports adult males are usually intolerant of pubescent males; when the former approach, the latter flee in terror.

Adolescent blackback gorillas are subordinate to adult silverbacks and dominant over all other males in an age-graded and strength-based hierarchy. In actuality, there are few direct physical contacts or dominance interactions between the two classes of males; the hierarchy is clearly set and recognized (Schaller, 1963).

Both adolescent male and female chimpanzees rank near the bottom of the group dominance hierarchy (Goodall, 1968). If an adolescent's mother is a high-ranking individual, then he or she may be dominant over some low-ranking matures. The female adolescent rarely engages in dominance interactions, despite the fact that she is in a precarious position in the group and likely to be threatened by adult males and females, as well as by adolescent and juvenile males.

During late adolescence, males enter into dominance interactions on a consistent and sustained level. At first they threaten low-ranking chimpanzees. This signifies that the adolescent apprenticeship is over, as is also maternal protection and male tolerance of insubordination. Severe retributions are likely to occur once a male is sexually mature. Apparently, the more sexually mature a young male is, the more likely he is to receive aggressive attacks from adult males (Albrecht & Dunnett, 1971). Yet, he continues to associate with adult males, often sitting and watching from a slight distance (Pusey, 1978). Goodall (1968) believes that the adolescent male needs to be on good terms with the adult males, desiring reassuring contact after feuds that promote his status and group bonding as well.

Conclusion

The frequency of dominance behaviors, roughly catalogued as threats, aggressive contacts, and supplantations, increases during the pubescent period in male nonhuman primates. An individual not only has the motivation (sex drive, power motif, biochemical disequilibrium), but also the means (strength, canines, vocalizations) by which to gain status. Until this time adult males by-and-large ignore young males. But, with pubescence,

141

young males begin to assert themselves, and adult males respond in kind to their potential rivals. Although the increased frequency of antagonistic interactions at pubescence correlates with increased levels of androgens produced by the enlarging testes (Dixson, 1980), there is no simple, direct casual relationship between the specific level of sexual maturity in males and the amount of aggression received from other group members. The adult male's intolerance of maturing males often results in scars, tears, and bruises for the latter. But because of previous social experiences, including play activities, "there are more dominance fights avoided by one animal slipping quietly away than there are actual fights or chases" (Dolhinow, 1972; p. 363).

It is not clear why an adult male is provoked to aggress against the young group males—unless, perhaps, in response to their increased sexual interest in "his" females, or to the threat of losing dominance status to these insurgents. On the other hand, he may merely be responding in kind to the aggressive behavior initiated by the adolescents. The primate literature provides few resolutions to these critical behavioral and motivational issues.

The adolescent's first place in the adult dominance hierarchy is usually last. But by late adolescence or young adulthood he enters into dominance interactions, first defeating adult females and lowly ranked males. When he establishes a semipermanent position, he is an adult. That position is seldom bequeathed to him by the status of his mother, as is often the case for adolescent females. While rank seldom gives breeding power, it does orient group leadership, cohesiveness, travel arrangements, peaceful existence, and food gathering.

The pubescent female rarely engages in dominance interactions, in continuity with both her juvenile and adult patterns. She seldom asserts herself; neither is she the recipient of antagonism from others. As a potential mate and as a mother, both are beneficial.

Dominance Interactions Among Human Adolescents

Overview

It first occurred to me in a University of Chicago class taught by noted human ethologist Daniel G. Freedman that the kinds of behavioral interactions and social structures described above might also be characteristic of human adolescents interacting with each other in naturalistic settings. The current report is a synthesis of the work that followed, and summarizes the importance of these studies for understanding intrasex aggression and control among human adolescents.

Theoretical Review

As noted in the review of nonhuman primate adolescents, it is not uncommon for adolescent individuals to engage in social interactions that can be construed as dominance behavior. The net effect of these behaviors on a group level is a system of status differentiation that is necessary for group formation and maintenance (Rowell, 1966). The alternative to "fitting in" is to become peripheralized to the group as a solitaire or as a member of a bachelor group, or to leave one's natal group for another.

Ethologists such as Lorenz (1966) and Tinbergen (1968) argue that humans genetically harbor a number of behavioral propensities that predispose us to form hierarchical dominance relations when we engage in interpersonal behavior within the context of a social group. Tiger (1970) also maintains that it is "human nature" to create hierarchical orders based on dominance and submission behaviors:

> The nub of the historical argument is that during the formative periods of human anatomy and bodily structure—which are broadly replicated in today's model of the human—patterns of social differentiation in the dominance form were also developing, and it is this prior phenomenon which governs the occurrence of dominance hierarchies in contemporary societies, rather than only a variety of formed or historical circumstance (p. 295).

Mechanisms

An arrangement into a dominance hierarchy is one of two structural mechanisms—the other being territoriality—prevalent in vertebrates for controlling intraspecies aggression. These mechanisms have evolved to reduce the harmful effects of aggression without negating its useful aspects such as protection from predators, population regulation, and habitat utilization. This reduction of overt aggression renders the most potentially

143

harmful aspects of aggression—injury, death, energy waste —ineffectual by engendering intragroup, multisensory familiarity and by enhancing reliable expectations through fostering predictable intragroup behaviors.

Wilson (1975) notes that animals who depend for survival on relatively stable group units use dominance rather than territorial behavior to control aggression, adjust mutual relations and determine priority access to resources: "Dominance behavior is the analog of territorial behavior, differing in that the members of an aggressively organized group of animals coexist within one territory (p. 279)." This does not imply that group-living animals do not have territories; rather, their geographic area is compressed into personal space (Hall, 1966), with the center being one's own body rather than a relatively set location.

Evolutionary Significance

An essential question for ethological investigators is the survival value of the phenomenon studied. The evolutionary significance can be viewed from either an individual or a group selection level of analysis, in either case, focusing on the functional aspect. Rowell (1966) concluded that the evolution of dominance hierarchies had a three-dimensional basis: 1. the immediate advantage to the dominant animal, such as access to resources such as food, sexual mates, sleeping sites, attention and locomoter position; 2. the genetic or sexual selection advantage; and 3. the social advantage of group order, peacefulness and security. Group cohesion is not only maintained because a dominance hierarchy serves to dissipate aggression and overt fighting. Dominance hierarchies also facilitate average expectable behavior of individual group members, determine commodity acquisition if the supply is limited, and structure the limited resource of attention. They thus eliminate waste, provide for division of labor and, in turn, aid efficiency, organize activities for an enhancement of group competence and performance. Finally, they establish social distance while still maintaining sufficient proximity for "groupness." Poirier (1974) summarizes: "Since each animal knows its position vis-a-vis others and acts accordingly, and as long as each stays in its place, there is minimal disruption."

There has been less systematic thought given to the benefits or compensations of being subordinate. McGuire (1974) suggests that it is adaptive for some individuals to be submissive in order to avoid stress and the fear of real or imagined physical, social, or psychological harm. The potential for stress may be quite high in animals who lack the physical or temperamental equipment —biologically or environmentally induced—to defeat others. Physically losing may have costly consequences and so, too, may stress. Under stress, individuals waste energy, face the prospect of acting "irrationally" or non-adaptively, suffer disease and physical system breakdown (digestive problems, endocrinological imbalances), and are less capable of breeding.

In other ways, being subordinate is advantageous to an individual. By displaying submissive behavior, one's fitness is considerably higher than if one were to make an all-out effort to dislodge the most dominant group member. Alexander (1974) notes that, like other group members, a subordinate individual is informed by the various group dyadic interactions "when and how to display aggression, and when and how to withhold and appease and withdraw" (p. 330). With such knowledge, one increases his or her survival and reproductive chances by remaining in the group. In many social species, individuals face little hope of survival if alone, and, in addition, are almost universally excluded from breeding (Wilson, 1975). But a submissive group male will probably survive, eating with the group and benefitting from predator protection, with the outside chance of occasional breeding opportunities. Also, by staying with the group, a subordinate individual may enhance his or her inclusive fitness by aiding the survival opportunities of closely related kin. Furthermore, because top ranking individuals migrate or die; in most instances, the dominance ordering is not rigid. Thus, by staying with the group as a subordinate or peripheral member, one has a chance to advance in dominance status.

On a group selection level of analysis, West-Eberhard (1975) points out that subordinate group members, because they are dispersed from the core of the primary habitat, are the ones most likely to pioneer new ecological niches, and thus, learn new species forms of adaptation. They are the "cutting edge of evolution" (Wilson, 1975).

Hierarchy

The notion of hierarchy is "the principle by which the elements

145

of a whole are ranked in relation to the whole" (Dumont, 1970; p. 66), or, more concisely, "a set of ordered levels" (Whyte, Wilson & Wilson, 1969; p. vii). Thus, hierarchy marks the conceptual integration of the larger and the smaller, of that which encompasses with that which is encompassed (Dumont, 1970). Hierarchical rank is a societal category—much like age, sex, in-out, normal-abnormal, etc.—global in application because it reflects the dilemmas, experiences, and associations that are intrinsic in constructing and maintaining a conceptual framework of the social world.

Pattee (1973) maintains that:

> It is a central lesson of biological evolution that increasing complexity of organization is always accompanied by new levels of hierarchical controls. The loss of these controls at any level is usually malignant for the organization under that level. Furthermore, our experience with many different types of complex systems, both natural and artificial, warns us that loss of hierarchical controls often results in sudden catastrophic failure (p. xi).

The central assumption is that "nature loves hierarchies":

> Hierarchical organization is so universal in the biological world that we usually pass if off as the natural way to achieve simplicity or efficiency in a large collection of interacting elements. If asked what the fundamental reason is for hierarchical organization, I suspect most people would simply say, "How else would you do it?" (Pattee, 1973; p. 73).

The empirical observation of hierarchy is well documented, but the explanation of hierarchical structure is more speculative. Most researchers believe that hierarchical structure facilitates the survival of complexity, due to its enhancement of integration. By ordering parts in terms of the whole, the complexity of the whole is established. Thus, not to see hierarchy, regardless of the level of empirical concern, would be surprising because it would imply chaos.

Dominance

In comparative and social psychology, social dominance has

traditionally had its reference in such concepts as competition and aggression: one controlling the behavior of another by force or fighting (Schneirla, 1951; Scott, 1953). Wilson (1975) equated dominance and aggression hierarchies: "the set of sustained aggressive-submissive relations among these animals" (p. 279). In the more phylogeneticaly "advanced" species, few researchers are so inclined to equate dominance and aggression, noting that a multiplicity of factors other than aggression mediate dominance behavior, including the behavior of the subordinates (supplantation, avoidance, attention). McGuinness (1983) distinguished the two by noting that aggression is the "intention" to harm, while dominance is the "intention" to gain control.

Social psychologists have referred to a dominant individual as a leader (Glidewell, Kantor, Smith, & Stringer, 1966), an egotist (Whiting & Edwards, 1974), a headship (Gibb, 1969), and an authoritarian (Adorno, Frenkel-Brunswik, Levinson, & Stanford, 1950) among others, in large part depending on how dominance is asserted or expressed. One may attempt to exert dominance from various motivational desires: to serve one's own interests, to gain desirable prerequisites, to counter domination, to humiliate or to aggress against another, or to assume leadership over a group (Maccoby & Jacklin, 1974). A dominant person desires power, prestige and material gain, and manifests ascendance, assertiveness, and social boldness (Gibb, 1969).

In this chapter, *dominance* is eclectic, referring to specific varieties of behavior occurring in a dyad, in which one pair member asserts or expresses power and/or authority over the other. In the process, influence may have preceded, and leadership in a larger group may result. Aggression may or may not be behaviorally involved. In fact, as the frequency of aggressive behavior decreases after early childhood, it is necessary to define dominance in a non-physical fashion during adolescence (Weisfeld & Weisfeld, 1984). Thus, dominance is primarily a relational term that can be utilized to describe a person ("a dominant individual") or to indicate a social role or position ("the most dominant in the group"), without reference to responsibilities or obligations.

Dominance Hierarchy

The joining of the two concepts, dominance and hierarchy, has

147

primarily been undertaken by primatologists and ethologists who consider that, among social animals with the capability of individual recognition, a dominance hierarchy will be the result of the residual or inevitable inequalities of aptitudes of group members, thus enhancing a "chain of command" (Dumont, 1970). Alcock (1975) asserts that social animals that did not evolve a system of interindividual dominance relations became extinct because "their excess members lived longer during hard times, devoured the countryside, and caused the downfall of the entire group" (p. 229).

Method for Research

Settings and Participants: My research on human adolescents began after my first year as a human development graduate student at the University of Chicago. During the summers of 1973–1979, 13 groups (Table 1) were observed at the same 5-week leadership camp setting in Michigan. In 1980–1981, groups 14 and 15 were observed on a New England bicycle travel trip sponsored by a private youth organization; the females in group 16 were at a Jewish camp in New York State.

The 60 male and 36 female participants were between the ages of 11 and 17 years, and were in groups ranging in size from 4 to 10 (see Table 1). The sample is predominantly Caucasian (94%), Protestant or Catholic (except group 16), and middle- to upper-middle class.

Measures and Procedures: The instruments and means for collecting data varied from one study to the next, but all included observational *and* sociometric measures and procedures. An underlying theme of the research was the comparison of ethological and traditional psychological methods of collecting data (see Savin-Williams, Small, & Zeldin, 1981).

Observation Measures: Eight types of dominance behaviors measured the assertion of one individual (X) over another (Y). These behaviors, not necessarily synonymous with aggression, wins, or conflict, were derived from field studies of primatologists, social psychologists, and human ethologists, and were pretested in a pilot study (Savin-Williams, 1977). Only dyadic interactions between cabin members were recorded.

Index behaviors were divided into overt (notated with an *) or

Table 1

Summary of the Groups Studied

Group No.	Year	Number	Sex	Age	Publication
1	1973	6	male	13	Savin-Williams, 1977 & 1980a
2	1974	6	male	12–13	Savin-Williams, 1976, 1979 & 1980a
3	1975	6	male	12–14	Savin-Williams, 1979 & 1980a
4	1976	4	male	11–12	Savin-Williams, 1979
5	1976	4	male	12–13	Savin-Williams, 1979
6	1976	5	female	12–13	Savin-Williams, 1979 & 1980b
7	1976	5	female	13–14	Savin-Williams, 1979 & 1980b
8	1976	5	female	12–13	Savin-Williams, 1979 & 1980b
9	1976	5	female	12–13	Savin-Williams, 1979 & 1980b
10	1977	6	male	15–17	Savin-Williams, 1980c
11	1978	5	male	14–16	Savin-Williams, 1980c
12	1979	6	male	14–16	Zeldin, Savin-Williams, & Small, 1984 Savin-Williams, Small, & Zeldin, 1981 Small, Zeldin, & Savin-Williams, 1983
13	1979	6	male	14–16	Zeldin, Savin-Williams, & Small, 1984 Savin-Williams, Small, & Zeldin, 1981 Small, Zeldin, & Savin-Williams, 1983
14	1980	10	coed	15–17	Small, Zeldin, & Savin-Williams, 1983 Zeldin, Small, & Savin-Williams, 1982
15	1980	9	coed	15–16	Small, Zeldin, & Savin-Willaims, 1983 Zeldin, Small, & Savin-Williams, 1982
16	1981	8	female	16–17	Paikoff & Savin-Williams, 1983

indirect subcategories, depending on the degree to which dominance was initiated by X (overt) or Y (indirect), or was expressed through direct (overt) or subtle (indirect) means.

1. Verbal Directive: X verbally communicates to Y what to do and Y complies.

*a. direct order or request

b. indirect directive or suggestion of behavior

c. giving unsolicited advice or information

2. Verbal Ridicule: X raises his/her status or lowers Y's status by verbally abusing Y or by putting himself or herself in a good light at the expense of Y. Y does not contradict, usually withdrawing from further interaction.

*a. name calling, teasing—usually through direct confrontation

b. talk about, verbal put-down, gossip, cattiness-usually through a third person

*c. bragging or boastful behavior

3. Physical Assertiveness with Contact: X pushes, shoves, kicks, or hits Y. Y takes a submissive posture, flees, or, if asserts self in turn, loses.

*a. overt aggressiveness, in earnest

*b. play fighting, in fun, with a smile

4. Recognition: Y acts in such a way as to place X in a more powerful position. X becomes a social monitor for Y.

a. imitating or modeling behavior, appearance, speech; agree with

b. ask for approval of behavior or appearance; to apologize

c. give compliments or favors; ask where is; defend

d. ask or solicit information or advice; divulge information; wait for

5. Physical or Object Displacement: X takes an object away from Y, or X approaches Y and Y moves away.

*a. direct removal or supplantation

*b. indirect control; not asking to borrow; moving into space; maintain privileged position.

6. Verbal or Physical Threat: X asserts verbal or physical authority over Y with Y not countering.

*a. verbal challenge, usually with threat of bodily harm

*b. physical challenge without making actual physical contact; glaring.

7. Counter Dominance: X, commanded by Y, assertively or passively disobeys and Y does not pursue the demand.

*a. ignoring a direct order or request

b. ignoring the other; shunning; spatial exclusion

8. Verbal Control: X verbally argues or battles with Y and gets the last word or monopolizes the content and structure of the verbal interaction

*a. arguments or battles; direct refutation
b. monopolizes a conversation; interrupts the other's speech
c. contradictions without anger; corrections

In all studies, the indices of dominance were significantly intercorrelated, indicating that they rank ordered group members in a similar fashion. Thus, the behaviorally based hierarchy in each group is a summation of these eight indices. Observation data were also collected on prosocial behavior, athletic ability, leadership, hiking position, and bed position in the various groups.

Observation Procedures: Nine undergraduate or graduate students conducted observations (I collected data on 6 of the 16 groups). Again, the exact procedures varied depending on the study, but most characteristic were the procedures described below and in Savin-Williams (1979).

Those who collected the observational data on dominance interactions also assumed counselor functions. This dual role as participant-observer enabled a direct but unobtrusive recording of behavior without hindrance or suspicion. For example, observers recorded dominance interactions among group members during athletic games as they kept score, during cabin meetings as they took minutes, and during rest hour as they wrote letters. A premium was placed on unobtrusively observing naturally occurring behavior in the ongoing life of the group.

For 3 hours per day during the 5-week camping sessions, the observers recorded all episodes of dyadic dominance that occurred between members within each cabin group. Observations entailed the use of an event-sampling technique, "all occurrences of some behavior" (Altmann, 1974), and were made during five behavior settings: 1. rising from and going to bed (rest periods), 2. meals, 3. cabin cleanup, 4. cabin discussions and meetings, and 5. athletic activities.

Prior to camp, the observers were trained by me on data-collection techniques and behaviors to be recorded. Due to the nature of data collection, the camp setting, and camp policy, reliability checks during the camping session were not possible. Post-camp observer reliability scores were obtained from an audio tape and accompanying written transcript of a cabin discussion session.

The approval of the executive director of the camps was procured prior to the collection of data. This approval was received only after the following human subject conditions were guaranteed: 1. the study would in no manner interfere with normal camp procedures or camper behavior; 2. confidentiality of the participants would be strictly maintained by coding all behavioral records to mask the identity of the adolescents and by eliminating all personal references from subsequent oral and written presentations of the data; and 3. participants would be debriefed in language appropriate for their level of understanding as to the nature and purposes of the project and their role in the project, and would also be given the option of having their data deleted from the study (all willingly participated).

In some groups, a time sampling technique was employed in which all occurrences of dominance acts were recorded within a limited time span (Wright, 1960). This was necessary because of the nature of the activities: a wilderness travel camp.

Sociometric and Other Measures: In all groups, the adolescents were asked to rank group members in order of dominance. The term was defined as when someone exerts power, authority, or influence over others. This was usually completed during the first and last weeks of the camping session.

Many other attributes were assessed through either peer rankings, counselor rankings, tests, or measurements. These included friendship, popularity, athletic ability, pubertal maturation, chronological age, physical size, socioeconomic status, overtness of behavior, frequency of interactions, leadership, camping ability, intelligence, creativity, cooperativeness, camp spirit, self-esteem, physical attractiveness, and empathy.

Results

From the 16 groups, there are many detailed results that are specific to a particular group(s). This brief presentation of the data will focus on general research findings as they relate to developmental change and stability in the two sexes.

Males: Male adolescents between 11 to 17 years of age interacting in same-sex and same-age groups, share with other primates a system of structuring interpersonal relations that can be characterized as a dominance hierarchy. This hierarchical group structure was recognized by group members (including one's self rank) both verbally and behaviorally within days if not hours of coming together. Relative status remained temporally stable during the 3 to 5 weeks of camp and was cross-situationally consistent in the various camp settings (e.g., discussions, athletic games, mealtimes). Friends were usually closely-ranked individuals.

The most frequent expression of dominance was verbal ridicule. Over time, the frequency of dominance acts within a group decreased as the hierarchy became more clearly linear; the expression of one's status also became more overt. One male group countered this trend by becoming less overt over time, but the frequency of dominance interactions increased.

There were several notable age differences in dominance interactions. Early adolescents were more likely than late adolescents to physically assert themselves over cabinmates, and to argue. Physical variables such as pubertal maturation, athletic ability, and physical fitness predicted relative rank among early adolescents; among late adolescent males mental abilities, camp experience, and social skills were more important correlates of dominance status. With age, dominance interactions were less overt, less physical, and more often based on recognition of another's status through submissive behaviors.

Females: While 9 of the 16 groups studied were all-male, only 5 were all-female (2 were coed). Thus, our findings are more tentative in regard to dominance systems among females. A system of status differentiation was prevalent among the adolescent females, although this group structure differed from that of adolescent males and across the adolescent years.

In contrast to the male dominance hierarchy, the group structure among early adolescent females was less stable. Relative dominance among dyads was likely to fluctuate during the course of camp. This occurred not among low status individuals as in male groups, but among middle and even high ranked individuals. There was also considerable disagreement among the females on relative rank within the group and the rank order derived from these sociometrics did not always correspond with the behavioral observations of intragroup interactions. There was also no temporal decrease in the frequency rate, and occasionally there was an increase of dominance acts within a female group.

The females in our groups seldom asserted their influence through physical means or by verbal argument. Rather, verbal ridicule, ignoring, shunning, and giving unsolicited advice were the most prevalent means of dominance expression. This sex difference increased dramatically among the older adolescent females. Dominance behavior was more likely to be subtle than it was to be overt; overtness of expression decreased over time in the early adolescent females. Compared with adolescent males, the females were more likely to underrank themselves on dominance status. Athletic ability, pubertal status, leadership skills, and peer popularity predicted the rank order in early adolescent female camp groups.

The level of instability found among early adolescent females was not characteristic of our one group of late adolescent females. Relative dominance status among the dyads increased in directionality over time as dominance behavior became more overt during the camp setting. The females recognized relative dominance status among themselves on the sociometric exercise.

Rather than a linear, hierarchial status rank-ordering, the late adolescent females formed a "cohesive dyarchy". A group structure based on coalitions with a dual system of leadership was formed—some females assumed the role of instrumental leader, while others became expressive leaders. The cabin functioned as a cohesive group manifested through a complex and stable form of social interactions. Least predictive of relative status were physical attributes or self-report abilities; characteristics perceived by peers—such as well known, friendship, camp spirit, and empathy—significantly predicted relative group rank among late adolescent females.

Conclusions

Dominance Behaviors

A diversity of behaviors are used by primate adolescents to

assert or recognize relative differences in status. The eight indices of dominance and submission that were incorporated in the research on human adolescents reported above are not equivalent in content or form, but in effect: one individual being dominant over another. In content many of the behaviors may also be indicative of other constructs, such as friendliness; in form, dominance may range from overt to subtle and from vocalizations to physical acts. This variety of forms encourages cross-species and cross-cultural comparisons. For example, supplanting others, gaining access to priorities, displaying threat gestures, and receiving attention from others are behaviors that connote dominance in both human and nonhuman primate adolescents. In all human groups studied, however, the primary mode of expressing status was verbal, thus highlighting the symbolic, linguistic skills of humans. Any definition of dominance that is applicable to only one species is doomed to obsolescence as a narrow and ungeneralizable tool. At least this is an ethological view.

Individual adolescents varied considerably in the way they expressed their status. For example, some primate adolescents appear to be "bullies," physically asserting themselves in a rather overt and aggressive manner. Others display more finesse, using subtle, nonthreatening behaviors such as shunning or ignoring to indicate their status.

Although these behaviors may reflect a style or "personality trait," it is also true that different situations elicited different response styles. For example, during athletic games and rough-and-tumble play activities, physical threats and acts were frequent means of expressing dominance. In the human groups, verbal argument and interruptions were common dominance behaviors during group discussions.

Thus, the specific behaviors used to express one's dominance status may vary with an individual's style, the situation in which the act occurs, one's age (discussed below), and one's sex (discussed below), among many possibilities. These variations should not, however, disguise the fact that a conceptualization of dominance as a higher order phenomenon than specific behaviors is warranted. In all human studies reported above, the specific indices of dominance were significantly intercorrelated.

Group Structure

The empirical research justifies the conclusion that primate adolescents behave in dyadic situations with other same-sex, same-age adolescents in a fashion that can be summarized on a group level as a dominance hierarchy. This stable and ordered, but not invariant, group structure can be assessed not only through observations of interpersonal behavior, but also from verbal reports within human groups.

The dominance hierarchy may exist within a play group, a bachelor group, or an adult hierarchy, enduring over time as members enter and exit the group. In the human studies, the incorporation of new group members or the exchange of cabin counselors for a day did little to disrupt the dyadic behavior patterns.

While it is not possible to determine the exact point in the life of an ongoing group that relative dominance status is recognized by group members, in new groups (such as the human camp groups) "end anchoring," the identification of extreme stimuli in a series and the judgment of others relative to those extremes (Sherif & Sherif, 1964), occurs within a relative brief (perhaps an hour) period of time. In the camp studies, the behavioral dominance hierarchy became more stable over time, with most dyadic relationships becoming firmly entrenched. The contested or flexible dyadic relationships were predictable, resulting in occasional shifts in relative status occurring between adjacently ranked group members (one up, one down). This basic hierarchical stability may extend over a long period of time. Weisfeld, Omark, and Cronin (1980) found that children studied in first- and third-grade (Omark and Edelman, 1976) maintained their relative dominance positions 8 years later as high school freshman and juniors.

Aside from major disruptions, the dominance hierarchy remains stable over time and settings, increasing in stability as group members more clearly distinguish relative status. Challenges become more selective, respecting clearly established dyadic relationships while challenging the flexible ones. This plasticity would appear to be prevalent in most adolescent groups.

Individual Characteristics

Nonhuman primate research has seldom undertaken the task of predicting the group dominance structure by reference to individual characteristics of its members. Research on humans has occasionally undertaken such procedures, but with little success since few of the physical, behavioral, and social measures consistently or significantly relate to dominance status, e.g., age, body size, aggression, sociability, experience, popularity.

During the early pubescent years, physical traits may be most important in distinguishing relative rank. One explanation for this is the dramatic saliency of physical variability during this time. For example, among the 12 to 13 year olds in the human male adolescent groups 1–5, pubertal maturation stage (Tanner, 1962) ranged from 1 to 4; among the 14 to 17 year old boys in groups 10–11, the stages were either 4 or 5. Relative differences in height and weight were just as marked: from 58–71 inches and from 81–140 pounds among the early adolescents, but from 66–73 inches, from 121–165 pounds among the late adolescents. When physical features become more equalized at the conclusion of pubescence, other variables such as intelligence, peer popularity, and camp experience are emphasized, demarcating individual variation and, consequently, importance in regard to group dominance status. The drop in the use of pushing and shoving, and of overt categories of behavior among late adolescents, underscores this deemphasis of physical modes of asserting dominance position. The finding that girls develop this deemphasized pattern earlier could be attributed to their earlier physical maturation or to an earlier learning of the importance of social and mental characteristics, or to both.

The nonhuman primate literature suggests that, rather than relating the entire rank order to some dimension, a more productive technique is to examine the characteristics of individuals at the extreme points of the hierarchy. Nonhuman primate adolescent alpha males tend to be morphologically larger and physically stronger than other group members. "Social graces" with a "pleasing personality" are as important as physical size and strength in many primate species for attaining a prominent position in the group. An alpha is the center of attention, a focal animal for unification of the group. Although not always the leader in trail progressions, a top ranked individual leads in the sense of initiating and directing group movement. Such an individual defends the group against both internal and external sources of disturbance. Dominant chimpanzees are not only stronger, but also more highly motivated, coordinated and "ingenious" than are subordinates (Goodall, 1968).

The data do not, however, answer *how* an individual has his/her "degree" of dominance or submission. Most likely, there is a plurality of determinants, some tied to morphological and temperamental inheritance and others to socialization factors. This "degree" is probably flexible and defines a range of possibilities rather than a precise positional placement. The range is dependent on who else is present and on characteristics of the setting. If six alphas were placed together in a group, it would be obvious that not all could be "most dominant"; if an omega adolescent were placed in a group of juvenile individuals two to three years younger, then it would be doubtful that she/he would reside at the bottom of the new dominance hierarchy.

The position taken in this paper is that, when individuals freely interact, some are more likely to rise to the top of a hierarchy, while others will fall to the bottom. This is also the position of McGuire (1974), who argues that, in many primate groups, some animals are compelled toward achieving a high dominance status. He outlines the role of genetic and environmental factors in his "idiosyncratic male hypothesis":

> The hypothesis assumes that certain males are particularly assertive and aggressive by virtue of their genetic makeup. One essential element of this hypothesis, therefore, is genetic. Depending upon conditions of upbringing, such as mother's rank, social structure, etc., a certain amount of aggressiveness is more or less likely to manifest itself. But no conditions have been found which would suggest that continual intense aggressiveness, as seen in the fission process, is environmentally determined. Males that exhibit this continual intense aggressive behavior are called *idiosyncratic males*, i.e., their behavior does not appear to be the result of social conditions alone (although given condi-

tions would theoretically enhance or suppress such behavior) (p. 124).

Other group members—whether for biochemical, morphological, temperamental or socialization reasons—seem "satisfied" with low status.

Sex Comparisons

In primate groups, a non-estrous female adolescent rarely engages in dominance interactions, usually ranking near the bottom or next to her mother in the group dominance hierarchy. While, at pubertal onset, she may decrease, maintain, or increase her radius of social contact in relation to former standards, her relations with peers of either sex dramatically decrease during adolescence. Adult females now become her "reference" group and infants become her focus of attention. Perhaps due to social contact and hormonal changes (Baldwin & Baldwin, 1977), the adolescent female becomes more passive and withdrawn from aversive contingencies. She seldom asserts herself or is the recipient of antagonism, an adaptive strategy for protecting genetic potential. Unlike her male counterpart, the female adolescent seldom becomes a solitaire, forms a unisex group, relocates, or becomes peripheralized. Staying with the natal group is the norm; if this is abridged then it is usually just after the onset of pubescence and before first parturition.

Among human adolescents, the two sexes diverged considerably in their manifestation of dominance behavior. Boys in the cabin groups were more likely to physically assert themselves, argue with others, and, to a lesser extent, verbally/physically threaten and displace cabinmates; girls were more likely to recognize the status of others, give unsolicited advice and information, and shun and ignore. This reflects the general trend for boys to be direct and girls to be indirect in dominance encounters. Young adolescent males thus *asserted* their status by utilizing the "power" related components of dominance behavior; girls *expressed* their status through vertical, evaluative behavior.

As the camp session progressed, most male dyads decreased their frequency but increased the overtness level of dominance encounters. This supports the position that a hierarchical arrangement of group members abets antagonistic interactions, thus enhancing the prospects for group order and harmony. The female pattern was of a different nature and thus, perhaps, had different effects. Rather than reducing the frequency and raising the overtness of dominance relations, female dyads tended to increase the frequency rate and to make the interactions less visible, i.e., more indirect.

The female pattern of expressing or recognizing authority in an indirect fashion is considerably more conducive for developing and maintaining close knit relationships than is the more competitive and direct assertion of power by males. In the camp studies, the adolescent females varied this frequency rate of dominance interactions in accordance to the situation. This indicates their greater willingness to accommodate behavior to the particular activity, implying a greater sensitivity to the surroundings and to the complexity of the social environment. Male status seldom changed; fluctuations in the dominance hierarchy occurred primarily among the followers. An alpha girl during the middle camp often slipped to the beta position before regaining her prominence during the last week of camp. There is female flexibility, temporarily as well as situationally.

There is also some evidence to raise doubts that the dominance hierarchial structure, so prevalent in male adolescent groups, is adequate to describe status differentiation among adolescent females. As noted above, primate adolescent females seldom congregate in groups; when they do, they are more likely to form cliques of twos or threes (Savin-Williams, 1980c) than the relative large groups that may be artifically imposed by a camp setting among human adolescents.

There is some indication, based on our groups of human adolescent females, that a different structure, which we termed a "cohesive dyarchy," is more descriptive of dominance relations among adolescent girls. One way in which this structure differs from the dominance hierarchy is that individuals are ordered in a less linear arrangement. The horizontality of the cohesive dyarchy implies that more than one person can be at one rank. For example, two girls may be equally effective in asserting dominance, but do so in different ways. This reflects the greater division of labor in accordance with female needs of expressivity; it acknowledges the equal importance of looking out for each others' feelings and of "getting the job done." In the sociological literature, the concepts of instrumental and expressive leaders are employed (Parsons & Bales, 1955). An instrumental leader reduces the likelihood of group conflict due to lack of direction, by giving structure to group activities; an expressive leader reduces the likelihood of conflict between individuals, and thus allows the group to function as a cohesive unit.

This dichotomy may be helpful in understanding the behavioral differences between Alice and Betty in Group 16. Alice, as the instrumental leader, was successful in overt behaviors involving ridicule and control, while Betty filled the expressive role, successful in subtle behaviors, involving others' recognition of her status and her own counter dominance. The girls approached Alice and Betty for different reasons. They were far more likely to ask Betty for advice on friendship, clothing, and hairstyle, and to approach Alice to ask her to do something with them (e.g., go swimming, take a walk) or to seek approval of ideas for group activities. It is plausible that in male groups the instrumental leader is the alpha-ranked individual; if there is an expressive leader, he is clearly subordinate in the dominance hierarchy since instrumentality is highly valued in male socialization (Parsons & Bales, 1955).

The male bonding theory of Tiger (1969) and the female contingency hypothesis of Angrist (1969) both account for the sex differences noted above. In primate groups, Callan (1970) has noted that dominance relations among females tend to be relatively unorganized and unstructured when compared with intermale behavior:

> I should like to suggest, roughly, that one structural feature common to a good deal of human and animal social life is that the males are the conspicuous participators, the upholders of the contours and corners of the social map, and that the position of the female is characteristically more subtle or even equivocal with respect to this map (p. 144).

While females may not be regularly engaged in dominance interactions among each other or with males, they are the "keepers-in-being" of the system as a system by concerning themselves with the interpersonal aspects of group life.

The greater male proclivity for formulating and maintaining hierarchical and cohesive same-sex groups is empirically congruent with Tiger's (1969) speculations on group bonding and evolutionary theory. He proposes that male-male bonding is a positive valence or attraction, serving group defense, food-gathering and social order maintenance purposes that are a direct consequence of pre-hominid ecological adaptation:

> The two critical adaptations were the development of patterns of hunting large animals which may have involved tools and, more significantly, a propensity to form co-operative bonds which (as I will later argue) would have to be all-male (p. 35).

Male-female physical and behavioral differences oriented the male toward participation in the hunting-gathering manner of exploiting the environment.

Because of early socialization experiences adolescent males are more likely to adapt to mega-structural situations, such as camp. On the other hand, according to Angrist (1969), females are oriented toward a contingency sex role development. Rather than simply fitting into a highly organized and rule enforced structure, females negotiate interpersonal relationships in face-to-face interactions. Such a linear system is dysfunctional because it negates the informal, socioemotional aspects of interpersonal relationships for cohesive and compatible female adolescent groups. The cohesive dyarchy form allows for these unique female characteristics.

Effects of a Dominance System

Ethologists assume that a systematic group structure, whether patterned as a dominance hierarchy or as a cohesive dyarchy, develops and is maintained because individuals and/or the group benefit(s) from such a structure. Alexander (1974) concluded that groups "form and persist" because all group members gain genetically.

Given the ethological studies conducted to date, the genetic advantage of a particular status position is a matter of speculation. It is possible, however, to demonstrate "personal benefits" an individual may derive from a dominance position. For example, high ranking human adolescents at camp frequently ate the biggest piece of cake at mealtimes, sat where they wanted to during discussions, and slept in the preferred sleeping sites during camp—outs (near the fire)—all "scarce resources" at camp. These are not unlike the benefits other primate adolescents gain from high status. Subadult male langurs base accessibility to food, right of way, and tree position on relative dominance rank (Yoshiba, 1968).

Perhaps the most salient benefit from high status is internal. Levi-Strauss (1951) noted that, even in cultures where being a leader may result in personal loss or death, some individuals strive for the position because of its "intrinsic reward," an enhanced self-esteem. Chance (1967) suggested that the most dominant male individual is the focus of attention within the group. Others imitate him, seek his support, and allow him to innovate without inhibition from other group members (McGraw, 1972). In nonhuman primates, Washburn and Hamburg (1968) have noted that "being dominant appears to be its own reward —to be highly satisfying and to be sought, regardless of whether it is accompanied by advantage in food, sex, or grooming" (p. 473).

There is little speculation as to the personal benefits of a subordinate rank. Sherif and Sherif (1964) suggest that all group members seek to belong to and be approved by the peer group. To achieve this security some group members are willing to submit. Alexander (1974) is more explicit:

> The subordinate also gains by his behavior: like the dominant he is informed, by the interactions of the hierarchy, when and how to display aggression, and when and how to withhold and appease and withdraw, so as to stay alive and remain in the group and be at least potentially reproductive for the longest period (p. 330).

Many of the subordinate adolescents in the camp studies appeared to identify with the group's success and to accept their status as a way of life. They avoided, with a passion, making decisions and being responsible for others. Deciding which way to travel on a strange path or which of several foods to take on a camp—out is not an enjoyable or sought after task or some adolescents. Perhaps the maxim, "everyone cannot be a leader" should be altered to include the words, "nor wants to be."

In primate groups, the advantages of a dominance hierarchy are to alleviate the damaging aspects of aggression without decreasing its survival value (defense of self and group, predator protection, altruism, delineation of habitat) and to add stability and expectancy to social living (Eibl-Eibesfeldt, 1975).

Because of their group status, particular individuals have specialized group obligations and roles to perform, expected of them by other group members. Failure to carry out these duties implies loss of the prestige that has been bestowed by the group (Thrasher, 1927). From a more egotistical point of view, Alexander (1974, p. 327) notes: "Whenever individuals derive benefits from group functions, they may be expected to carry out activities that maintain the group, and thereby serve their own interests as well."

High ranking male human adolescents played a crucial instrumental role within the camp group. Arguments during athletic games were reduced to a minimum when the alpha individual, by assessing everyone's athletic skills, told each where to play and for how long. Few objected to his authoritarianism, even those low ranking cabinmates who frequently had to play undesirable positions. The most dominant males initiated and determined group movement; they also made the important decisions within the cabin group, e.g., deciding the theme of the cabin flag or where to camp on the beach. The subordinates' role was to do the necessary work for the implementation and completion of tasks, and to follow.

As previously discussed, the female pattern was to differentiate the instrumental and expressive dominance status positions within the group. When intermeshing properly, the net effect of this behavior and the behavior of subordinates was the stabilization of interpersonal relations and enhanced group performance.

The level of serious fights in the human cabin groups was extremely low, 1% of the over 7000 dominance encounters observed in groups 2–9, and less in the older adolescent groups. In male adolescent groups the number of recorded dominance encounters dropped precipitiously during camp; even though the level of antagonistic behavior tended to increase in female adolescent groups, became more indirect in form as camp progressed. Thus, with stabilization of the group structure, antagonistic behavior became either less frequent or less overt.

The group thus benefits by having dominant individuals within the group: decisions are made, activities are organized, intragroup friction is avoided or reduced and intragroup relationships are negotiated. The group structure assigns roles and obligations to particular group members—which enhances a cohesive and well-functioning group—and regulates interindividual behavior in such a way so as to reduce the level of intraspecific aggression, which is beneficial to individuals and to the survival of the group.

Dominance and War

Although a system of dominance relations acts most effectively in controlling aggression within a small unit, it is not readily apparent how much of this research literature can be extrapolated to larger issues such as the control of war among nations. As noted by McGuinness in the Introduction, modern warfare is not usually rooted in interpersonal anger or aggression, and thus, dominance hierarchies among individuals can do little to explain or prevent larger-scale, multinational war. My best estimate is that the phenomenon of hierarchical arranging of individuals within a group is a vestige of an evolutionary time when warfare was prevented or reduced in likelihood of occurrence by interpersonal status differentiation. Nations were unknown and kinship groups remained separated and at peace due to the mechanism of territorial spacing.

Whether males or females have higher levels of aggression and, if there is a difference in absolute level, whether the difference is due to biological or socialization considerations are not issues that the current review and research addressed. Rather, sex differences in how power and influence are expressed within a dyad and a group structure were illustrated. Aggression appears in both sexes; how it is expressed and how it is controlled vary between male and female adolescents, perhaps due to basic biological (hormonal, morphological, physiological) and socialization differences between the sexes.

Placing women in charge of nations might counter rampant sexism but there is little in my research to give us hope that it will prevent warfare. The reasons for this are because 1. even assuming females are less aggressive than males, some women are more aggressive than most men; 2. wars are not usually caused by aggressive tendencies of the nation's leaders; and 3. dominance hierarchies tell us little, if anything, concerning modern warfare. The value of the current chapter thus resides in its importance for the day-to-day life of individuals. Within groups of adolescents, aggression is frequently controlled by a system of status differentiation, whether in the form of a dominance hierarchy, a cohesive dyarchy, or some other form yet to be described.

Primate Adolescence

The concepts of dominance and submission behavior, and of dominance hierarchy are frequent assumptions in studies of children and nonhuman primates. Beyond middle childhood, however, the view of Collins and Raven (1969) is prevalent: Whereas among groups of animals and human children a *simple* rank ordering based on power is characteristic, by adolescence, the processes of socialization and cognitive experiences enhance the development of social systems—e.g., authority, leadership, friendship, coalitions—with a complexity far more sophisticated than a dominance hierarchy.

The present research casts doubt on the upper age restriction claims made for a "simple" dominance hierarchy being descriptive of group structure, at least for male adolescents. This is not to imply, however, that behavior that expresses power and authority, or that the physical, behavioral, and social predictors of status do not change developmentally. Unfortunately, such age trends are difficult to assess given the dearth of naturalistic observation studies on dominance and submission in children and adolescents. Apparently, and most generally, with age, verbal and subtle indicators of status gradually replace physical and overt behavioral manifestations.

Although athletic ability is a good predictor of relative dominance rank from childhood through adolescence, it is during adolescence that sexual maturation first becomes instrumental in predicting status. Sade (1967) has pointed this out for primate males:

> I speculate that at about puberty, physiological differences between males become more important in fighting and that the differences that derive from past experiences and continued association with

adults of different rank become less overriding in determining the winner of fights (p. 113).

During pubescence, sexual dimorphism becomes most pronounced, separating the "men from the women"; during preadolescence both sexes tend to look alike. Counter to Darwin's belief that secondary sex characters evolved as sexual lures, Guthrie (1970) views them as having evolved as social signals, functioning as threat displays after pubescence. For example, the genital area, undergoing radical changes during pubescence, may serve as a social signal. Pubic hair, a darkened scrotum and enlarged testes and penis are visible signs of one's approaching maturity, and hence signify to adult males that one is now potentially a sexual and status competitor (Wickler, 1967). In some primate species, there is a direct relationship between the progress of pubescent development and the amount of male aggression that one receives. Pubic and auxillary hair function not only as visual displays but also as olfactory signals of threat.

Thus, for primate adolescent males, the connection between physical maturation and dominance rank has been theoretically and empirically made. Due to vast deficiencies in studies of primate adolescent females within a group setting (Savin-Williams, 1980c), it is not clear what role pubescence has for female adolescent status. Perhaps, female secondary sex characters also serve as threat displays among same-sex peers. Or, they may be held in awe or high esteem because of their role as sexual attractants.

The present study focused on adolescence because it is during the age of pubescence or sexual maturation, regardless of the primate species, when social competitive behavior increases, and group bonding and allegiance are formulated and consolidated. More specifically, human adolescence is a time when the peer group becomes influential in the establishment of self-concept (Hartup, 1983), identity (Erikson, 1959), and norms or standards of comparisons by which an individual evaluates his or her own behavior, attitudes and values as well as those of others (Kelley, 1952). Hence, the importance of dominance behavior (competitiveness) and hierarchical status (identity, self-concept, norms and standards) in the adolescent peer group (group bonding and allegiance) becomes understandable.

From an ethological stance, the end of adolescence is adulthood. Dominance behavior thus has a new importance during pubescence: the net outcome of one's dominance encounters with other group members may well determine one's relative adult status. This status may have significance for one's relative genetic potential in both the number and the quality (potential to survive) of offspring produced. At some point in the primate's evolutionary history, the outcome of such encounters may well have shaped what adolescents are today.

References

Adorno, T.W., Frenkel-Brunswik, E., Levinson, D., & Stanford, R.N. *The authoritarian personality.* New York: Harper, 1950.

Albrecht, H. & Dunnett, S.C. *Chimpanzees in Western Africa.* Verlag, Munchen: R. Piper, 1971.

Alcock, J. *Animal behavior: An evolutionary approach.* Sunderland: Sinauer Assoc., 1975.

Aldrich-Blake, F.P.G. & Chivers, D.J. "On the genesis of a group of siamang." *American Journal of Physical Anthropology,* 1973, *38,* 631–636.

Alexander, R.D., "The evolution of social behavior." *Annual Review of Ecology and Systematics,* 1974, *5,* 325–383.

Altmann, J., "Observational study of behavior: Sampling methods." *Behaviour,* 1974, *49,* 227–267.

Angrist, S.S., "The study of sex roles." *Journal of Social Issues,* 1969, *25,* 215–232.

Baldwin, J.D., "The ontogeny of social behaviour of squirrel monkeys *(Saimiri sciureus)* in a seminatural environment." *Folia Primatologica,* 1969, *11,*35–79

Baldwin, J.D., "The Social behaviour of adult male squirrel monkeys *(Saimiri sciureus)* in a seminatural environment. *Folia Primatologica,* 1968, *9,* 281–314.

Baldwin, J.D. & Baldwin, J.I., "The role of learning phenomena in the ontogeny of exploration and play." In S. Chevalier-Skolnikoff and F.E. Poirier (Eds.) *Primate bisocial developement: Biological, social, and ecological determinants.* New York: Garland, 1977.

Benson, P., Dehority, J., Garman, L., Hanson, E., Hochschevender, M., Lebold, C., Rohr, R., & Sullivan, J., "Intrapersonal correlates of nonspontaneous helping behavior." *Journal of Social Psychology,* 1980, *110,* 87–95.

Boggess, J., "Immature male and adult male interactions in bisexual langur *(Presbytis entellus)* troops." *Folia Primatologica,* 1982, *38,* 19–38.

Boice, R. *Human ethology.* New York: Plenum, 1983.

Bourliere, F., Hunkeler, C., & Bertrand, M., "Ecology and behavior of Lowe's guenon *(Cercopithecus cambelli lowei)* in the Ivory Coast." In J.R. Napier & P.H. Napier (Eds.), *Old World monkeys.* New York: Academic Press, 1970.

Bronfenbrenner, U., *The ecology of human development.* Cambridge, MA: Harvard University Press, 1979.

Budnitz, N. & Dainis, K., "*Lemur catta:* Ecology and behavior." In I. Tattersall & R.W. Sussman (Eds.), *Lemur biology.* New York: Plenum, 1975.

Callan, H., *Ethology and society: Towards an anthropological view.* Oxford: Clarendon Press, 1970.

Carpenter, C.R., *Naturalistic behavior of nonhuman primates.* University Park, Pa.: Pennsylvania State University Press, 1964.

Chalmers, N.R., "Group composition, ecology and daily activities of free living mangabeys in Uganda." *Folia Primatologica,* 1968, *8,* 247–262.

Chance, M.R.A., "Attention structure as the basis of primate rank orders." *Man,* 1967, *2,* 503–518.

Chandler, C.F., "Development and function of marking and sexual behavior in the Malagasy prosimian primate, *Lemur fulvus.*" *Primates,* 1975, *16,* 35–47.

Chivers, D.J., "The siamang and the gibbon in the Malay Peninsula." In D.M. Rambaugh (Ed.), *Gibbon and siamang, Vol. I.* Basel, Switz.: S. Karger, 1972.

Collins, B.E. & Raven, B.E., "Group structure: Attraction, coalitions, communication, and power." G. Linzey & E. Aronson (Eds.), *Handbook of social psychology, Volume 4.* Reading, Mass.: Addison-Wesley, 1969.

Darwin, C., *The expression of emotions in man and animals.* London: D. Appleton, 1872.

Dittus, W.P.J., "The evolution of behaviors regulating density and age-specific sex ratios in a primate population. *Behaviour,* 1979, *69,* 265–302.

Dolhinow, P. *Primate patterns.* New York: Holt, Rinehart & Winston, 1972.

Drickamer, L.C. & Vessey, S.H., "Group changing in free-ranging male rhesus monkeys." *Primates,* 1973, *14,* 359–368.

Dumont, L. *Homo Hierarchicus: An essay on the caste system.* Chicago: University of Chicago Press, 1970.

Dunbar, R. & Dunbar, P., "Social dynamics of gelada baboons." In H. Kuhn (Ed.), *Contributions to primatology, Volume 6.* Basel, Switzerland: S. Karger, 1975.

Eibl-Eibesfeldt, I. *Ethology: The biology of behavior,* revised edition. New York: Holt, Rinehart & Winston, 1975.

Erikson, E.H., "Identity and the life cycle." *Psychological Issues,* 1959, *I,* I.

Galdikas-Brindamour, B., "Orangutans, Indonesia's "people of the forest." *National Geographic,* 1975, *148,* 444–473.

Gibb, C.A., "Leadership." In G. Linzey & E. Aronson (Eds.), *Handbook of social psychology, Volume 4.* Cambridge: Addison-Wesley, 1969.

Glidewell, J.C., Kantor, M.B., Smith, L.M., & Stringer, L.A., "Socialization and social structures in the classroom." In L.W. Hoffman & M.L. Hoffman (Eds.), *Review of child development research.* New York: Russell Sage Foundation, 1966.

Goodall, J., "The behavior of free-living chimpanzees in the Gombe Stream Reserve." *Animal Behaviour Monographs,* 1968, *I,* 161–311.

Graham, C.E., "Reproductive physiology of the chimpanzee." In G.H.

Bourne (Ed.), *The chimpanzee* (Vol. 3). Basel, Switzerland: S. Kargar, 1970.

Guthrie, R., "Evolution of human threat display organs." In T. Dobzhansky, M.K. Hecht & W.C. Steere (Eds.), *Evolutionary biology*. New York: Appleton-Century-Craft, 1970.

Hall, E.T. *The hidden dimension*. New York: Doubleday, 1966.

Hall, K.R.L. & DeVore, I., "Baboon social behavior." In I. DeVore (Ed.), *Primate behavior*. New York: Holt, Rinehart, & Winston, 1965.

Hartup, W.W., "Peer relations." In P.H. Mussen (Ed.-in-Chief) & E.M. Hetherington (Ed.), *Handbook of child psychology*, Fourth Edition, *Volume IV*. New York: wiley, 1983.

Holden, C., "More than the faces are familiar." *Science*, 1980, 55–59.

Jay, P.C., "The common langur of North India." In I. DeVore (Ed.), *Primate behavior*. New York: Holt, Rinehart, & Winston, 1965.

Jolly, A., *Lemur behavior*. Chicago: University of Chicago Press, 1966.

Jones, C.B., "The functions of status in the mantled howler monkey, *Alouatta palliata gray:* Intraspecific competition for group membership in a folivorous neotropical primate." *Primates*, 1980, *21*, 389–405.

Kelley, H.H., "Two functions of reference groups." In T.M. Newcomb & E.L. Hartley (Eds.), *Readings in social psychology*, Revised Edition. New York: Holt, Rinehart, & Winston, 1952.

Koyama, N., "On dominance rank and kinship of a wild Japanese monkey troop in Arashiyama., *Primates*, 1967, *8*, 189–216.

Kreuz, L.E., Rose, R.M. & Jennings, J.R., "Suppression of plasma testosterone levels and psychological stress." *Archives of General Psychiatry*, 1972, *26*, 479–482.

Levi-Strauss, C. *Tristes Tropiques*. Translated by J. Russell. New York: Criterion Books, 1951.

Lorenz, K. *Evolution and modification of behavior*. Chicago: University of Chicago Press, 1965.

Lorenz, K., "Oer Kumpon in der umwelt des vogels." *Journal of Ornithology*, 1935, *83*, 137–413.

Lorenz, K.Z., *On aggression*. New York: Harcourt, Brace & World, 1966.

Loy, J., "Estrous behavior of free-ranging rhesus monkeys *(Macaca mulatta)*." *Primates*, 1971, *12*, 1–31.

Loy, J. & Loy, K., "Sexual harassment among captive patas monkeys *(Erythrocebus patas)*." *Primates*, 1977, *18*, 691–699.

Maccoby, E.E. & Jacklin, C.N. *The psychology of sex differences*. Stanford: Stanford University Press, 1971.

McGrew, W.C. *An ethological study of children's behavior*. New York: Academic Press, 1972.

McGuinness, D., "The emotions: Focus on intermale aggression and dominance systems." In *Absolute values and the new cultural revolution*. Twelfth International Conference on the Unity of the Sciences, Chicago, Illinois, 1983. New York: I.C.U.S. Books, 1984.

McGuire, M.T., "The St. Kitts vervet." In H. Kuhn (Ed.), *Contributions to Primatology*, *Volume 2*. Basel, Switzerland: S. Karger, 1974.

Medin, D.L., "The comparative study of memory." *Journal of Human Evolution*, 1974, *3*, 455–463.

Mitchell, G. & Brandt, E.M., "Paternal behavior in primates." In F.E. Poirier (Ed.), *Primate socialization*. New York: Random House, 1972.

Montemayor, R. & Savin-Williams, R.C., "Parent and peer relations among adolescent nonhuman primates: The development of independence." In preparation.

Omark, D.R. & Edelman, M.S., "The development of attention structure in young children." In M.R.A. Chance & R.R. Larson (Eds.) *The structure of social attention*, Wiley, 1976.

Omark, D.R., Strayer, F.F. & Freedman, D.G., *Dominance relations: An ethological view of human conflict and social interaction*. New York: Garland, 1980.

Owens, N.W., "A comparison of aggressive play and aggression in free-living baboons," *Papio anubis. Animal Behaviour*, 1975, *23*, 757–765.

Paikoff, R.L. & Savin-Williams, R.C., "An exploratory study of dominance interactions among adolescent females at a summer camp." *Journal of Youth and Adolescence*, 1983, *12*, 419–433.

Parsons, T. & Bales, R.F., *Family socialization and interaction process*. London: Routledge & Kegan Paul, 1956.

Pattee, H.H., *Hierarchy theory: The challenge of complex systems*. New York:; George Braziller, 1973.

Poirier, F.E., "The Nilgiri langur *(Presbytis johnii)* of South India." In L.A. Rosenblum (Ed.), *Primate behavior, Volume I*. New York: Academic Press, 1970.

Pusey, A.E., "The physical and social development of wild adolescent chimpanzees *(Pan troglodytes schweinfurthii)." Dissertation Abstracts International*, 1978, *38*, 5791–5792.

Redican, W.K. & Taub, D.M., "Male parental care in monkeys and apes." In M.E. Lamb (Ed.), *The role of the father in child development, Second Edition*. New York: Wiley, 1981.

Richard, A.F. & Heimbuch, R., "An analysis of the social behavior of 3 groups of *Propithecus verreauxi."* In I. Tattersall & R.W. Sussman (Eds.), *Lemur biology*. New York: Plenum Press, 1975.

Riesen, A.H., "Comparative perspectives in behavior study." *Journal of Human Evolution*, 1974, *3*, 433–434.

Rodman, P.S., "Population composition and adaptive organisation among orang-utans of the Kutai Reserve." In R.P. Michael & J.H. Crook (Eds.), *Comparative ecology and behaviour of primates*. New York: Academic Press, 1973.

Rosenblum, L.A., Coe, C.L. & Bromley, L.J., "Peer relations in monkeys: The influence of social structure, gender, and familiarity. "In M. Lewis & L.A. Rosenblum (Eds.), *The origins of behavior: Peer relations and friendships*. New York: Wiley, 1975.

Rowell, T.E., "Social organization of wild talapoin monkeys." *American Journal of Physical Anthropology*, 1973, *38*, 593–598.

Rowell, T.E., "Hierarchy in the organization of a captive baboon group." *Animal Behaviour*, 1966, *14*, 430–443.

Sade, D.S., "Determinants of dominance in a group of free-ranging rhesus monkeys." In S.A. Altmann (Ed.), *Social communication among primates*. Chicago: University of Chicago Press, 1967.

Savin-Williams, R.C., "Dominance and submission among adolescent boys." In D.R. Omark, F.F. Strayer, & D.G. Freedman (Eds.), *Dominance relations: An ethological view of human conflict and social interaction.* New York: Garland, 1980(a).

Savin-Williams, R.C., "Social interactions of adolescent females in natural groups." In H. Foot, T. Chapman, & J. Smith (Eds.), *Friendship and social relations in children,* London: Wiley, 1980(b).

Savin-Williams, R.C., "Dominance hierarchies in groups of middle to late adolescent males." *Journal of Youth and Adolescence,* 1980(c), *9,* 75–87.

Savin-Williams, R.C., "Dominance hierarchies in groups of early adolescents." *Child Development,* 1979, *50,* 923–935.

Savin-Williams, R.C., "Dominance in a human adolescent group." *Animal Behavior,* 1977, *25,* 400–406.

Savin-Williams, R.C., "An ethological study of dominance formation and maintenance in group of human adolescents." *Child Development.* 1976, *47,* 972–979.

Savin-Williams, R.C. & Montemayor, R., "A characterization of primate adolescence: An ethological perspective." In preparation.

Savin-Williams, R.C., Small, S.A. & Zeldin, R.S., "Dominance and altruism among adolescent males: A comparison of ethological and psychological methods." *Ethology and Sociobiology,* 1981, *2,* 167–176.

Schaller, G.B., *The mountain gorilla.* Chicago: University of Chicago Press, 1963.

Schneirla, T.C., "The levels concept in the study of social organization in animals." In J.H. Rohrer & M. Sherif (Eds.), *Social psychology at the crossroads.* New York: Harper, 1951.

Scott, J.P., "Implications of infra-human social behavior for problems of human relations." In M. Sherif & M.O. Wilson (Eds.), *Groups relations at the crossroads.* New York: Harper, 1953.

Sherif, M. & Sherif, C.W., *Reference groups.* Chicago: H. Regnery, 1964.

Simonds, P.E., "The bonnet macaque in South India." In I. DeVore (Ed.), *Primate behavior.* New York: Holt, Rinehart, & Winston, 1965.

Small, S.A., Savin-Williams, R.C. & Zeldin, R.S., "In search of personality traits: A multimethod analysis of naturally occurring prosocial and dominance behavior." *Journal of Personality,* 1983, *51,* 1–16.

Snyder, P.A., "Behavior of *Leontopithecus rosalia* (golden-lion marmoset) and related species: A review." *Journal of Human Evolution,* 1974, *3,* 109–122.

Southwick, C.H., Beg, M.A., & Siddiqi, M.R., "Rhesus monkeys in North India." In I. DeVore (Ed.), *Primate behavior.* New York: Holt, Rinehart, & Winston, 1965.

Struhsaker, T.T., "Social structure among vervet monkeys *(Cercopithecus aethiops)."* *Behaviour,* 1967, *29,* 83–121.

Swartz, K.B., & Rosenblum, L.A., "The social context of parental behavior." In D.J. Gubernick & P.H. Klopfer (Eds.), *Parental care in mamals.* New York: Plenum, 1981.

Tanner, J.M., *Growth at adolescence, Second Edition.* Oxford: Blackwell Scientific Publications, 1962.

Tenaza, R.R., "Territory and monogamy among Kloss' gibbons *(Hylobates* klossi) in Siberut Island, Indonesia." *Folia Primatologica*, 1975, *24*, 60–80.

Thrasher, F., *The gang*. Chicago: University of Chicago Press, 1927.

Tiger, L., *Men in groups*. New York: Random House, 1969.

Tinbergen, N., "On war and peace in animals and man." *Science*, 1968, *160*, 1411–1418.

Tinbergen, N., "On aims and methods of ethology." *Zeithschrift fur Teirpsychologie*, 1963, *20*, 410–433.

Washburn, S.L. & Hamburg, D.A., "The implications of primate research." In I. DeVore (Ed.), *Primate behavior*. New York: Holt, Rinehart, & Winston, 1965.

Weisfeld, G.E., "An ethological view of human adolescence." *The Journal of Nervous and Mental Disease*, 1979, *167*, 38–55.

Weisfeld, G.E., & Berger, J.M., "Some features of human adolescence viewed in evolutionary perspective." *Human Development*, 1983.

Weisfeld, G.E. Omark, D.R., & Cronin, C.L., "A longtudinal and cross-sectional study of dominance in boys." In D.R. Omark, F.F. Strayer, & D.G. Freedman (Eds.) *Dominance relations: An ethological view of human conflict and social interaction*. New York: Garland, 1980.

Weisfeld, G.E., & Weisfeld, C.C., "An observational study of social evaluation: An application of the dominance hierarchy model." *Journal of Genetic Psychology*, 1984, *145*, 89–100.

West-Eberhard, M.J., "Evolution of social behavior." *The Quarterly Review of Biology*, 1975, *50*, 1–33.

Whiting, B. & Edwards, C.P., "A cross-cultural analysis of sex differences in the behavior of children aged three through eleven." *Journal of Social Psychology*, 1973, *91*, 171–188.

Whyte, L.L., Wilson, A.F. & Wilson, D., *Hierarchical structures*. New York: American Elsevier, 1969.

Wickler, W., "Socio-sexual signals and their intra-specifie imitation among primates." In D. Morris (Ed.), *Primates ecology*. Chicago: Aldine, 1967.

Wilson, E.O., *Sociobiology: The new synthesis*. Cambridge: Harvard University Press, 1975.

Wright, H.F., "Observational child study." In P. Mussen (Ed.), *Handbook of research methods in child development*. New York: Wiley, 1960.

Yamada, M., "Five natural troops of Japanese monkeys on Shodoshima Island: II. A comparison of social structure." *Primates*, 1971, *12*, 125–150.

Yoshiba, K., "Local and intertroop variability in ecology and social behavior of common Indian langurs." In P.C. Jay (Ed.), *Primates*. New York: Holt, Rienhart, & Winston, 1968.

Zeldin, R.S., Savin-Williams, R.C. & Small, S.A., "Adolescent prosocial behavior in a naturalistic context." *Journal of Social Psychology*, 1984, *123*, 159–168.

Zeldin, R.S., Small, S.A. & Savin-Williams, R.C., "Prosocial interactions in two mixed-sex adolescent groups." *Child Development*, 1982, *53*, 1492–1498.

Zucker, E.L. & Kaplan, J.R., "A reinterpretation of 'sexual harassment' in patas monkeys." *Animal Behaviour*, 1981, *29*, 957–958.

Commentary: Dominance Systems and Primate Adolescence: An Evolutionary Approach

Joseph Shepher

Professor Savin-Williams' excellent presentation is a comprehensive summary of research on dominance hierarchies among human adolescents. The summary, however, is much more than the survey and reanalysis of his experiments. This time he integrates his research on humans into the wider framework of primate research, opening up the possibility of cross specific comparison, and establishing a sound theoretical framework for both his own and other researchers work on adolescent dominance hierarchies.

The relevance of his topic can hardly be exaggerated. Modern human life is basically a study in dominance hierarchies: we spend most of our waking hours in hierarchies that range from corporate industry to government administration, from supermarkets to department stores, from the elementary school to the university. Even our clubs, associations, churches, and hospitals are hierarchically organized, all displaying a wide variety of dominance systems. This is much more than Dumont's Homo hierarchicus, and modern adolescents can hardly find a more important system to adjust to than dominance hierarchies.

Because I think that dominance systems in primates are at least a corollary, if not integral, part of mating systems, and largely a part of ecological adaptations, I suggest that an ecological typology, in addition to taxonomy, might be equally fruitful for the

174

understanding of the evidence. Here are some examples. Although gibbons are apes, and marmosets, platyrrhine monkeys, they both are arboreal monogamists and this last fact has more influence on their dominance systems than does their place in the primate taxonomy. They are closer to each other in their dominance systems than are marmosets to howler monkeys, although both are in the same suborder, or gibbons to chimps, again both in the same suborder. Moreover, when the relevant variable is dominance hierarchies, langurs are too wide a taxon to be dealt with as a single group. There are langurs that live in multimale groups and langurs that live in a strict harem system. In such a harem, the statement: "During puberty, as a male matures in size and strength, he asserts himself first over low-ranking females, and then as a young adult, over low ranking males," makes no sense, since adolescent males live in a separate male group and have no access to females at all, except if and when they are successful in taking over a harem.

The primate evidence in Savin-William account is largely focused on male behavior, whereas excellent new material is available on female dominance hierarchies (Hrdy, 1981). It is extremely important for the understanding of both nonhuman and human dominance hierarchies to establish whether there is a separate hierarchy for males and another for females, or one that is all encompassing. As I hope to show later, the impact of females on male hierarchies, and vice versa, is crucial. One such instance is mentioned by the author who indicates that a macaque male's status is largely determined by the rank of his mother during juvenile and early adolescence. But, he adds, later after puberty, physical strength, ability and assertiveness become more influential. But physical strength, ability and assertiveness are not independent of mother's status; a dominant mother's son has more access to food, and will therefore be stronger, more self assured and more assertive than the son of a subdominant female. Differential status placement has certainly not been invented by human primates, however prevalent it may be among them.

Also, the author later points out, the status of the mother is bequeathed, not to the male offspring, but to the female offspring, and he summarizes: "While rank seldom gives breeding power, it does orient group leadership, cohesiveness, travel arrangements,

175

peaceful existence and food gathering." But again, are group leadership and food gathering, to say the least, irrelevant to breeding success? The closing statement on female assertiveness is, to my knowledge, contrary to recent evidence.

Whereas my comments on the nonhuman primate evidence focused on organization of the material, suggesting some additions, I have nothing to add to the rich material on humans that is a result of the author's long-standing research. Here, my comments will be directed more to the theoretical interpretation.

The Theoretical Review section relies on an impressive series of authors who would not easily agree among themselves on a theoretical platform: Lorenz and Tinbergen represent the group selectionists of classical ethology, whereas McGuire and Alexander, and certainly Tiger (though he did not say so in his 1968, Men in Groups), would prefer individual selection. But, it is important to decide which basic assumption is accepted. If we accept the group selectionist position, we may be pushed toward a naïve functionalism. An example: "These mechanisms (of dominance hierarchy J.S.) have evolved to reduce the harmful effects of aggression without negating its useful aspects such as protection from predators, population regulation and habitat utilization" (page 13). Nobody would doubt that dominance hierarchies do these things and have these effects on the group. That does not mean, however, that they have evolved *in order to do these things*. They may have evolved as a result of vectorial interaction of individual animals, the behavior of which became fixed through evolution in order to adapt to the physical and social environment. Adaptation has the function of assuring self replication, that is, reproduction. The vectors of individual behaviors are different in power and usually, but not always, contrary in direction. I say not always, because there is kinship altruism and sometimes, reciprocal altruism. The outcome of this series of vectorial interactions is the dominance hierarchy which may or may not have the above mentioned beneficial effects on the group. Thus, if a baboon group faces a leopard, the group is maintained, its dominance hierarchy intact. But, if it is confronted with a lioness, the group disintegrates and each individual animal tries to save itself. There is nothing mysterious about the integration of the individual into the group. It is the evolutionary outcome of not deviating from the well known cold calculation of natural selection: if an animal is flexible enough to be aggressive at the right place, in the right time, it will survive and reproduce; an animal that is either too timid or too aggressive will die or be outreproduced.

This approach seems to me more fruitful and more parsimonious than the group selectionist one, in yet another important feature of dominance hierarchies: intersex differences. In both human and nonhuman primates, we witness a conspicuous difference between male and female hierarchies. Savin-Williams' summary of those differences is exceptionally revealing:

> "The female pattern of expressing or recognizing authority in an indirect fashion is considerably more conducive for developing and maintaining close-knit relationships than is the more competitive and direct assertion of power by males," and later, "There is female flexibility, temporally as well as situationally" (page 29).

A somewhat different pattern emerged during the course of my research on female hierarchies in a kibbutz (Shepher and Tiger, 1978, 246). The difference stemmed from the fact that these hierarchies were comprised of adult women in task oriented groups, and were problematic structures, very different from male hierarchies. There was wide reluctance to accept authority and rather strained relations among the individuals. Authority was often concentrated in one single, usually menopausal, older female per work group and there was usually no gradation of authority.

Why should female dominance hierarchies be so different than male hierarchies? The answer, I think, is to be found again in the individual selectionist evolutionary thinking. I suggest the following line of explanation:

1. The only single criterion of life is self replication. All living things replicate themselves through different *mechanisms: division, halving, self–fertilization and sexual reproduction.*

2. Since evolution is genetic change, its main vehicle is reproduction. The living individual's adaptation is aimed at replicating itself, that is, its genes.

3. Individuals, in sexually reproducing animals, must combine their genes with those of another individual to create a zygote, an offspring. The reproductive strategy of the individual will be determined by its proportional contribution (investment) in the future offspring.

4. In mammals, parental investment is highly asymmetrical: males always invest less than females. Consequently, females become a limiting factor of male reproductive success. Males mammal tend to be polygynous; female mammal would opt for the mating system that promises the best male investment in the future offspring.

5. The ultimate function of male dominance is reproduction, though there may be several proximate functions: food, status, power. The striving of the mammalian male for reproductive success will be checked by other males and by the number of consenting females. An ecological situation that calls for high male investment in offspring will result in a monogamous (in humans, very rarely polyandrous) mating system; otherwise the system would be polygynous. Eighteen percent of primate species are monogamous, the rest polygynous. In human cultures, 29% are monogamous, less than 1% polyandrous, the rest polygynous, or having at least the option for polygyny—though it may not be present functionally.

6. Consequently, male dominance hierarchies will be aggressively oriented, well graded, triangular and stable, and more prominent in polygynous species than in monogamous ones. Dominance will be a central point in male life because what is at stake is very high: access to the ultimate limiting factor of reproductive success: consenting females. Variance of male reproductive success will be high, reflecting the triangular dominance hierarchy.

7. Female dominance hierarchies will be manipulatively oriented, flat, nongraded and unstable. Females are interested in guarding the precious product of their high parental investment by nesting themselves among supportive kin and soliciting and preserving male parental investment. Hence, the manipulative orientation of female dominance systems. Female variance of reproductive success is low, reflective of the flat hierarchy.

All this seems to contradict the author's statement that, "Given the ethological studies conducted to date, the genetic advantage of a particular status position is a matter of speculation" (page 32). The problem is methodological: in the nonhuman primate case, calculation of reproductive success is extremely difficult, primarily due to an inability to demonstrate paternity, and difficulty with multigenerational follow up research. In the human case, other difficulties arise, especially in modern mass society. Most of the data on mass societies refers to birth rates and it is obvious that birth is only part of the story. In a yet unpublished paper, D.R. Vining, Jr. (1983) of the University of Pennsylvania declares: "In short, until evidence is presented to the contrary, I think we can take, as one of the universals characterizing modern culture, the idea that social and reproductive success are inversely related." While I do not think that Vining's data convincingly demonstrates what he says, he himself finds an explanation of why and how this contradiction came about. Whereas, more often, culture follows biological predispositions; there is not less, and sometimes more drift in cultural evolution than in genetic evolution. And because cultural evolution is Lamarckian and works through group selection, the impact of such a cultural evolutionary drift is both more rapid and more comprehensive than the impact of genetic drift in biological evolution. Two such drifts, I claim, could bring modern society to the brink of extinction: the invention of hormonal birth control and the invention of nuclear weapons. The first contradicted the epigenetic rule of parental investment and therefore created a separation between social-cultural and reproductive success. This ultimately can (and I think does) undermine human mating systems and result in a demographic extinction. The second created a means of destruction against which the genetically evolved solution of dominance hierarchies are powerless. If we could have a world dominance hierarchy, the horrible spectre of nuclear holocaust would probably disappear. Without it the threat of the extinction of the human species is too obvious.

Adolescents, in learning to adopt adult social and biological roles are primed to act according to epigenetic rules that have evolved through millions of years of the coevolutionary process. If and when they grow up, they will have to face a new cultural environment with the Pill and nuclear bombs and missiles. Let us hope that they will do a better job than did their parents and grandparents.

References

Shepher, J. and L. Tiger, "Female Hierarchies in a Kibbutz Community" in Tiger, L. and H. Fowler (eds.) *Female Hierarchies*, 1978, Chicago: Aldine.

Vining, Daniel R. Jr., "Social *versus* Reproductive Success: A Conundrum for Sociobiology", Unpublished manuscript, 1983.

6.

War in the New Guinea Highlands: Theory and Ethnography in Conflict

Edward Li Puma

Introduction[1]

Although anthropologists, political scientists, and an assortment of fellow travelers have spent pen and ink on phenomena they variously designate as warfare, armed conflict, or feuding, they seldom attempt to pinpoint what they are describing. The reason for this evasion is that there are no true definitions, only different perspectives, each having their own criteria. Thus, the orchestrated, semi-ritual warfare of New Guinea tribesmen or Plains Indians seems distant from the warfare of nuclear conflagration.

Nonetheless, it seems that human warfare has certain recognizable characteristics which set it apart from non-human conflict:

1. Warfare involves groups which are organized in terms of principles of social organization. This may encompass kinship, the legal system, or concepts of nation-state. Accordingly, the conflict takes place between two groups as groups.[2]

2. Warfare is a recognized species of event which stands in contrast to accidental homicide, murder, and other forms of causing death. There is indeed an implicit agreement between factions on the legitimacy of fighting with the intent to kill.[3]

3. The motives for warfare include not only territoriality and the

allocation of scarce resources (both of which are historically determinate), but a plethora of immediately social motives, ranging from religious affiliation to rites of initiation. More, warfare can be multi-motivated, with different factions of the same group fighting for very different reasons.

4. Warfare may be triggered by the manipulation of symbols and indicies, rather than by overt aggression. So, for example, defacing the burial grounds of a rival or failing to sign a peace accord may trigger aggression.

5. The categories of warfare (e.g., categories of combatants) have a influential linguistic component insofar as these categories are inflected by the semantic structure of the language and its rules for the use of linguistic items.

6. Acts of warfare, like all human actions, have a belief, a desire, a judgement, and an intentionality component. This expressly implies a concept of the future and ability to construct an image of future events based on the outcome of present ones.

Many of those who analyze warfare allow themselves to be trapped in fruitless oppositions, particularly the oppositions between cause and effect, and between independent and dependent variables. Almost invariably, these analysts forget—or perhaps never understood—that warfare brings together two states of history: the history that is objectified in buildings, technology, codified laws, traditions, and books; and the history that is embodied in practices and dispositions of agents (Bourdieu, 1982,305). Warfare only ignites when societies, predisposed by their own history, aware of their outstanding investments, endowed with compatible dispositions and attitudes, take an interest in its prosecution.

Part of the popular philosophy of the West is the notion that we have understood a social or natural phenomena when analysis discovers its most primitive cause. Analysts have thus generated biologically-based theories of warfare on the unspoken premise that the biological ontologically precedes the social. Such theories are rarely content to illustrate how biological factors, such as hormonal balance, may interact with social and psychological factors. Eschewing modesty, they often proclaim that biological variables and their realization determine human warfare. The most general defect of such theories is that they are based on a pre-scientific logic, one which operates from the standpoint of underdetermination. Theories, such as that advanced by Wilson

(1972), are notable because they cannot account for the social organization of war, its conceptualization or imbrication of motives, the categories of warfare, and indeed all of the features listed above.[4]

It is quite clear that, on the rebound, warfare will affect the biological profile of warring groups. Hulse (1961), Divale (1970), and others have shown that in many primitive societies, war alters the age and sex composition of the population. It is clear also that the effects of depopulation vary dramatically from one group to the next, depending on their mode of production, rules for the transmission of land and other resources, marriage practices, and much more. Hulse (1961) has also demonstrated that warfare, for a variety of reasons, can stimulate or retard shifts in gene frequencies. So, returning warriors may carry back new diseases, captured females may introduce new genes as may conquerors, and the flight of a population to a new homeland may generate a new genetic mix. By the same token, it is likely that a call to war has a biological impact on the warriors, altering their willingness and ability to risk their life in what may be a mindless cause.

A Perspective on Warfare

An adequate, comparative theory of warfare must start with well-developed specific cases, and then synthesize these cases without doing violence to historical truths. In other words, the theory must be able to account for the production of warfare in specific instances, and, with equal dexterity, for the similarities of warfare across cultures. The starting point must be a theory which asserts that social action, especially as warfare, is never a mechanical causality. Rather, there must be a fundamental integration between the agents and the practices and institutions. The same history must inhabit both the soldiers and the institutions of war, so that in the words of Bourdieu (1982,306), history "is reflected in its own image," and soldiers, appropriated by a state of war, unquestioningly appropriate things inhabited by the same state. It is not only, for example, that ethnocentrism (or in-group, out-group relations) drive societies to war but the potential to initiate war leads societies to draw lines of demarcation. In the same vein, those who are involved in war (soldiers of various ranks) are imprisoned by the nets they cast over one another, motivating one another to combat even if they only reluctantly accept the reason given for the combat. An account of warfare must, in other words, be specific and move on several fronts at once, without unduly weighting any one factor.

I would like, at this point, to take up a specific case study and try to illustrate a situation where a society which had not engaged in war for more than a generation, indeed had embraced the understanding that economic development required the renunciation of war, is moving towards conflict once again. Hopefully, focusing on a specific circumstance, and adopting a non-reductionist viewpoint, will offer some insight for the development of a more general model.

The New Guinea Highlands

The Maring form a distinct cultural and linguistic group living in the interior Highlands of Papua New Guinea (located in the Western Pacific, and the second largest island after Greenland). Their homeland consists of some 350 square kilometers of steep, rugged, and heavily forested terrain straddling the slopes of the Bismarck Mountains and the border between the Western Highlands and Madang provinces. Those who live in the Jimi Valley are affiliated politically with the Western Highlands, and those of the Simbai Valley, with Madang. Land ownership follows the geometry of the mountainous environs and territorial units cultivate vertically banded strips that extend from the valley floor to the mountain crest. Considerable variation in altitude and heavy forestation permit production of a wide variety of crops and practice of a classical form of swidden agriculture. The society is internally organized into more than twenty clan clusters whose constituent clans are aligned through a history of intermarriage and material exchange. Marital and material alliances between Simbai and Jimi clan clusters are the rule and constant traffic between valleys has accelerated with pacification.

Introduction to Maring Warfare

The sweep of recent years has witnessed a resurgence of violence in the Western Highlands that recalls an older tradition. But the threat is not of a return to tradition—the resurrection of an earlier practice—but that clansmen will enlist violence in the service of modernity. I have interviewed more than one weekend warrior; Mt. Hagen men who work for government and business during the week, only to leave on Friday afternoon to fight (see Meggitt, 1977).

Traditional warriors, the Maring have for the past quarter of a century been at peace, a peace they perceive as lasting and durable despite the memorable accounts of conflict which are emblazed in their oral history. Nonetheless, violence is never out of the question altogether and occasional homicides still do occur. More importantly, many clansmen are again coming to see violence as an effective political and economic tool. Indeed, I have heard it said that the success of the Mt. Hagen Melpa in gaining concessions from the national government lies in their return to warfare. In 1980, both Banz and Kol, the two cardinal centers which lie between Mt. Hagen and Jimi Valley, were trapped in political dispute, spilling over into violence. And talk of warfare again has a place at the night fires when men of power talk about the problems and politics that beset them. For now it is "tok tasol," the mere whirring of the imagination, but within this decade it may be a reality if government initiates do not release the social pressures which well within Maring society. Economic development and the encroachment of modern institutions are generating pressures for which there are no peaceful indigenous solutions.

Traditionally, war erupted when a clansmen of one cluster killed a member of another cluster. In such cases, a principle of balanced reciprocity prevails and the clan cluster of the victim is compelled to seek revenge. This principle also encourages the continuation of violence, as a side which has suffered more deaths in a particular round of warfare feels obligated to initiate a new round of fighting. More than a strictly military affair, warfare activates the ritual system. Warriors try to align themselves with the Red Spirits, or the spirits of those who have died in previous battles, by performing a complex ritual in which fighting stones are hung from a center post of the special ritual house. The ritual formally states that the relationship between combatants is one of sanctified enmity and that it is moral to kill the opposition.

In many instances, the war dragged on sporadically for months. Oral histories tell the occasional rout of one of the parties, and the destruction of enemy grounds by the victor. This entailed the uprooting of pandanus trees, killing of pigs, burning of houses, to cite only the most prominent. However, warfare does not lead to an appropriation of the lands of losers, because victors are fearful that the spirits of their enemies will seek revenge if they use the territory.

In terms of its social position, the material, psychological and ritual preparations, the staging of the battle, the impact of victory or defeat, warfare was central to the making of Maring society. The status and self-image of a clan cluster rode on its military prowess. For men, warfare was integral to their construction of gender identity. It was a wholly male undertaking that was not only a statement of power, but a performance, made more significant by the fact that in local epistemology the truth of the word remains ever unknown until the deed.[5]

Warfare was the culture's social means of exemplifying maleness just as gardening is its natural means of exemplifying femaleness. Accordingly, men say, in moments of candor, that the distance between male and female lines converges as one moves into the present. One aspect of this more remarkable statement, which is no less than a summation of sexual identity in modern times, is that men fought not only to display power and dispell any traces of uncertainty as to their manhood, but to insure the certainty of its rewards: for the economy of power increases with and in proportion to its expenditure.[6]

National government was imposed on the Maring in 1955 and the last wars date from this period. These wars were apparently the most violent ever fought, the death toll sometimes eclipsing a hundred as tactical innovations, such as ambush and flanking maneuvers, were brought to bear. Not surprisingly, the clan clusters who were driven from their land have not easily forgotten their wounds.

The first order of business for the Australian government was the institution of a permanent peace, the surpression of warfare, rightly perceived as the key to local submission to a higher polity. Increasingly, and with less reservation, people came to accept formal legal remedies, and acquired the skills to use them to their own best advantage. Almost overnight, the court became a political arena in which old wars were renewed on new terms. A persuasive ideology flowered around this promise of legality; the attitude towards violence was used to draw a sharp horizon between traditional and modern life, as if "the law" was a ladder to a higher social world. Thus, the equation so often announced at public meetings: tradition equals warfare, modernity equals peace. In fact, there is much historical revision afoot, for the negotiation of dispute and the levy of compensation have always existed, though not in such a codified version. More to the point, traditional enmities have not died peacefully; and a hard-eyed assessment is that the court room, the local government council chambers, and the gaming boards are the current battle grounds. In essence, the new ideology belies a more enduring tradition.

All of this does not mean that the culture must choose between war and legality, for there is always the option to integrate them into a more encompassing set of strategies. Indeed, this is always the case with practice which uses the generative schemes of culture to shape itself to everchanging social conditions. Warfare must thus be seen as an articulate cultural response that draws on many social resources and traditions. It is what I call a consolidating or assimilative practice, one whose major purpose is to fashion elements from separate domains into a social form capable of accomplishing the current cultural objectives. There is both a theoretical and practical implication to this understanding. Without going into detail, a structuralism which perceives warfare as a conspicuous outpouring of social anomie, or a functionalism which looks to an underlying ecological reality, always underestimate the totalizing significance of war. The problem is not to discover the causes of warfare—any more than to discover the causes of ancestor worship, an axe, or a kin term; all are instruments in the service of goal-directed behavior. The task for indigenous advocates of peace, as well as outsiders, is to find ways of accomplishing the same objectives at lower social cost.

The Pressure of Modernization

The size of Maring groups, especially those in the vicinity of a health center, is on the upswing. Consider the demographic profile for the Kawatyi cluster whose pyramidal structure indicates a population boom. The advent of health facilities, changing attitudes towards hygiene and medicine, and the belief that numbers translate into social power have ignited this trend. Significantly, the benefits of watchful sanitation, health care, and good nutrition have all become associated with the modern world view, the campaign for these improvements publicly promoted by elected officials. By the same token, family planning has received little notice, both because Western medicine is traditionally clinicly oriented and because clansmen hold that the power and prestige of a group demand an upward population spiral. In addition, health centers are under the auspices of the Anglican church, which is never anxious to encourage birth control. Population growth is a function of the convergence of indigenous and external beliefs and practices.

FIGURE 1

AGE STRUCTURE OF KAUWATYI CLUSTER

```
                        2 - 75 - - 3
                      4 - - 70 - - 3
                    8 - - - - 65 - - - - 8
                17 - - - - - - - 60 - - - - - - - - - 15
            24 - - - - - - - - - - - 55 - - - - - - - - - - - - 20
        32 - - - - - - - - - - - - - - 50 - - - - - - - - - - - - - - 23
        33 - - - - - - - - - - - - - - - 45 - - - - - - - - - - - - - - - - - 32
      37 - - - - - - - - - - - - - - - - - - 40 - - - - - - - - - - - - - - - - - - - 37
  44 - - - - - - - - - - - - - - - - - - - - 35 - - - - - - - - - - - - - - - - - - - - - - 42
    40 - - - - - - - - - - - - - - - - - - - - 30 - - - - - - - - - - - - - - - - - - - - - 39
45 - - - - - - - - - - - - - - - - - - - - - - 25 - - - - - - - - - - - - - - - - - - - - - - - 44
49 - - - - - - - - - - - - - - - - - - - - - - - 20 - - - - - - - - - - - - - - - - - - - - - - - - 47
50 - - - - - - - - - - - - - - - - - - - - - - - 15 - - - - - - - - - - - - - - - - - - - - - - - - - 48
50 - - - - - - - - - - - - - - - - - - - - - - - 10 - - - - - - - - - - - - - - - - - - - - - - - - - 50
52 - - - - - - - - - - - - - - - - - - - - - - - 05 - - - - - - - - - - - - - - - - - - - - - - - - - 50
```

Totals males 496
      females 470

The relationship between population size and land pressure is defined by the principles of land use and their practical manipulation to serve social ends. One aspect of pacification was that the boundaries of clan clusters were frozen at that point in time. Seemingly necessary, and fair besides, this act has proven troublesome (LiPuma, 1982b). Formerly, boundaries fluctuated with the expansion and contraction of neighboring groups. Spatial discontinuity at the border made it possible to encroach on foreign land. Moreover, the borderland was often ambiguous, thus encouraging the use of neighboring lands on the grounds that it was one's own, if not for gardens, then at least as a source of raw materials. This zone of ambiguity, once a social mechanism for modulating man-land ratios, is now the scene of much legal confrontation. Often it is very possible for both sides to claim legitimately that their forefathers cultivated a certain tract of land. To make matters worse, because it is usually impossible to establish primacy, the issue cannot be easily resolved through legal channels.

Modernization has also seen the advent of cash cropping on a major scale, with coffee dominating production. From the standpoint of the community's welfare, coffee is protein on the vine inasmuch as growers use the monetary return to purchase tinned fish and meat. As a Maring diet is deficient in protein (Buchbinder, 1973), this is clearly a boon to nutrition so long as vegetable foods remain available. But coffee not only aids and abets population growth, it consumes appreciable and valuable garden land. I estimate that producers allocate as much as 10% of such land for coffee production. Cash cropping in conjunction with population increase means that greater and greater amounts of land must be put under cultivation. And Maring are very much aware that fallow periods are falling rapidly, dropping as dangerously low as three years for some. This shortening of fallow naturally reduces fertility which forces more land to be cultivated. So the inevitable cycle of less yield for more acreage begins, a cycle which induces land pressure in the absence of countervailing measures. The current local thinking is that the Jimi Valley people must mobilize enough political muscle to convince provincial authorities to send them fertilizer. Such action is unlikely and would not, in any case, resolve the contradiction.

Many clansmen, particularly those belonging to the larger clans, admit that they face a severe and growing land shortage. A scarcity of land takes on a deeper significance because its effects reverberate throughout the system. In that land is the social issue on which the organization of kinship and marriage depends, any specific disruption to the practices of land use undermines social reproduction in general. Land is instrumental to the construction of kinship. Maring believe that the confluence of male semen and female blood creates a child in the image of its parents (LiPuma, 1980). Bodily substances and tissue diminish or weaken with time and thus, individuals must replenish these substances for the sake of their well-being. Food is the principal means of renewing the body; it is the object of mediation which transmits the substance of the land to those who live from it. Thus, persons who eat the same food or food sown on the same land bear a co-substance relation. And, as the culture defines kinship in terms of co-substance, it follows that co-consumers are, to varying degrees, kinsmen. Within the clan, the free rotation of land, labor, and planting material is a primary means of binding its constituent subclans: of constructing a consubstantiality that defines agnation. Unfortunately for some clans, land shortages have seriously impeded this flow as the subclans vie to protect their rights and interests; some talk of second and third generation immigrants being asked to return to their original (and certainly now foreign) homeland; and there has been a rising incidence of intraclan land disputes: all unheard of scarcely a generation ago and all telling signs of social disruption.

The transfer of land is also crucial to the making and maintenance of affinal relations, for along with pigs, money, and military assistance, land is an indispensible element of affinal compensation. Such gifts usually take the guise of cultivation rights to some choice parcel of land, and the prospects of obtaining this return is a lending motive for the contraction of marriage. The flow and counterflow of land is part of the maintenance work which keeps the affinal relationship on course and running smoothly. The implications are magnified because the intermingling of gardens, cooperative production, and the trading of cultigens serve to unify the clan cluster. It oils the exchange relation at the same time that it promotes a co-substance tie. Thus, from all points of view, a land shortage disrupts social reproduction, making it all but impossible to fully realize the symbolic and material interests of the clan. To further inflame the situation, the end of warfare has permitted marriage relations to expand so that marriages between geographically remote clans now occur. This distance precludes the possibility of land transfers and thus, access to needed lands. This confers a greater significance on those land exchanges which can be made, and just at the point when such exchanges are most difficult. Thus it is that symbolic and material conditions conspire to make land pressure a pressing and progressively growing problem.

Local Perceptions and Perspectives

Although Maring tend to embrace modernization, perceptively aware they are making a virtue out of necessity, they are less than enthusiastic about the present state of affairs. They are particularly vexed by the fact that both national and provincial government display little concern for their well-being, offering neither political recognition nor practical assistance. The general feeling is that the people of the Jimi Valley have no political representation to speak of, no real voice in the making of their own future. This disaffection has crystalized around the conspicuous failure to complete the proposed road linking Koinambe with Mt. Hagen, thus cutting them off from economic and social benefits they hold dear. The road is an elegant and appropriate symbol of this knawing disaffection in that modernity is often called the "new road." Its absence is thus a symbol of the failure of an idea as well as practice. It is quite understandable, then, that the Jimi Valley people have expressed a wish to withdraw from the Western Highlands and become part of Madang Province. In essence, Maring believe that the government has turned a deaf ear to their pleas for recognition and essential services, concerned only with townspeople and never the rural communities.

With the development of rural education, a growing knowledge of the outside world, and a taste of the material benefits which lie ahead, the social expectations raise people's vision of the minimal conditions for a good life. Where before nearly everyone was content with the labor of cultivation and a sparse technology, today modern goods and services are in demand. What was several years ago a luxury item, now is seen as a necessity, the content of the economic categories shuffled upwards—and quickly acquiring not only a cognitive but an emotive basis in the psychology of desire. The lines redrawn on the economic plane continue into the social, heavily affecting the processes of socialization.

Perhaps the most significant example is that school leavers (usually from grade six) are seldom content to make their life in the village even when they have little chance of finding employment elsewhere. The result is a floating contingent of young men with no future in town and wanting none in the village. Concomitant with modernization and rising expectations is a dependence on exogenous conditions and organizations beyond local control. So, there is a growing sense of impotency as people see the bottom fall out of the coffee market or the price of imported goods skyrocket. The Maring have been forced to strike a bargain with the modern world: a better standard of living in exchange for a lower standard of control and personal involvement.

Conclusions

Specific

One way to assess the future of violence is, that given the prevailing social conditions and current interests and objectives, warfare is a highly practical response, especially should the state of affairs continue to edge the system closer to its social limits. Consider that the wisdom to abandon the ways of war, at first imposed on an unwilling people, was later embraced wholeheartedly by them as the practical road to a better life. Just as warfare was a pragmatic judgment, a decision that cultural objectives could best be achieved through violent means, so the swing of the pendulum towards a peaceful legality was made for the very same reason. The awful possibility is that a return to warfare might again be thought practical, and not with the intention of forsaking the gains of a legal system, but of including both as complementary means in a more encompassing political strategy. The possibility is that people will again see violence as a means of resolving the imbalance between a desire for more land and its unavailability; of reviving the now dying distinction between men and women; of finding a sense of purpose for the young men now adrift between traditional and modern lifestyles. Also, the influence of the Anglican mission, always a strong voice for peace, is waning, itself associated with the failing promise of the past two decades. Understand that my purpose here is not to justify conflict, less to see it as anything but destructive to community and country alike, but to appreciate from a Maring point of view why conflict may reignite in the Jimi as it has in so many other areas of the Highlands.

191

It should be clear from the foregoing discussion that if future conflict erupts, the following factors will be implicated:

1. Population expansion of a kind previously unknown.

2. Increased land pressure as clansmen devote more and more land to cash cropping, and fallow periods fall.

3. Rising community frustration over the impotency of the local leadership to obtain government support.

4. The disruption in food and land redistribution reverberating through kinship and marriage practices.

5. The symbolic linkage between warfare and definitions of manhood and status (see Lowman, 1971).

6. A tradition of warfare coupled with the perception that war will be effective in attaining desired objectives.

7. Lack of employment opportunities for semi-educated youths.

8. The unpredictable and uncontrollable fluctuations in the price of commodities, particularly coffee exports.

It is certainly not too late to ventilate the pressures which are brewing within the Jimi political sphere. It may even be the case that local leaders will find within their own culture the means to prevent violence—whether or not the government plays an active part. But the most likely scenario is that government failure to address the growing problems, such as promoting birth control and employment opportunities through road construction, will allow the political system to continue on its downward trajectory into violence.

Conclusions:

General

Maring warfare is organized in terms of kinship and principles of social organization. But the relations of kinship differ greatly from those of biology, and there is only a general correspondence —based, of course, on different principles—between genetic affinity and military alliances. In fact, a common feature of Maring warfare is that a clan which is allied to two other clans, who are themselves enemies, may wind up with its membership on both sides of the battle field. Sometimes this serves to repress or inhibit fighting as the "relatives in between" will act as intermediaries. But often as not, the conflict occurs.

For Maring, as for other groups, warfare is a named species of event; indeed it is subdivided into types of warfare based on the relationship between combatants and the severity of the fighting. There is a clear-cut difference between homicide and deaths due to warfare. This difference, which has great consequences for practical action, may be generated by a linguistic performative. That is to say, there are certain grammatically distinct linguistic forms which have the power (when uttered in the correct social context under the aegis of the proper authorities) to declare a change in the state of affairs. The ability of such words as "This country declares war" to generate such changes, is rooted in conventionally understood criteria and the structure of the grammar of the language in question.

The example from New Guinea also illustrates the broader point that, even in the most circumscribed cases, warfare synthesizes a variety of motives. Maring fight because they possess a sense of honor and live in a society where acts of honor have economic and political implications. And, given the power of society to define the terms of peoples' dispositions, this sense of honor which compels clansmen to seek revenge, possesses clansmen as much as clansmen possess it. Warfare is also the activity which exemplifies what it is to be a man. The rituals of war, which differentiate men from women also, because they reverberate throughout the social economy, differentiate men's tasks from women's tasks. By the same token, wars were fought for reasons more familiar to the West, such as disputes over the ownership of a tract of land.

There is also clear evidence that as two groups move closer to warfare, the level of aggression between individual members needed to ignite the conflict, becomes less and less. Indeed, what counts as aggression is itself part of the semiotics of social interaction. These may include a hostile gesture, increased military preparedness, a spoken word, and much more. Observe that what counts as an act of aggression depends on the coordinated intentionality of the parties in question. An ally who courts a woman is making a gesture intended to deepen the alliance; an enemy who courts a woman is committing an act of hostility. Similarly, the state of war may itself be signalled through a variety of signals, such as the sacrifice of a pig to the ancestor spirits of war, which bear no intrisic connection to the act of war itself. To summarize what I have said, human systems of warfare and aggression are based on a structure of mediations; that is, they are mediated by historical, linguistic, semiotic, economic, and psychological factors, and as importantly, by the interaction of such factors in specific contexts.

References

Bell, F.L.S. "Warfare Among the Tanga." *Oceania, 1935* 5:253-79.

Benedict, Ruth F., "The Natural History of War." In *An Anthropologist at Work*, ed. M. Mead, pp. 369-82. Boston: Houghton Mifflin 1934.

Bram, Joseph, *An Analysis of Inca Militarism*. American Ethnological Society monograph no. 4 1941.

Buchbinder, G., *Maring Microadaptation: A Study of Demographic, Nutritional, Genetic and Phenotypic Variation in a New Guinea Highlands Population*. Unpublished doctoral dissertation, Columbia University 1973.

Chagnon, Napoleon A., "Yanomamo—The Fierce People." *Natural History* 1967, 76:22-31.

Divale, William T., "An Explanation for Tribal Warfare: Population Control and the Significance of Primitive Sex-Ratios." *New Scholar*, Fall, 1970 pp. 173-92.

Ekvall, Robert B., "Peace and War Among the Tibetan Nomads." *American Anthropologist*, 1964, 63:1119-48.

Ellis, Florence H., "Patterns of Aggression and the War Cult in the Southwestern Pueblos." *Southwestern Journal of Anthropology*, 1951, 7:177-201.

Goldman, Irving, "Status Rivalry and Cultural Evolution in Polynesia." *American Anthropologist*, 1955, 57:680-97.

Kiefer, Thomas M., "Tausug Armed Conflict: The Social Organization of Military Activity in a Philippine Moslem Society." Philippine Studies Program, Research Series no. 7. Chicago: Department of Anthropology, University of Chicago, 1969.

Koch, Klaus-Frederich, "Cannibalistic Revenge in Male Warfare." *Natural History* 79, 1970, no.2: 41-50.

Leach, Edmund, "The Nature of War." *Disarmament and Arms Control*, 1965, 3:165-83.

LiPuma, E., "Economy and Society Among the Maring." *Anthropology Tomorrow*, 1979, 1:1-15.

———"Sexual Asymmetry and Social Reproduction among the Maring of Papua New Guinea." *Ethnos*, 1980, 1-2:34-57.

———"The Spirits of Modernization: Maring Concept and Practice." In *The Use and Abuse of Alcohol in Papua New Guinea*. Ed. Mac Marshall. Boroko, Papua New Guinea: IASER, 1982a.

Lowman, C., "Maring Big-Men." *Anthropological Forum*, 1971, 2:199-243.

Mead, M., "Alternatives to War." In *War: The Anthropology of Armed Conflict and Aggression*, ed. M. Fried, M. Harris and R. Murphy, 1968, pp. 215-28. Garden City, N.Y.: Natural History Press.

Meggitt, M., *Blood is Their Argument*. Palo Alto, California: Mayfield Publishing Company, 1977.

Paul, Benjamin D., "The Direct and Indirect Biological Costs of War." In *War: The Anthropology of Armed Conflict and Aggression*, ed. M. Fried, M. Harris and R. Murphy, 1968, pp. 76-80. Garden City, N.Y.: Natural History Press.

Rappaport, R., *Pigs for the Ancestors*. New Haven: Yale University Press, 1968.

Service, Elman R., *Primitive Social Organization: An Evolutionary Perspective*. New York: Random House, 1962.

"War and Our Contemporary Ancestors." In *War: The Anthropology of Armed Conflict and Aggression*, ed. M. Fried, M. Harris, and R. Murphy, 1968, pp. 160-67. Garden City, N.Y.: Natural History Press.

Vayda, Andrew P., "Expansion and Warfare Among Swidden Agriculturalists." *American Anthropologist*, 1961, 63:346-58.

Wallace, Anthony F.C., "Psychological Preparations for War." In *War: The Anthropology of Armed Conflict and Aggression*, ed. M. Fried, M. Harris, and R. Murphy, pp. 173-82. Garden City, N.Y.: Natural History Press, 1968.

Notes

1. Fieldwork for the current paper was conducted for 18 months in the Jimi Valley, and 4 months in the Simbai Valley under grants from the National Science Foundation and Wenner Gren. A preliminary version of this paper was delivered at the University of Papua New Guinea. I would like to thank Sarah Meltzoff and William Heaney for comments which have served to improve the end product; and Gou whose patience and understanding improved the original one.

2. Much of the anthropological literature has focused on the relation between warfare and social organization. The evidence indicates that warfare may be instrumental in promoting cohesion, stratification, and disorganization depending on both circumstance and culture. There is a general concensus that warfare is linked to the maintaining of identity and social boundaries, to the increase of internal cohesion, to the

definition of the group and the relative involvement of the members, and to a redefinition of power and authority. Note, for example, that Chagnon (1968) describes how a village headman will attempt to subdue internal warfare or conflicts because he fears that a fragmentation of the village will render it more vulnerable to attack. Similarly, Goldman illustrates how warfare was a major contributor to stratification in Polynesia. Benedict (1959) argues that warfare may have very decisive disorganization effects, noting that in many indigenous societies, warfare is relatively non-lethal with respect to the existence of that society.

3. Mead (1968) has spelled out the social and psychological sanctions surrounding homicide as opposed to warfare. In fact, she considers the legitimization of murder for war as one of war's primary defining features.

4. Speaking generally about theories of war, Otterbein (1973) writes that "sixteen approaches are used to classify the various studies of primitive warfare. As half of the approaches treat war as a dependent variable (i.e., as a phenomenon to be explained by independent variables), and the other half treat war as an independent variable (i.e., as a phenomenon that explains certain dependent variables, the theories can be grouped into two major categories: (1) causes of war and (2) effects of war. It is possible to pair the approaches and discuss a cause of war approach and then an effect of war approach . . . . The paired theoretical approaches are these:

Causes of War (Dependent Variable)	Effects of War (Independent Variable)
Innate aggression	On species
Frustration-aggression	Ethnocentrism
Diffusion	Acculturation
Physical environment	Ecological adaptation
Goals of war	Patterns and themes
Social structure	On social organization
Military preparedness	Survival value
Cultural evolution	Origins of the State

5. Rappaport (1968) has described Maring warfare with detail and depth, though perhaps underplaying the complexity of the motives involved. Vayda (1961) has also written about Maring warfare from the highly reductionist standpoint of ecological adaptation.

6. Other major anthropological studies of warfare include Bell (1935), Bram (1941), Ekvall (1964), Ellis (1951), Leach (1965), Paul (1968), Richardson (1960), Kiefer (1969), Hunt (1940), Kock (1970), Service (1962, 1970), and Wallace (1968).

Commentary: Sociological Analyses of Human Conflict

James A. Schellenberg

Sociological Analyses of Human Conflict

The paper by Edward LiPuma on "Warfare in the New Guinea Highlands: Theory and Ethnography in Conflict" seems to me to consist of two rather different parts. First, we have some general reflections on the nature of human warfare. Then, we have a discussion of the particular case of warfare in the highlands of New Guinea, with special attention to the Maring. I will comment on both of these topics in turn.

I find myself applauding the perspective that Edward LiPuma initially lays out for the consideration of human warfare. Although we might quibble over a few of his points about distinctive features of human warfare (some chimpanzees, for example, may engage in conflicts between groups as groups), in general it is good to get out on the table, so to speak, the awareness that organized human conflict is fundamentally different from fighting among other animals. And LiPuma gives us a good listing of the ways that human warfare is different. In so doing he also makes us aware of the variability of human motives and actions included in warfare, and properly warns us against any simple reductionism in explaining warfare.

However, I am a bit disappointed not to have a clearer theoretical statement about the nature of the type of warfare to be examined further in the paper. To say that:

Warfare only ignites when societies, predisposed by their own history, aware of their outstanding investments, endowed with compatible dispositions and attitudes, takes an interest in its prosecution.

does not take us very far in predicting or explaining outbreaks in group hostilities. In the end, we have a withdrawal from theorizing in favor of induction. "An adequate, comparative theory of warfare must start with well-developed specific cases, and then synthesize these cases without doing violence to historical truths." We then turn to the case of warfare among the Maring.

The key question implicit in most of LiPuma's paper is: why is there now a resurgence of warfare between local groups in the New Guinea highlands? Apparently the Maring have not yet returned to the patterns of warfare known before pacification in 1955; but some of their neighbors have shown a return to previous patterns of conflict, and there is at least a concern that the Maring are also headed in that direction. Why?

Before we deal further with the question of why the resurgence of warfare, let us note that the New Guinea highlands are not the same as they were thirty years ago. The modern world has arrived, and many people associate modernity with peace. We have in LiPuma's paper both a good summary of traditional warfare patterns and how the influences of the modern world are now placing new strains in Maring life. The threat of a return to violence, we are told, "is not a return to tradition—the resurrection of an earlier practice—but that clansmen will enlist violence in the service of modernity."

How could a revival of warfare be used "in the service of modernity"? Here, I do not find the paper providing a very clear answer. We have the suggestion that some neighboring tribes have caught the attention of the national government with a return to violence, which assumes that the attention of government is critical in resolving local distresses. And we have the suggestion that litigation over local issues, such as land boundaries, is frequently a very cumbersome process. But I still do not feel that the way warfare could effectively serve modern purposes for the New Guinea highlanders is very clearly indicated in the paper.

Why then do we have a resurgence of warfare in parts of the New Guinea highlands? After first admitting that I don't know (even after reading the helpful papers of LiPuma and Meltzoff), I would join LiPuma in assuming that strains of population growth and land pressures might be sources of instability and that traditional forms of social organization might still be strong enough to enlist fighting loyalties. However, it seems to me that a major return to a general pattern of warfare could only come if the power of the national government was losing its hold in the highlands and was being replaced by more traditional and localized centers of authority. But this would be quite different from fighting to gain concessions from the national government. The alternative possibility would be that there is a resurgence of sporadic violence, but that this is not really equivalent to the organized warfare of the old days.

I must confess that I am still, in the end, mystified by the resurgence of violence in the New Guinea highlands. Perhaps if I had been there, as LiPuma has, I would understand it better. But not having been there, my mind tends to wander to other forms of conflict with which I am more personally familiar, and in some of these there are similar themes of a resurgence of violence after a period of relative peace. I think of American race relations—of the riots after World War I and during World War II, of the relative calm, and then the outbreaks in the late 1960s. I think of conflict in Northern Ireland, which returned to violence about fourteen years ago after a generation of relative stability. And I think of my own studies of "county seat wars" in America—where local conflicts erupted (mostly toward the end of the nineteenth century) into sporadic violence over the issue of county seat location. Of course none of these forms of conflict is properly called a war; they have little in common with either modern international wars or more traditional and localized forms of warfare. But I do at least see some common threads running through these various forms of conflict, and I wonder if some of these might also apply to the New Guinea highlands. One common thread is that of social change unleashing new popular aspirations. Another is that of mobilization (using both traditional and nontraditional channels) for group action to achieve new aspirations. A third is the divided or uncertain role of governmental authority in relation to either supporting or repressing the movements afoot. Here is not the place to develop a theoretical structure for those considerations, only to wonder if they might not also apply to instances like the revival of violence in the highlands of New Guinea.

Finally, let us recognize that the question we have been pursuing can be refocused in another way. Given the strength of the

warfare complex in the highlands of New Guinea and its significance for manhood—as is well indicated by both the LiPuma and
Meltzoff papers—we might perhaps better ask: how can we
explain the generation of relative peace? How can we explain why
these tribes generally abandoned warfare? An answer is partly
given by LiPuma, but I am still not satisfied that I fully understand the pacification process and why it was generally effective.
The understanding of this question is, I think, the key to the
secondary question of why we see some of the patterns of warfare
returning. That is, what particular elements of the pacification
process may no longer be working, and why? It is within the
framework of this question that I believe we can most profitably
examine the return of warfare in the New Guinea highlands.

The Social Psychology of Aggression

Two of the points I especially appreciate about LiPuma's paper
are: 1. his insistence that warfare must be seen not only in terms
of collective institutions, but also as the actions of concrete
human beings; and 2. his pointing to the importance of the
linguistic component in warfare. Perhaps the point is obvious
once made, but we still need to be reminded that the institutions
of a society do not speak for themselves, but become expressed in
the beliefs, motives, and actions of living people. Warfare, too,
requires an incorporation into the everyday life activities of men
and women—especially of men. And linguistic forms may be
critical in this process of incorporation. A man becomes a "soldier," and immediately a whole host of new associations
—actions, motives and, yes, even beliefs—are triggered by this
entry into a new category of personhood. We cannot fully understand the actions of persons engaged in structured social conflict
unless we understand the linguistic conventions that define the
conflict and the primary roles played by its participants.

7.
Lethal Dance

Sara Keene Meltzoff

Introduction

Pulling the leaf wad plug out of his bamboo tube, Bambilai shook out the glossy red Bird of Paradise tail plume. He joined the growing gathering of newly washed and oiled clansmen preparing for that night's ceremonial dance. Men discussed everyday affairs, the potential power of rival dancers, and where each of the clansmen had obtained the necessary body decoration for the upcoming performance. Some of the men had hunted successfully in the virgin forest where the human settlement ended; others had borrowed well from other clansmen, drawing on trade relations built up during the year. The range of paraphenalia assembled was consistent with their pre-arranged theme, although telling individual differences were apparent to anyone skilled in the social semiotics of dance. Each participant weighted the sheen and brilliance of the others' furs and feathers, the rarity of jungle plants, and whether the golden crescent and other shells and beads were plentiful. And each dancer begged audience approval, desiring appreciation of his "grease" or radiance of health and magnetism to attract more such power symbols.

The most powerful and awe-inspiring dancers drew women to them, and created new allies for future dances, exchanged relations central to the economic system, and warfare (or, more likely, nowadays, for local government considerations). Though the dancers were concerned with their own appearance, they took great pains to insure that the clan group danced intact and

201

maintained a common front, for men are evaluated less on the basis of individual merits than on the merits of their clan as a whole. And, from a religious standpoint, the men would dance as a unit to demonstrate that their living dead (ancestor spirits) were present and supportive of their efforts. Indeed, it was only with the assistance of ancestor spirits, and thus by virtue of the sacrifices made in their honor, that a clan was able to pyramid its strength and wealth. In a strong sense, dances paralleled warfare, pitting one group against another, and were also a correlary of warfare in that relations created at ceremonial dances became the main alliances of war.

The Highland Setting[1]

New Guinea Highlanders are intrinsically competitive and live within the fold of competitive societies. The competition is all the more intense because there are no rigid hierarchies (Strathern, 1966) or hereditary offices (Berndt, 1962). Political enclaves and factions are relatively small; they are led by self-made leaders who must compete with one another. A principal sphere of competition for big-men is ceremonial exchange, and less dramatically, the numerous smaller transactions that fill daily economic activity. A second domain of competition between men and groups is ceremonial dancing. Frequently, ceremonial exchanges and dancing are combined into a single event.[2]

Men controlled warfare in the bygone days just as they control ceremonial exchanges and dances today, and indeed they perceive the control of the latter as a logical extension of the former. What is essential about the dance is that the message is conveyed in terms of acts and substance, implicit recognition that all communicative media are not equal. The characteristic decorations of dancers and the forms of dance, which emphasize power and strength, communicate more and in a different way than words alone. Dance and dancers do not simply state that they are powerful, but performs acts of power and strength. They index a social state and are thus that much more convincing than language alone.

There is also something intrinsically important about the use of the body, as opposed to words. As Rappaport (1979) suggests in another context:

I . . . propose that the use of body defines the self of the performer for himself and for others. In kneeling, for instance, he is not merely sending a message to the effect that he submits in ephemeral words that flutter away from his mouth. He identifies his inseparable, indispensible, and enduring body with his subordination. The subordinated self is neither a creature of insubstantial words from which he may separate himself without loss of blood, nor some insubstantial essence or soul that cannot be located in space or confined in time. It is his visible, present, living substance. . . . As "saying" may be "doing," "doing" may also be an especially powerful—or substantial—way of "saying" (page 200).

More than simply drawing a strong connection between physical acts and social efficacy, this viewpoint expresses the indigenous Highland view of the power of acts over speech. It is no accident that in very many Highland languages a single verb embraces both "to know" and "to see." And if we embrace the advanced theoretical perspective of Bourdieu, the point has even deeper significance; for Bourdieu writes that the "principle generating and unifying all practices, the system of inseparably cognitive and evaluative structures which organizes the vision of the world in accordance with the objective structures of a determinate state of the social world . . . is nothing other than the socially informed body" (1977,124). In other words, the socially informed body becomes the perfect medium for unifying thought and practice, the individual and the social, which allows for the construction of an individual aesthetic that is also a social commentary. This further points out that in human societies, the relationship between form (e.g. the use of dance and body decoration) and function (to index the state of political affairs) is open to history and creativity.

Dancing and Fighting

Highlanders are frequently involved in ceremonies where pigs and shell valuables are exchanged. These "gifts" are couched in terms of compensation for allies or former enemies as a result of their losses in past combat. They have the spirit of war indemnities. An ally who has lost some of its men fighting on behalf of the main combatant will receive death compensation. "Exchanges are ostensibly made to keep the peace; but they contain a latent rivalry, expressed in the size of the gifts, in speeches, and in decorations themselves" (e.g., type and size of bird plume). These payments invite reciprocal exchanges between groups (Strathern, 1971,14).

The entire process of dancing against one's enemies and potential allies is an aggressive action, and is so viewed by the participants, even as they appreciate its other qualities. Without the presence of guests, the dance is essentially meaningless, being drained of its social content. Dancers dress like warriors. Over cleaned skin goes charcoal to heighten the vision of strength and spirit participation. Blackness is felt to be a sign of ferocity and stealth, necessary for successful combat. Dancers—perhaps assisted by a helper—will paint red and white geometry to blend with the features of the human face. The dancer's nose is made more prominent, the eyes are enlarged by color contrasts. The head is transformed by large headdresses or elaborate wigs. For the Simbai Valley people, the most prized part of their costume is the bonnet wig, enlarging their short stature by several feet once the feathers are set into place on the top. The bonnet is encrusted with iridescent green scarab beetle thoraxes strung onto bamboo spits and set on a turban-shaped frame. In other areas of the Highland, wigs adorned with feathers is the custom.[3]

For any dance ceremony, the guests are a key element precisely because the structure of the dance is to recreate the rivalries of warfare. The Australian Administration penetrated the dense, steep terrain of the interior only after the finale of World War II. The first act of the administration was to seize control by prohibiting the endemic warfare. In the most easily accessible areas, the Pax Australianus (as pacification was called) was established in the late 1940's. In the Bismarck mountain area, pacification came in 1956, though not without some bloody encounters. And, finally, the most remote areas of the Highlands have only been contacted in the late 1970's, though now no longer under the auspices of Australia but an independent Papua New Guinea Government. Ironically, there has been a resurgence of warfare in the regions pacified first in 1945.

Throughout the Highlands, warfare was rarely, if ever, fought to appropriate the land of a neighbor. When the loser was routed from their homeland, the territory remained deserted for a number of years and then was slowly repopulated by the previous owners. In this way, the ownership of land remained relatively stable over long periods of time despite the disruptions of frequent wars. It was only at the border of the two territories, where boundaries were not clearly established by the presence of gardens (because of the tendency of clans to concentrate in the center of their territory), that land shifted back and forth between rivals. Indeed, planting at the border commonly provoked warfare. It was one of the ways that a clan could signal hostile intentions.

In Highland social systems, the center of gravity is the clan or group rather than the individual. Accordingly, if members of one clan murdered a member of another clan, revenge was likely to be taken on any of the members of the perpetrator's clan. The system of balanced reciprocity was, in other words, calculated on a clan basis. Prior to pacification, men would frequently be slain or injured for walking across enemy clan territory.

Young men preparing for a dance today are well versed in the stories of war, for the outcome of past encounters is inscribed in present status and authority of the different clans. Endless hours are spent recounting the glories of the days before pacification, and young men know the details of wars they could not have witnessed. Inter-clan aggression, which is part and product of the coming-of-age for men, is nowadays channelled into gambling (particularly dice and card games), sports such as soccer (which often assume a violent spirit never intended by their inventors), and dancing.

In a calculated attempt to harness and control, the Australian Administration developed the Mt. Hagen and Goroka Shows, where clans stream in from across the Highlands in full regalia to compete. As in other contexts of dance, a key element is that the aggression exhibited by dancer-warriors is not an uncontrolled, anti-social rage, but a highly ritualized form of social practice. That is to say, the dancing is stylized, repetitive, stereotyped, and highly distinctive. There is a full sense of identification between the dancers and the dance: the dancers are identified with the dance.

The dance is ritual because it does not simply have an audience, in the same way that all drama does, but a congregation which participates as an act of social definition. Dancing in this sense is a cultural mode of communication which operates simultaneously on several channels and with different types of signs. In one dimension, the dance reveals the current psychic, social, or practical state of the participants; in the other dimension, the structure of the dance and the activities which surround it are a backdrop, themselves amenable to manipulation in the quest to communicate and create social situations. Note that there is no intrinsic linkage between dancing in the present ceremony and fighting in a future war, other than a symbolic connection where the dance functions as a promise, and those who have danced but failed to fight are held accountable by the community at large. Note also that it is the difference in time between dancing and fighting, and thus the introduction of risk, which crystalizes the social relation. The time lag between the promise (made by the dance) and its fullfilment, is always social time, to be manipulated by the parties in the pursuit of their own interests. To put this in a pan-primate perspective, it is between the relatively automatic, instinct-based reactions of non-human primates and the total arbitrariness possible for human agents that the coherence of social practice is constructed. It is for this reason that human aggression seems to encompass all of the forms of aggression available to non-human primates, and then some. It is also for this reason that dancers not only pledge support in future rounds of fighting, but do so with a degree of delicacy that explains where they stand on the continuum from provision support to unconditional assistance. They indicate their position in terms of the possibilities for variation within the context of the ritual. For example, it is always possible to vary the number of dancers such that an ally who sends a small contingent probably harbors an equally small commitment (unless, of course, this message is countervened by another message—in this case a meta-commentary). Or, another group of allies may dance particularly strongly to indicate their willingness, perhaps eagerness, to sponsor a war. As the concept of meta-commentary tries to illustrate, the communication may be multi-layered; this layering either made possible directly by a linguistic channel or indirectly by analogy to this channel. In essence, the gestures, postures, and ornamentation of the dancers are cultural. Their meanings are determined by a socially informed body and the meta-communication which languages makes available.

This structure allows Highlanders to selectively appropriate the behavior of different animals. Thus, Highlanders say that they imitate the Bird of Paradise in their elaborate displays and songs. Paradise, unique to Papua New Guinea, are the most prized feather; they are wild because they come from the jungle where humans do not inhabit. Hard to shoot with bow and arrow, living in remote areas over great areas, hunting the Paradise demands archery skills and the assistance of the ancestor spirits. The Bird of Paradise clears a tree branch and puts on daily displays to attract females. Their cultural correlary is the building of dance grounds, the grand display of plummage, and the chorus of cries sounded by the males. Bird of Paradise are graced with irridescent body capes, tail and head wires, and tail plumes. Highlanders are intimate with the habits of the Paradise and by paralleling its behavior, they exhibit the wild, and thus only barely controlled, part of their own nature. One of the primary aspects of the art forms of dance and ornamentation is that they mediate between men and nature, bridging the chasm which culture has created.[4]

In practice, ceremonial exchanges, ordinary business dealings and warfare compensations are intertwined. This interdigitation of exchanges is possible because all are based on the principle of reciprocity. Thus, an exchange given in one round of presentations will be reciprocated in the next. The Stratherns explain:

> . . . there is a further factor involved in the relations between exchanging groups, which is important: where groups are in a reciprocal exchange relations, they are likely to have been both allies and enemies to each other on different occasions in the past. They are rivals, and in their exchanges they try to outdo each other by the total size of their gifts. Rivalry is built into the . . . transaction as a premise, since the main gift should exceed the solicitory gifts in value and should also exceed previous gifts given by those now receiving. We are dealing with groups which confront and test each other over time with demonstrations of their wealth (Strathern and Strathern, 1971,48-49).

In essence, though the ceremony pivots around dancing and its clear implications for alliance, much, much more goes on which influences the outcome of the dance, and the future strategies which flow from it.

Warfare Decorations and Dress

All of the decorations worn for formal ritual occasions are meant to communicate to members of the clan, and to outsiders, information concerning the strength of the wearer. In so doing, they mark off a ceremonial occasion from those of ordinary affairs which are more concerned with pragmatic affairs, such as the tending of gardens, rather than the process of social differentiation. On these ritual occasions, the relationship between the hosts and the guests is one of both friendship, as indicated by the invitation and the offering of food, and hostility, as demonstrated by the nature of the dancing and dressing. Naturally, the relative proportions of friendship and hostility will depend on the seriousness of previous warfare, and projected state of future relations. The consolidation of common interests in the present may override disagreements and deaths of the past. There is a direct connection between the elaborateness of the finery donned by the dancers and the seriousness of the wars conducted previously. There is thus a strong association between the donning of headdresses and situations of hostility. Strathern (1971) notes that the warrior's entire body was charcoaled because, in local eyes, such darkening of the body made the warrior appear frightening and powerful. Poison is associated with the darkness of the color black, and poison is often brewed in stone hollows in which charcoal remains. Accordingly, black is connected with the two major forms of inflicting death: sorcery and violence. Since warfare springs from the motive of revenge, black is also related to revenge, to the reestablishment of an equilibrium between clans.

The Mechanics of Warfare

Many Highlanders believed that war was essential to their well-being. As women determined themselves as women by working in their gardens, so men exemplified themselves as men by engaging in warfare and related activities. In many instances, the ancestors demand that the living avenge their death. Unappeased ghosts may harass delinquent kinsmen by not shielding the living from the attacks of evil spirits or assistance in the fertility of the gardens. Recall that almost all deaths in New Guinea societies are attributable to actions of other men, be this action actual physical attack or the poison administered by sorcerers. Once an incident sparks a war, the bigmen from both groups call upon their allies to join them in battle. And those who have danced together now join one another on the battle field. After the call has been issued, the men of the central clan cluster and their allies prepare themselves with feathers and paint and assemble on the field of battle. Ritual preparations leading up the convening on the battle field are frequently elaborate.

War leaders conduct divinations to determine the course of the battle. Often this involves incantations which call upon the wisdom of the ancestor spirits. Through the intermediary of a shamen, the ancestor spirits identify those opponents upon whom the propitiants should concentrate their arrows.

In many instances, the fighting begins by agreement of both sides, on a battleground of common choice. Both combatants may, in fact, have spent time and energy the previous day clearing the field of debris. The warriors of both parties meet with arrows and spears in a skirmish, and having exhausted their energy and munitions, retire for refreshment. New groups of warriors replace the retiring outfit, the fighting being intermittent. As the fighting intensifies and the combatants draw closer and closer, the warriors underline their bravery and agility by dodging spears and arrows. Both groups use barbed arrows, especially designed for warfare, whose points break off when they become embedded in the flesh. After a day of fighting, the two sides withdraw, sometimes because the afternoon rains have unleashed their torrential downpour. A series of such engagements may continue for weeks on end, with neither side gaining a clear advantage or, for that matter, suffering more than light casualties. Most deaths do not occur as a result of formal encounters, but as a consequence of ambushes and raids when a small party is set upon by much greater numbers.

Maintaining the support of allies becomes increasingly difficult as the fighting drags on. Not only do allies become tired of participating in a fight not of their making, but they are unable to make exchanges and carry on their necessary business. Victories, in many cases, went to the allies who could continue to mobilize and motivate their allies the longest. In very large measure, then, the entire nature of fighting strategy depended heavily on an antagonists capacity to judge the level of commitment of allies. In this respect, judging a groups commitment during a festival, and the cementing of the alliance, was central to the political fortunes of the clan. It is little wonder then that clansmen took the dance ceremonies very seriously. For defeat generally meant being forced to flee to the clan homeland for the ground of a distant ally, and to suffer the indignity of being treated as a guest for the years to come.

When the opposing forces have exhausted their desire to fight or one side has been defeated, the combatants can call a halt to the exchange of raids, injuries, and deaths by agreeing to a truce. This may be a permanent halt or a temporary respite between rounds of warfare. Throughout the Highlands, pigs are exchanged to terminate the fighting. Other potent symbols, such as replanting of *rumbim* which was uprooted to signal a state of war, may also be activated. Pigs are the food of formal exchange or the cultivation of human relationships, while plants indicate that the clan has returned to a state of gardening and material reproduction, rather than the time out of time that is warfare.

Retaliation and Compensation

Throughout Papua New Guinea, the establishment of Australian control led to the creation of patrol posts or government outstations. This lead to the appointment of local headmen in the early years, and later to elected local government councilors whose main office included reporting fights and bringing disputants to patrol headquarters for trial. This action served to repress fighting, as the perpetrators were either jailed or fined. Nonetheless, such action did little to relieve the causes of fighting or to give any solice to the victims.

A principal reason why Western remedies had little effect on war in the Highlands is a difference in principle. A fundamental premise of Western law, upon which the law of New Guinea is based, is that an injury or death may be due to entirely accidental causes. But for the people of the Highlands, the question is not whether a clansmen was struck down by malaria or some other sickness, but why *he* was struck down rather than some other individual. The general understanding is that misfortune is always due to sorcery, spiritual cause, or other forms of intervention. This is especially true when a young man or a woman in her prime is struck down. Such deaths, like those which result from direct physical action, demand revenge and redress.

After noting that there have been many recent outbursts of war and vengence fighting, and resulting demands for compensation, Brown (1979) quotes the following passage from the Papua New Guinea Newsletter of July 2, 1975:

> After more than 50 years of fighting and bitter feelings, members of the Niniga and Kumai clans have settled their differences as a mark

of respect for Papua New Guinea's Independence year. At a meeting in Minj (a Highland's town) recently, attended by 4000 warriors, the Ninigas made a settlement of 200 pigs, four cassowaries (a large flightless bird used in compensation payments), and K2000 in cash (about US$3000), and the long-standing feud was over. Most of those present could not remember what the years of fighting were all about and only a few old men remembered the day when a Kumai man was killed in a food garden by a party of Niniga warriors. It was thought to be a Niniga garden, but no one could really remember after so long. Certainly no one remembers the man's name (a sign that a certain era has passed in New Guinea chronologies). Assistant District Commissioner at Minj, Don Simmons, who attended the ceremony, said the compensation payment was the second by the Ninigas. The first, made many years ago, consisted of 500 pigs and traditional riches, but was considered inadequate. Fighting had continued until this meeting and compensation payment had been arranged. Mr. Simmons said the two clans would now live in harmony and understanding.

One of the most distinctive features of fighting in the Highlands is that almost every culture has its own means of initiating offenses, assembling support, counting and assessing damage, etc. The Maring, for example, conduct a major festival, called a *kaiko* (meaning dance), which confirms the termination of hostilities. At the conclusion of a war between major enemy clan clusters, a preliminary truce is made. In the following few years, the two sides accumulate sufficient pigs to hold a major slaughter. Territory abandoned during the hostilities, is reclaimed and new planting stakes are put in to mark off boundaries. Preparations for the *kaiko* include the planting of special gardens and fattening of pigs, as well as the assumption of taboos and ceremonies of fertility. The ritual lasts for an entire year, with a variety of special events. The events embrace ritual sacrifices to the ancestor spirits, songs to commemorate the war, and elaborate dancing in full regalia. It is, ironically, the creation of the dance which generates new alliances and establishes the terms for the next round of warfare. The killing and sharing of pigs is the culmination of the cycle of war and peace, indicating that a clan is wealthy, has strong, clearly-defined relations to allies, and has paid its compensation.

Causes/Effects of Warfare

Because of the intimate and intrinsic connection between a

211

clan and its membership, warfare frequently starts following violence of some sort between members of the two clans. The likelihood of warfare is directly correlated with the number of previously fought wars. The most proximate "causes" of warfare are, as deduced by local people:

1. The marriage, or taking, of a woman without the consent of the woman's agnates.

2. Sexual misconduct between members of opposing groups; the woman's group feeling that their integrity has been violated by the act. In modern terminology, Highlanders sometimes describe such acts as "rape" even when they occur with the woman's consent, for given the groupism which pervades Highland society, a woman's consent was not, strictly speaking, her's to give.

3. Shooting a pig which has invaded a garden, stealing crops, or poaching game and appropriating wild resources. Given the extremely strong attachment between clansmen and their ancestral lands, an attachment which is rooted in the clan cycle of material reproduction, such actions as stealing crops represent a symbolic invasion as well as a material one.

4. The causing of death through sorcery. As noted earlier, one clansmen may cause the death of a member of another clan through the use of magic.

In a strong sense, the underlying motivation for warfare in all of New Guinea Highlands is land. This does not mean land in the simple sense of appropriation for increased productivity. Rarely is land directly taken from the defeated and, in many instances, such appropriation would not offer any opportunity for increasing productivity. Different clans usually live in similar ecological zones and they grow exactly the same products. Warfare over land centers on land as a structural element in a complex of structural relations, constituting social reproduction. By social reproduction, I mean the capacity of a clan to physically reproduce and, more importantly—because more problematic—to reproduce a way of life. As the main source of male continuity, land represents and embodies the temporal continuity of the clan. Throughout the Highlands, mythology, ritual ceremony, and common wisdom depicts men as the great trees of the primary forest, their roots deeply entrenched in the soil and their permanence assured. This is reflected also in marriage practices where the woman moves to the clan lands of her husband on marriage. There is also a material attachment through the cycle of reproduction. In this cycle, the membership of a clan bear a common identity because they have eaten food from the same land, land upon which the bodies of the dead have been buried and returned to the earth. Note, here, that the conception that stealing food is justification for warfare stems from the premise that the eating of food is a means of making kin relations. In other words, the theft of food, quite apart from its material aspects, is a symbolic statement of disregard, a form of insult which challenges the sense of honor of the clan. Women are also intimately related to the clan's social reproduction, for they are not only the means of increasing its numbers, and of providing labor for the raising of gardens and pigs, but an essential gift of exchange between clans. Clans related by marriage bear an intrinsic connection. They dance at each other's festivals, serving as allies in warfare and friends in peace. It is for this reason that the taking of a woman is a cardinal offence against the clan as a social body. It is also why the consent of the woman is very irrelevant to the matter at hand.

It is here that the cycle of war and peace and the creation of allies through dance join hands at a deeper level. It is precisely at dance festivals, when men come from many clan clusters and display their wealth and attractiveness as allies, that theft and "rape" are most likely. It is why the circumstances for the generation of allies and friendships is also the forum for the making of conflict.

The Resurrection of Violence

An observer who toured the Highlands in the late 1950's and early 60's could easily come away with the impression that warfare had come to a decisive end under Australian administration. Below this surface of tranquility, many of the indigenous problems were reasserting themselves, unrelieved by the move into modernization, and perhaps even exaccerbated. Indeed, Meggitt (1977) notes for the Enga that the increasing frequency of fighting "was strongly rooted in conditions engendered by the earlier period of imposed peace and the extension of public services" (p.156).

Not surprisingly, the resurrection of warfare as a legitimate means of resolving problems has placed renewed emphasis on the festivals and dances of the modern era. This resurgence of warfare was actually a simple transformation of previous condi-

213

tions, to the extent that the period of peace could be seen in retrospect as a hiatus between hostilities. As soon as peace was imposed, a flood of legal cases began to engulf the newly created courts and adjudicators. People viewed the courts as the modern equivalent of battle, with each side pressing home its claims for compensation in land or money or pigs. This turn to legal debate also fit into the Highland tradition of oratory, where big-men mobilized community sentiment by virtue of their speaking abilities.

However, the courting process soon began to break down in some areas. The limits of the court system became apparent first in those areas which were pacified first. As this modern form of warfare failed to resolve the problems resolved by war, people quickly returned to the older forms of dispute settlement. Thus, warfare is again commonplace in some areas of the Highlands.

References

Allen, M., *Male cults and secret initiations in Melanesia* Melbourne: Melbourne University Press, 1967.

Berndt, C., "The ascription of meaning in a ceremonial context in the Eastern Highlands of New Guinea," in *Anthropology in the South Seas*, ed. J. Freeman and W. Geddes, Avery Press, 1959.

Berndt, R. M., *Excess and Restraint*, Chicago: Univ. of Chicago Press. 1962.

Brown, P. *Highland Peoples of New Guinea*, Cambridge: Cambridge University Press, 1978.

Bulmer, R. "The strategies of hunting in New Guinea," *Oceania*, Vol. 38., 1968, pp.302-318.

Forge, A., "Art and society in the Sepik", *Proceedings of the Royal Anthropological Institute, 1966, pp. 23-31.*

"*The Abelam artist.*" In *Social Organization*, ed. M. Freedman, London: Frank Case, 1967.

Gilliard, E., "New Guinea's rare birds and stone age men." *The National Geographic Magazine*, 1953, vol.53. pp.421-88.

Meggitt, M., *Blood is their Argument* Los Angeles: Mayfield Publishing, 1977.

Pouwer, J., "Review of Van der Veen, the Merok Feast of the Sa'dan Toradja," Journal of the Polynesian Society, 1967, vol.76, pp.104-8.

Simpson, C., *Adam in plumes.* Sydney: Angus and Robertson, 1955.

Rappaport, R., *Pigs for the Ancestors*, New Haven: Yale Univ. Press, 1968.

Strathern, A., *Ceremonial exchange in the Mount Hagen area*, Unpublished Ph.D. dissertation, Cambridge University, 1966.

Strathern, A. and M. Strathern, *Self-Decoration in Mt. Hagen*, London: Duckworth and Co., 1971.

Notes

1. The archaeological record indicates that men first crossed from the Asian mainland into New Guinea some 30,000 years ago. The earliest sites date from about 25,000 when even the highest New Guinea mountains, stretching 15,000 feet upwards, were glaciated. A decisive turn in the history of the island came about 5000 years ago when the sweet potato was introduced. This allowed larger settlements to flourish in the Highlands and was no doubt instrumental in the rapid population diffusion.

2. Fuller accounts of ceremonies and festivals can be found in Allen (1967), Berndt (1959), Simpson (1955), Pouwer (1967), and Forge (1966).

3. For Highlanders, dances are meant to express their desires for health, strength, and fertility—fertility in the complex sense of total social reproduction. Paradoxically, dances not only try to solicit ancestral assistance and the help of allies, but also to demonstrate to the world at large that these goals have already been achieved. As a compounded communication, the dance is both a form of propitiation and a celebration of success. Decorations at dances embody these dual purposes. There is an internal logic to dance ceremonies, which stipulate that insofar as the dance is an indication of health and strength, individuals who have been beset by illness or economic misfortune should not join in. In some cases, a dance celebration is delayed because a clansmen of the host group has died. As Strathern and Strathern (1971,134) note: ". . . self-decoration is the antithesis of mourning. In mourning, the body is neglected, dirtied, even mutilated by the tearing-out of hair and the amputation of finger joints; by decoration, it is enhanced and made attractive."

4. A more complete account can be found in Bulmer (1968), Gilliard (1953), and Forge (1967).

Commentary: The Evolution of Violence and Aggression

Chet S. Lancaster

Aggressive behavior has been easily learned, practiced in play, encouraged by custom, and rewarded by most human societies for thousands, if not millions of years (Bigelow, 1972). It may be that the human organism in early life is "primed" to acquire with relative ease, certain elementary behavior patterns such as aggression, that there is a special facility for learning, along lines that have been adaptively valuable for the species over a very long time in the course of its evolution.

Stone Age humans originally evolved as hunter-gatherers and this has had immense significance on what we are today. (see Washburn and Lancaster, 1968). Unfortunately, there is a tendency in the popular media and in some versions of "sociobiology" to over-emphasize *male hunting* in our primal adaptive nature as hunter-gatherers, and to assume that aggression and dominance have always been key elements in our evolutionary struggles to survive. This emphasis downplays the female gatherer, along with the non-aggressive human capacity to maintain adaptive cooperative groups.

There are certain aspects of human evolution that may make aggressive behavior easy to learn, as Hamburg and van Lawick-Goodall (1974) noted in their studies of aggression in chimpanzees and humans. However the most impressive similarity is the deep and enduring quality of attachments in the higher primates, reaching a culmination in chimpanzee and human interpersonal bonds. As in humans, affectionate bonds between chimpanzee mothers and their off-spring, and between siblings, are commonly strong and long-lasting.

216

As complex organisms have evolved, behavior has become an exceedingly important way of performing adaptive tasks that contribute to species survival. The role of behavior in adaptation is not only a function of individuals, but of groups as well. This is strikingly true of the higher primates. Studies of non-human primates, and of hunting-gathering humans in their natural habitats, show that group living has conferred significant selective advantage upon the more highly developed primates. Derived from social organization, this selective advantage has probably included: protection from predators, meeting nutritional requirements, protection against climatic variation, dealing with injuries, facilitating reproduction, and preparing the young to adapt to the environment. Both non-human primates and early humans have organized themselves into small-scale societies that provide intimate, enduring emotional attachments. We feel comfortable and "well" when these attachments are present and uneasy when they are not. To a large extent, the presence of satisfying attachments defines what we mean by "mental health." These attachments also engender mutual assistance in difficult or emergency situations. They provide clear guidelines for individual behavior that are highly relevant to survival requirements (Washburn & Harding, 1975).

The important adaptive functions of primate groups alerts us to the evolutionary significance of the interindividual attachments that make group life possible and meaningful. Individuals have evolved to seek and find gratifying those situations that have been highly advantageous in the past survival of the species (Hamburg, 1963). Emotional attachments and motivations necessary for species survival tend to be quite pleasurable; they are easy to learn and difficult to extinguish. Their blockage or deprivation leads to tension, anger, substitutive activity, and depression. Such blockage is often accompanied by emergency-type physiological responses that support actions necessary to correct the situation, leading to repair or replacement of the threatened attachments.

In human beings, a conjunction of behavior patterns very early in life fosters the formation of deep interpersonal bonds. As Hamburg and van Lawick-Goodall (1974) put it, "A perceptual preference in the visual sphere (for the human face), another preference in the auditory sphere (for the human voice) and a simple motor pattern (the smile), come together in such a way as to elicit caretaking, affectional responses from the mother, and to facilitate a deeply satisfying ongoing transaction between mother and infant that deepens the mutual bond between them over time."

Similarly, human *adults* have a tendency to form highly adaptive, fairly long-lived mating pairs or attachments which are quite unlike the sexual relationships and reproductive arrangements of other primates. Both mates make unusually large parental investments for many years while bringing their slowly maturing children to the point of successful reproduction in the next generation (Lancaster & Lancaster, 1983). Like the initial mother-infant attachment, the human mating attachment and indeed the father-child, sibling-sibling, and other close family attachments, are quite pleasurable. They have become easy to form and both difficult and painful to extinguish, because of their obviously important evolutionary advantages.

In humans, there is an inverse relationship between attachment and aggression. The strength of a bond will determine the effort against any threat to sever it. While we can be aggressive creatures, and it is fashionable to take note of this, much of our aggression comes in response to threatened life-supporting attachments whose proper functioning is critical for mental and physiological well being. In our evolutionary past, and therefore in our present evolutionary nature as human beings, a capacity for peaceful attachment, sharing and caring, has probably been more important than aggression (J. Lancaster, 1978). Attachment enables us to form and maintain the cooperative relationships and groups necessary for survival and well being. Bowlby (1975) has emphasized that anger is one of the most common responses to unwilling separation or threats of separation in the mother-infant relationship. His main focus is on the child's anger towards its mother, though he recognized that other targets are possible. To the extent that mother-infant attachment is a prototype for all subsequent human attachment, anger experienced in this context early in life paves the way for anger later in life in the context of jeopardy to other important attachments, especially those between mates, between parents and children, siblings, and other intimates habitually enjoying multi-faceted interdependence in human groups.

In all human societies, our most intense attachments are concentrated together in the family, where their partial or total blockage and deprivation may eventually lead to tension, anger, depression, when there is a threat to these attachments, such as fear of being replaced by another loved one, or if there is undue stress in the environment, jealousy and frustration can erupt into violence within the family. People today are more likely to be hit, physically injured, even killed, in their homes by another family member than by anyone else (Gelles, 1979; Straus, Gelles & Steinmetz, 1981). Each year, as many people are murdered by relatives in New York City as have been killed in all the disturbances in Northern Ireland since 1969. Nearly 1 out of every 4 murders is a family affair in the United States, Great Britain, Denmark, and Africa. Often the ratio is substantially higher. In America each year, at least 6 million men, women, and children are victims of severe physical attacks at the hands of their spouses and children. That is twice the population of Los Angeles. Each year 2,000 American children are killed by their caretakers. Violence toward children is the leading cause of injury, disablement, and death among American children. Rather than individual pathologies or aberrations, this is part of the pattern of family relations, emerging from the psychological tensions and outside stresses afflicting all families at all social levels, rich or poor. In the United States, police answer more calls involving family violence than for all other criminal incidents combined; more police die answering family calls (22% of all police fatalities) than die answering any other single type of call. Much as we may blame current U.S. or world conditions for this situation, there is no reason to think that we emotional humans today love less or hate more than our ancestors of other times and places.

Our evolutionary history as a species influences our vulnerability to environmental pressures. Several major categories of frustration are particularly effective in eliciting severe aggressiveness in humans (Hamburg & van Lawick-Goodall 1974). Survival threat is of course always a major stimulant to aggression in all times and places. For survival, it has always been important to be a securely integrated member of a human group. For millions of years, human survival has depended upon attachment to other human beings belonging to organized groups oriented toward adaptation, thus explaining our strong need to conform and belong.

Another basic motivation, frustration of which is likely to stimulate aggression and violence, is self-esteem, recognition, and status, related in evolution to the adaptive value of having a place in the group. Maintenance of human dignity and self-worth has great cross-cultural generality in all human societies (Turnbull, 1972). One important sub-category here is threat to self-esteem of young males, especially the issue of manliness in young transitional males who have been so important in warlike activities.

Finally, in addition and closely related to family affiliation, is threat to the sense of belonging to some larger group or groups beyond the family. These would consist of occupational unit like Polish Workers' Solidarity, a subculture, tribal units like the Masai and Maring, or ethnic groups like the Irish-Americans. These group alliegences contribute to self-esteem, well being, and the adaptation of its members. It is at the level of the group that we can trace the roots of larger-scale bouts of inter-male violence or war. As the center of sociopolitical gravity shifts from the hunter-gatherer's campsite, where women are key actors because of their major roles in food collecting and reproduction, we increasingly enter a male world in matters of violence and warfare no less than in matters of diplomacy, politics, economics, and religion (Lancaster 1983).

With their comparatively high population densities and larger-scale sociopolitical systems, the agricultural peoples of the New Guinea Highlands provide excellent examples of situations where male-male aggression has developed far beyond the levels that probably were normal when our species first evolved as low-density hunter-gatherers. Warfare in the New Guinea Highlands is motivated by the competitive need for land. Group integrity is severely threatened when landless losers in warfare must flee from their territories (see Meltzoff: this volume). A male-supremacist attitude has come to be exemplified by warfare and related activities (see Divale & Harris, 1978; Lancaster & Lancaster, 1978). Political life centers on military coalitions. Since the New Guinea Highlands have "pacified" by outside forces, though with no alleviation of land pressure, groups continue to express their aggressive reactions through political action and competitive gift-giving and sports, and above all, through the ritual of competitive dancing. Dancers dress like warriors, and alliances formed through ceremonial exchanges replace former military coalitions.

These major categories of motivation are important in all human cultures. Threats to these fundamental human motivations, such as our need for a sense of security and sustaining group membership, can lead to hateful, destructive, violent attitudes and actions. Nevertheless, among humans, such threats may also lead to non-violent ways of coping, to assertive behavior and personal initiative, to persistent efforts toward problem-solving and organizational manipulation that are perhaps aggressive in some sense, but not necessarily destructive (see Gluckman, 1963, 1965). Persistent, instinctive human efforts towards peace-keeping derive from our ancient innate abilities, and needs, to form and maintain interpersonal attachments and develop wider adaptive coalitions. They have served us, intermittently, until now. The species as a whole survives, though countless subgroups have perished in violence. Modern peace-keeping desperately needs a technology to match the killing power now at the disposal of our negative aggressive reactions.

In our modern large-scale, high-technology world, the men who run the "military-industrial-political" system are essentially the same as the men in primitive small-scale societies. We can understand them by understanding their sociopolitical situations, their ambitions, their competitions, and their positions in the system. Their ability or inability to live without violence is the same as anyone else's. Like our earliest ancestors, who forged links between small hunter-gatherer bands, we need organizational structures to unify conflicting power blocs, structures which can place these rival factions into one system with vital common interest in non-aggression.

Dominance and dominance hierarchies, popular topics in recent years, are concerned with status and rank, the real phenomena of importance in understanding primate behavior. What is generally observed as dominance, is the result of some threat to status. The real issue in understanding primate behavior, both human and otherwise, is to discover how status and rank are assigned and the clustered networks of roles associated with each actor's status that form adaptive cooperating groups and coalitions. The threat to status, producing aggression, may not have evolved so much for positive adaptive reasons, as in having the ability to preserve rights and territory, but as a negative residual fuss when the real stuff of life is threatened or lost. The real stuff is a sense of well-being and self–esteem, emotional attachment, and commitment to important others and to various kinds of supportive "home" groups.

Chet S. Lancaster

References

Bigelow, R., *The Evolution of Cooperation, Aggression and Self-Control.* Lincoln: University of Nebraska Press, 1972.

Bowlby, J., "Attachment Theory, Separation Anxiety and Mourning." In *New Frontiers, American Handbook of Psychiatry*, 1975, Vol. 6, eds., D. Hamburg & K. Brodie. New York: Basic Books.

Divale, W.T. and M. Harris, "Population, Warfare, and the Male Supremacist Complex." *American Anthropologist*, 1978, 78:521-538.

Gelles, R., *Family Violence.* Beverly Hills:Sage, 1979.

Gluckman, M., *Order and Rebellion in Tribal Africa.* London:Cohen & West, 1963, *Custom and Conflict in Africa.* Oxford:Blackwell, 1965.

Hamburg, D., "Emotions in the Perspective of Human Evolution." In *Expression of the Emotions in Man*, ed., P. Knapp. New York: International University Press, 1963.

Hamburg, D. and J. van Lawick-Goodall, "Factors Favoring Development of Aggressive Behavior in Chimpanzees and Humans." In *Determinants and Origins of Aggressive Behavior*, eds., J. DeWit & W. Hartup. The Hague: Mouton, 1974.

Lancaster, C., "The Evolution of Human Social Systems." In *Proceedings of the Eleventh International Conference on the Unity of the Sciences.* New York:International Cultural Foundation Press, 1983.

Lancaster, C. and J. Lancaster, "On the Male Supremacist Complex: a reply to Divale and Harris." *American Anthropologist*, 1978, 80:115-119.

Lancaster, J., "Caring and Sharing in Human Evolution." *Human Nature*, 1978 1: 82-89.

Lancaster, J. and C. Lancaster, "Parental Investment." In *How Humans Adapt*, ed., D. Ortner. Washington, D.C.:Smithsonian, 1983.

Meltzoff, S., *Lethal Dance.*

Raleigh, M. and S. Washburn, "Human Behavior and the Origin of Man." *Impact of Science on Society*, 1973, 23:5-14.

Strauss, M., R. Gelles and S. Steinmetz, *Behind Closed Doors:Violence in the American Family.* Garden City:Anchor Books, 1981.

Turnbull, C., *The Mountain People.* New York:Touchstone, 1972.

Washburn, S. and R. Harding, "Evolution and Human Nature." In *New Frontiers, American Handbook of Psychiatry*, Vol. 6, eds., D. Hamburg & K. Brodie. New York:Basic Books, 1975.

Washburn, S. and C. Lancaster "The Evolution of Hunting." In *Man the Hunter*, eds., R. Lee & I. DeVore. Chicago:Aldine, 1968.

8.
Form and Intention in East African Strategies of Dominance and Aggression

John G. Galaty

Introduction

We are accustomed to using the same terms to describe aggressive behavior between human individuals, groups and collectivities such as nations, and we often use the same terms, as well, to depict such behavior, both in small scale rural societies and highly complex urban settings, and for animal and human populations. An everyday vocabulary exists, drawn from quasi-scientific developments in Psychology and Ethnology, Anthropology, and Political Science, which concerns itself with systems of conflict among primates, non-Western societies and nations. Notions such as 'dominance hierarchies,' 'blood feuds,' and 'balance of power' are commonly used together with the sort of metaphorical exactitude which characterizes most ordinary language, communication by suggestion and nuance. All too often, however, the *use of such concepts* as 'dominance,' 'threat,' or 'aggression' to label behaviors across diverse levels and cases, seems to suggest the proof of their validity for comparative analysis. In this essay, and drawing primarily on examples from East Africa, I would like to address the problems and possibilities of comparison between dominance and aggression systems at several levels, while critically reflecting on the nature of the models we use in bridging diverse cases and disciplines.

The thesis which will be discussed in the next section can be depicted in condensed form; it will serve as a set of guidelines for a discussion of ethnography in the third section. The thesis is:

1. Structure and Intentionality:

a. That behavior should be understood as involving aggression, conflict or dominance within the context of 'systems' that are internally structured;

b. that the significance of each element of the structure (which may relate directly to actions) derives from a level of 'intentionality' which depends in part on the actors intention or meaning, and in part on the elements' meaning within the structure and in the context of its enactment.

2. Form and Analogy:

a. That there are useful analogies to be drawn between the subject matter of non-human primate dominance and aggression, conflict and warfare in small-scale pre-industrial societies, and the military strategies of highly mechanized armies in nation states, for which similar terms may be used out of convenience and for constructive comparison; but

b. that many of these analogies cannot be demonstrated to represent homologies, stemming from a common primate heritage, but are more formal than substantive, deriving from either formal constraints on social interaction or on the reasoning underlying these analogies or more elaborated explanatory logic.

In the third section, the question of form and intentionality will be applied to several issues in the ethnography of East African societies, with special reference to the Maasai;[1] each of these issues will yield useful analogies to primate and strategic studies, but, I will argue, require a structural and meaningful (intentional) account, rather than a behavioristic one, and may result from formal rather than substantive relations to those other fields of study. The issues to be discussed are aggression and symmetry, dominance and power, and the motives and functions of dominance and aggressor systems.

Interpreting Conflict

A baboon chases a rival away from a section of bushland, a group of warriors deters a herder from crossing a river to reach a section of pasture each claims, and an alliance establishes a transnational military line across which the army of the opposing alliance must not cross. Are these examples of 'territoriality'? In Maasai society, a ritual village may be divided in half by moieties, the pasture outside a cattle gate reserved for the livestock of the family of the gate, and a water source may be identified with a given clan. Territoriality?

A large, young male baboon offers its rear to an aged 'alpha' male, a proud warrior waits expectantly for a tired elder to recognize him in greeting, and a small nation waits to see the opinion of a large and powerful nation before voting. Are these examples of 'deference' and 'dominance'? In one society, a wife may wait for a husband's opinion before offering her own, a child will refuse to sleep in the same house as its father, and a seat is left vacant during a council for the spokesman to occupy. 'Deference,' 'dominance,' all?

Such parallels are compelling for those who seek unified patterns of behavior across human communities, and between human and animal populations. They suggest common processes, perhaps within primate species, with diverse manifestations. Yet these parallels are remarkably unsatisfying for students at each level, or observers of particular ethnographic settings, who feel that what may be gained is far outweighed by what is lost: understanding of the particular phenomena. The tension between the particularizers and the generalizers is quite intractable, in large part because their interests differ and their common ground is weak. When the division between those who seek law and those who seek reality also crosses disciplines, the possibility of tension becoming warfare is high. Yet any anthropologist must recognize the complementarity of the two projects, of providing an ethnographic account rich in detail and reminiscent of a history, while entertaining the validity of regional cultural systems and a general social science to which each ethnographic case contributes.

The opposition between particularizing and generalizing is, in short, not fundamental, despite the sniping of the former and the condescension of the latter. Their argument raises, however, at least one fundamental issue which challenges both positions with the obligation to collaborate. What 'particular' form of behavior is to be used to 'compare' between cases? As previously suggested, generalizing concepts—such as 'aggression' or 'dominance'—seem to suggest the problem does not exist, that what is to be compared is self-evident, that we all know aggression or dominance, or whatever, when we see it. However, the methodology of ethology was dramatically advanced when it adopted certain procedures of behavioral psychology, and began to define general notions in behaviorally specific ways, operationalized as behavioral 'indicators' rather than as general impressions. Even controversy between those advocating controlled versus naturalistic observation could not hinge on the desireability of defining 'rage' or 'deference' behavior in explicit terms. Comparison, then, could depend on behavioral indicators rather than on general concepts, providing a point of rapprochement between generalizers and particularizers, since the subject matter of the latter becomes the data of the former. The fundamental issue, however, remains: how to define a behavioral indicator, especially for creatures with culture?

An epigramatic critique of behaviorism in the social sciences might suggest that a method which is a necessity in ethnology and animal psychology has been wrongly taken as a virtue by anthropologists and sociologists. Without even considering subtlety in animal behavior, one who studies human language use, knows that meaning can change dramatically with context, that in the same language, *behavior* means one thing if uttered to a lover and another thing to a friend. There may be useful behavioral indicators of rage or anger, but what if forceful articulation is used in a speech, as part of a form of political discourse, or as parody, with a gleam in the eye? Children do not learn literal use and then alter it, but grasp the essentials of language and culture through play, by 'pretending' to be angry or through elaborate games which provide practice. Such a moderate criticism of defining actions in behavioral terms, which assumes an intrinsic link between an indicator and a process which may under circumstances be transformed, reversed, or parodied, should not be allowed to mitigate the strong criticism that different cultures express rage, anger, dominance, etc. in different ways that must be given specific account, or that different cultures tend to emphasize quite different social forms, and that even a universal underlying process of 'dominance', for example, may not be assumed.

The challenge of accounting for aggression and dominance systems in a comparative setting is to understand, first, whether such systems are appropriately seen in given contexts; second, to understand how their elements are manifested and indicated in each universe of expression; and third, to grasp broad commonalities between such systems, without reifying analogies or yielding to the compelling, yet potentially superficial, evidence of behavior indicators.

Structure and Intentionality

What does it mean to suggest that it is within a *system* that behavior can be seen as aggression, etc., and that such a system will also be internally structured? At an initial level, the question of behavioral units raises the image of units with which they can be contrasted, or similar units which convey different messages. Correct identification of a unit implies grasp of a larger system of units of varying form and meaning. The way such systems fit units together represents their internal structure. Two examples may be useful in describing a 'system'.

Among the Maasai, all males carry sticks, the form of which signifies their age, status and activity. One stick is used for herding, for beating animals into a line, or for waving in front of a herd to keep it from approaching water until the source has been cleared of other animals. The theme of beating is ever-present in the society, with sticks often being raised to chase away even small children, as well as to threaten other adults when conflicts arise. Actual beatings might be rare, but the theme underlies the perpetual carrying of sticks and their use in gesture and threat. Now, most of these threats are in humor, and most people who flee a raised stick do so with laughter; indeed, a pattern of flight is one way of expressing deference. When a minor fight does erupt, a stick is the usual weapon employed. It signifies, however, not only conflict but also restraint, since a stick is not a sword or a spear, and can stun but will rarely kill. Sticks are also used as symbols of authority, and are wielded by speakers during council meetings, for histrionic effects and emphasis. Sticks become symbols of elderhood in general, and evoke divinity through being carved from certain species of trees and being pointed at the sky at the time of blessings.

Thus the carrying of an apparent weapon, a stick, requires an understanding of the system in which it is embedded: the system of different sticks, and when they are used and what they imply;

the system of occasions when different sticks are used, and how their impact may change if the context is an exchange of words between two angry men or a council; and the system of persons who use sticks, and how their positions and statuses are signified. Further, to evoke aggressive acts in which sticks may be used, the same gesture may imply inter-generational play, a dramatic accompaniment to discourse, or a real threat.[2]

A second example follows. Leadership among the Maasai may be described very generally in terms of authority and deference, similar terms used to describe authoritarian kingships or chieftainships. Maasai 'spokesmen' (*Ilaiguenak*) are separated from their age peers when chosen, become individuals set apart from everyday familiarity and conflict, and receive respect and deference more appropriate to elders. Their authority is supported by a set of sanctions and curses. However, these attitudes must be seen within an overall system of quasi-democratized politics, carried out primarily in local councils, in which the spokesman speaks first and last, but where any eligible male can speak freely. The process of speaking requires articulation, presence and poise, and can be seen not only as involving decision-making and consensus-building, but also a pattern of display, oratory and recreation of intrinsic interest and enjoyment. Speaking involves the use of logic and argumentation, but also the use of verbal force and aggression, all to the end of persuasion. Spokesmen may be those with particular abilities of oratory and persuasion, but their techniques do not differ from those of lesser ability. There is no behavioral indicator to identify the spokesman at council when he is speaking, other than the fact that he carries a smaller, highly polished black stick, an emblem of office, and has a seat reserved for him when he sits. Dominance is implicit rather than explicit, and exists; but to use the same term for a spokesman and a despot is to misunderstand the situating of Maasai leadership within a *context* of consensual decision-making and an equalitarian ideology, a system quite different from that of a highly stratified political order.

I suggested that the significance of each element of such a system should be seen in terms of the intentionality of actors. At one level, human behavior is often a means of accomplishing intentional acts, that is, acts embodying purposes which can be either communicated by actors or are implicit in those acts. To grasp those acts as meaningful is to reconstruct the intentions behind them.[3] A Maasai may raise a stick, which is recognized not as a prelude to a beating but as an assertion of age, a humorous retort, or as a means of gaining space for another elder to sit, all intentional meanings immediately transparent in context. That is, an *aggressive behavior is merely a communicative token to achieve any number of diverse ends.*

At another level, human behavior embodies culturally codified 'intentionality,' or significance which transcends or is assumed by actors, without contributing to their situationally-specific aims. The spokesman carries a black stick as a token of office, but does not do so specifically to assert the greater weight of his contribution to dialogue in a given meeting. His 'dominance,' then, is an outcome of cultural intentionality (in a specifically Maasai sense), resulting in part from the significance of his office and in part from his intentions of the moment. One spokesman's style is to actively intervene with arguments and wit, another's style is to remain aloof, speak rarely and with parsimony, or even to absent himself when mundane matters are considered. Although behaviorally divergent, both styles depend on and achieve 'dominance.'

It is a commonplace to observe that human languages achieve a virtually infinite scope of expression through the combination of a quite finite number of sounds. The even greater limitation on the gestural repertoire should be apparent, facial expressions being well-captured in a small number of discrete images and emotions, and forms of social interaction in a few modes of behavior or response. Of course, behaviors are compounded in sequences and any set of activities might appear complex, but the essential aim of ethology is to reduce complex sequences and motions to a set of interactional functions. Humans, we know, use their finite number of behavioral forms—waving sticks at each other, for example—to achieve a far greater number of intentional ends. Among the Maasai, 'aggression'—taken in some sort of general sense—is a cultural theme, as is 'respect' and 'dignity,' which is not simply signified by various gestures, but becomes itself a signifier or a conveyer of information far from any intrinsic value of the aggressive form. 'Dominance,' however, is not pervasive, and while multiple forms of deference exist, they are not replicated and transformed into a cultural theme by Maasai, as has been done by, for example, the Amhara of Ethiopia. If we are to grasp the structure and intentionality of human acts, it must be within their universe of discourse, rather than in terms of the vagueness of general comparative concepts.

Form and Analogy

Obviously, if forms of behavior are few, and largely similar, then the possibilities for a comparative behavioral science are increased. Inversely, if forms of behavior were many and largely unique to given species, then the possibility of developing such a comparative science would be decreased and its problems magnified. The question of the behavioral range of primate species is beyond the scope of this paper, though it is clear that significant behavioral differences between primate species do exist. The theoretical question, however, is clear: do different behavioral patterns between species merely represent different ways of achieving a few essential functions, perhaps identified as a single underlying primate pattern of social and emotional needs and drives; or do those essential behavioral patterns and functions serve as a repertoire for expressing or enacting a more diverse and complex set of aims, motives and acts? Of course, the first solution seems appropriate to species without language, the second to the single species with language, and thus the question is largely irresolvable. Clearly, analogies between species, especially between sub-human and human primates, must be based on explicit behavioral criteria, with all the pitfalls previously enumerated, or on postulated underlying drives, emotions or organic functions, the identification of which depends on a logic of inference from empirical phenomena. In most cases, the comparison made *assumes* the underlying commonality between species, and the successful comparison in turn seems to verify and validate the commonality in a not unusual exercise of circular reasoning. That is, the very process of comparing seems to support an assumption of a common bio-behavioral structure, presumably a genetic heritage, manifested in behavioral homologies.[4]

Unfortunately, the strategy is ill-suited to determining whether or not the observational concepts and analytical analogies do or do not identify underlying homologies between species. The alternative hypothesis is that analogies represent formal rather than substantive parallels, and result not from genetic constraints but from formal constraints, either on the social and behavioral process or on the process of model-building. In human societies, the symbolic capacity tends to intervene in both the shaping of social interaction and the creation of models after behavior, so the formal constraints may well coincide. That is to say that, unlike the study of animal psychology, the study of human societies and cultures tends to involve processes of observation, creative inference and interpretation not unlike the processes of social life itself, and presumably model-making and model-following are implicated in the genesis of behavior, along with formal patterns of constraint.

One sign of the power of symbolic processes is the tendency to overdetermine that which they observe or define: choice of object, focus, observation, and report tend to be carried out by the same agent with a single lens or motive, and thus it is not surprising that we humans often see a world of our own making. The awareness one might have of ethnocentricity, bias, or simply powerful expectation serves, in part, to control distortions in perception for the common man or for the social scientist. Anthropologists have, to a large degree, elevated the problem of observer bias into a sub-field of methodology, and emphasize the importance of the "viewpoint of the other" and entering into a culture's "universe of discourse," both as means of control and as means of access into its very subject matter. Thus it is not surprising that Anthropology reacts with suspicion and reservation at claims of analytical accuracy based primarily on the transparent adequacy of descriptive concepts of common currency in our own culture applied to other cultures, other species, or human collectivities. Reservation is not refutation, but, in the absence of further evidence, makes avid pursuit of the comparative research program difficult unless placed on firmer foundations, such as awareness of the formal nature of our comparative constructs and results.

What, for instance, is 'dominance'? It may represent a pattern of activity whereby one individual's behavior tends to be determined by that of another, the converse not being so. A 'linear' dominance hierarchy would be one in which a set of transitive dominance relations were obtained, each individual subordinated to any other individual being also subordinated to those the other is subordinated to. However, the research strategy may involve eliciting a series of paired conflicts which result in dominance being ascertained between individuals; the results may not approximate the actual social dynamics of dominance relations, but may, rather, represent a result *formally determined* by the nature of the planned situation and the expectation of the research design. The question of dominance, posed to a pair, is equivalent to a question answerable by a yes or a no, posed to an informant; the results are clear-cut, but it is unclear what they mean.

This critical discussion points, in actuality, in one direction, towards the investigation and analysis of a given society, with the following questions in mind. If general interest in dominance, aggression and conflict systems exist, in what systematic relations to each other does each element have, and what structures of significance, meaning and intentionality define each behavior or more general element, and by what internally-generated definition can each be seen as representing the general comparative concept? Second, on the basis of what principles can analogies between levels or species be suggested, and what formal constraints might exist which would account for those parallels, before attribution of genetic, historically-based homologies are made? Third, if such formal principles are identified, how can they be used in a constructive manner for the purpose of comparison without their being taken for signs of a single bio-behavioral inheritance?

Form and Conflict In East Africa

The question of inter-group conflict and warfare in East Africa has interested observers from outside the region for centuries. Chinese texts from the 9th century A.D. refers to East Africa: "From olden times they were not subject to any foreign country. In fighting they use elephants' teeth and ribs and the horns of wild oxen made into halberds, and they wear armour and have bows and arrows." (Hirth, 1909,48). An early missionary reference to the Maasai states that "when cattle fail them they make raids on the tribes which they know to be in possession of herds (Krapf, 1867,359), continuing that:

> . . . they are dreaded as warriors, laying all waste with fire and sword, so that the weaker tribes do not venture to resist them in the open field, but leave them in possession of their herds, and seek only to save themselves by the quickest flight (Ibid.).

The East African interior was the last explored by Europeans, and at an astoundingly late date of the 1880s, was a void on the map of Africa due to outside ignorance of its even most rudimentary geography. This was in large part due to the avoidance of the region even by Arab slavers until the latter half of the century, which in turn inhibited European adventurers and missionaries, and this reluctance has largely been attributed to the military strength of the Maasai.

The above citations reveal several factors in the militarism of the Maasai and other East Africa groups, that is, the relation between specialized pastoralism, with its inevitable fluctuations due to an unpredictable climate, and livestock raiding, necessary for immediate subsistence as well as to build up herds necessary for continuing pastoral viability. It has been suggeested that the exigencies of pastoral production, including highly autonomous and reliable young herders and an opportunistic and responsive economic strategy, represent adaptive pressures towards individuals with personalities characterized by overt aggressivity, open expression of emotions, and obedience to authority (Edgerton, 1971). In actuality, early caravans and European exploration through the Maasai interior were carried out with little bellicosity (Thomson, 1883), and violent clashes that did occur were invariably precipitated by pugnacious yet uncertain Europeans (Peters, 1891). While the notion that Maasai were "peaceful pastoralists" may be overstated (Jacobs, 1979), the opposite view, that the Maasai, and other East African pastoralists, were congenitally rapacious, is surely exaggerated and inaccurate. The fact is that armed conflict was common, but primarily carried out in the process of cattle raiding, a specific, limited and largely reciprocated form of aggression. If, in the specific case, livestock raiding provided an opportunity for individuals to build up herds sufficient for domestic life, in the aggregate, raiding provided a mechanism for evening out the radical shifts in livestock numbers due to drought, famine and pestilence.

Most East African pastoralists, however, entertain a military tradition and could be said to harbor an ethos of assertive masculinity. This ethos may be, to a large extent, due not to a pastoral practice, but to elaborated age organizations which lend codification and regimentation to a period of 'warriorhood' for adolescent and young adult males. Such age organizations are found among most Nilotic, Cushitic and Bantu-speaking peoples of East Africa, and include groups practicing animal husbandry, hunting, and cultivation. It is clear that such Bantu-speaking groups as the Kikuyu (Leakey, 1977), Embur (Saberwal, 1970), and the Meru (Bernardi, 1959); combined sedentary agriculture with age-sets and age-grading, and developed highly assertive warrior classes. Certainly, it is today recognized that relations of armed conflict and raiding between these groups and nearby pastoralists were reciprocal (Muriuki, 1974), and that if pastoralists such as the Maasai dominated East Africa, politically and militarily, prior to the advent of colonialism, it was due to an economically-based capacity to occupy huge areas of savannah through nomadic practice and to use age-organization as a means of lateral mobilization, beyond the capacity of sedentary groups bound to limited and fixed locales, between which enmity existed.

Among the Maasai, "warriorhood" or "young manhood" (*Ilmurran*) has its own sub-culture. Young uncircumcised boys are largely occupied with tasks of herding, and because of their unfinished state, are considered of little consequence culturally, especially by circumcised warriors. They in turn look forward to when they will become *Ilmurran* through circumcision, which can occur anytime between the ages of 12 and 22, and practice in secret the forms of warrior practice denied them in public. When one age-set has graduated from the grade of junior warriors, the group of older boys began to acquire the accoutrements of that grade and to publically assert warrior prerogatives. They grow their hair long, braid it and smear it with red ochre and fat; they dress in red robes, wear certain styles of jewelry, and begin carrying weapons. Dances and songs which were previously denied them are now practiced and sung, together with the courting of young uninitiated girls, theoretically denied them by the now graduated warriors. But of most consequence here, they begin to *form small neighborhood cadres* and *sub-sectional warrior groups*, and *to identify with them in opposition to other neighborhood and sub-sectional groups*. A pattern of tension, raised by taunts, challenges and competition for the favors of young girls, begins to dominate relations between boys, which culminates in beatings and clashes between individuals and small groups.

This period of transition, during which the new warrior group is being formed, is ritually marked by collective ceremonies that officially open the age-set, to which boys will be recruited by initiation. The ceremony of *Enkipaata*, signified by a great skipping dance the boys carry out in long lines, in actuality does three things. First, it formally creates an age-set, by endowing the group with a name (I will not elaborate here the complexities involved in the question of whether the age-division, *olporror*, is of the "right-hand" or the "left-hand," (Galaty, fr. press). Second, it begins to weld disparate neighborhood and sectional groupings into a single age-set, through physically congregating the boys, acquainting them with each other, and celebrating the unity of the age-set and the overall section. This level of integration becomes progressively more important and more salient as the life of the age-set proceeds. Thirdly, it defines the terms of symbolic unity which must be obtained between members of the same age-group. Through sharing the "three calabashes" of the collective ceremony, drinking the blood of the sacrificial ox, eating its meat, and later drinking milk together, they are bound by an oath to collective life. They must put age-set solidarity above all division, must always offer hospitality to an age-mate, and must demonstrate respect to the "fathers" of the age-set, the sponsoring elders' set. In fact, during the initial period of warriorhood, the young males seal their solidarity through additional prescriptions, to always travel and stay in groups, to take milk with other age-mates, and not to eat meat seen by initiated women, that is, to slaughter outside of the domestic villages in special meat camps, or *olpul* (Rigby, 1979). This is a period during which warriors form intensive friendships, involving mutual grooming, play, physical wrestling and competition, confidences, collaboration in courting, and mutual trust built up through joint escapades, such as cattle raiding. Of importance is the edict that age-mates should never allow women to come between them, though this often applies more to those in a local group than in a larger arena where jealousy does occur. The establishment of generalized solidarity with the entire age-set and a set of close male friendships with age-mates at the time following *Enkipaata* and the opening of the age-set, inevitably implies that when the strictures of warriorhood are loosened, when the group graduates at the collective ceremony of *Eunoto*, great emotion is felt as warriors fear they will lose the intensity of experience and comradeship of that period.[5]

The process of establishing an age-set relates to systems of conflict and aggression in several ways. The sub-sectional cadres form great villages composed of houses made by the mothers of warriors, and these *Manyata* represent military batallions. The age-grade of junior warriors represents, in effect, a standing army, charged with the defense of the country. It is also expected, however, that they will also engage in offense, through carrying out of small and large-scale cattle raids. While, theoretically, solidarity obtains across the entire age-set (which provides the major mechanism for social relations across groups), the pattern of conflict and armed clashes involves opposing territorial units of the same age-set. It is expected, and warriors internalize and act out this expectation, that they will initiate and accept aggressive encounters; this readiness is, of course, exploited by the rest of the society for their own ends, as in generalized conflict over pastures.

This warrior complex is situated within a network of meaning, implied by this discussion, whereby actions are shaped and defined through terms of expectation and orientation regarding age-group solidarity and competition, norms of respect and familiarity, and motives of defense and aggression. One way to grasp this intentional pattern is through forms, through patterns which seem to emerge and which appear to represent a structure underlying meaning and activity. In the succeeding pages, the formal aspects will be revealed in systems of aggression and symmetry, dominance and power, and motives of conflict.

Aggression and Symmetry

Evans-Pritchard's classic study of *The Nuer* (1940) suggested that this acephalous group carried out its system of "ordered anarchy" through an implicit structure of "segmentation," which defined degrees and qualities of relations between individuals and groups. A genealogically-based lineage system defined relations between lineages in terms of their relative distance in time from their common ancestor; given conflict or question, siblings would unite against cousins, based on descent from two different brothers, while the entire group of siblings and cousins would unite as one against second cousins, based on a common grandfather. In actuality, such a system operated with respect to lineages which understood their respective relations to one another in terms of quite distant ancestors, but in terms of a comparable system of simultaneous alliances and oppositions, which depended on the genealogy of the actors in question. Such a "segmentary structure" involved a certain "complementary opposition" between lineages, since groups opposed to each other in one context might unite in a complimentary form in another, to oppose yet a more distant group.

Evans-Pritchard perceived that such a genealogical structure of lineage also occurred within an implicit political system of relations between territorial groups, both directly, because territorial groups were identified with dominant lineages, and indirectly, since the system of political segmentation had a resilience and a permanence beyond the lineage base; indeed, in some sense, the political system was understood in terms of genealogy and lineage, as much as constituted by it. "Segmentary theory" predicted a pattern of coalitions and alliances, and seemed to account for just how serious conflict between groups could become, since relations between closer groups were kept under greater control and constraint than those between more distant groups. In the Maasai case, it is well understood that conflict within a section (*Olosho*) should involve only clubs, while conflict between members of different sections, especially more distant sections, might involve mortal weapons, such as swords and spears (c.f., Galaty, 1981).

In some sense, segmentary theory suggests that political units will grow and then split (fission), much as kin groups grow until more distant lines of a family separate, perhaps by no longer celebrating common feasts. But if kin groups and lineages do not grow at even rates, what of territorially based groups? An outgrowth of segmentary theory suggests that smaller groups tend to identify with larger groups, or even unite with them in a process of fusion. Smaller lineages will, over time, tend to identify themselves with the ancestors of those lineages which dominate a local area, or will tend to act in concert with those lineages through an idiom of marital alliance, and may tend to lose their own distinct identities with regard to their own apical ancestor. Thus a segmentary system will represent not just a mechanical tree of growth and splitting, projected from the dimension of time onto the dimension of space, as groups expand and colonize new lands, but rather, *will represent a more stable and highly domesticated tree,* with a more finite number of branches, whose shoots are pruned. In large part, this constraint on segmentation is probably due to a certain demography and structural limit born out of processes of conflict, since smaller lineages or political units may not have the strength or resistance to exercise themselves as autonomous entities over time, but will maintain themselves only within a larger branch.[6]

It seems evident that segmentary theory, while born out of an anthropology of non-centralized societies, in effect, resembles a theory of balance of power more salient in the strategic study of modern warfare and the diplomacy of nation-states. First, there is an inherent dualism in both models, since alliances tend to congregate units of disparate and varying interests into large blocs; and when conflict occurs, units which attempt to sit on the fence tend to be pushed to one block or the other. Similarly, segmentary theory rests on the premise that a multitude of diverse political units tend to become organized according to a dualistic logic of opposition, which replicates itself at each level. Second, the various sides tend towards balance, in part because smaller groups gravitate towards alliances with or assimilation into the larger, and in part because an asymmetry in relations between the two might produce a form of instability that will lead to diplomatic realignments. If one bloc decisively prevails or absorbs the other, a process of fission within may well replicate the dualistic opposition within the bloc that formerly existed between it and another.

Implicit in a notion of balance is a concept of appropriate response to hostilities, or a "limitation" on warfare. The feud, which underlies the system of relations between opposed units in a segmentary system, represents a system of justice based on the appropriateness of response, in a sort of "tit-for-tat" form. If an individual from one group murders one from another, the second group will be honor bound to avenge the murder, through taking the life of someone from the first group. Since action is considered to be collective, a murder may be seen not as an individual act for which responsibility is borne by the murderer, but a collective act for which the murderer is simply the active hand of a group. In Western understanding, the essence of the feud is that it is a permanent relation between two conflicting groups, irresolvable because any retribution calls for yet another round of retribution. In systems such as the Nuer, the feud is a mechanism not just of justice but of stabilization. Without organized systems of courts, the threat of retribution—combined with notions of pollution of a murderer—acts to deter violence, in theory at least.

The threat of retribution is a major incentive, as well, for resolution of the crime through the payment of compensation to the family or lineage of the victim. The notion of balance, of life-for-a-life or material payment for a life, is intrinsic to the system of the feud. Among the Nuer and the Maasai, the murderer is polluted until cleansed, and the family of the murdered person is also polluted, both until cleansing ceremonies have been held and until rectification occurs. The blood-wealth payment does not represent a mercenary assessment of human life in material terms but rather, a cosmological mandate of restoration. In practical terms, livestock are seen to mediate human reproduction through bride-wealth, and thus can serve in the form of blood-wealth payments to make possible the acquiring of a bride by the lineage who will then produce offspring to replace the lost individual.

The feud, then, is not an institution directed at meaningless retribution but is a mechanism for restoring order after it is disrupted; it is aimed at resolution rather than continuance of hostilities, and represents an intrinsically limited notion of conflict, since an act of aggression calls for a balanced and specific, rather than an unpredictable and generalized, response. It is not unlike the diplomacy between political and military blocs in the west, whereby careful discussion and analysis goes into determining an "appropriate" and "balanced" response to given political and military torts.

In Maasai history, warfare itself has usually been dictated by principles of limitation, in some ways reminiscent of the formal procedures of pre-20th century European warfare. Conflict has largely been seen as involving warrior batallions, who fight in daylight in long opposing lines using the same weapons. Women and children were excepted for the process, and often carried on trade between lines of hostilities. Some engagements resembled tournaments or duels, sometimes with champions, where the manner of engagement and the honor with which one fought was seen as important as the outcome. Cattle raids are themselves described in terms evocative of escapades and adventures, and were clearly directed towards acquisition of stock rather than the killing of human beings, although this inevitably did occur.

However, mortal clashes between sections did occur, in which the rules of limited conflict seemed to be disregarded in a series of escalations matched on either side. A series of 19th century wars saw autonomous sections of Maasai-speakers come to conflict over a series of years, with defeated sections in effect ceasing to exist. Myth and recent history describe the demise of the Lose-kelai, the Uasin Gishu and the Laikipiak, all north of present-day Maasailand in Kenya. Under threat, perhaps heightened because of devastating plagues and famines of the latter half of the 19th century, sections of the central Maasai banded together to oppose these sections and, ultimately, to disperse them. Even with this loss of restraint and limitation in warfare, it would appear that the disappearance of the opposed sections as political units does not imply wholesale massacre, but merely indicates that they were assimilated into the body of the victorious group and the political-military threat removed. Perhaps the threat of uncontrolled esca-lation always represents an apparent deterrent to ignoring the proper rules of limited conflict, but when such a turn towards unlimited warfare occurs, with fear of defeat and opportunity of victory motivating both participants, it is difficult to see anything being deterred. These events, in one case of small-scale warfare, are the only possible analogues to the "mutual assured destruc-tion" (MAD) theory behind the nuclear deterrence of NATO and the Warsaw Pact, which appears effective insofar as it is not acted on, but will have assuredly failed if it ever is.[7]

Dominance and Power

The warrior pattern is in many ways directed towards achieving certain effects on others, and in the Maasai case has been quite effective. It was suggested earlier that the political dominance of pastoral groups, especially the Maasai, in East Africa, was in part due to their ability to extend their influence over vast regions through the practice of nomadic pastoralism. If effective military control of pastureland represented one necessary condition for successful and highly productive pastoralism, the practice of pastoralism itself made possible that form of extended control, since animals represent mobile subsistence which can support warrior cadres inhabiting or extending themselves into marginal lands. Another factor in pastoral dominance was their ability to sustain political cooperation between sections, largely through mechanisms of segmentary alliance previously discussed. While each regional skirmish may have had the appearance of a certain balance between forces, in a regional perspective, the Maasai clearly dominated the central Rift Valley and its surrounding highlands. This was true to the point at which an ethos of superiority was clearly established, echoed in every 19th century record of virtually all East Africa groups, which recorded that fear of Maasai raids became a material factor in determining where groups would live, how they would live, and how they would use their resources. Intimidation kept Maasai neighbors off the plains and in the highlands, stimulated larger and more concentrated villages, and shaped a more cautious and limited form of animal husbandry, including stall feeding.

Fear may be based on rational apprehensions, but becomes a motivating force in itself. Indeed, dominance as a concept implies not the use of force by a superior to keep an inferior in line but precisely the opposite: the largely symbolic determination of an inferior's behavior by the superior, without the use of force. The Maasai reputation may have been earned, but it served in following as a factor itself in producing the dominance that it reflected. In Psychology, theories of response to punishment have shown how strongly fear of punishment is resistant to extinction, since every occasion on which a punishment may have been received and is not, becomes, in effect, a reward through the relief it produces; and since organisms tend to practice forms of behavior which are rewarded, punishment avoidance responses tends to be perpetuated even in the continued absence of the aversive stimulus. Similarly, a devastating Maasai raid could produce specific defensive responses on the part of their victims, which would be perpetuated even in the absence of continuous and sustained threat. In this way, a pattern of dominance relations could have been established, even in the absence of a sizeable enough Maasai population to thoroughly monitor and police the vast regions they were able to seasonally exploit through pastoral use, or the even greater regions they were able to occasionally terrorize through raids.

At a more micro-level, the issue of "display" arises. If a pattern of violence and raiding is feared and has been experienced, it is only necessary for a group to sight a member of the threatening group for it to experience intimidation. The force of the Maasai visual display is heightened by its elaboration. The young warriors wear their hair long and ochred a bright red, a fact interpreted by some as an incident of a more general' phenomenon of long hair signifying lack of restraint and expressive sexuality and aggressivity (c.f., Leach, 1958). In full regalia, many warriors wear head-dresses of lion mane and ostrich feathers, which sweep up above the head in an imposing arch. Painted shields, made of buffalo skin, are three feet high and can be used not only to cover but to extend the body into a more projective force. For ceremonies and ritually sanctioned raids, warriors paint their bodies with white or red substance, in swirls up the legs, and across the face, to form images or spectres of themselves equally horrific and beautifying. Audible, as well as visual, imagery is used. Warriors wear bells on their ankles, so a long line of approaching warriors is accompanied by a melodious clanking and ringing, strong, loud and evocative. At the same time, a grunting chant magnified over tens or even hundreds resembles a drum with all its resonance and reverberation. One can only imagine the effect of such display on those whom it was intended to intimidate; perhaps the obverse effect we can observe is equally as interesting, for the effect of such dramatic synesthesia on participants themselves is such as to produce fits of paroxysm and gripping urges to fight those who might oppose them, in order to justify the audacity of their warrior postures, to others and themselves.

Threat, then, can be experienced directly through attack, or indirectly through signs which evoke past or future attacks. If Maasai attacks were carried out with some frequency, the signs associated with raids were displayed even more frequently, in the very garb and appearance of warriors whose role included long journeys and explorations, as well as raids. Here at the individual level we find a form of intimidation through display comparable to the placement of Maasai age-set Manyatta and cattle camps near the boundaries of pastures. If the forces of threat are not known, they cannot be experienced; but insofar as they are seen as well as known, they will invariably have an added impact. In strategic analysis, assessment is often made of a nation's military potential rather than their military intentions, though intentions are combined with capability in the last analysis. Since the value of much military force is in persuading others you will use it, its visibility is also a factor in its influence. For instance, the presence of troops from the United States are, according to NATO theory, less intended as material factors of intimidation of the Warsaw Pact forces, since they are too few for that purpose, but more as a factor of reassurance that given hostilities, the United States will be bound to assist Germany. One can also suggest several solutions to the perceived problem of mutual vulnerability to ICBM attack by the United States and the Soviet Union. But one factor in the United States' decision to deploy the MX missile is apparently visibility; smaller missiles or submarine-borne missiles will not have the political impact that huge, land-basedmissiles will have, especially when viewed through satellites.

Dominance is not, then, a matter simply of force, but of influence, which may be effected by visible display as well as by invisible yet tangible threats. Threats may, however, be utterly unspoken or even unintended; indeed, a capability rather than an aim, may underly the experience of threat by a subordinate party, even to the surprise of a superordinate. Much dominance rests on a set of relations which are rarely questioned, and are not subject to the sort of reduction to vulgarity which overt intimidation or threats represent, but rest on differences of power accepted by both parties. Instability occurs when the ground of dominance shifts over a long period of time.

If Maasai long exercised dominance over East Africa, within Maasai society, elders assert a certain dominance over the society and over younger warriors which is unquestioned, and only challenged *ad hoc* rather than in principle. The major axis of dominance is between sponsoring elders, who in effect hold political power during the period when a sponsored group is coming into being and moves through the age-grades of warriorhood (a period of perhaps twenty years), and the group of sponsored juniors. The relationship is established when the youths are uninitiated, most in their early teens, and rests on the assumption by the elders of the symbols of "fatherhood," as they initiate the boys and accept them into the new age-set. Obedience to their "fire-stick" elders is a primary tenet of initiates, one implied by the shared instruments of ritual and assumed by comparable obligations of solidarity to the group of age-mates, whose unity is defined for them by their mutual age-set parentage. This obedience is sanctioned, however, by the power of the curse held by elders over the juniors, somewhat equivalent to the power of the curse a parent has over a child. A curse is a largely unmentioned principle of the relationship, entailed by the fact that the elders have "given birth" to the juniors and thus hold power over them. These obligations to obey, however, are mentioned in councils which seek to instill the proper attitudes of respect on the part of the boys, including specific forms of behavior, avoidance and circumspection. Of great importance is the prohibition on any sexual relations between the wives of sponsoring elders and the juniors, for these women are considered their "mothers," although they may be only slightly older or even of the same age as their symbolic "sons".

Behavior between elders and juniors reflects the dominance of the former, with the juniors inhibited from speaking in the presence of the former, and bound to wait patiently for recognition before greeting or audience with their "fathers". Key decisions about the age-set and its activities are made by elders, and are carried out by juniors. This relationship is culturally given rather than negotiated, and clearly does not depend on overt force, since in such a case, warriors would certainly prevail. Indeed, any resort to wrangling or conflict, especially of a physical order, would be considered extremely shameful for an elder to engage in, and a scandal for a warrior to initiate. If forms of disobedience do occur, boys are harrangued by their elders in general and fined, and they invariably accept their lot with silence and hanging head, if not apologetic then not resentful. The dominance of elders is sanctioned by the curse, which may be evoked when disobedience is experienced; but the curse clearly expresses as well as supports the lines of asymmetrical dominance between the two groups, and is surely most effective when not asserted.

Form and Function

In this discussion of forms of East African aggression and dominance, analogies have been drawn to concepts familiar in strategic studies and primatology. To summarize, East African political systems involve structures of segmentation and symmetry which act to produce a certain military balance, and most often reflect assumptions of appropriate or limited response in warfare. Dominance systems exist which reflect the determination of one individual's or group's behavior by another, but which rarely involve overt force, relying on the more persuasive influence of assumed threat or simply relations of power. These forms of symmetry, limitation, dominance and power can be shown to occur at the East African macro-level, in relations between groups, and at the micro-level, in relations between individuals and in local communities.

Systems of aggression and dominance often result in specific material functions being served, that is, warfare may result in territory being taken and controlled, new resources being opened up, livestock being taken, while dominance may result in power for individuals, benefit for groups, wealth for the dominant. However, I would suggest that as systems, they *are internally motivated* and cannot be accounted for by the specific functions which they serve, or the particular benefits which they appear to have obtained, at certain points in historical time. If territory is taken in one case, in another case territory is left vacant after a decisive battle. There is no evidence that the Purko occupied the Laikipia plateau after they decimated the group of the same name, and there is evidence from the lower Omo valley that land vacated by one group after a defeat was not occupied by the victors. Yet, on other occasions, military conflict is part of an expansionary process of a pastoral system, and new land is occupied and its previous occupants pushed out or assimilated.[8]

Systems of aggression and dominance have their own rationale, which leads to the exercise of force or the exercise of will, apart from specific benefit or return. Much of the debate over the two political blocs in Europe concerns the military realities and the possibilities of confrontation, rather than the issues which divide them. In short, political division becomes its own motivation, as the structure of segmentary alliance and the existence of latent coalitions may demonstrate. Further, a military or warrior ethos becomes internally motivating as well, as readiness for battle incites battle, and defensive maneuvers are interpreted as provocative. The age-set system involves an ethos of assertive masculinity and an organization of warriors, which implies a set of assumptions about the value and the desireability of certain forms of conflict.

Thus it is not towards the functions of aggression and dominance that I turn, which may often concern fairly mundane interests and returns, but to the structure of those systems and their explanation.

Analogies between levels and species suggest, as previously asserted, a commonality of origin or a genetic base. Alternative arguments could assert various situational or motivational factors or factors of form, and factors of form can be attributed to constraints on social interaction or on the making of models, both inflected by the symbolic process. The symmetries involved in a segmentary structure, or one described as a balance of power, can be seen to bear the imprint of systems of social relations, which often involve coalitions in equilibrium, or the imprint of logical analysis, wherein a complex field is reduced to a structure of dualism or a series of oppositions. There is a definite logical constraint implied by the question of which of two complementary and mutually exclusive sides an individual or group belongs. Similarly, the very posing of the question of limited or appropriate responses in conflict vis-a-vis unlimited or massive response, reveals a two-fold yet exhaustive typology of possibilities which determines the logic of modeling as well as orientation to action. Dominance systems are constrained, as previously cited, by the transitive nature of linear series, which underlie any interpersonal relationship, short of notions and experiences of ideal reciprocal intersubjective relationships. The very generality of a notion of dominance in terms of asymmetrical determination of behavior suggests that wherever it is sought, it will be found. Of course, the question of "display" behavior producing certain results is matched by the inverse case, where "non-display" produces similar results, where patterns are deeply ingrained or power makes display redundant. In short, underlying this discussion of Maasai and East African systems of aggression and dominance has rested a set of formal relations, which have helped elucidate and develop the relevant factors, and may well have represented not only heuristically valuable notions but also forces at work. But to use the concepts which are associated with these forms as major dimensions of comparison, rather than as useful analogies, may misconstrue their formal nature, constrained as they are by logic rather than species nature.

Conclusion

This paper represents a body of case material, developed with the expressed intention of providing comparative material for the analysis of aggression and dominance systems, and with the aim of reflecting on the nature of concepts used in such comparison. The social sciences are characterized by the fact that they utilize vocabulary and insights derived from ordinary experience rather than controlled experimentation. Many of the most profound insights they have developed stem from creative use of analogies, which places subject matter in new light, bringing novel perceptions to bear on old problems or redefining fields of thought and study. Where analogies bridge levels proper to given societies, species or families of species, the temptation exists to attribute their convincing nature less to a stimulating principle of symbolic connection, which yields the iight of ancillary lines of rapport, and more to an underlying genetic commonality. Without refuting the possibility of such biogenetic connections, mainly because they cannot be demonstrated, I have suggested that necessary factors, from underlying analogies should be accounted for before more substantive factors are evoked. If levels and species look alike, the commonality may well be in our eyes and minds, and in the models we construct and apply; further, the similarities may well exist in the constraints on social interaction which face agents of comparable forms of action, as is surely the case, in part, with the segmentary structure which may underly primate, human and nation-state behavior. If such possibilities are not carefully considered, Anthropology runs the risk of reducing itself to a sort of evocative bio-journalism, rather than a science advancing through the self-reflective use of general concepts to better understand the human situation, of being both within and outside the universe of human meaning.

References

Bernardi, B. "The Mugwe: a failing prophet." London: Oxford Univ. Press, 1959.

Dyson-Hudson, Rada, "Review of: Warfare among East African Herders," (K. Fukui & D. Turton, eds.). *Science*, 1980, 207, 170–171.

Edgerton, Robert, "The Individual in Cultural Adaptation." Berkeley: University of California Press, 1971.

Evans-Pritchard, E.E., The Nuer. Oxford University Press, 1940.

Fukui, K. & D. Turton, eds. "Warfare among East African Herders." Senri Ethnological Studies 3. Osaka: National Museum of Ethnology, 1979.

Galaty, John G., "Models and metaphors: on the semiotic explanation of segmentary systems." In L. Holy & M. Stuchlik, eds., *The Structure of Folk Models*. A.S.A. Monograph 20. London and New York: Academic Press, 1981.

——Review of: "Warfare among East African Herders (K. Fukui & D. Turton, eds.). *American Anthropologist*, 1981.

——"Being 'Maasai'; being 'people-of-cattle': ethnic shifters in East Africa." *American Ethnologist*, 1982, 9 (1), February: 1–10.

————"Ceremony and society: the poetics of Maasai ritual." *Man* (N.S.), 1983, 18:361—82.

————Ainesse et cyclicite de l'organisation des ages Maasai. *In* M. Abeles & C. Collard, eds., Ainesse et generation en Afrique. Montreal & Paris: Presses de l'Universite de Montreal & Presses Universitaires de France in press.

Hirth, Friedrich, "Early Chinese notices of East African territories." *Journal of the American Oriental Society*, 1909—10, Vol. 30.

Jacobs, Alan, "Maasai inter-tribal relations: belligerent herdsmen or peaceable pastoralists?" *In* Fukui, K. and D. Turton, eds., *Warfare among East African Herders*, 1979.

Krapf, J.L., *Travels, Researches and Missionary Labours*. London: Trubner and Co., 1867.

Leach, E.R. "Magical hair." *The Journal of the Royal Anthropological Institute 88*, 1958 (2): 147—64.

Leakey, L.S., "The Southern Kikuyu before 1903." London: Academic Press, 1977.

Muriuki, G., "A History of the Kikuyu: 1500—1900." Nairobi: East African Publishing House, 1974.

Parks, Robert, "Carrying Culture: an analysis of Maasai sticks and clubs." Unpublished paper, 1979.

Peters, Karl, "New Light on Dark Africa." London: Ward, Lock & Co., 1891.

Ricoeur, Paul, "The Conflict of Interpretations." Evanston: Northwestern University Press, 1974.

Rigby, Peter, "*Olpul* and *entoroj:* the economy of sharing among the pastoral Baraguyu of Tanzania." In Pastoral production and society. Equipe ecologie et anthropologie des societes pastorales, eds., Cambridge University Press, 1979.

Sahlins, Marshall, "The use and abuse of biology: an anthropological critique of sociobiology." Ann Arbor: University of Michigan Press, 1976.

Saberwal, S., "The Traditional Political System of the Embu of Central Kenya." East African Studies 35. Nairobi: East African Publishing House, 1970.

Schelling, T.C., "Arms and Influence." New Haven and London: Yale University Press, 1966.

Schutz, Alfred, *The Phenomenology of the Social World*, (1932) Evanston: Northwestern University Press, 1967.

Thomson, Joseph, "Through Masailand, 1885," London: Frank Cass and Co. (1968).

Weber, Marx, *The Theory of Social and Economic Organization*. New York: The Free Press, 1947.

Wilson, E.O., *On Human Nature*. Cambridge: Harvard University Press, 1978.

Winch, Peter, *The idea of a Social Science and its relation to Philosophy*. London: Routledge and Kegan Paul, 1958.

Notes

1. Case material from the Maasai is drawn from field research carried out in 1974—75 with the support of NSF Doctoral Dissertation Research Grant

No. 74–24027, in a brief field trip in 1981 made possible by the support of the Graduate Faculty of McGill University, and during research on Maasai ritual in 1983, supported by the Social Sciences and Humanities Research Council of Canada and the F.C.A.C. of Quebec. Research affiliation with the Bureau of Educational Research, of the University of Nairobi and Kenyatta University College has made possible and greatly facilitated this work.

2. I have elsewhere described, in brief, symbolism associated with Maasai sticks (Galaty, 1981), a topic pursued at greater length by Parks (1979).

3. I evoke here, but do not review, a literature, spanning sociology, philosophy and anthropology, on the meaningful nature of social action and its symbolic construction (c.f., Weber, 1947; Ricoeur, 1974; Schutz, 1967; Winch, 1958).

4. Sociobiology represents the least subtle variant of this mode of reasoning, in which the assertion of the adaptive character of behavioral traits is assumed, since it cannot be demonstrated, to represent group selection of biological traits (e.g., Wilson, 1978; but c.f., Sahlins, 1976).

5. For an elaboration of the social and symbolic dynamics of *Eunoto*, which underly the system of Maasai segmentation, see Galaty (1983).

6. For further discussion and analysis of the Maasai system of political segmentation, see Galaty (1981; and in press).

7. One excellent, though somewhat dated, example from the literature on deterrence theory is Schelling (1966).

8. The excellent set of cases studied in the collection *Warfare among East African Herders* (Fukui and Turton 1979) offers no explicit conclusions regarding the territorial motive of warfare. However, several contributions lend themselves to the interpretation that these cases of warfare rest most immediately on factors of political competition and competition for livestock, rather than the factor of control of territory or use of pastures. In the long run, warfare surely involves shifts of regional power between groups and processes of territorial expansion and retraction, but usually as later, secondary and often unintended consequences (c.f., Galtay, 1982; but c.f., R. Dyson-Hudson, 1980 for the opposite interpretation).

Commentary: Some Parallels with Modern War

Armand Clesse

$\mathcal{A}$ main thesis put forward by Prof. Galaty in his paper states that there are useful analogies to be drawn between the subject matter of non-human primate dominance and aggression, conflict and warfare in small-scale pre-industrial societies and the military strategies of highly mechanized armies in nation states. At the same time he makes clear that many of these analogies are more formal than substantive.

Being neither an ethologist nor an anthropologist, I would like to confine myself to some cautious remarks on those analogies which have a more or less direct link with the problems of peace and war among states from the point of view of strategic analysis.

Professor Galaty asks whether the establishment of a transnational military line, across which the army of the opposing alliance must not cross, can be considered as an example of 'territoriality.'

Probably it can. But the comparison would perhaps be more accurate for communities as defined by Toennies[1] or Easton[2] or pluralistic security communities (according to the terminology of K. Deutsch[3] than for alliances.

Indeed, even if, for example, paragraph 5 of the North Atlantic Treaty provides that an armed attack against one or more of the parties in Europe or North America shall be considered an attack against them all, this does not mean that in real life each of the members of the alliance will react should any of the other members become victim of aggression, in the same manner as if his own territory were attacked. The United States, for example, as the main guarantor of the security of other alliance members would certainly not react in the same way after an attack against Turkey or France as it would after an attack of W. Germany (Turkey appearing less important than W. Germany from an overall strategic point of view). The US has stronger historical ties and socio-cultural affinities towards W. Germany than towards Turkey, and more than 200,000 American troops are deployed in W. Germany, while only a few thousand are in Turkey; France is not a member of the integrated military system of NATO, and so forth. And of course, it would not react in the same way after an attack on W. Germany as it would after an attack on American soil. This difference in behavior results from the fact that the alliance does not form a monolithic entity the way a nation, state or a community does.

Professor Galaty writes that the sticks carried by male Maasai signify not only conflict, but also restraint. I wonder whether it may not be possible to compare, in some sense, the stick in Maasai society and the Western nuclear doctrine called 'Second Strike Strategy' which is based upon a posture called 'Second Strike Capability.' (Professor Galaty himself does not make such a comparison.) A 'Second Strike Strategy' signifies, as does the stick in the hand of a male Maasai, a capacity for retaliation but also restraint. Indeed, such a 'Second Strike Strategy,' which also appeared under the name of 'Assured Destruction,' or 'Mutual Assured Destruction' (MAD), intends to show the potential adversary that one will not try to disarm him (i.e., to prevent him from dealing a full retaliatory blow) by striking first, but only to inflict unacceptable damage (i.e., damage exceeding by far whatever the adversary could reasonably expect to win[4]) upon him, should he not stick to the tacit rules of the game, i.e., should he try a first strike (be it counterforce or countercity or both at the same time).

If a 'Second Strike Capability,' which is most dreadful in itself, i.e., by its sheer physical potentialities, is seen in the context of the system of mutual strategic deterrence existing between the superpowers, it appears only as an instrument for fostering strategic stability, for preserving the status quo. Of course, one can argue with Oppenheimer that such a restraint is not more than a restraint of two scorpions in a bottle.[5]

Professor Galaty writes about the Maasai spokesman who carries a smaller, highly polished black stick, an emblem of office, and who has a seat reserved for him when he sits; his dominance,

according to Professor Galaty, is an outcome of cultural intentionality and is more implicit than explicit.

A similar pattern of dominance can be found in the society of
states. France and Great Britain, even if they are no longer great
powers, but at best middle powers, are permanent members of the
Security Council of the United Nations (together with the USA,
USSR, China) and play a role in world politics that goes far beyond
their real power. Their nuclear capacity is a symbolic expression
of this role rather than a genuine power instrument which would
allow them to impose their views by threatening the use of this
instrument. In fact, this capacity can be useful as long as it will
not be pushed towards a showdown, as long as its dominance
remains implicit.

Resemblance between segmentary theory and a theory of balance of power: Professor Galaty writes that there is an inherent
dualism in both models, since alliances would tend to congregate
units of disparate and varying interest into large blocs; when
conflict would occur, units that attempt to sit on the fence would
tend to be pushed to one bloc or the other.

The latter part of the statement is not necessarily true for
neutral states: it would certainly not hold true for Sweden,
Austria or Switzerland. A state such as Finland, on the other
hand, would probably tend to be pushed to one block or the other
in case of serious East-West conflict.

The statement might prove correct for states which, without
being neutral by international law or international behavior,
show no strong interest, in time of detente, in supporting clearly
the aims and actions of an alliance whose general political and
ideological objectives and world outlook they share.

Intensified conflict may, however, have in this case an opposite
effect: the fear of states which sit on the fence, of being entangled
in the conflict and of running (especially in the nuclear age) a
greater risk of annihilation, might lead these states to turn
further away from the bloc.

The statement made by Professor Galaty may be correct from an
intra-alliance perspective, i.e., for states which are legally and
materially committed to an alliance. In periods of rising tensions
(see Cold War) there is reinforcement of alliance solidarity, alliance cohesion, there may even be progress towards greater
integration; whereas in times of lessening tensions (see Detente)

there is a lessening of alliance harmony, mounting discontent, disputes on political aims, on strategic foundations, and on economic burden-sharing.

One must notice, however, that there are today, in a time of renewed East-West confrontation, strong neutralist tendencies in several formally committed West European countries, i.e., tendencies towards withdrawal from the Atlantic alliance and a policy of appeasement towards the Soviet bloc.

Prof. Galaty writes that the various sides tend towards balance because smaller groups gravitate towards alliances with, or assimilation into, the larger, and because an asymmetry in relations between the two might produce a form of instability that would lead to diplomatic realignments.

I think that this is too mechanistic a view of international relations and that, while being attractive from a theoretical point of view, it does not take into account the complexities of these relations (interstate activities do not take place under ideal conditions).

First, states do not always have the opportunity to align or realign according to their preferences. They do not always have this opportunity in the US sphere of influence and they certainly do not have it in the Soviet one (Yugoslavia and Albania are exceptions; moreover, they defected but did not realign themselves with the West).

Second—and this seems quite natural—states sometimes tend to realign themselves with the stronger block (or the one they think will be stronger in the future), increasing, in the same vein, the risk of global imbalance, i.e., of the preponderance of one power bloc.

Appropriate response to hostilities, limitation on warfare: According to Prof. Galaty, the feud represents a system of justice, based on the appropriateness of response, in a sort of "tit-for-tat" form; it is aimed at resolution rather than continuance of hostilities, and represents an intrinsically limited notion of conflict since an act of aggression calls for a balanced and specific, rather than an unpredictable or generalized response.

This analogy goes to the heart of the strategy debate of the Western alliance ever since its inhibition in 1949. When Dulles proclaimed, in 1954, the doctrine of 'massive retaliation'[6]—which in fact never was a doctrine of massive retaliation but, as Dulles himself was to explain afterwards, a doctrine of selective retaliation—the US was in a situation of clear nuclear superiority. But even in this situation the credibility of this doctrine was soon to be doubted: would the US really risk a general nuclear war because of a minor Soviet encroachment somewhere in the world? The doubts and critiques were summed up in Maxwell Taylor's "The Uncertain Trumpet,"[7] and led finally to a doctrine of 'Flexible response' adopted by NATO in 1967 (MC 14/3). The essence of the new doctrine was that NATO would react, in case of Soviet aggression, with those means that were just necessary to stop the attack and make clear that it was up to the Soviets to make the next steps in the ladder of conflict escalation. The purpose is to terminate eventual hostilities at the lowest possible level.

Secretary of Defense, McNamara declared in June, 1962, in Ann Arbor: "The US has come to the conclusion that, to the extent feasible, basic military strategy in a possible general nuclear war should be approached in much the same way that more conventional military operations have been regarded in the past. That is to say, principal military objectives . . . should be the destruction of the enemy's military forces, not of his civilian population."[8]

One of his successors, Schlesinger, said in his Annual Defense Department Report, FY, 1975: "What we need is a series of measured responses to aggression which bear some relation to the provocation, have prospects of terminating hostilities before general war breaks out, and leave some possibility for restoring deterrence."

The Presidential Directive No. 59, issued by Carter in 1980, affirmed selective and limited nuclear options as American strategic policy. The Reagan Administration has also offered some rather loose talk about limited nuclear war, protracted nuclear war, fighting a nuclear war, winning a nuclear war.

These reflections and statements, as well as new technological achievements, have aroused much public concern. Some people think that all this could lead to an official posture of nuclear war-fighting and to a destabilization of the existing delicate balance of terror. Nuclear war could thus, they fear, lose part of its horror, become more thinkable and therefore more feasible. In fact, as Ian Clark has written, "the attempt to create the infrastructure of the future convention of limited nuclear warfare could easily be interpreted by the opponent as threatening and

254

provocative, and as being more aggressive than the simple espousal of total war threats."[9]

Professor Galaty writes that defensive responses tend to be perpetuated even in the absence of continuous and sustained threat.

One can observe this kind of perpetuation of defensive responses also in the behavior of nation states, at least on a political, if not on a military, level. The USSR and France have spoken of a terrifying German threat in the years following the Second World War (in the case of the USSR, even into the Sixties, and to the Ostpolitik of the Brandt/Scheel government) when this threat had long since gone and Germany had no longer by any rational account, even after its—purely conventional—rearmament in the middle of the Fifties, the slightest physical possibility of attacking these states. The same seems to have been true for China v. Japan after 1945.

On the other side and in a positive sense, a commitment (by a state for the security of another one) can persist long after it has expired on a legal level, has been terminated on a material one, and has even faded away on a psychological one.[10]

The issue of "display": Professor Galaty writes that if a pattern of violence and raiding is feared and has been experienced, it then is only necessary for a group to sight a member of the threatening group for it to experience intimidation. He also stresses the importance of the visibility of the military force as a factor in its "influence". As examples he mentions the presence of American troops in NATO-Europe and land-based intercontinental missiles.

This observation certainly is quite accurate. It might be partially for this reason that the Soviet Union keeps such enormous numbers of troops and tanks, especially in its Western military districts, even if it knows that part of the troops have a poor combat readiness and many of the armoured forces are of inadequate quality—and could even impede a rapid advance of the better ones. In addition they prefer to deploy land-based missiles rather than sea-based ones; they build huge missiles which can carry enormous megatonnages when smaller missiles could serve the strategic objectives as well or even better (at least for eventual preventive counterforce strikes). This might also be the reason why big military parades are organized all over the world (but especially in capitals like Moscow and East Berlin), that huge military manoeuvres regularly take place in East and West (and that even the East has agreed, in the context of the Conference on Security and Cooperation in Europe, that observers can be present at such manoeuvres).

Notes

1. Toennies, Ferdinand: Gemeinschaft und Gesellschaft, Darmstadt, 1970.

2. Easton, David, *A System Analysis of Political Life*, New York, 1965, p. 185.

3. "Political Community and the North Atlantic Area," by Karl W. Deutsch, Sidney A. Burrell, Robert A. Kann, Maurice Lee, Jr., Martin Lichtermann, Raymond E. Lindgren, Francis L. Loewenheim, Richard W. Van Wagenen in *International Political Communities. An Anthology*, New York, 1966, p. 2–4.

4. In the sixties, unacceptable damage was sometimes defined as meaning the destruction of about one-fifth to one-third of the population and one half to two-thirds of the industrial capacity.

5. Robert Oppenheimer in mid-1953: "We may anticipate a state of affairs in which the two Great Powers will each be in a position to put an end to the civilization and life of the other, though not without risking its own. We may be likened to two scorpions in a bottle, each capable of killing the other, but only at the risk of his own life." Atomic Weapons and American Policy, Foreign Affairs, July 1953, p. 529.

6. In a speech of January 12, 1954, Dulles declared that the Eisenhower Administration had decided a strategic policy according to which the US would "depend upon a great capacity to retaliate, instantly, by means and at places of our choosing." Department of State Bulletin, 30, January 25, 1954, p. 107–110.

7. New York, 1960.

8. Address given at Ann Arbor, Michigan, June 16, 1962, Department of State Bulletin July 9, 1962, p. 64–69.

9. Clark, Ian, Limited Nuclear War, Oxford, 1982, p. 145.

10. Schelling, Thomas C., *Arms and Influence*, New Haven, 1966, p. 52.

9.
Nuclear Weapons and the Control of Aggression

Armand Clesse

Is war in the nuclear age obsolete or does it remain an inescapable mode of regulation of conflicts between sovereign states?

Osgood and Tucker noted in their "Force, Order and Justice" that the question of military power includes more than the obsolescence or utility of war.[1] By military power, the authors mean the "ability of states to affect the will and behavior of other states by armed coercion or the threat of armed coercion."[2]

Stated in such terms, military force may remain a useful instrument of the power politics of nations. But this does not solve the essential problem of whether such a use could also sensibly encompass the physical employment of thermonuclear weapons, or if, on the contrary, these weapons are suited exclusively for purposes of deterrence. Certainly, nuclear weapons may be used for the more or less subtle power objectives of states in the same way that other weapons have been used in the past. But what will happen if the power game gets out of control, if deterrence fails, if the first missiles leave their silos? Will the possessors of nuclear weapons be able to remain in control of events or will they watch, helplessly, to the very last bomb, the awesome exchange of systems of mass extermination?

Is man, in collusion with a technique he invented, capable of devising a means of retaining control after the outbreak of war? And would such an effort be useful? Or would it be wiser to proclaim the impossibility of keeping a nuclear war limited, to make plain that the release of one single nuclear weapon will signify the first step in an inescapable process leading to all-out war, and thus try to maximize the incentives against any first use of nuclear devices?

How does one get the most effective deterrence? Is it by showing that one is able to remain in control of events after deterrence has failed, or by making plain that one would be completely overrun by events?

This dilemma lies at the core of the "nuclear debate" of the past decades, years and months, and it will probably confront the world for an indefinite period of time.[3]

Functions and Causes of War

War is not normally the product of pure aggressiveness; aggressiveness is intermingled with other elements such as fear, or lust for power. And generally, war is not normally caused by an impulse, but by calculation: a war is undertaken if the attacker thinks he has a fairly good chance of being better off after the war than before.

So, the conduct of war between territorial entities has traditionally been more or less proportional to the stakes involved, to the intended level of violence, to the political intentions of the combatants.[4] A certain amount of aggressiveness, plus a certain amount of greediness, leads one state to attack another in order to improve its own chances of survival through eliminating a dangerous, actual or potential, rival, by annexing his territory, or by exploiting his economic resources. "Throughout recorded history, violence has served as a major mechanism for changing the intercommunity status quo; and the intercommunity war, and the threat of such war, have been the major forms in which violence has been employed toward effecting changes in power relationships, in political boundaries, and in the allocation of many values figuring in intercommunity conflicts of interest."[5]

While most observers do not attribute the waging of war to one single cause, many do perceive a basic motive in man's innate aggressiveness and pugnacity.[6] For them, the important causes of war are found in man's nature: wars result "from selfishness, from misdirected aggressive impulses, from stupidity."[7] Reinhold Niebuhr saw man's quest for absoluteness as the ultimate cause of war: "It is the human effort to make our partial values absolute which is always the final sin in human life; and it always results in the most bloody of human conflicts."[8]

Hans Morgenthau distinguished two main roots of conflict: the competition for scarce goods and the animus dominandi: "In a world where power counts, no nation pursuing a rational policy has a choice between renouncing and wanting power; and if it could, the lust for power for the individual's sake would still confront us with its less spectacular yet not less pressing moral defects."[9]

According to E.I.M. Durbin, war is due to the expression in and through group life of the aggressiveness of individuals. There are only two ways, he thought, to reduce war in its frequency and violence: a slow, curative and peaceful one, a new type of emotional education to remove the ultimate causes of war in human character, and an immediate, coercive one, aimed at symptoms, namely the restraint of the aggressor by force.[10]

In his monumental study of the phenomenon of war, Quincy Wright tried to be as comprehensive as possible regarding the causes of war: he distinguished five general causes which were connected to political, sociological, psychological, technological and legal factors,[11] and five additional and more specific causes: reaction to perceived threats; enthusiasm for ideals; frustration over unsatisfactory conditions attributed to a foreign scapegoat; belief in the utility of threats of war, or war itself, as instrument of independence, policy, prestige or power; conviction that military self-help is necessary to vindicate justice, law, and rights if peaceful negotiation proves ineffective.[12]

Traditional Warfare

In traditional warfare, the risk involved in the attack of another country did not appear excessive, as the assailant was able to choose the place, moment and means of attack, to some extent the dimension of the warfare, prepare avenues for retreat and decide the moment of retreat (cease-fire). While waging war, states could be more or less confident of remaining in control of affairs, regulating the level of hostilities by mobilizing more or less troops, pouring in or retiring armaments, advancing or retreating, and through diplomatic exchanges, announcing the war aims or underlining the declared intentions through practical steps. The pressures upon the attacker, as upon the defender, to make a rapid decision about escalation or deescalation were relatively weak. Many built-in constraints existed which offered time to think about the consequences of a decision, increase inputs, strike a balance, and reach a compromise—either inside one's own political system, with allies, or with the opponent through intermediaries.[13]

In the Middle Ages, war was "more a way of life than a calculated instrument of policy."[14] The armies were small and they lacked the weapons and logistics to overcome the defensive advantage of castles and fortresses. Wars were fought for the status and enrichment of kings, and for the economic gratification of the nobility. They were mostly permeated by the chivalric values of personal honor, glory and vengeance.

Napoleon, by creating a "nation in arms" (levée en masse), transformed warfare into a national crusade[15] profiting from popular nationalism and ideological fervor. The wars from 1815 to 1914 were relatively limited: they were fought for limited objectives, they were localized and quickly terminated.

Even the two World Wars, with their introduction of innumerable new weapons such as airplanes, tanks, submarines, poison gas, the mass slaughtering of men (s. Verdun), and the annihilation of enormous quantities of war material, were still encounters which were, to a certain degree at least, controlled by the warchiefs and where one seldom lost sight of the overall political objectives.

The Nuclear Revolution

The advent of nuclear weapons appears to have dramatically changed the basic conditions of warfare. In the past, when certain conditions were fulfilled, war could be considered a useful instrument of policy for states in relation to those of inferior power: when, for example, military technology favored the offensive and was not excessively destructive; when the international system was a loosely organized balance of military power providing no forum in which economic, legal, or moral arguments might prevail against an opponent with a superior power position; when policies generally aimed at territorial adjustments, nationalistic integration, imperial expansion, increase of power, or other tangible interests, with little attention to human welfare or world stability.[16]

Now, nuclear power seemed to have made traditional war aims obsolete: "Thus far, the chief purposes of our military establishment has been to win wars. From now on, its chief purpose must be to avert them. It can have almost no other useful purpose," wrote Bernard Brodie in 1946,[17] and again thirteen years later: "Clausewitz's classic definition, that the object of war is to impose one's will on the enemy, must be modified, at least for any opponent who has a substantial nuclear capability behind him."[18]

The thesis that nuclear weapons have made war obsolete has been defended with particular vigor by Walter Millis, who wrote that war "can no longer serve its greatest social function—that of ultima ratio in human affairs—for it can no longer decide."[19] Many politicians have shared this view: "War is obsolete," said President Johnson in 1964, "obsolete because there can be no winner. War is obsolete because the progress in mankind's abilities and knowledge make possible and imperative a new measure of national greatness, the measurement of how men are served by their system."[20]

Others don't agree—or at least not completely—with the thesis of the obsolescence of war in the nuclear age. They criticize it—a bit unfairly as we have seen—for failing to appreciate the "subtle and varied role of military power short of war." Without dealing with the utility or uselessness of actual war among highly industrialized states, they think that the fearful prospect of war and the policies for using, deterring, controlling, and disarming armed forces in the shadow of this prospect, play a decisive role in international politics. This role may even be more pervasive than previously, when war was less dangerous.[21] Their thesis, therefore, is that military power, far from losing its relevance to international politics, has even expanded its role in many respects—not in opposition to politics, but through politics: "Political and military factors have come to suffuse each other in a way that makes the conventional distinctions of previous eras irrelevant."[22]

Hence, nuclear weapons may have brought a technical revolution, but not a political one: "The political revolution that was so widely expected in 1945 would have made international politics more like domestic politics by abolishing anarchy, and so, by placing supreme power in the hands of a single authority, would have abolished war. This revolution has not taken place."[23] In fact nuclear weapons may not have changed the international system:

"Relations among sovereign states are still governed by the principle of anarchy. War is still possible."[24]

Because of their revolutionary properties, the emergence of nuclear weapons fundamentally altered the possibilities of warfare itself. These properties include: an enormous increase in the scale of destruction, the enormous technological superiority of offensive over defensive forces, the greatly enhanced uncertainties about the capabilities of military forces and about relationships of military power, the dramatically increased—and indeed global reach of nuclear weaponry, and the fabulous speed with which nuclear weapons could reach their targets.[25]

In fact, as Churchill noted, it was the fusion bomb, far more than the fission bomb, that triggered a genuine revolution in warfare: "The atomic bomb, with all its terror, did not carry us outside the scope of human control or manageable events in thought or action, in peace and war. But . . . (with) the hydrogen bomb, the entire foundation of human affairs was revolutionized."[26]

The difference between the military force available before and after 1945 was so enormous that it fundamentally altered the character of military operations: "To compress a catastrophic war within the span of time that a man can stay awake, drastically changes the politics of war, the process of decision, the possibility of central control and restraint, the motivations of the people in charge, and the capacity to think and reflect while war is in progress."[27]

Familiar moral categories, ideas of right and wrong in warfare, do not fit all-out nuclear war; cultural mechanisms for coping with death do not work on the scale of death and destruction that nuclear weapons make possible. Whereas battles of the past have been conflicts of will between soldiers, a large-scale exchange of nuclear force would be a contest in the endurance of annihilation by civilian populations.[28]

The excess of force that has resulted from the possession of nuclear weapons has certainly placed severe constraints upon the possibilities to wage war. This scale of destruction has impinged upon the options to resolve, by violent means (not only of nuclear, but also of conventional character), disputes on ideological, territorial, economic issues, and questions concerning the behavior of the other superpower in a still bipolar international system, that is, its way of assuring power within its direct sphere of influence, of trying to obtain influence in other parts of the world through destabilization tactics, and in the struggle for superiority.

Without doubt, nuclear weapons have, at least under most imaginable strategic configurations and as far as the relations between the present nuclear powers are concerned, a strongly inhibitory effect upon aggression.[29] There remain, of course, the problems of aggression between non-nuclear states (s. Iran v. Iraq), between a nuclear and a non-nuclear state (s. China v. Vietnam), of catalytic war (a war brought about by a third party), and of spill-over from a non-nuclear conflict between non-nuclear states to a nuclear conflict between nuclear states.

Few people would contest the assumption that only in the most extreme situations, such as the expectation of a great unimpaired gain or fear of a great irreparable loss, would the leadership of the superpowers resort to the massive employment of strategic nuclear weapons. But then, the key question is: where is this all-decisive threshold located and could it shift under certain circumstances so that the use of nuclear weapons could—for one side or both—become less unacceptable? What would these circumstances be and how could one change the "nuclear system" to render it immune against such destabilizing tendencies?[30]

This leads to the question of unintentional nuclear war, of accidental nuclear war: could a nuclear war break out because of technical malfunction, because certain signals are misread, because of psychological breakdown? What would happen if, despite all the measures of prevention and control, something goes wrong between the nuclear superpowers? What kind of reactions would their doctrines prescribe, and their weapon systems provide or allow? How would they cope with the predictable, the unpredictable? Would they try to end the war as quickly as possible on any terms, as some have suggested, or would they strive for a kind of meaningful victory in such a war, as others demand? And if they would like to, would they be able to remain in control of the war or would this war irresistibly escalate to the extreme,[31] to an all-out war ending up in total mutual annihilation?

American Strategic Policies

If there has existed a basic continuity in American thinking about national security since the forties, in the sense that the central issue always has been to determine the best way for establishing and maintaining deterrence, the implementation of this thinking has undergone many transformations. The dominant beliefs of any period have always been heavily challenged by a certain number of theoreticians and practicians, i.e., there has never been a national consensus on how best to secure national security.

In the late forties, despite the scarcity of the available atomic bombs, and the means for delivering them,[32] and prior to the arrival of hydrogen weapons, war operations were conceived in a World War II framework. Strategic airpower "was expected to function as a blunting instrument that might succeed in purchasing time for the United States to mobilize on a World War II scale."[33] The Finletter Report of 1948 emphasized the increased importance of airpower.[34]

Whereas the National Security Council Paper NSC-68 of April, 1950, asked for a balanced military build-up of the United States and its allies; NSC-162/2 of October, 1953, came to reflect the policy of the Eisenhower Administration (the so-called "New Look"), whose main characteristic was a pronounced reliance upon nuclear weapons in order to save money—nuclear arms being relatively cheaper than conventional ones. "In the event of hostilities," said this document, "the United States will consider nuclear weapons to be as available for use as other munitions."[35] The paper asked for a capability for inflicting massive retaliatory damage by offensive striking power, thus anticipating the "massive retaliation" speech by Foreign Secretary Dulles. At the same time, NSC-162/2 anticipated the arguments of the opponents of a "massive retaliation" strategy by forecasting a time when the two major powers would have reached "a stage of atomic plenty and ample means of delivery," which in turn could result in a "stalemate, with both sides reluctant to initiate general warfare."[36]

The determination of the administration to use nuclear weapons was proclaimed by Eisenhower in the State of the Union Message on January 7, 1954: "While determined to use atomic power to serve the usages of peace, we take into full account our great and growing number of nuclear weapons and the most effective means of using them . . . if they are needed to preserve our freedom."[37] A few days later, on January 14, 1954, Foreign Secretary Dulles declared that the basic decision had been made "to depend primarily upon a great capacity to retaliate, instantly, by means and at places of our own choosing."[38] As this statement was largely misinterpreted, or as Dulles was disturbed by the way it was interpreted, he felt obliged to issue a clarification, in a *Foreign Affairs* article of April, 1954, stating that a "massive atomic and thermonuclear reaction is not the kind of power which could most usefully be evoked under all circumstances."[39] Still later, he explained that this doctrine was to be "a policy of deterring war by a capacity for selective retaliation."[40] Despite this attempt at clarification, SAC's war plans in the early and mid-1950s provided exclusively for all-out war.[41]

During this time, some experts began to think about the possibilities of limited nuclear war. Tactical nuclear weapons might favor the position of the West because they favored the position of the defender. Henry Kissinger, among others, advanced a doctrine for limited nuclear war in which he developed the idea of building units for tactical nuclear warfare: these units should be small so as not to offer worthwhile targets to the enemy, mobile to avoid detection and early destruction, self-contained because the supply system of World War II appeared to be vulnerable to interdiction.[42]

The availability of tactical nuclear weapons, the ever growing accuracy of strategic nuclear systems, and the realization of the rapidly increasing Soviet strategic arsenal, producing fears (as in the missile gap debate) of a decisive Soviet superiority, led to a recognition that any massive counter-city attack would engender a devastating and inescapable counter-strike. In addition, the fears that the balance of terror could be less stable than presumed,[43] and an increasing awareness of a new societal vulnerability (after the launching of the first Soviet Sputnik,[44] directed new attention to thoughts about preventive and preemptive war) and also to demands for steps to improve the protection of the offensive systems, as well as the population.[45]

The Kennedy Administration pronounced "survivability" as a primary strategic goal. Defense Secretary McNamara explained that, in the age of nuclear-armed intercontinental missiles, "the ability to deter rests heavily on the existence of a force which can weather and survive a massive nuclear attack, even with little or no warning, in sufficient strength to strike a decisive counter-blow."[46] In the first weeks of 1961, Kennedy ordered a permanent alert status for half of the airplanes of the Strategic Air Command, invested heavily in the Polaris and Minuteman systems, that is, those weapons which appeared capable of riding out a massive nuclear attack.[47]

The "Basic National Security Plan" was redrawn. Contrary to earlier plans, the US war plan, called SIOP (Single Integrated Operation Plan), provided that thermonuclear hardware would no longer be released in a single, awful "spasm"; instead, the nation would withhold strategic forces in reserve, even after the shooting began. The distinction between military and non-military targets was emphasized and provisions were made for sparing Soviet command and control systems to give the Soviets the chance to maintain that distinction even during a nuclear exchange.[48]

McNamara announced the change in American tactical plans in June, 1962: "Principle military objectives, in the event of a nuclear war stemming from a major attack on the alliance, should be the destruction of the enemy's military forces, not of his civilian population." Nuclear conflict should, from now on, be approached "in much the same way that more conventional military operations have been regarded in the past."[49]

But the limited potential of the Minuteman missiles as hard-target killers, the increasing number of Soviet ICBMs (intercontinental ballistic missile) after 1963, the prospect that the Soviet Union would soon construct hardened silos and deploy SLBMs (sea-launched ballistic missiles) aboard strategic submarines, as well as strong bureaucratic opposition, led the Department of Defense to shift its "declaratory doctrinal emphasis" from counterforce to assured destruction.[50] ". . . In the event of nuclear war," McNamara declared in 1965, "attacks might be directed against military targets only, against cities only, or against both types of target, either simultaneously or with a delay. They might be selective in terms of specific targets or they might be general."[51]

Assured Destruction was, for McNamara, more important than damage limitation: "it is our ability to destroy an attacker . . . that provides the deterrent, not our ability to partially limit damage to ourselves."[52] McNamara thought that a potential to destroy at least 25 to 30 percent of the USSR's population, and two-thirds of its industrial capacity, should serve as an effective deterrent. Later, he lowered the assured destruction levels to 20 to 25 percent population fatalities and one-half the Soviet Union's industrial capacity.[53]

Contrary to what he had proclaimed during the electoral campaign, Richard Nixon returned, one week after assuming office, to the concept of strategic sufficiency, which had been introduced by Eisenhower.[54] At the same time, his administration worried about the vulnerability of the American arsenal in view of advancing Soviet technology. The ICBMs were threatened by the Soviet SS-9 and the development of MIRV (Multiple independently targetable reentry vehicles) for the SS-9. The B-52s were vulnerable because of Soviet SLBM, and the American SLBM became targets for Soviet anti-submarine warfare.[55] Nixon announced in March, 1969, that the Sentinel ABM (which had been initiated by the Johnson administration to provide a thin area defense of the United States against small-scale missile attacks and defend American ICBMs if necessary) would be changed into the Safeguard System (which called for ABM sites to be deployed at Minuteman ICBM fields in the first stage and for a nationwide coverage in a second stage).[56] But the Nixon Administration was soon to lose interest in ABM.

At the same time, the MIRV program was pursued to offset possible future Soviet ABM expansion and provide a greater number of surviving Minuteman warheads if a portion of the U.S. force was destroyed by a counterforce strike; MIRV would also give U.S. sea-based forces greater deterrent power.[57]

In his first foreign policy message, Nixon asked whether an American president should really be left "with the single option of ordering the mass destruction of enemy civilians, in the face of the certainty that it would be followed by the mass slaughter of Americans."[58] In view of the rigidity of the U.S. strategic war plans, the Administration wished to develop operational plans for using strategic forces selectively.

Defense Secretary Schlesinger, in a testimony of March 4, 1974, exposed a new targeting doctrine which emphasized flexibility and which was intended to provide pre-planned small strikes against a variety of targets, including military targets, with the option of limiting these strikes down to a few weapons.[59] In his Fiscal Year 1975 Report, Schlesinger explained that the aim of the new targeting doctrine was to reinforce deterrence across a wide spectrum of situations by having sufficient options that ranged from massive response to no response, or, if deterrence should fail, to limit the chances of uncontrolled escalation by being able to respond selectively before having to consider the ultimate option of assured destruction strikes against cities.[60]

The "Schlesinger Doctrine" was slightly modified by the Carter

Administration which adopted the so-called "countervailing strategy"; this strategy found its official expression in the July 25, 1980 Presidential Directive 59 on Nuclear Weapons Employment Policy. The new policy provided that the United States must have countervailing strategic options "such that at a variety of levels of exchange, aggression would either be defeated or would result in unacceptable costs that exceed gains."[62] In a November 1980 Nuclear Planning Group Communiqué, the Allies agreed that this strategy, coupled with force modernization efforts, "enhances NATO's strategy of deterrence by adding to the credibility and flexibility of its forces."[63]

The Reagan Administration has largely endorsed the doctrinal approach of its predecessor even if it introduced in its 1982 Defense Guidance statement, the concept of "prevailing" in a protracted nuclear war.[64]

American Civilian Strategists Against "Assured Destruction"

Elements of the countervailing strategy appeared in the works of American civilian strategists more than two decades ago. Wohlstetter argued that deterrence would not of itself remove the danger of accidental outbreak of war or limit the damage in case it failed; nor would it be at all adequate for crises on the periphery. A protected retaliatory capability, on the other hand, would have "a stabilizing influence, not only in deterring rational attack, but also in offering every inducement to both powers to reduce the chance of accidental war."[65] In his path-breaking study on thermonuclear war, Herman Kahn proposed that, since deterrence was not absolutely reliable and since it would be possible to survive a nuclear war, we must buy time, that is, make preparations to limit damage, to facilitate recuperation, to get the best military result possible, or to prevail somehow, even if one could not win.[66]

For Fred Charles Iklé, the American strategic policy was full of contradictions: "On the one hand, we brush aside the immorality of threatening to kill millions of hostages, assuming that the threat will deter and that to deter means to prevent nuclear war. On the other hand, we argue that we must be poised to carry out 'retaliation' swiftly and thus convey determination for irrational vengeance, since all rational purpose of retaliation would have disappeared when its time had come. We want to maintain a vague threat of using nuclear weapons first to deter massive conventional attack; yet, to stabilize mutual deterrence we must not threaten Soviet nuclear arms nor defend against them . . ."[67] Instead of what he termed the strategy of "assured genocide," Iklé proposed a policy to eliminate the vulnerability of the strategic arms to surprise attack. This was intended to break the vicious circle inherent in the argument that these arms "must be ready for prompt launching because they are vulnerable, and that they are vulnerable because they must be ready."[68] One could jointly decide with the Russians to replace the "doomsday catapults" invented in the 1950s with arms that would be incapable of being launched swiftly, and thus reduce the fear of surprise attack.

Henry Kissinger also launched a caustic critique at the strategy of Assured Destruction, which he charged with irrationality, immorality and inefficiency: "It was all very well to threaten mutual suicide for purposes of deterrence, particularly in case of a direct threat to national survival. But no President could make such a threat credible except by conducting a diplomacy that suggested a high irrationality . . . And if deterrence failed and the President was finally faced with the decision to retaliate, who would take the moral responsibility for recommending a strategy based on the mass extermination of civilizations? How could the United States hold its allies together as the credibility of its strategy eroded? How would we deal with Soviet conventional forces once the Soviets believed that we meant what we said about basing strategy on the extermination of civilians?"[69]

Theories of pre-war deterrence cannot guarantee, Colin Gray explained, that the United States will never slip into a crisis, wherein the President has to initiate the use of strategic nuclear weapons or surrender. In such a situation, a president would need "realistic war plans that carried a vision of the war as a whole and embodied a theory of how military action should produce desired political ends. In short, he would be in need of strategy."[70]

These criticisms and proposals have of course come under the heavy fire of those who believe in the utility and feasability of a stable strategic balance which would guarantee mutual assured destruction. For Bernard Brodie, "the notion that in an extremely tense crisis, which may include an ongoing theater war, any useful purpose is likely to be served by firing off strategic nuclear weapons, however limited in number, seems vastly to under-estimate both the risks to the nation in such a course, and the burden upon the person who must make the decision." And he remains convinced that, "any rigidity which keeps us from entering the new horrors or from nibbling at it in the hopes that a nibble will clearly be seen as such by the other side, is a salutary rigidity."[71]

Michael Howard, in a critique of Gray and also of PD-59, questions the adequacy of the command and control structure for the execution of a strategy of flexible operations. He asks about the situation in Europe during such a limited war and raises the issue of the effects of a limited nuclear exchange upon the United States. To use strategic nuclear weapons for war "would be to enter the realms of the unknown and the unknowable, and what little we do know about it is appalling."[72]

The critics of such tactical strategies remain convinced like McNamara that "nuclear weapons serve no military purpose whatsoever," that "they are totally useless—except solely to deter one's opponent from using them."[73]

Soviet Strategic Policies

In the Soviet Union, there has never existed a strategic debate comparable to that of the United States. As in all matters linked to sensitive ideological issues, the Soviet debate which, contrary to the American one, was led by military people, has been of a cautious, tentative, incremental character. So it seemed that early on, Soviet leaders were reluctant to accept the revolutionary impact of nuclear weapons on inter-state relations and on the possibilities of waging wars.

For many years, the "five permanently operating factors" pro-nounced by Stalin in 1942[74] (the stability of the rear, the morale of the army, the quantity and quality of divisions, the armament of the army, and the organizational ability of the army command-ers), determined the strategic outlook of the Soviet state. After the death of Stalin, the importance of this doctrine was relativized by one of the most influential Soviet writers on military affairs, Major General Talensky.[75] Contrary to capitalist military science, Talensky wrote, Soviet military science assumes the "objective" character of the laws of war; these laws apply to concrete but changing historical situations; the formula of the permanently operating factors is important but not basic: it is not a law of war.[76]

Talensky defined the basic law of war as follows: "Victory in modern war is attained by the decisive defeat of the enemy in the course of the armed conflict through the employment of successive blows accumulating in force, on the basis of superiority in the permanently acting factors which determine the fate of war, and on the basis of a comprehensive exploitation of economic, moral-political, and military potentialities in their unity and interaction."[77]

Two years before his death, Stalin had declared, in an interview with *Pravda* of February 11, 1951, that war was no longer inevitable because the "aggressive forces" in the United States, Great Britain and France could not be contained by the peaceful forces in these countries.[78] After the death of Stalin, Premier Malenkov evoked the possibilities of a peaceful coexistence between the two systems.[79] On March 12, 1954, he declared that a new world war fought with the terrible new weapons would mean the destruction of world civilization.[80]

But Malenkov's advocacy of a "minimal" nuclear strategic capability for deterring a U.S. attack was countered by other Soviet leaders, especially by Defense Minister Nikolai Bulganin, who warned against reliance on the "humaneness of the imperialists," and it seems that Malenkov was compelled to retreat.[81] After Malenkov had been deposed, K. Voroshilov stated squarely: "We cannot be intimidated by fables that in the event of a new world war, civilization will perish."[82] The importance of strategic surprise—treated by Stalin as an unreliable, temporary factor that could not under any circumstances play a decisive role in war—was revised. The Marshal of Tank Troops, P.A. Rotmistrov explained that the advent of nuclear weapons and jet aviation greatly enhanced the role of surprise in war and rendered surprise attacks particularly dangerous.[83]

Krushchev, after having strongly criticized the views of Malenkov, later took over many of his ideas on war and peace. His basic tenet was that nuclear war would signify a catastrophy for humanity: "In our days", wrote Talensky in 1965, "there is no more dangerous illusion than the idea that thermonuclear war can still serve as an instrument of politics, that it is possible to achieve political aims by using nuclear weapons and still survive."[84]

In the basic Soviet work on military doctrine, "Military Strategy," edited by a team directed by Marshal Sokolovsky, the colossal and unacceptable consequences of a world nuclear war, not only for NATO but also for the socialist countries, were clearly exposed.[85] Sokolovsky recognized that "the greater the buildup of means of mass destruction, the greater the conviction in the impossibility of their use," and that the "growth of nuclear-missile power is inversely proportional to the possibilities for its use." In this situation of a nuclear stalemate, both sides would find themselves in a position of "mutual deterrence."[86]

The Soviets usually express this concept of mutual deterrence in terms of assured retaliatory capability.[87] But if Soviet authors speak of a "nuclear balance" which would guarantee mutual deterrence—and if, since the 24th Party Congress of April, 1971, Soviet leaders no longer ask for strategic superiority—they also warn of the danger of a disruption of this balance, for example, through the American Ballistic Missile Defense.[88]

Despite the recognition, however, that nuclear war would constitute an unprecedented catastrophe for mankind, many Soviet commentators declare that socialism would be the ultimate victor in any nuclear confrontation. General Bochkarev, for example, in an influential article in 1968, after having stated that one of the primary tasks of Soviet foreign policy must be to prevent a world nuclear war, was unambiguous about this: ". . . if international imperialism unleashes a nuclear war, the progress of the socialist states and their Marxist-Leninist Parties will not be paralyzed in terror and they will not drop their arms as the enemies of peace and socialism would desire."[89] The conclusions of Bochkarev were repeated by Maj. Gen. V.I. Zemskov in another important article in *Military Thought*, the confidential Soviet general staff journal.[90]

If, in general, Soviet political leaders and civilian spokesmen tend to agree that the Soviet Union could not avoid unacceptable damage, nor obtain a meaningful victory in nuclear war, other military spokesmen have criticized this position.[91] But it seems that their criticism is due above all to concerns about ideological conformity and the preservation of morale (indeed, the prospect of high casualty rates and the end of civilization is not likely to strengthen the morale of the troops).[92]

Some Western commentators have counterposed a Soviet military interest in "war-fighting" and "war-winning" capability to a "deterrent" capability. Other Western observers think that this distinction is not accurate because the Soviets would see the former capabilities as providing the most credible deterrent as well as a "contingent resort if war should nevertheless come."[93] General Talensky, himself, made clear that for the Soviets, deterrence is not inconsistent with a war-fighting capability.[94] Soviet military writers even seem to blur the notions of deterrence and preemptive defense.[95]

Soviet strategists tend to put operational concepts at the heart of their military doctrine. This tendency leads them to put damage-limitation ahead of all other considerations.[96] To deny the United States the capacity to destroy the Soviet society, and to preserve their own capabilities of waging traditional war upon the United States, is of greatest importance.[97] This view has a strong unilateral component which makes some Western observers think that the Soviets have no confidence in Mutual Assured Destruction.[98] Soviet writers stress, on the one hand, the importance of surprise and preemption, of a strategic disruptive strike; on the other hand, the capacity of fighting a protracted war, survivability and sustainability.[99]

The Soviets seem not to be, according to the best available evidence, interested in the control of a nuclear exchange, in the limitation of such an exchange, in the flexible and selective use of nuclear weapons, or in intrawar bargaining.[100] Already, in the early sixties when McNamara advanced the idea of a city-avoidance strategy, Soviet spokesmen described this as a cynical U.S. ploy to legalize nuclear war, and as a clever but hopeless effort to provide the United States with the key to a quick and easy victory.[101]

The Schlesinger proposals were depicted by Brezhnev himself as showing an American willingness to fight a nuclear war and the search for a disarming first-strike capability against the USSR.[102] The countervailing strategy was also attacked by Brezhnev who declared that this strategy "actually boils down to making the very idea of nuclear war more acceptable . . . to public opinion."[103] The Soviet expert on strategic affairs, H. Trofimenko, wrote that this "American course replaces a calm opposition between the two leading powers. Now one of the sides in the strategic equation proclaims that it does not simply intend to deter the other from attack, but to wage a war, or at least, to pressure the opponent from the positions of counterforce superiority. This superiority is to be used as a cover for local military actions. In other words, the inevitable tendency of a unilateral emphasis on counterforce is to turn political rivalry into acute military confrontation."[104]

If Soviet spokesmen now seem more disposed to accept threshold distinctions (for example, between theater and intercontinental nuclear war), and threshold restraints within the different categories of war, they show no inclination of endorsing, within the categories of theater nonnuclear war, theater nuclear war, or central nuclear war: "any concept of restraint in the tempo and intensity of combat and no inclination to refrain from attacking certain target categories in the interests of collateral-damage avoidance or intrawar coercive diplomacy."[105] If the refusal of limited strategic options could be an attempt to deny the United States some practical strategic options, as, for example, the enhancement of the credibility of its strategic commitment to Western Europe, it also appears to be consistent with traditional Soviet strategic thinking.[106]

Can Strategic Nuclear War be Controlled?

As the control of a nuclear war would require that all those participating in such a conflict be both willing and able to exercise restraint, the Soviet attitude regarding the possibility of limiting strategic nuclear war is not a promising omen for a successful war limitation. If the Soviets were to make true their announcements that they would start any nuclear exchange with the massive use of strategic weapons against the most vital assets, such as the C^3I (Command, Control, Communications and Intelligence) systems, the physical foundation of any limitation would perhaps be decisively damaged or even wiped out, right from the start of a nuclear conflict. The same argument would of course hold true for the United States if it came to adopt a strategy of "decapitation." If such doctrinal concepts were applied in the course of a nuclear exchange, both superpowers would probably grope about like blind monsters and destroy, in a senseless effort, themselves and the world with their gigantic guideless bludgeons.

But even if they showed the best will would the superpowers be able to control a nuclear conflict? Perhaps the most critical variable in such a situation would be the command and control systems which are all more or less vulnerable to direct physical attack and to operational failures. Physically, they are vulnerable to nuclear effects, i.e., to blast and radiation (transient radiation effects on electronics, electrical or electromagnetic pulse which both can seriously damage electrical and electronic equipment), to attack with conventional weapons, and to sabotage. Operationally, they are vulnerable to unintended effects such as human error, natural phenomena (solar-induced ionospheric disturbances, changes in the earth's magnetic field, etc.), equipment failure and to intentional jamming (emission of electro-magnetic radiation on the same frequency as the targeted command and control systems) or exploitation of failures in communications security.[107]

Because of these manifold vulnerabilities, it is likely that "beyond some relatively early stage in the conflict, the strategic communications systems would suffer interference and disruption, the strikes would become ragged, uncoordinated, less precise and less discriminating, and the ability to reach an agreed settlement between the adversaries would soon become extremely problematical."[108]

It would probably take only a rather limited number of warheads to destroy the fixed facilities of the national command systems or to effectively impair the communication links between the National Command Authorities (NCA) and the strategic forces.[109]

The Soviet Union could even try to annihilate the NCA, which consists of the President and the Secretary of Defense or their duly deputized alternates or successors, before orders for retaliation could be issued to the U.S. strategic nuclear forces. Indeed, the warning time for a Soviet SLBM attack—Soviet strategic submarines routinely patrol off the U.S. coasts—could be less than five minutes.[110] It is doubtful whether the NCA could be transported to the NEACP (National Emergency Airborne Command Post) aircraft within this warning time, and doubtful whether this aircraft could take off even if the NCA managed to arrive at the Andrews airforce base by helicopter. A Soviet surprise attack would probably include strikes against all relevant airfields in the Washington D.C. area.

And even if the systems of command and control could be maintained, the question is whether a nuclear exchange could remain limited by the amount of damage created. Of course, there exist, for example, some Soviet targets which could be attacked without causing enormous collateral damage (naval vessels at sea, some of the SS-18 ICBMs in south-central USSR, bomber bases in the Arctic, isolated industrial facilities in Siberia etc).[111]

But already an attack on Soviet or American oil refineries would cause several million casualties.[112] In the case of a Soviet attack against American ICBM silos, estimates of collateral damage fatalities range from 800,000 to 50 million.[113] A comprehensive Soviet counterforce attack that would also involve strikes against the SAC bomber bases, FBM (Fleet Ballistic Missile) submarine support facilities and command-and-control centers (in addition to the ICBM silos) would of course raise these figures.[114]

The effects of American counterforce attacks against the Soviet Union would probably be even greater than those of Soviet attacks. If, on the one hand, American warheads are smaller than the Soviet ones, Soviet strategic forces, on the other hand, are generally ill-based from the point of view of minimizing collateral damage. About half of the 26 Soviet ICBM fields are located west of the Ural Mountains, several of them near some of the most densely populated areas of the USSR; prevailing wind patterns at any time of the year would cover areas with the highest population density with fallout.[115] Since two of the three Soviet FBM submarine bases are located within urban areas, since more than 70% of the Soviet air bases are in the western USSR, south of Leningrad, and since several hundreds of IRBMs (intermediate range ballistic missile) and MRBMs (medium range ballistic missile) are deployed west of the Urals, a comprehensive U.S. counterforce attack could well bring the Soviet fatalities to anything between 5 and 50 million people and, in all events, twice as much as in the case of a single ICBM attack.

These weaknesses, constraints and uncertainties regarding command and control systems,[116] the difficulty—if not impossibility—of executing limited counterforce strikes without causing severe collateral damage, the apparent unwillingness of the Soviets to engage in limited strategic nuclear exchanges, make the prospect that a nuclear conflict could be controlled at will and remain limited, appear extremely shaky.

Can strategic doctrine evade what technology offers, and from a certain political point of view, imposes? Weapons are becoming ever more accurate and more apt for strategic fine-tuning. How could strategic planners resist the invitation and even the apparent necessity to adapt their targeting plans to these new possibilities—as long, at least, as the involved actors do not explicitly consent to arms control agreements to renounce voluntarily, for the sake of a greater long-term mutual benefit, the development of a certain technique?

A Soviet-American Doctrinal Rapprochement?

Better chances, for the comprehension of the fears and the wishes, the capabilities and the intentions of the other side, which might lead to the regulation of conflicts short of war as well as for the (preventive) control of weapons developments, might result from a greater compatibility of American and Soviet strategic objectives.

As we have seen, the American and Soviet strategic doctrines —especially the American one in the last ten years—have undergone some modifications which might foretell a kind of rapprochement[117]—not of convergence and not of "reverse convergence"[118] of these doctrines.

American strategic doctrine has moved from a conservative stance, which treated—prior to thermonuclear devices—nuclear bombs as "weapons as usual," or as "all or nothing" instruments as in the period of "Massive retaliation," or in the heyday of "Assured destruction"), towards a more rational, thoughtful, balanced approach which takes into account intrinsic potentialities but also internal determinants of these weapons. This has meant a shift from a conservative military posture towards a purely technical one; as well as from an abstract to a more genuinely strategic approach, which tries to integrate technical, operational, psychological, political aspects.

On the Soviet side, there has been an evolution from a disdainful disregard of the impact of nuclear weapons, deriving from a purely voluntaristic attitude, towards a slow recognition of the real physical and hence strategic potentialities of the new weapons.[119] This has finally led to a growing concern over the mastering of this weapon and the constraints upon its possible use. Having moved from an exclusively ideological and classical military posture to a more reality-related and equilibrated view, the Soviets now recognize the deterrence effects of nuclear weapons for both superpowers.

In conjunction with these elements of rapprochement, there are also elements of dissociation, due to the fact that the United States has not reached any unequivocal conclusions regarding its national security strategy. It still hesitates between "Assured Destruction" and selective options. On the other side, the Soviet Union is still refraining from the idea of flexibility and selectivity, and from intra-war bargaining.

A rapprochement of strategic doctrines would, of course, not by itself constitute an absolute, or even a good, guarantee against the outbreak of nuclear war and the escalation of such a war to an all-embracing catastrophy. It might even lull the nuclear super-powers to a false sense of security—and of confidence that one could, in some circumstances, for some objectives, engage in a nuclear fight because one would somehow be able to manage that fighting, keep it under control and extricate oneself at the right moment. A certain dose of ambiguity and uncertainty about the other's posture and doctrine can sometimes reinforce the deterrent effects.

At any rate, and even if nuclear weapons may have made war among those who possess them an absurd, insane undertaking, a self-defeating and self-destructive operation, with costs grossly disproportionate to any rational objective of foreign policy,[120] they cannot eliminate, by their sheer existence, the possibility that war might break out. Even if intentions are not bellicose and if preventive controls are very efficient, there remains a certain danger that things will get out of hand.

The American doctrine of "Assured Destruction" cannot be a definitive answer to the agonizing questions raised by the existence of nuclear weapons, nor can a "Countervailing" or "Prevailing" strategy. Assured destruction has been above all a theoretical effort to block aggression and, with it, nuclear power; but, in blocking aggression, it could also dam this aggression up, causing volatile conditions.

Nuclear weapons in general have not erased aggression, they have only deflected it, displaced it—from superpower confrontations to "wars by proxies", from the homelands of the superpowers and the fringes of these homelands to the Third World, from direct armed clashes to rhetorical confrontations.

The notion of deterring an attack by announcing the will and the capability to wage war successfully at every imaginable stage, can be as dangerous as the threat of assured destruction if it is not inserted into a congenial, receptive, political and strategic environment. Otherwise, to make war thinkable could only make it appear either feasible, i.e., winnable or unavoidable. Strategic planners must remain conscious of the fact that, despite the best preparations for calibration, control and termination, crossing the nuclear threshold may confront them and their mechanical systems with unbearable stress.

Some useful efforts at diminishing the risk of a controlled or uncontrolled nuclear conflict might begin by banking on the rational forces in the "opponent's camp;" and by preventing nuclear proliferation, by developing more efficient procedures for crisis management, by improving national command and control systems, by relying more strongly on invulnerable second-strike weapons with no (or only minimal) counterforce potential, and above all, by making sure that the "opponent" always has something to lose.

For, deterrence in the last decade and a half of the century will prove true what Albert Wohlstetter said about deterrence in the sixties: "it is neither assured nor impossible, but [it] will be the product of sustained intelligent effort and hard choices, responsibly made."[121]

Notes

1. Osgood, Robert E.; Tucker, Robert W., *Force, Order, and Justice.* Baltimore, 1967, p. 3.

2. Ibid.

3. Tucker, S.; Robert W., The Nuclear Debate, *Foreign Affairs.* Fall, 1984, pp. 1–32.

4. "So wird also der politische Zweck, als das urspruengliche Motiv des Krieges, das Mass sein, sowohl fuer das Ziel, welches durch den kriegerischen Akt erreicht werden muss, als fuer die Anstrengungen, die erforderlich sind." Clausewitz, Carl von: Vom Kriege, Erstes Buch: Uber die Natur des Krieges. Berlin, 1853, p. 13.

5. Knorr, Klaus, "On the Uses of Military Power in the Nuclear Age." Princeton, N.J., 1966, pp. 138–139.

6. See for ex., Freud, Sigmund, *Civilization, War and Death.* London, 1953.

7. Waltz, Kenneth, M., *Man, the State, and War.* New York, 1954, p. 16. See also William James, who wrote that war is rooted in man's bellicose nature, which is the product of centuries-old traditions. *Memories and Studies.* New York, 1912, pp. 262–272.

8. Niebuhr, Reinhold; Sherwood, Eddy, *Doom and Dawn.* New York, 1936, p. 16.

9. Morgenthau, Hans J., *Scientific Man versus Power Politics*. Chicago, 1946, p. 200.

10. Durbin, E.F.M.; Bowlby, John, *Personal Aggressiveness and War*. New York, 1939, pp. 40–48.

11. See *A Study of War*, 2nd edition. Chicago and London, 1965, pp. 1284–1295.

12. Ibid., pp. 1512–1514; also 720–727.

13. See also Knorr, op. cit., p. 87.

14. Osgood; Tucker, op. cit., pp. 42–43.

15. See Rothenberg, Gunther E., *The Art of Warfare in the Age of Napoleon*. Bloomington, Indiana; 1978, for ex. p. 100.

16. See Wright, op. cit., pp. 1521–1522.

17. Brodie, Bernard, *Implications for Military Policy*, in *The Absolute Weapon*, ed. by Bernard Brodie. New York, 1946, p. 76.

18. Brodie, Bernard, *Strategy in the Missile Age*. Princeton, N.J.; 1959, p. 313. At about the same period, Raymond Aron wrote: "La théorie, meme la plus abstraite, suggère que l'énormité du risque est de nature à conseiller la prudence alors que l'indétermination du rapport des forces, dans le passé, tentait les audacieux." Le Grand Débat, Paris, 1963, p. 232.

19. Millis, Walter et al., *A World Without War*. New York, 1961, p. 55; See also his *An End to Arms*, New York, 1964, p. 20.; White House Press Release, June 23, 1964.

21. See Osgood; Tucker, op. cit., p. 26.

22. Ibid., p. 28. Knorr also remarks that the great nuclear powers, if they do not use, in the pursuit of their foreign policies, nuclear war, they nevertheless exploit the fear of it: "They exploit the risk of war rather than relative military power; they negotiate less from strength than from relative susceptibility to fear and worry." Hence strategic power remains, even at a time of nuclear parity and under conditions of the "competitive manipulation of a deadly risk" of instrumental value and therefore of some political utility. Knorr, op. cit., pp. 109, 113.

23. Mandelbaum, Michael, *The Nuclear Revolution: International Politics Before and After Hiroshima*. Cambridge, Massach., 1981, p. 7.

24. Ibid., p. 8.

25. See Knorr, op. cit., pp. 82–87. Henry Nash sees four decisive changes in the war environment brought about by nuclear weaponry: 1) change in geographical accessability, which lead to a new sense of vulnerability, which in turn produced a new sense of responsibility for world affairs; 2) change in weapon speed and destructive capabilities; 3) change in weapon control practices; 4) change in relative superiority of offensive over defensive capabilities. Nash, Henry T., *Nuclear weapons and International Behavior*. Leyden, 1975, pp. 59–63. John Herz had already previously described the diminishing impermeability of nation-states. Herz, John, *International Politics in the Atomic Age*. New York, 1959.

26. Quoted in Moss, Norman, *Men Who Played God.* New York, 1968, p. 5.

27. Schelling, Thomas C., *Arms and Influence.* New Haven, 1966, p. 9.

28. Mandelbaum, op. cit., p. 4.

29. Mandelbaum writes that the relative peace since 1945 may be due to the bipolar distribution of power, the margin of superiority of the two superpowers having made it easier for them to manage their rivalry so as to avoid war. Ibid., p. 8.

30. Osgood; Tucker think that the danger of a war by miscalculation is counterbalanced by greater caution stemming from the fact that the cost of political miscalculation, added to the cost of military miscalculation would be enormously greater than at any time before the nuclear age. At the same time, the authors noted that "lower risk-taking propensities have not dissuaded the nuclear states from boldly confronting each other in crises short of war. Quite the contrary, for the threshold of provocation, below which the nuclear powers will confidently compete by threats of war, has been raised by their knowledge of each other's great reluctance to fight." Osgood; Tucker, op. cit., pp. 125–126, 144–145.

31. Clausewitz thought that, in principle, any war would necessarily mount to the extreme: ". . . der Krieg ist ein Akt der Gewalt und es gibt in der Anwendung derselben keine Grenzen; so gibt jeder dem Andern das Gesetz, es entsteht eine Wechselwirkung, die, dem Begriff nach, zum Aeussersten fuehren muss." Clausewitz, op. cit., p. 6.

32. See Polmar, Norman, *Strategic Weapons: An Introduction.* New York, 1982, pp. 10–11.

33. Gray, Colin S., "Strategic Studies and Public Policy," *The American Experience.* Lexington, 1982, p. 34.

34. See Yergin, Daniel, *Shattered Peace. The Origins of the Cold War and the National Security State.* Boston, 1977, pp. 339–341.

35. Statement of Policy by the National Security Council on Basic National Security Policy, Document 18 (NSC–162/2), October 30, 1953, in the Pentagon Papers, Boston, 1971, p. 426.

36. See the analysis by L. Freedman of NSC–162/2 in Freedman, Lawrence, *The Evolution of Nuclear Strategy.* London, 1981, pp. 81–84.

37. *Public Papers of the Presidents of the United States,* Dwight D. Eisenhower, 1954 (1960), pp. 10–11. In May, 1953, Eisenhower indirectly let Chinese leaders know of his willingness to resort to the use of nuclear weapons against Chinese military bases if the Korean truce negotiations broke down. See in Eisenhower, Dwight D., *The White House Years: Mandate for Change, 1953–1956.* Garden City, New York; 1963, p. 181.

38. See "The Evolution of Foreign Policy," Department of State Bulletin, vol. 30, January 25, 1954, pp. 107–110.

39. "Policy for Security and Peace," *Foreign Affairs,* April, 1954.

40. Untitled document, NATO. draft no. 1., July 18, 1956. Dulles Papers,

File IX, July-December 1956, NATO Meeting, December 8–15, 1956, Princeton University Library, Princeton.

41. See Friedberg, Aron L., "A History of US Strategic 'Doctrine'—1945 to 1980," *Journal of Strategic Studies*. December, 1980, pp. 40–41, 146–147.

42. Kissinger, Henry, *Nuclear Weapons and Foreign Policy*. New York, 1957, pp. 174–202. For a critique of Kissinger's ideas, see for ex. Kaufmann, William, "The crisis in military affairs," *World Politics*. July, 1958, p. 594.

43. Albert Wohlstetter wrote in his influential article, "The Delicate Balance of Terror": "The notion that a carefully planned surprise attack can be checkmated almost effortlessly, that, in short, we may resume our deep pre-Sputnik sleep, is wrong and its nearly universal acceptance is terribly dangerous." *Foreign Affairs*, January, 1959, p. 234.

44. The Gaither Report concluded that "by 1959, the USSR may be able to launch an attack with ICBMs carrying megaton warheads, against which SAC will be almost completely vulnerable under present programs." Security Resources Panel of the Science Advisory Committee, "Deterrence and Survival in the Nuclear Age," November 7, 1954, p. 14.

45. The Gaither Committee (see note 44) proposed measures to enhance the survivability of U.S. strategic bombers, such as a shortened reaction time, further base dispersion, the protection of SAC bases through active and passive defense and the deployment of a ballistic missile warning net; it also emphasized the need for acquiring the highly survivable Polaris system as soon as possible and for rapid installation of hardened sites for land-based missiles.

46. Department of Defense Appropriations for 1962: Subcommittee of the House Committee on Appropriations, 87th Congress, 1st Sess., vol. 7, part 3, p. 102.

47. The Minutemen were stored underground in concrete shelters, see Mandelbaum, Michael, *The Nuclear Question: The United States and Nuclear Weapons, 1946–1976*. Cambridge, Mass.; 1979. p. 77.

48. Ibid., p. 108.

49. McNamara, Robert S., "Defense Arrangements of the North Atlantic Community," Address given at the University of Michigan, June 16, 1962, Department of State Bulletin, vol. 49, July 9, 1962, p. 67. J. Kahan writes that "the new doctrine affirmed that the United States was prepared to use nuclear forces to defend Western Europe and implied that it might be possible to "fight" a strategic war without necessarily sustaining catastrophic damage—points, it was believed, that would enhance the credibility of our nuclear commitments, decrease the motivations for independent nuclear forces, and provide our allies with greater incentives to expand their conventional forces." Kahan, Jerome H., *Security in the Nuclear Age*. The Brookings Institution, Washington DC; 1975, p. 92.

50. See Gray, op. cit., p. 100–101.

51. Statement by Robert S. McNamara on Department of Defense Appropriations, on the Fiscal Year 1966–1970 Defense Program and 1966 Defense Budget, in U.S. Congress, Senate Committee on Armed Services, Military Procurement Authorization, Fiscal Year 1966, Hearings, 89 Cong., 1 sess. (1965) p. 42.

52. Statement by Secretary of Defense Robert S. McNamara before the House Armed Services Committee on the Fiscal Year 1968–72 Defense Program and 1968 Defense Budget, January 23, 1967, (processed), p. 39.

53. See Kahan, op. cit., p. 96.

54. On March 2, 1955, Eisenhower had declared: "There comes a time, possibly, when a lead is not significant in the defensive arrangements of a country. If you get enough of a particular type of a weapon, I doubt that it is particularly important to have a lot more of it." News Conference of March 2, 1955, in Public Papers of the Presidents of the United States, 1955 (1959), p. 303.

55. Secretary of Defense Laird in March, 1969, before the Senate Foreign Relations Committee: the Soviet Union is "going for a first-strike capability. There is no question about it." Strategic and Foreign Policy Implications of ABM Systems, Hearings before the Sub-Committee on International Organization and Disarmament Affairs of the Senate Committee on Foreign Relations, 91 Cong., 1 sess. (1969), pp. 1. 196.

56. See Kahan, op. cit., p. 151.

57. Ibid., pp. 153–154.

58. "U.S. Foreign Policy for the 1970's: A New Strategy for Peace," A Report to the Congress by Richard Nixon, President of the United States, February 18, 1970, p. 122.

59. See in Wolfe, Thomas, "The SALT Experience: Its Impact on U.S. and Soviet Strategic Policy and Decision-making," A report prepared for the U.S. Air Force Project Rand, R–1686–PR, September 1975, p. 123.

60. Ibid., p. 122.

61. The strategy had been outlined before by Secretary of Defense Brown in his Defense Report in early 1979 and then again in January, 1980; in June 1980, at a meeting of the NATO Nuclear Planning Group in Norway he briefed the Allies on the conclusions reached.

62. According to the description of W. Slocombe in Slocombe, Walter, "The Countervailing Strategy," International Security. Spring, 1981, p. 21.

63. Ibid., p. 22.

64. See Tucker, op. cit., p. 9.

65. Wohlstetter, op. cit., p. 230.

66. See his On Thermonuclear War, Princeton, N.J.; 1960.

67. Iklé, Fred Charles, "Can Nuclear Deterrence Last Out the Century?" Foreign Affairs. January, 1973, p. 285.

68. Ibid., p. 283.

69. Kissinger, Henry, The White House Years. London, 1979, p. 216.

Kissinger added that Assured Destruction was "one of those theories that sound impressive in an academic seminar but are horribly unworkable for a decision-maker in the real world and lead to catastrophe if they are ever implemented." Ibid.

70. Gray, Colin S., "Nuclear Strategy: the Case for a Theory of Victory," *International Security*. Summer, 1979, p. 87.

71. Brodie, Bernard, "The Development of Nuclear Strategy," *International Security*. Spring, 1978, p. 82.

72. Howard, Michael, "On Fighting a Nuclear War," *International Security*. Spring, 1981, p. 14.

73. McNamara, Robert S., "The Military Role of Nuclear Weapons: Perceptions and Misperceptions," *Foreign Affairs*, Fall, 1983, p. 79.

74. See in Dinerstein, Herbert, *War and the Soviet Union*. Westport, Connecticut; 1959, p. 6.

75. "On the Question of the Laws of Military Science," *Military Thought*. September, 1953.

76. Dinerstein remarks that since Stalin's "permanently operating factors" formula had usually not been described as a law, technically Talensky was not rejecting Stalin's theory when he denied that it constituted a law of war. Dinerstein, op. cit., p. 39.

77. See also Col. M.P. Skirdo, who wrote that war develops "on the basis of objective laws which are independent of man's volition" and that leadership in war "can be successful only if crucial decisions are in conformity with the demands of the laws of war." *The People, the Army, the Commander (A Soviet View)*, transl. U.S. Air Force, *Soviet Military Thought Series*, No. 14. Washington D.C., 1978, p. viii.

78. In an interview with J. Reston of the New York Times, December 21, 1952, Stalin declared that the Soviet Union and the United States would be able to live in peace.

79. Pravda, March 10, 1953.

80. Pravda, March 13, 1954.

81. See Horelick, Arnold L.; Rush, Myron, *Strategic Power and Soviet Foreign Policy*. Chicago, 1965, p. 19 ff.

82. Pravda, March 27, 1955.

83. See in Horelick; Rush, op cit., p. 24.

84. Maj. Gen. N.A. Talensky, "The Late War: Some Reflections," *International Affairs*, no. 5. May, 1965, p. 23; this conviction had been expressed two years earlier in a still more drastic way by Boris Dmitriyev who had written in Izvestiya of September 25, 1963: "War can only be the continuation of madness."

85. "The losses in a world nuclear war would be suffered not only by the United States and its NATO Allies, but also by the socialist countries. The logic of a world nuclear war is such that in the sphere of its effect would fall an overwhelming majority of the world's states. As a result of the war many hundreds of millions of people would perish, and the

majority of the survivors would in one or another degree be subject to radioactive contamination." Marshal V.D. Sokolovsky, ed., *Military Strategy*, 3rd edition. Moscow, 1968, p. 239.

86. Sokolovsky, op. cit., 1st ed. 1962. p. 74–75.

87. R. Pipes thinks that as long as the Russians persist in adhering to the Clausewitzian maxim on the function of war, mutual deterrence does not really exist. Pipes, Richard, "Why the Soviet Union Thinks it Could Fight and Win a Nuclear War," *Commentary*. July 1977, p. 34.

88. Garthoff, Raymond L., "Mutual Deterrence and Strategic Arms Limitation in Soviet Policy," *International Security*. Summer, 1978, pp. 125–129.

89. Maj. Gen. K. Bochkarev, "The Question of the Sociological Aspect of the Struggle Against the Forces of Aggression and War," *Military Thought*. September, 1968. pp. 3–4.

90. Zemskov wrote that "a possible nuclear war would, undoubtedly, bring unprecedented disaster to all mankind"; but, if "international imperialism unleashes a war, the peoples of the socialist states and their Marxist-Leninist parties will not cringe in terror and will not lose heart, as the monopolists would like. The peoples of the world socialism will engage the enemy decisively, filled with confidence in the triumph of their just cause. This would be a just and victorious struggle." "Characteristic Features of Contemporary Wars and Possible Means of Conducting Them," *Military Thought*. July, 1969, p. 23.

91. For example, Col. V.F. Khalipov; General-Major A. Milovidov; Rear-Admiral Shelyag; all three members of the Lenin Military Political Academy.

92. See Arnett, Robert L., "Soviet attitudes towards nuclear war: do they really think they can win?" in Baylis, John; Segal, Gerald, *Soviet Strategy*. London, 1981, p. 60; also Lambeth, Benjamin, "How to think about Soviet military doctrine," in Ibid., p. 112.

93. See Garthoff, op. cit., p. 122. Ken Booth writes that in Soviet thinking the concepts of "deterrence" and "defense" are interrelated or even synonymous, and that the Soviet conception conforms with the traditional military view everywhere in the world which comprehends deterrence in terms of a threat by an impressive war-fighting capability: "There is no mutual blockage in Soviet thinking . . . caused by the thought of deterrence 'failing'. If war breaks out, the Soviet attitude is then to move onto the next stage. In preparation for this possibility, Soviet military planners have given much more explicit attention to fighting and winning a nuclear war than Western (especially civilian) strategists." Booth, Ken, *Strategy and Ethnocentrism*. London, 1979, p. 82.

94. See in Dinerstein, op. cit., p. 36 ff.

95. See Snyder, Jack L., "The Soviet Strategic Culture: Implications for Limited Nuclear Operations," A Project Air Force report prepared for the U.S. Air Force, R–2154–AF, Rand Corporation. Santa Monica,

September 1977, p. 18. Snyder thinks that Soviet fears of an American war-fighting capability in the fifties and sixties made Soviet military theorists develop their own war-fighting concepts., Ibid., p. 27.

96. See Ermath, Fritz W., "Contrasts in American and Soviet Strategic Thought," *International Security*. Fall, 1978, p. 152.

97. See Legvold, Robert, "Strategic Doctrine and SALT: Soviet and American Views," *Survival*. January/February, 1979, p. 10.

98. See Erickson, John, "The Soviet View of Deterrence: A General Survey," *Survival*. November/December 1982, p. 245. Garthoff is of a different opinion, and to corroborate this opinion he quotes a statement by the Soviet delegation at the SALT preparatory talks in Helsinki in November 1969: "Even in the event that one of the sides were the first to be subjected to attack, it would undoubtedly retain the ability to inflict a retaliatory strike of crushing power. Thus, evidently, we all agree that war between our two countries would be disastrous for both sides. And it would be tantamount to suicide for the ones who decided to start such a war." Garthoff, op. cit., p. 126.

99. See Erickson, op. cit., p. 246.

100. D. Ball writes that "the evidence that Soviet military doctrine now incorporates the possibility of control, selectivity and restraint in a strategic nuclear conflict is actually very fragmentary. It derives principally from some statements that stand somewhat apart from the overwhelming thrust of Soviet military literature . . ." Ball, Desmond, "Can Nuclear War be controlled?" Adelphi Paper 169, IISS, London, 1981, p. 33.

101. In fact, as Lambeth writes, the Soviets had at that time no choice: their strategic arsenal was not only numerically inferior but it consisted also of cumbersome and slow-reacting ICBMs and IRBMs deployed in vulnerable soft-site configurations: "Given this primitive and inflexible strategic capability, the Soviets plainly lacked the wherewithal for underwriting the sort of sophisticated strategic targeting concepts envisaged by the McNamara policy and had every reason to refrain from attempting to compete with the United States on the latter's terms." Lambeth, Benjamin S., Selective Nuclear Operations and Soviet Strategy, in Holst, Johan J.; Nerlich, Uwe, *Beyond Nuclear Deterrence*. New York, 1977, p. 85.

102. See in Wolfe, op. cit., pp. 149–154.

103. *Pravda*, August 30, 1980.

104. Trofimenko, Henry A., "Counterforce: Illusion of a Panacea," *International Security*. Spring, 1981, p. 47. At the same time, Trofimenko, who is head of Department at the Soviet Institute of U.S.A. and Canadian Studies, asserts that the American declarations with regard to counterforce options are irrelevant from the viewpoint of safeguarding the interests of the USSR and protection of its population in case of "aggressive use" of American strategic forces because the "Soviet Union evaluates the external threats to its security in categories of

objective material potentials and possibilities, not pronouncements of this or that statement." Ibid.

105. See Lambeth, "Selective Nuclear Operations," op. cit. p. 87.

106. See Snyder, op. cit., p. 39.

107. See Ball, op. cit., p. 9–14.

108. Ibid., p. 35. J. Steinbruner writes that "regardless of the flexibility embodied in individual force components, the precariousness of command channels probably means that nuclear war would be uncontrollable, as a practical matter, shortly after the first tens of weapons are launched." Steinbruner, John, "National Security and the Concept of Strategic Stability," *Journal of Conflict Resolution*. September, 1978, p. 421.

109. Ball estimates that 50 to 100 warheads would suffice for this purpose. Ball, op. cit., p. 35.

110. According to a testimony by General Royal B. Allison, the worst case estimates range from about 4½ to 8½ to 9 minutes, Senate Armed Services Committee, *Military Implications of the Treaty on the Limitations of Anti-Ballistic Missile Systems and the Interim Agreement on Limitation of Strategic Offensive Arms*. 1972, p. 345.

111. See Ball, op. cit., p. 27.

112. See "The Effects of Nuclear War," Office of Technology Assessment. Washington DC, 1979, p. 64–80.

113. The estimate of 800,000 comes from a Department of Defense study of September 1974; another study of the DoD, done with different assumptions, came to an estimation of 18.3 million casualties; a study of the U.S. Arms Control and Disarmament Agency advanced an estimate of 50 million casualties. See Senate Foreign Relations Committee, Briefing on Counterforce Attacks, Secret Hearing held on September 11, 1974; sanitized and made public on January 10, 1975, pp. 13–14; 32–33; Senate Foreign Relations Committee, "Effects of Limited Nuclear Warfare," September 18, 1975, p. 31.

114. The 1975 DoD study estimated the fatalities resulting from such a comprehensive attack at 21.7 million.

115. See "The Effects of Nuclear War," op. cit., pp. 91. 143.

116. See also the pessimistic judgement of P. Bracken in Bracken, Paul, *Command and Control of Nuclear Forces*. New Haven 1983.

117. Colin Gray sees such a rapprochement when he writes: "Over the past several years, the United States government has recognized that at the core of its nuclear deterrence policy has to be an ability to deny victory to the Soviet Union." Gray, *Strategic Studies and Public Policy*, op. cit., p. 159.

118. D. Hanson defines such a "reverse convergence" as "the view expressed that the better course may well be for American strategic thought to converge with Soviet doctrine." Hanson rejects such "reverse convergence" because he thinks it is logically incoherent (the United States cannot be the Soviet Union), because "strategic asym-

metry may be healthy" and because "Soviet doctrine is bad advice." Hanson Donald W., "Is Soviet Strategic Doctrine Superior?" *International Security*. Winter, 1982/83, pp. 61–83.

119. After the first tests of the H-bomb, this weapon was said to be a terror and propaganda weapon, but it was then soon admitted that it had military utility; see Dinerstein, op. cit., p. 223.

120. "The arbitrament of war has become too costly for practically all rational purposes of statecraft, if by "rational" we mean no more than that governments will not choose an action from which, in terms of probabilities, they stand to lose a great deal more than they can hope to gain." Knorr, op. cit., p. 134.

121. Wohlstetter, op. cit., p. 211.

10.
On Human Dominance Systems[1]

James A. Schellenberg

ℐt is appropriate to bring together persons of different back-grounds to discuss intellectual issues which they have in common. We should recognize, moreover, that our disciplinary differences offer opportunities for insight as well as barriers inhibiting easy communication. Different approaches to explanation do not necessarily invalidate each other. In focusing upon the aggressive behavior of humans and other higher primates, we should be alert to the possibility of multiple explanations of what we observe. Nevertheless, this does not mean that all explanations are equally useful for our understanding. For some purposes of understanding, one mode of explanation may be clearly more helpful than others—but without detracting from the value of such other purposes.

Let me illustrate my general point with special reference to human aggressive behavior. If we have a very large time span for our analysis of variations in aggressive behavior shown by humans—such as a 100,000 years or more—I see no alternative to viewing such behavior in relationship to the biological survival of the group or species. We thus come to understand differences in terms of biologically-based propensities which are rooted in genetic determinants and developed through interactions with other life forms in the particular niche occupied by the group.

represented by a few decades or a century. Differences in aggressive behavior by members of a society within such a time span are unlikely to be very well explained by biological differences. What we might broadly call sociological variables—including those of cultural background and access to technological resources, as well as social organization variables—are much more likely to help us explain the variations in aggressive behavior between different persons and groups in society and between different periods of time.

Let us now narrow the time span to one of a few days and take the individual as the focus of our analysis. We need not rule out completely the value of biological or sociological variables in order to recognize that another set of variables is much more likely to help us explain the differences in the individual's behavior. These variables have to do especially with self-conceptions, including a sense of social identity, and how different events are seen as enhancing or thwarting these conceptions of the self. Thus, the variables which are especially important for explaining aggressive behavior in this context are those which might be broadly labeled as social psychological.

I have said enough to justify, I believe, the variety of disciplinary approaches brought to bear on a subject such as human aggression. But I do not want to leave the impression that everything is simply relative to the purposes and scope of explanation. There is not only the organization of the questions asked, which limits how interpretations are to be made; interpretations are also limited by the organization of the phenomena to be observed. Living cells contain molecules, but they have characteristics which call for more than simply a chemical analysis. Likewise, organisms have properties of behavior which take us beyond the activities of cells. And human collective systems require an understanding which transcends that of the behavior of particular individuals. All of this is not to discount the importance of chemical analysis for cytology, of neurology for psychology, or of psychology for cultural anthropology. But we must be aware that new levels of organization in phenomena to be studied call for new forms of explanation in our quest for understanding. A major point of the present paper is that much human aggression cannot be well understood without seeing its collective pattern of organization.

In a Small Town in Iowa

To give a concrete illustration of the collective focus of much human aggression, let us attempt in our imaginations to recreate some events which actually happened in a small town in Iowa on the day of January 11, 1859. That was one of the most exciting days which the citizens of Marietta, Iowa, ever experienced. Conversations throughout the community showed agitation, which would have been apparent to any careful observer. It is reported that a lady named Mrs. Boardman marched out of her house with a gun and threatened to shoot one of the men she found on the street. Meanwhile, a Mr. Daly emerged with a huge sausage-stuffer which he used to spray muddy water upon some men of the local militia.[2]

The objects of the wrath of Mrs. Boardman and Mr. Daly that day were not their Marietta neighbors, but the men who had come into town from nearby Marshall. The Marshall men had come for the purpose of transporting the county records to a newly selected location in their own town. The citizens of Marietta did not favor such a move. Indeed, so much were they against it that they were said to have planted a keg of powder under the county safe in their temporary courthouse—threatening to blow up the records if the invaders from Marshall should succeed in entering the building.

The visitors from Marshall were organized as a company of militia under orders of the county sheriff, and they were led by a man named Shurtz. Captain Shurtz established his headquarters just outside Marietta and then moved his men to the public square. There, as a local historian has recounted:

> A barricade was constructed within a few feet of the Court House and the cloud of battle began to lower . . . all about could be heard the "click, click" of the rifle locks.

However, there was not an immediate attack on the courthouse. Hours passed without either side actually firing a shot at the other. Finally, Judge James Thompson provided an order to cease hostilities, leaving the county records temporarily housed at Marietta.

There is, of course, more to the story of the Marshall County,

Iowa, courthouse battle of 1859. Both before and after that January day there was severe conflict between the towns of Marshall and Marietta. An election had been held on April 5, 1858, to decide the county seat question, but the results had remained in dispute. Both towns claimed victory, with the outcome depending on whether certain disputed ballots were counted or not. For nearly another year after the day we have described, the election remained in dispute; but after the Iowa supreme court helped to decide how the ballots were to be counted, a final recount was made on December 29, 1859. Two days later Marshall publicly celebrated the arrival of the county records drawn by eight yoke of oxen, for they had been finally and officially declared the new county seat.

Today neither "Marshall" nor "Marietta" can be found on an Iowa road map. "Marshall" has since become "Marshalltown," and it remains the county seat of Marshall County. Marietta gradually disappeared as a town after losing the county seat fight in 1859.

This case of a county seat fight actually ended without physical violence. Most of the approximately four dozen cases of severe "county seat wars" which I have traced through local histories have not been so fortunate, and in a few cases deaths have been recorded in similar conflicts.[3] But the point is not so much whether or not actual personal injuries were recorded as a result; rather, our purpose in raising the Marshall County case is to give us a sense of the fundamental nature of collective conflict in the aggressive actions of human beings.

The Nature of Human Conflict

Human conflict has many forms. It includes arguments over the breakfast table and haggling at the marketplace, as well as barroom brawls and international wars. It includes many means of pursuing a conflict, from the polite discourse of a diplomat to the physical violence of an armed force. Many motives may be embedded in a conflict—even within the same conflict—to say nothing of the diversity of motives in very different conflicts.

In all the diversity of forms of human conflict, there is a commonality in the impulse to hit or to hurt. This is the rising up in anger which we associate with acts of aggression—whether expressed offensively or defensively, whether politely subdued or openly displayed. It is this impulse which links us to other

Suppose, however, interest is more in a time span, such as that animals, for an emotionally based tendency to show aggression under certain stimulus conditions (as we are reminded in Kenneth Moyer's fine paper) is a very common pattern among mammals.

But despite the continuity of human aggression to that of other animals, there are also some distinctively human features shown in our patterns of aggression. It is only humans who have the brains—or the foolishness—necessary to engage in bloody carnage in support of a high principle. The jihad or crusade —whether blessed by religious personages or secularized in form, such as in a "war to make the world safe for democracy"—is a distinctively human endeavor. Such conflicts over principles would be impossible without the complex symbol systems within which humans fashion their lives. Also, it is only among humans that complex group interests can serve as the rallying point for prolonged struggle.

It is tempting to note the common animal forms of aggressive behavior and see them as somehow more basic than the distinctively human patterns. The objective then becomes that of reducing the complex forms of human aggression to the basic animal impulses involved. Such a reductionism is as misguided as the opposite tendency of suggesting that we are somehow immune from our animal ancestry—that such impulses to respond aggressively may somehow be eliminated from human behavior by acts of individual will or by legislation. What I believe is to be preferred to either tendency is to study human conflicts in primarily human terms—but allowing for a recognition of the role that raw emotional involvements may play in our human struggles.

To return to our illustration of the Marshall County, Iowa, case, I suppose that Mrs. Broadman's righteous anger as she came out with a gun had something in common with the baring of teeth of some other mammal defending a territory. But to reduce her behavior to her genes or her glands would miss the distinctively human focus. She was the wife of one of the leading citizens of the town of Marietta, and unless someone showed some resistance, the town was about to lose its county seat. Furthermore, this was a matter of principle, for it had not yet been finally settled exactly how the ballots for the county seat election were to be properly counted. Here we have an issue of legitimacy—so common in human conflicts—which heightens the forcefulness with which the struggle is pursued. It was believed in Marietta that one of the county officials had been coerced into signing a paper certifying Marshall as the victor in that election, and now the sheriff was illegally following this up with a sneak attack to forcibly seize the county records. Of course, from the standpoint of the Marshall men, they were simply laying claim to what rightfully belonged in Marshall—now officially certified—over the stubborn opposition of the people of Marietta.

Most human conflicts are a product of complex forms of human association. To understand them thoroughly, we need to understand the forms of association in which they are embedded. The conflict in Marshall County, Iowa, can be understood only if we know something of the meaning of counties in the American framework of local government. In rural areas of America—which in the nineteenth century included clearly most of the United States—the county was the main unit of local government. And county government was centered in a town known as the county seat. The town which was named as the county seat had a certain political dominance over other towns of the same county, and with this also came certain economic advantages as well. On the other hand, a town that lost out in a county seat contest was often at a disadvantage; and in many cases such towns, like Marietta, Iowa, quietly disappeared. Finally, we need to understand that one of the legacies of democracy in America has been the resolution of many local issues by the ballot box, and in most states, including Iowa, this has meant that the county seat was to be permanently established (or removed) by an election. Such elections could be focal points of great local controversy, especially when the election was between towns just in the process of establishing themselves as permanent centers. One of the features of such an issue, which heightened the sense of conflict, was that only one town could be the county seat; this was not something which could be divided or shared. Also, once established, the county seat was usually not apt to be easily moved.

All the above points need to be parts of our understanding about the Marshall County, Iowa, conflict of 1859. They are more directly relevant than knowledge about the emotional makeup of particular individuals—even though it might be interesting to know more personally about Mrs. Broadman or Mr. Daly or Captain Shurtz.

Another point which a case such as our illustration may help us understand is that of the close intertwining of conflict with its resolution. Our simplified imagery identifies war and peace as opposite patterns; however, in reality the processes of conflict and the resolution or control of conflict are very closely tied together. Seldom is a conflict pursued "with no holds barred"—some control is typically a part of its pursuit. Conflict, in other words, is always to some degree managed by those who engage one another. And the way it is managed bears a close relationship to the issues at hand. Likewise, its ultimate resolution bears a close relationship to both the issues involved and the way parties pursue and manage their engagement in the conflict. In the case of Marshall County, Iowa, the central issue was the correct interpretation of the county seat election. There were well founded suspicions that certain officials were trying to use their influence to invalidate some of the ballots, thus assuring one side or the other of the victory. Both sides felt that if the ballots were counted correctly, they would be shown as the proper winner. The fundamental issue was therefore one of due process and proper legitimacy. The Marshall forces believed that the issue was now officially settled and that they could claim the county seat legitimately. The Marietta forces saw the same actions as an invasion, completely without proper legal sanction; for them the signing of a piece of paper in the wee hours of that morning did not constitute a proper conclusion for locating the county seat. So both sides felt legally justified in opposing each other. But, despite some threats, they did not feel justified in carrying out the full potential of physical force for their cause. Both sides showed some significant control of the conflict. The Marshall forces held back from actually shooting their way into the courthouse, and the Marietta forces held back from doing physical harm to the men from Marshall. So the physical confrontation proved to be a standoff. And finally it was another piece of paper which provided the immediate resolution—a court order for the Marshall men to leave the county records, for the time being, in Marietta. Ultimately the courts would then be able to decide just how the ballots for the 1858 election would be counted.

We have tried to illustrate several general ideas about human conflict with the backdrop of the confrontation between two towns in Iowa. First, most important human conflicts are not simply expressions of individual aggressive impulses; rather, they are socially motivated and controlled. They are organized around group objectives, and they are patterned by complex symbolic identifications. Second, the patterns of dominance which are displayed in most human conflicts are not simple matters of individual competition; rather, they are matters of group dominance. It is because group interests are primary (even when these involve individual interests) that parties to the conflict can pursue it with such a sense of justification. Third and finally, the pursuit of conflict proceeds hand-in-hand with the pursuit of its resolution. And both depend on the standards of legitimacy present in that particular framework of human social organization.

A Broader Perspective

It may be protested that I have made too much out of a few insignificant events which took place more than a hundred years ago in a small town in Iowa. I of course do not claim that this isolated case can represent the full range of human conflict. But I have chosen it because it includes, in rather simple form, many of the features we find in other human conflicts—economic interests, political dominance, territoriality, issues of legal due process, and so forth. But now it remains for me to bring the points I have been making into a broader historical framework. I shall attempt to do this at two levels: first, within the framework of human history, in the sense of a written record of human endeavors; and second, within a broader evolutionary perspective.

Some of the most bitter human conflicts have been conflicts between communities. In the ancient days of Europe, these communities were often identified with cities, and few wars have been fought with the zeal as that between ancient Athens and Sparta. With the emergence of the modern world, a city became too small a unit for ultimate loyalties or for military defense. The sense of community shifted to other forms—to one's regional or ethnic group, often rooted in either a religious or a racial consciousness, or to a larger political entity. Gradually the larger political entity of the nation-state took on some of the loyalties which previously had been focused on the ethnic group or local community, and we thus obtained the peculiarly modern phenomenon of nationalism. The most severe conflicts of the world today are between those very large "communities" which we call nations.

The expanding scope of human loyalties has brought with it a greater potentiality for massive destruction. With greater concentrations of power, there can be greater damage inflicted upon adversaries. But with such power, there also comes a mechanism for the resolution of smaller conflicts. For example, within a modern nation it is almost unthinkable that a conflict between two local communities can come to a point of actual physical violence.

Moving now more speculatively into the mists of time beyond human prehistory, we may perceive something of a parallel process setting the stage for humanity. I refer to the movement to established local bands which became the basis for self-conscious cooperation between individuals. Surely this must have been associated with the socially protective contexts which nurtured the emergence of the human species. We see something of this process suggested in some of our nearest relatives among the primates, and here I turn in particular to the paper by Junichiro Itani.[4] Professor Itani recognizes the paradoxical links between humanistic characteristics and what he calls "negated coexistence" as he concludes his paper with a specific discussion of aggression. Aggression within the group seems relatively well controlled in most primate societies—either by the dominance system, by the mutuality fostered by what he calls the equality principle, or by both. But aggression against those outside the group is something else; it is often bitter and occasionally murderous. And here we come to the paradox: as cooperation becomes more fully developed within the group, the potential for systematic attack upon outsiders seems to grow, too. Of course this is only a paradox if we expect the mutuality within the group to be extended beyond it. Our studies of the chimpanzees at Gombe show that these unusually peaceful primates can be quite ruthless in seeking the extermination of a rival group. Itani suggests that only groups with a strong male bond can successfully pursue or resist in such violent intergroup contests, leading to the natural selection of those not only inclined to band together with the group but also willing and able to fight against outsiders. This last point, I believe, is rather speculative. What is quite clear is that the mutuality within the group sets the stage for more systematic conflict and aggression between groups.

From Individual to Collective Dominance Systems

When we discuss the problems of human aggression, there are two kinds of images which most commonly come to mind. One is that of one individual violently attacking another. The other image is that of the devastation of modern war. In the first case we have an individual acting in a fashion generally conceded to be anti-social. In the second case we may note the destruction of social values, but the actual process of modern warfare is thoroughly social in its manner of organization and profoundly pro-social in the motivations of its participants. So different are these two kinds of behavior that it is questionable whether we should use a common term to refer to them both.

Kenneth Moyer has emphasized the distinction between emotional aggression and instrumental aggression.[5] Most experimental work on aggression with non-human animals is limited to emotionally-based aggressive behavior. The physiological bases of instrumental aggression are not as well understood. Of course, in reality the two forms are often mixed; strategic objectives may be involved in an angry outburst, and emotional involvement may show itself in carefully instrumental aggression. It is rather a question of what is primary. In most cases of criminal assault, it is the emotional response which is primary. In most actions of modern warfare, it is instrumental aggression which is primary.

A further distinction needs to be made among those forms of aggression which are primarily instrumental. This is the distinction between aggression which is instrumental for the purposes of the individual, and that which is primarily oriented to group objectives. Here again the distinction is often blurred in reality. Groups must provide individual incentives for those who are to pursue their purposes, and so, soldiers develop individual, as well as collective, reasons for their actions in battle. But, again, it is a matter of primary emphasis. Few soldiers would ever go into battle in pursuit of only their individual objectives. Modern warfare involves highly developed collective purposes more than it involves the summation of individual purposes.

This is not to say that nations may not be badly misguided in their collective purposes. They frequently are. For example, large accumulations of nuclear weapons may have no application which does not do enormous damage to the nation which launches them, as well as to those upon which they are exploded. In these circumstances, a strategy which threatens massive nuclear destruction upon a potential enemy becomes irrational. Nevertheless, among its believers, it still may be put forward as the acme of strategic rationality. Whether misguided or not, it is this instrumental pursuit of collective objectives which is the hallmark of modern military organizations.

It is sometimes instructive to look at human behavior in settings which neutralize the broader collective involvements. When this is done, we note remarkable parallels to studies of non-human primates. Ritch Savin-Williams' studies of interpersonal dominance among children and adolescents is a remarkably clear example of this.[6] But if our focus is on the collective dominance systems of humans, a quite different approach is required. We then have to start with examining the nature of the existing social organization, how it has developed and how it is now changing; and we must be sensitive to the particular cultural traditions involved.

Of course, it is still individuals who behave within the collective systems. We not only need to understand how the goals of groups may be in conflict, but there is also the need to explain how the conflict goals of the group become embodied in the motives of individuals. This is a very broad subject, and here I only wish to outline some of the questions which help to organize its pursuit:

1. How are the values of the larger group represented in the everyday actions of men and women, and how do these become accepted in the thinking of young children?

2. How are the social divisions of adult worlds recognized and assimilated by children?

3. How are rewards (material and otherwise) provided for certain roles in society, such as those of soldiers or political leaders? How do persons come to learn of these rewards and the behavior required to obtain them?

4. What happens when people are inducted into special social roles, such as that of a soldier? How does the conception of self change with the incorporation of this role? What new ranges of actions become morally permissible as part of this new role?

5. How are political leaders selected, and what characteristics help them to achieve success? How do these characteristics

influence the values they pursue in their positions of leadership? What particular values must they be seen to affirm—and what must they be against—if they are to maintain support for their leadership?

There is of course a growing literature on topics of this sort in the fields of sociology, political science, anthropology, and social psychology.[7] Some of the papers presented in this group provide some good illustrations of important insights for answering these questions.[8] But I do want to imply that we need far more systematic work on such questions if we are to try to close the gap between our understanding of the relationship between individual behavior and the aggression shown by human groups and organizations.

In Conclusion

We do not need to claim that only humans have a self conscious system of social organization. Some dawning self-consciousness must be present in the kin recognition shown by other vertebrates as simple-minded as toads;[9] and other papers in the present collection well identify some of the complexities of systems of social organization among non-human primates. But among humans, with our complex technologies and richly elaborated linguistic systems, so much more is possible than with any other species on earth. And human nature—including the propensities for dominance relations and aggressive behavior—is accordingly transformed. We are still animals, but animals addicted to ideological commitments, to passions of nationalism, and to the deployment of massively destructive weapons. Herein lies the peculiar genius—and challenge, if humanity is to survive —of human dominance systems.

Notes

1. Although drawing upon my paper prepared in advance for the Twelfth International Conference on the Unity of the Sciences and my oral presentation made at the conference, I prepared the present paper following the Chicago meetings. It represents my general reflections on the materials discussed by Committee V. It does not attempt to discuss in detail particular papers presented, as I did in my written and oral presentations for the conference.

2. In describing these events, I draw especially upon *History of Marshall*

County, Iowa by Gerald Schultz (Marshalltown, Iowa: Marshall Printing Co., 1955), pp. 35–37.

3. For further details, see the following articles by the present writer: "County Seat Wars: A Preliminary Analysis," *Journal of Conflict Resolution*, 14 (1970), 345–352; "Courthouse Coups d'Etat: County Seat Wars in the Old West," *The American West*, 10 (March 1973), 33–37 & 62–63; "County Seat Wars: Historical Observations," *American Studies*, 22 (Fall 1981), 81–95.

4. Junichiro Itani, "Inequality versus Equality for Coexistence in Primate Societies."

5. Kenneth E. Moyer, "The Biological Basis of Dominance and Aggression."

6. Ritch C. Savin-Williams, "Dominance Systems among Primate Adolescents."

7. See, for example, the review by Richard G. Niemi and Barbara I. Sobieszek, "Political Socialization," *Annual Review of Sociology*, v.3 (1977), 209–233.

8. As I pointed out in my remarks at the conference, I think that the paper by John G. Galaty on the Masai ("Form and Intention in East African Strategies of Dominance and Aggression") presents some especially good illustrative material on questions such as I have indicated above. I also believe there are rich insights to be gained from the papers by Edward LiPuma ("Warfare in the New Guinea Highlands: Theory and Ethnography in Conflict") and Sarah Keene Meltzoff ("Lethal Dance") on warfare among New Guinea tribesmen.

9. Roger Lewin, "Practice Catches Theory in Kin Recognition," *Science*, v.223 (9 March 1984), 1049–1051.

Conclusion

Diane McGuinness

    In the preceeding section, James Schellenberg has clarified several key issues which are critical in any attempt to discern regularities in behavior across species and cultures. These are the problems of the span of time under analysis, the nature of conflict and confrontation, the distinction between the regulation of within-group aggression and between-group aggression, and finally, he summarizes some of the most significant questions that must be addressed concerning how roles and values of a given society are adopted and enacted.

    I want to be more speculative and step back from the details and trappings of individual human cultures to develop some unifying themes. I feel that there are relatively few major variables that have led to turning points in our human history. These have determined a variety of cultural responses and the richness of their expression. However, I want to argue that beneath this complexity, the *reasons* for the human propensity to conflict are the same.

Mechanisms for Enhancing Male Dominance and Inter-Male Aggression

    Chet Lancaster, along with other anthropologists and archeologists, suggests that our evolutionary heritage is the hunter-gatherer way of life. In hunter-gatherer peoples in stable environments with an ample food supply, organized aggression *between* neighboring groups is virtually unknown. However, this

302

is not because these people have no propensity for violence. Jealousy and interpersonal disputes are as much a part of their existence as our own. Murders do occur and the group members take responsibility to stop violence and occasionally to condemn the murderer to death. Nevertheless, these murders are rare and seem to be the result of peculiarly aggressive tendencies on the part of unusual individuals (Lee, 1979). The parallel of these societies to that of the Pigmy chimpanzee, is notable. Sexual freedom is tolerated, food is freely available and there is a considerable amount of leisure time.

There appears to be one major reason for the absence of inter-group hostilities. There is no competition for land. All groups share equally in the land and move freely from place to place. This is extremely costly in terms of the amount of land required to feed an individual. Peoples such as the !Kung of South Africa and the Aborigines of Australia, have managed to perpetuate an ancient economic form because their apparently "marginal" lands can provide sufficient protein and vegetable foods. Some, like the !Kung, have a consistently better balanced diet than many Americans and need to put in only a three-day work week to achieve it.

In the absence of competition for resources, group size is maintained at around 20 to 30 individuals. This appears to be the magical number to insure group cohesion. When groups grow beyond this size, individuals split off to form other communities. Fissioning to form new groups is only possible if economic resources remain high. Once these resources are strained it becomes necessary to adopt other economic systems, and societies turn to other modes of subsistence such as herding or horticulture. This moves societies down the food chain to a more risky food source. The !Kung gather from an abundance of approximately 220 plant foods. Horticulture reduces this number dramatically to a few major crops. Should one of these crops fail for any reason, there will be dire consequences. As Mark Cohen (1977) points out, a shift down the food chain to horticulture or agriculture has one solitary advantage: It uses less land to feed more people.

A shift from a natural resource base to a man-controlled resource base has two consequences. First, the land, once freely available for all, becomes "property," a commodity that is owned and maintained by an individual or group. Ownership of land, especially in increasing scarcity requires vigilance and defense on the part of the owner. The second consequence is that people who are tied to the land become considerably less mobile. This has the effect of increasing the population. Part of this increase is due to dramatic changes in birth spacing, with women conceiving approximately every two years instead of every four. It has been suggested that this is due to a change in the fat/muscle ratio because of the more sedentary life style (see J. Lancaster, 19, in press). In addition, children become a valuable economic asset because of their labor in gardening and herding. Increasing population puts additional stress on the available land. This transition, I want to argue, initiates a *positive feedback* in which an increasing number of people require an increasing amount of land.

Peggy Sanday (1981) has documented the fact that when people are under severe economic stress, male dominance becomes exaggerated. In a comparative analysis of a large number of traditional societies, she discovered that in peoples who had undergone recent migrations or were experiencing chronic food shortages, women came under the control of men and the mutuality of the hunter-gatherer ethic ceased to exist. At the same time, endemic warfare became nearly universal. A similar theme is explored by Kay Martin and Barbara Voorhies (1975). Their cross-cultural survey shows that as men are required to contribute more and more of the labor in food production, societies become less and less egalitarian.

As land becomes a precious commodity and the need to defend it increases, the formation of male coalitions becomes essential. In small societies these male groups are frequently related by birth, but as societies increase in size, this group cohesion has to be maintained by other means. One way to solve the problem of inter-group conflict in small-scale societies is to shift to another level and incorporate the enemy into the "In-group." Thus two social units of the same race and culture can form an alliance for their mutual benefit. This process changes the boundaries and the conditions of what is considered to be "In" and "Out." If this larger group is stable, the economic base comes under control, and more egalitarian behavior will be in evidence.

The shift in boundary conditions between In-group and Out-group is entirely a *cultural* solution to a biological and economic problem, that of mutual survival. It also guarantees a measure of peace with an increase in comfort and security. What is of considerable interest is how "alpha males" function to expand these boundary conditions. Boundaries are not extended simply by group consensus, but require strong *dominant* leadership on the part of both parties. It is possible that unless the two leaders share some degree of mutuality in status and rank, this attempt will be thwarted.

Our history has attested to a gradual merging of boundaries within tribes, city-states, kingdoms and latterly, large nation-states. We have lost the face-to-face intimacy of our kinship structure but still need to maintain a sense of the group. It is in this process that values and beliefs come to constitute the framework for a viable group identity. This is as often structured in terms of group cohesion and a set of agreed beliefs as it is by identifying the out-group, the common enemy.

In searching out alien cultures and studying the beliefs and values of other nations we have before us in the twentieth century the entire panorama of human history in transition. What we observe in remote cultures, such as the New Guinea tribes, are *temporary* solutions en route to new forms. The Dani fight, they say, because they enjoy it. They rationalize their activities on the basis of the theme of retribution based on rights to the land. They cannot give up or share their lands because the blood of their ancestors dwells there. They practice retribution because they attribute the deaths of their kin to evil and magical practices on the part of their enemies. Is this merely ignorance of the cause of disease, or a rationalization based on a need to protect their source of livelihood? To study their behavior is to participate in an aspect of a society frozen in time. One might speculate that perhaps 500 or even 1,000 years ago there was a completely rational explanation for their behavior. A neighboring band may have begun to encroach on the land of the resident band. Someone may have been killed as a result. Retribution was demanded, and another and another, until the original incident was drowned in the sea of time. We cannot witness the historical facts that led to their enduring practice of blood feuds, but only the current solution for maintaining their boundaries and keeping inter-male aggression under control. And despite the fact that they are officially at war 365 days of the year, loss of life in battle is minimal.

Another force in transition is the alpha male himself. In

egalitarian societies, with an ample food supply, the people tend to adopt a more feminine solution, as outlined by Ritch Savin-Williams (this volume). Here, advice is sought from the experts, whoever they may be. Each individual is equally respected for whatever skills they possess or contribution they can make. Once this open economic system breaks down, the first transition to be observed is a shift to a male leader. In many horticultural and herding societies, the alpha male is called "The Big Man," a literal translation. Generally, the function of the Big Man is to share food and to orchestrate land use. The essence of the Big Man is generosity. He manages feasts and parties in which he can be seen dispensing food to his neighbors and kinsmen. He is harshly judged if the quantity and quality of his food is poor. It is not necessary that the Big Man actually labor to procure the food; this is the province of his wife (or wives), his children and kin.

At the point when we entered the realm of specialization and surplus economies, such as found in Agricultural societies, the Big Man took on a new personality. He was still in evidence managing distribution, but he seemed to have acquired the propensity to keep most of it for himself. He built palaces and temples inlaid with gems and decorated in gold foil. He built gardens full of rare imported plants and channeled precious water from the irrigation ditches to keep them flourishing. He commandeered enormous quantities of slaves captured from the enemy and pressed them into his service. The Big Man of the Agricultural revolution began to break the Golden Rule. He refused to share.

In order to claim authority for these selfish acts he advertised that he was allowed to exercise his control by "divine right." In the Babylonian myth "Enuma Elish," Marduk (symbolizing the city-state of Babylon) steals the sacred tablets from his "mother," Tiamat, the Goddess of creation and claims them for the people. As the tale unfolds, the author cleverly alters the character of the Goddess from the divine and benign creator of all beings, to a wretched, vengeful dragon. The kings of Babylon take their authority from the demise of the mother Goddess and the heroic act of Marduk that put the male in the supreme position and gave them control over the secrets of the Gods.

The benefit to the people was any economic improvement due to a strong leader, but more often, only the comfort that they too belonged to a social order that was sanctioned by divine authority. Such a contortion of reality attests to the malleability of the human mind. But selfish Big Men didn't last for long (even though the belief systems still linger on). In terms of evolutionary time, the capacity of Big Men to take everything and share nothing was short-lived. Other Big Men arose who argued that Kings refused to share. While people starved, they alone lived in extravagant abundance. These newcomers promised a different solution and many won approval and support. Some of them lived up to their word and some did not. When they did not, the people searched for a better Big Man. Often he was long in coming. The remainder of the story can be read in any history book, and any morning paper.

Finally, there is another important element in our transition from the hunter-gatherer stage. Human males have a particular propensity for inventing and manufacturing tools. Tools can be used to feed people, create a better life, but, also, to take life. Weapons used in human warfare, it has been suggested by anthropologists originated as extensions of the "anatomy of bluff." Male apes, for example, have large canine teeth. The females do not. As apes are largely frugivores, these large canines appear to have no function. Primatologists have suggested that large canines, in conjunction with elaborate muscle groups around the face, function in rituals of threat. Human males look threatening in proportion to their size and muscle mass. The Maasai paint themselves red and white and put on elaborate headresses to make themselves look taller. In addition, they carry weapons into battle.

The earliest weapons were spears and bows and arrows used in hunting. Over time weapons were developed specifically to maim or kill other humans. In the evolution of weaponry, it is apparent that one solution for neutralizing weapons is to manufacture weapons that destroy other weapons, and subsequently, other weapons that destroy those weapons. Here is an example of another positive-feed back loop, in which the escalation of weaponry runs out of control. We have just about reached the limit of this feed-back process in which we are now in a position of having to decide whether to escalate further into a Star Wars campaign or maintain the deadly status quo. Mutually Assured Destruction is indeed MAD, and far more irrational than any practices we could witness in the most bizarre traditional culture. The only hope we can cling to is that none of the alpha males and their coalitions want to die any more than we do. This hope is predicated on the

belief that national leaders are all basically sane, a shaky supposition.

How Important are Beliefs and Values?

The behavior of the Dani, or the Maasai, or the Maring seems peculiar to us. They dress up in funny costumes, paint themselves from head to foot, fight battles for silly reasons, and impose unnecessary stress on their communities. Most of these conflicts could be solved by a mutually cooperative stance, giving up a little pride or ego, and the codification of their agreements into laws giving equitable rights and privileges. They don't do this. Why not? Edward LiPuma writes that "war seems a highly practical response" to the Maring's dilemma over the shortage of land. Why? It would seem to us looking in from the outside, that the most highly practical response would be to determine exactly how much land was available, how many people needed to be fed and proceed to work out a solution that was maximally beneficial to all. This is what one would do in a family or in a kinship group. This is what one would do if New Guinea was a unified state, and only the professional farmers worried about food production. But the Maring have not yet been able to transcend local politics and formulate plans at the national level.

We in the civilized world are wise about these things. We would scarcely squabble over fields of sorghum or cabbage. Our problems, instead, are much more serious and highly rational. We have to deal with a nation and its satellites (coalition by coercion) who claim to want to remake the world on the basis of a particular political system. What we see instead are the machinations of male dominance games, where emissaries admit that one of the major issues is "Russian pride," whatever that may be. The Russians want to play global Big Man, but the American government won't let them. In addition, the American alpha male (Ronald Reagan) isn't taking them seriously enough. They are losing face. Meanwhile, the Russians are accused of being barbarians and they accuse the Americans of masterminding assassinations in foreign countries. The Dani raise their spears and shout abuse across a meadow that is about 500 meters wide. The East and the West hurl insults at each other over 10,000 miles with radio waves and printers ink. Is our behavior really different or is it only a question of scale?

All human social organization is due to the biological propensities of being a sharing primate, in combination with the male response to ecological constraints. Human *culture* reflects the way in which these behaviors are represented in consciousness and elaborated. Humans adopt an extraordinary amount of excess baggage in the form of rituals, rules and symbols. Cultures differ, not only because they are at different stages of economic transition, but because they have arrived at differing sets of reasons, rationalizations, and rules for a similar set of basic behaviors. Cultures also set different limits on the way in which these behaviors are expressed. Capitalism encourages material greed and rewards hard work. Socialism encourages a generous spirit and tolerates sloth.

When male alliances and belief systems combine, they result in a purely intellectual concept of the nature of a *common bond*. This is the key ingredient for the unity of the In-group. Human bonds are biologically based on familiarity (derived from "the family") that is, through face-to-face interaction. In complex societies where this face-to-face interaction with the entire social group is lost, bonds are built on extensions of intellectual "familiarity" such as common languages, common religious and ideological belief systems. Rationalizations can also function to forge a common bond or purpose. These involve invoking the will of God, or the "truth" of ideologies in combination with the active promotion of hatred for anyone who has a different God or ideology. It is belief systems and the rationalizations that derive from them that both maintain and divide human social groups.

Here, I would like to differ with James Schellenberg on the relative importance of studying values and beliefs. Understanding alien cultures, including their history and belief systems is of enormous importance in bridging our prejudices and in diplomacy. However, I want to argue that belief systems are *precisely* what get in the way of any attempt to understand the principles underlying human social behavior. Let us take a very cogent example. The Westerner is told that the reason we oppose Russia is because they practice "communism." Communism is said to be an errant or even evil belief system. Similarly, communists hate the West because we practice "capitalism." Focusing peoples' attention on beliefs instead of realities has always been the means to maintain group unity. It is a form of mind control. The dispute with the Soviet Union has nothing whatsoever to do with political beliefs or a system of government, not *even* the fact that it is a dictatorship. If the Soviet Union made no attempt to threaten and control other nations, and let people freely cross her borders, our concern with Russia would be minimal. What is really at issue has nothing to do with beliefs or values, but with territorial expansion masterminded by a coalition (gang) of dominant males. Each member of the gang has achieved his status by a slow ascent in a political hierarchy and together they maintain their power through fear. We may object to their record on civil rights, and protest the lack of freedom in their society as we do over South Africa (and these may be genuine feelings), but what is really at issue is the balance of power and which nation (male coalition) will control the world and its economic resources.

Rushing Towards Armaggedon

How can we halt the march towards our destruction and devise a solution that will take mankind to another level? If the peoples of New Guinea could unite and rise to a new group identity, then there would be so many examples to draw from. Morrocco would provide an excellent model of an emergent state, with farming as its major economic focus. But from the description of the Maring, it appears that they do not or cannot seek a solution in Nationalism. They neither understand it, nor trust the negotiators. They are trapped by their cultural baggage and belief systems, just as we are by our belief systems and the endless friction between nation-states. As long as we focus on beliefs instead of working toward novel solutions, we may be doomed.

Throughout this volume, we have been exploring the nature and function of male dominance hierarchies. They represent a biological solution to the stress arising from an increased population that puts pressure on land and resources. But they are a cumbersome solution because they generate hostility and get bogged down in rituals of bluff. They are immensely costly in terms of time, effort and human lives. We can no longer afford the luxury of slowly evolving solutions. I want to argue that male dominance behavior is holding us back from moving on to a new social awareness, one that would be embodied in a global economic unit, with outer space as the only national boundary.

We already have the answer in the alternatives of science and technology. Most peoples no longer fight wars, because of a superstitious belief that disease and death are caused by the ill will of the enemy. Science has taught us the causes of disease. Science and technology have given us the solution to hunger through the techniques of modern farming, and to overpopulation in effective contraception. Human ingenuity in technological innovation and in business acumen have developed economic systems that function with perfect efficiency *despite* intervention from governments. Even the Russians play at multinationals. Hayek (1975) has described the free marketplace as the central "morality" in human affairs. Trading is an extension of sharing and the principle of sharing is fairness. In short, science, technology and trade have obviated the need for the biological solution of male dominance.

We see all of these alternative solutions at work *within* the boundaries of nation states. Here, competition over land and resources no longer leads to war. Japan is the most over-populated country in the world, yet has one of the highest living standards. Russia is not overcrowded, nor lacking in natural resources. And should crops fail, her greatest "enemy" supplies her people with grain. Internal strife, is almost exclusively caused by the failure to provide previously autonomous "In-groups" with sufficiently compelling reasons (new beliefs) to transcend their ancient "Out-group" hostilities. America's strong emphasis on religious freedom provides a unifying "belief system." And so, too, does Russian communism.

Beliefs are important, but only if we are continually reaching towards the ultimate belief that we "do not have to believe" to be a member of a unified world. What is holding us back from implementing a viable global strategy is the perpetuation of this In-group/Out-group mentality through the mechanism of male dominance. We can no longer afford the luxury of this behavioral dinosaur. Rituals of bluff have escalated from a hand waving a spear, to a silo clutching a nuclear warhead. The most frightening aspect of allowing our world to be governed by male dominance coalitions is that a coalition of alpha males (politicians) is inherently unstable. It is for this reason that male politicians spend an inordinate amount of energy managing shifting coalitions. Each one of these men is currently, or was formerly, an alpha male. The alpha status is not absolute. It is entirely relative. As one ascends the ranks from party member to local and to national candidacy, each "alpha male" will inevitably meet his match. At this point, he will accept a lesser rank by joining in a coalition dominated by another alpha male. But when so many alpha males are concentrated in one location, these coalitions are fragile, *even* when the leading alpha male is strong. Incoming members, the demise of older members, transfers to new posts or divisions, create a constant hubbub of shifting alliances to maintain or to gain status.

In recent history we have been able to see the influence of male dominance and, in particular, the impact of an "alpha male" on the escalation or containment of international conflict. What is notable from these observations and from research, is that the characteristic of the "alpha" male is specific to an ability to control others and convince them to follow a pattern of action. Being an alpha male has nothing whatsoever to do with being right or wrong, or good or evil. Hitler and Churchill were both alpha males who were able to inspire and control the people around them. Yet Churchill could not convince Roosevelt of the importance of keeping Russia out of Eastern Europe. Again, alpha status is relative. The real challenge is to find leaders who are both right *and* good. Because we do not understand how the alpha male functions, we often succumb to "style" instead of content and good will. This appears to be especially true of men, where voting records indicate that they are more likely to base their decision on alpha status, whereas women focus more on content and the "sincerity" of the candidate.

This volume is only a beginning. Its ultimate message is that we must become aware of the nature of male dominance systems and male dominance games, how they originate and how they perpetuate themselves. We can only control what we understand, and we need to understand in order to search for alternatives. Male dominance systems and hierarchies function according to the rules of the zero-sum game, with an inevitable winner and loser. For a man who has a vested interest in maintaining or improving status, overt cooperation is always considered a sign of weakness. Compromise is won through confrontation, and confrontation is not only inefficient, but dangerous. We must move instead towards a **heter**archical mode, reflecting our initial heritage as hunter-gatherers. When decision-makers function with equal power, this makes it possible to effect a non zero-sum game in which everyone works toward the most creative solution to benefit the maximum number. The Japanese have used this approach, especially in business, with great skill. But, so far, they seem unwilling to be "maximizers" in the international marketplace, as their record on protectionism indicates. Nevertheless, they have taken the lead within their own borders and have at least provided a model for the possibility of a new global perspective, where the entire human race becomes the "In-group."

Bibliography

Cohen, M.N., *The Food Crisis in Prehistory*. New Haven: Yale University Press, 1977.

Hayek, F.A., "The Rules of Morality are not the Conclusions of our Reason" in: D. McGuinness, ed., *Evolution: The Trans Disciplinary Paradigm*. New York: Paragon House Press, 1985.

Lancaster, J.B., "Evolutionary perspectives on sex differences in the higher primates" in: A.S. Rossi, ed., *Gender and the Life Course*. New York: Aldine (in press).

Martin, M.K. and Voorhies, B., *Female of the Species*. New York: Columbia University Press, 1975.

Sanday, P.R., *Female Power and Male Dominance: On the Origins of Sexual Inequality*. London: Cambridge University Press, 1981.

Contributors

Walter Angst is a primatologist in Salem, West Germany.

Armand Clesse is a nuclear strategist in Eschdorf, Luxembourg.

Jose M.R. Delgado is Director Emeritus of the Department of Research, Ramon y Cajal Center, Madrid, Spain.

John G. Galaty is Associate Professor of anthropology, McGill University, Montreal, Canada.

Junichiro Itani is Professor of primatology, Laboratory of Human Evolution Studies, Faculty of Science, Kyoto University, Japan.

Takayoshi Kano is Professor at the Department of Human Ecology, School of Health Sciences, Faculty of Medicine, University of Ryukyus, Nishihara, Okinawa, Japan.

Chet S. Lancaster is a NIMH postdoctoral fellow, College of Medicine, Division of Community Medicine, University of Oklahoma, Oklahoma City, Oklahoma.

Edward Li Puma is with the Department of Anthropology, University of Miami, Miami, Florida.

Diane McGuinness is Assistant Professor at the Department of Psychology, University of South Florida, Ft. Myers, Florida.

Sarah Keene Meltzoff is with the Department of Marine Affairs, University of Miami, Miami, Florida.

Diane Lopez-Mendoza is in the Department of Psychology Research, University of Seville, Spain.

Kenneth E. Moyer is Professor of Psychology Emeritus, Carnegie-Mellon University, Pittsburgh, Pennsylvania.

J. Martin-Ramirez is Professor of Psychobiology, Department of Psychology, University of Seville, Seville, Spain.

Peter C. Reynolds is co-founder, Corporate Anthropology Group, Sausalito, California.

James A. Schellenberg is Professor of Sociology, Indiana State University, Terre Haute, Indiana.

Joseph Shepher was formerly Professor of Sociology and Anthropology, University of Haifa, Haifa, Israel. (Deceased.)
Ritch C. Savin-Williams is Associate Professor, Department of Human Development and Family Studies, Cornell University, Ithaca, New York.

Sources

The source of this volume was derived from papers presented in Committee V ("The Emotions: Focus on Inter-Male Aggression and Dominance Systems") at ICUS XII ("Absolute Values and the New Cultural Revolution".) This symposium, one of six sponsored by ICUS, of the International Cultural Foundation, Inc., was held at the Chicago Marriott Hotel, November 24–27, 1983, and had as its organizing chairman, Diane McGuinness. The honorary chairman was Karl H. Pribram.

Index

This index is of persons referred to in the book (including references) and of major themes in the text. A number in brackets [ ] behind a page number refers to a footnote on that page. Numbers in **bold face** refer to pages written by the person indexed.

Roe, A. 29
Rohr, R. 168
Rohrer, J.H. 172
Roosevelt 312
Rose, R.M. 22-24, 32, 131, 170
Rosenblum, L.A. 58, 135, 171, 172
Rosvold, H.E. 16, 29
Roth, E.M. 71, 72
Rothenberg, Gunter E. 280 [15]
Rotmistrov, P.A. 271
Rowell, T.E. 66, 74, 139, 143, 171
Ruffer, D.G. 12, 32
Rush, Myron 284 [81, 82]
Russell J. 170

Saberwal, S. 234, 248
Sackett, G.P. 57, 62, 70, 74
Sade, D.S. 21, 29, 33, 51, 62, 138, 166, 171
Sagan, Carl 120
Sahlins, Marshall 248, 249 [4]
Sanday, P.R. 304, 313
Sands, D.E. 25, 33
Savin-Williams, Ritch C. **131-173**, 174, 175, 177, 299, 301 [6], 306, 316
Schaller, G.B. 104, 141, 172
Schellenberg, James A. **197-200**, **289-301**, 302, 309, 316
Schelling, Thomas C. 248, 249 [7], 256 [10], 281 [27]
Schenkel, R. 6, 33
Schlesinger 254, 267, 273
Schneiria, T.C. 147, 172
Schultz, Gerald 301 [2]
Schutz, Alfred 248, 249 [3]
Scott, J.P. 19, 29, 33, 41, 62, 135, 147, 172
Sears, R.R. 4, 33, 67, 74
Segal, Gerald 285 [92]
self replication 177-179
Selznick, P. 3, 29
Sendor, M. 29
Service, Elman R. 195, 196 [6]

Seward, J.P. 7, 33
sex comparisons 159-162
Shagass, C. 30
Shelyag 285 [91]
Shepher, Joseph **174-179**, 316
Sherif, C.W. 156, 163, 172
Sherif, M. 156, 163, 172
Sherwood, Eddy 279 [7]
Shin, Y. 101
Shirek-Ellefson, J. 51, 63
Shurtz 291
Siddiqi, M.R. 104, 172
Siddiqui, M.F. 63, 138
Sigg, E.G. xiv, 28, 74, 99 [2], 104
Silk, J.B. 90, 104
Simmons, Don 211
Simonds, P.E. 137, 138, 172
Simpson, C. 214, 215 [2]
Simpson, G.G. 29
Singh Pirla, R. 74
Singh, M. 74
Skirdo, M.P. 284 [77]
Slocombe, Walter 283 [62]
Small, S.A. 148, 172
small towns (in Iowa) 291-292
Smith, J. 172
Smith, L.M. 147, 169
Smith, M.H. 9, 29
Smythies, J.R. 41
Snowdon 66
Snyder, D.R. 16, 33, 137, 287 [106]
Snyder, Jack L. 285 [95]
Sobleszek, Barbara I. 301 [7]
social
bonds 68-69
deprivation 69-70
psychology 200
regulation in primate societies 105-118
structures of primates 76-79, 97
sociology
biology versus xii-xiv
human conflict and 197-200, 289-301